KEATING's & KELTY's
SUPER LEGACY

The Birth and Relentless Threats to the
Australian System of Superannuation

Mary Easson

Connor Court Publishing

Connor Court Publishing Pty Ltd

Copyright © Mary Easson 2017

PO Box 7257
Redland Bay Qld 4165
sales@connorcourt.com
www.connorcourt.com

ISBN: 9781925501414 (pbk.)

Cover design by Amanda Easson utilising an image by iStock (Getty images)

Printed in Australia

For Michael, Louise and Amanda who, when the need was greatest, proved inspiring.

"My will is back'd with resolution:
Thoughts are but dreams till their effects are tried."

William Shakespeare

CONTENTS

ILLUSTRATIONS

A NOTE TO THE READER

I was a member of Paul Keating's government from 1993 to 1996. Thus I was elected a year after the historic Superannuation Guarantee Charge (SGC) legislation (1992) that ensured basic, legislative minimum standards for superannuation, including the phasing-in of the 9 per cent of salary minimum guarantee. It was an adventure to be part of the Keating government. I had known him since becoming President of Victorian Young Labor in 1976. I saw that the development of superannuation, one of Labor's great achievements, was vitally due to his leadership along with others I knew from the Victorian union movement, particularly Bob Hawke, Bill Kelty, Simon Crean, and Greg Sword.

After I recovered from a serious illness in 2009/10, I decided to begin my research so as to write something permanent on the issue of superannuation. It seemed important to get the stories down before those present at the creation of the modern system passed on.

I am extremely grateful for the incredibly interesting insights yielded through interviews with the main protagonists. Most of them I have known for decades, and they all shared ideas and perspectives that, so far as I can see, were mostly free of egotistic claims for "my place in history".

I have found out things I never knew. In the 1980s and early 1990s, Kelty and Keating, from its two wings, drove the labour movement[1] to excel in policy development like never before. The modern superannuation system was crafted through their combined efforts.

I came to realise how close in the early days all those reforms had come to perishing. Indeed, Paul Keating's winning of the "unloseable election"[2] of 1993 consolidated the gains that had been freshly won in industrial awards and in the SGC legislation. Had Labor lost in 1993,

---

[1] Throughout this book, consistent with common usage in Australia, "labour movement" is spelt with a "u", and "Labor Party" without.

[2] It has now passed into folklore that in 1993, starting well ahead in the opinion polls, the then Liberal Opposition Leader faced winning an election where he was odds-on favourite. But on 13 March 1993 Labor won, including in the seat of Lowe in Sydney, where I defeated Dr Bob Woods, the sitting member.

the system might never have evolved to what we see today. That victory was therefore more significant than many realised at the time. After 1996, the phase-in of the SGC minimums were enacted by the Howard government only because it could not secure a majority in the Senate to defeat them. Before Labor's defeat in 1996, the incoming government, then Opposition, canvassed freezing the SGC at its then current level (as it proposed at the 1993 election). But Shadow Treasurer Peter Costello reversed that stance for the 1996 campaign. Radical moves to dismantle what had been created were successfully resisted.

I am very appreciative to the surgeons Dr Anil Keshava and Professor John Hollinshead, as well as Margaret, Helen, Margaret, David, the other nurses, doctors and professional staff who kept me alive at Concord Hospital for six months in 2009. A year after recovery, Associate Professor John Evans, then Head of the School of Risk & Actuarial Studies at the University of New South Wales, encouraged me on this journey. I am grateful to him and to Professor Hazel Bateman for her guidance in writing an earlier version of this account – for a Master of Philosophy degree at the School of Business at the University of NSW. The story told here, however, in this book, is much expanded. Thanks are also due to my husband, Michael, who has offered valuable advice and suggestions here and there – not always agreeing with my points of emphasis and interpretation. My friend Catherine Harding read through the manuscript with an eager eye for grammatical and flow-of-argument slips, and occasionally saved the day. Laura Goodin also offered editorial suggestions which I gladly accepted. But I am entirely responsible for what follows.

In this telling of the story, I have tried to explain matters in a readable, rather than academic, style. Bismarck was reputed to have said that if you like sausages, avoid seeing them made in the kitchen. But if you want to understand you had better observe. The recipe for the creation of Australia's superannuation has never been written down. But I have looked at the untidy parts of the making of the Australian system to understand what really happened. Now we know - ingredients, cooks, plates, and all.

1. INTRODUCTION: FILLING THE GAP

Background

Australian superannuation funds[1] typically take one of five institutional forms: 1) corporate funds, which are sponsored by a single employer or group of related employers and cover employees; 2) public sector funds, which cover public sector employees; 3) industry funds, which cater for employees as a result of the certification of the industrial tribunal[2] of an enterprise agreement[3] or industrial award[4] – which typically draw members from a large number of employers; 4) retail public offer funds, which allow members to join by purchasing investment units or policies; and 5) self-managed (or "do-it-yourself") funds, called self-managed superannuation funds (SMSFs).

---

[1] See Appendices 5 to 8 for details on some of the major funds and organisations associated with them.

[2] The national workplace tribunal over the years was named: the Commonwealth Court of Conciliation and Arbitration 1907-1956; Commonwealth Conciliation and Arbitration Commission 1957-1973; Australian Conciliation and Arbitration Commission 1973-1988; Australian Industrial Relations Commission 1988-2009; Fair Work Australia 2009-2012; and the Fair Work Commission 2012 onwards.

[3] Since 1 July 2009, the various types of collective and individual workplace agreements that existed under the previous workplace relations system were replaced by a single type of agreement: an "enterprise agreement". This is simply an agreement between one or more national system employers and their employees, as specified in the agreement. Enterprise agreements are negotiated by the parties through collective bargaining in good faith, primarily at the enterprise level. Under the *Fair Work Act 2009*, an enterprise can mean any kind of business, activity, project or undertaking.

[4] Awards within the Federal sphere are made by the Commission – not as a result of agreement between parties – albeit some award clauses, including those nominating default superannuation funds are sometime dealt with by consent by major industrial parties.

As influential as the industry funds have been in the shaping of Australian superannuation policy and practice since the 1980s, they today represent only a minority of the industry total. Yet their impact has been and remains a decisive influencer for the entire industry. As at 30 June 2015, total superannuation industry assets were $2.0 trillion,[5] of which $1,246.0 billion were held by superannuation funds and $589.9 billion by SMSFs. The remaining $187.2 billion were held by public sector superannuation schemes ($131.1 billion) and life office statutory funds ($56.1 billion). Small funds – which include SMSFs and single-member approved deposit funds – accounted for 29.3 per cent of total assets. Retail funds held 26.5 per cent, industry funds 21.5 per cent, public sector funds 17.3 per cent, and corporate funds 2.7 per cent.[6]

The regulatory responsibility for the superannuation industry is split between the Australian Prudential Regulatory Authority (APRA), the Australian Securities and Investments Commission (ASIC), and the Australian Tax Office (ATO). ASIC and APRA are principally responsible for the supervision of the *Corporations Act 2001* and the *Superannuation Industry (Supervision) Act 1993* respectively. The ATO has a regulatory role in relation SMSFs. Superannuation funds also have important reporting and administrative obligations to the ATO. It is curious, though, that there is not one combined regulator of the whole industry.

The most significant change in Australian superannuation policy and practice, the origins of what is in place today, occurred in the 13 years between 1983 and 1996, coinciding with the Hawke-Keating Labor governments and considerable trade union movement efforts to establish industry funds. A host of factors – everything from sectoral advances in key industries, universal principles concerning vesting, portability, minimum contributions, life insurance – were legislated

---

[5] Unless otherwise stated, all dollar figures in this book are in Australian dollars (AUD).
[6] Australian Prudential Regulation Authority (APRA) (2016) *Annual Superannuation Bulletin*, APRA, Sydney, June 2015, reissued 23 August 2016, p. 3.

and formulated into standards that applied to the whole industry. In this period, the Australian trade union movement, backed by the Federal government, campaigned for occupational superannuation justice, and the government decided to universalise some of the changes unions were seeking across the whole workforce. This was in keeping with traditional social democracy – the practice of fighting for reforms in one sector and then attempting to consolidate them by ensuring that certain principles and standards applied to all.

In the early 1980s, there were many good reasons for change in superannuation, including what Howard Gill, an industrial relations observer at the time, noted: "The lack of vesting and portability are discriminatory against the mobile employee, restrict labour mobility and further disadvantage persons made redundant."[7] Changing the system, tackling the multitudinous issues and difficulties associated with different actuarial bases, benefit levels, problems of liquidity, discriminatory provisions, etc. in various schemes, rules, and processes, meant that radical reform was needed. "Industry, cure thyself" was never going to happen. A series of shocks and campaigns in the period led to the creation of a fairer, sustainable superannuation system. This book tells the story of the origins and development of Australia's modern superannuation system.

A comprehensive, well-researched history of the trade union and industrial origins of Australia's superannuation changes in the early 1980s demands the recounting – and explaining – of what really happened. This work fills the gap and, hopefully, will inspire other researchers to explore a fascinating topic in more detail.[8] I argue that the origins and development of the Australian superannuation system, though partly accidental, were brilliantly and vigorously pursued by

---

[7] Gill, Howard (1979) "Industrial Relations and Superannuation", *Superfunds*, No. 69, December, p. 8.

[8] At the time of writing, but without having sighted the book, I am aware that the industry funds have sponsored a history written by two RMIT academics, Mees, Bernard, & Brigden, Cathy (2017) *Workers' Capital. Industry Funds and the Fight for Universal Superannuation in Australia*, Allen & Unwin, North Sydney, which is expected to fill some important gaps and hopefully in turn will inspire other researchers to explore this rich history.

the union movement, which seized opportunities that arose from the then combative arena of industrial relations and the then government's desire to curtail inflation by moderating the growth in wages. When I spoke to him for this book, Labor luminary Simon Crean, former Storemen and Packers Union leader, ACTU President, and Labor government Minister, looked back on this time with just a hint of justifiable pride, saying simply, "... we have driven savings."[9] In other words, Crean considered that Australia's huge superannuation savings pool had been spurred by political and industrial labour working side by side. He said that national, portable superannuation, along with Medicare and the minimum wage, were important "safety nets,"[10] and were among the greatest contributions of the Australian labour movement to civilising Australian capitalism.[11] To the extent that such reforms represent the essence of labourism, they can be said to exemplify the Australian labour movement at its best. There is a vast literature on labourism much of it, however, written from a Marxist perspective denouncing the idea as opposed to socialism. A search through the academic critiques leads one to hanker for something more positive and consistent with what the labour movement has traditionally been on about. In part, it is noteworthy that the broad features of the (far) Left critique are correct. Labourism in Australia encompasses political and industrial labour (i.e., the unions and the Australian Labor Party), through collective and common action, campaigning for better working conditions, improving treatment from their employers, and curbing the depredations of capitalism – via a social safety net, welfare for the unemployed, training programmes for displaced workers, medical assistance, social insurance, and so forth. The goal of labourism is to protect and strengthen the interests of labour within capitalism. This is in contrast with the goal of socialism, as traditionally expostulated, which is to replace the

---

[9] Simon Crean interview, May 2013.

[10] *Ibid.*

[11] This is to appropriate a phrase by Bede Nairn (1973) *Civilising Capitalism, The Beginnings of the Australian Labor Party*, Australian National University Press, Canberra.

capitalist system entirely. The superannuation reforms of the 1980s onwards, in the Hawke-Keating governments, evidenced industrial and political labour at their peak.

With superannuation savings currently likely to double to over $4.0 trillion over the next decade,[12] there has been much celebration of the "Australian model", and even discussion of transferring it to other nations. There are doubts about whether this is feasible, given that the Australian experience emerged in such peculiar – perhaps unrepeatable – circumstances. In his 2011 book *The March of Patriots: The Struggle for Modern Australia*, Paul Kelly writes, "[h] istorians will be shocked to realise that universal superannuation had its origins in centralised wage fixation."[13] The achievement, however, was more than a footnote to the history of the Australian conciliation and arbitration: the fight for superannuation equity, as the unions saw it, was intense, arduous, sometimes bitter, never certain, and never simple. Throughout the 1980s, the policy and strategic environment relevant to superannuation and the range of potential outcomes were creatively dynamic and unpredictable.

Superannuation as a Major Industrial Issue

Superannuation emerged as an industrial relations issue from the late 1960s onwards. The Waterside Workers' Federation sponsored the Stevedoring Employees' Retirement Fund (SERF) (1967), and the Seamen's Union of Australia sponsored the Seafarers' Retirement Fund (1973). Separately, the Pulp and Paper Workers' Federation Scheme (1974), then in December 1978 LUCRF Super[14] was established. They were the early pioneers. Additionally some unions, such as the

---

[12] Rice Warner (2012; 2014) "Superannuation Market Projections Report 2012", Sydney and its update, "Superannuation Market Projections Report 2014."

[13] Kelly, Paul (2011) *The March of Patriots, The Struggle for Modern Australia*, Melbourne University Press, Carlton (first published in 2009, updated in 2011), p. 145.

[14] LUCRF's initials stood for the Labour Union Cooperative and Retirement Fund.

Federated Iron Workers' Association (FIA) had extended coverage of the BHP steel scheme to a broader range of employees. A decade later, the industrial relations academic Howard Gill bluntly commented that "... really, the wonder is it took so long."[15]

A survey of Australian workforce attitudes by Sentry Holdings Limited in 1979 "showed that retirement plans were regarded by 78 per cent of workers as the most important of a wide range of employee fringe benefits whereas only 56 per cent of workers were actually covered by retirement plans. Significantly 68 per cent of workers supported union action in this area ..."[16] From there the Australian Council of Trade Unions (ACTU), the peak or co-ordinating body of the union movement, began to strongly support superannuation as an industrial issue. But, in the early 1980s, this was on the proviso that a national scheme would eventually be created. As Garry Weaven, then a Senior Industrial Officer of the ACTU who reported to ACTU Secretary Bill Kelty on superannuation matters, stated:

> An essential element of the ACTU strategy is to attain government commitment to establish, at an appropriate time, a national scheme embracing contributions consistent with the productivity case, and equitable and socially desirable design features – such a scheme to be made compulsory for those employers who have failed to introduce or become party to an occupational scheme at an appropriate level of contribution and with appropriate features.[17]

Coming up with a viable plan was vital – as was the need for a breakthrough example of how superannuation reform could be managed. As is discussed later in the book, the building industry

---

[15] Gill, Howard (1979) "Industrial Relations and Superannuation", *Superfunds*, No. 69, December, p. 6.

[16] Cited in Solomon, D.J. (1979) "Wages Superannuation – Government, Union or Employer?", *Superfunds*, No. 68, September, p. 8. The author of this article was then a partner of Palmer Trahair Owen & Whittle (PTOW), consulting actuaries, which has since become absorbed into Russell Employee Benefits.

[17] Weaven, Garry (1985) "Superannuation: The Great Leap Forward. An Outline of the ACTU's Strategy for the Establishment of Universal Superannuation Coverage", *Superfunds*, No. 92, September, p. 12.

experience in 1983-84 was the transformative event that made everything else possible. As Weaven noted, "[i]n my view we ... have a simple, concrete and practical plan for the attainment of our goal. It does not pretend to solve all the problems or determine all the debates – indeed we could argue forever around alternative constructions of the perfect world – but it does present the mechanism for a great leap forward in this country's superannuation arrangements."[18] In one stroke, the fervour and practical drive to straighten out a broken system was crisply conveyed in Weaven's language.

It would be a mistake, however, to assume a slow, inevitable, bringing-to-boiling process leading to successful union superannuation campaigns. The early to mid-1980s was a period of wage and price inflation – during which restoring or maintaining real living standards was the main priority for most moderate union leaders – as well a time of some egregious claims for pay and conditions through the old "log of claims" process. Indeed, with respect to union inspired superannuation campaigns, one observer noted in the mid-1980s that:

> During 1980, however, the momentum slowed appreciably. This is thought to have occurred primarily as a result of a survey commissioned by the ACTU amongst its membership which disclosed, rather surprisingly, in July 1980 that superannuation was not considered an important issue by most union officials. Only 54 of the 140 affiliated unions bothered to reply to the survey and only half of those replying supported superannuation as an industrial issue.[19]

This underscored how removed the policy thinkers within the ACTU were from "here and now" objectives of most of their colleagues. What changed was the breaking down of orderly wage adjustment during the period of automatic indexation, the need to ensure the success of a new Labor government elected in 1983, and memories of the Whitlam

---

[18] *Ibid.*
[19] Devlin, Michael W. (1986) "Industrial Relations and the Superannuation Industry, Blushing Bride and Reluctant Bridegroom", *Superfunds*, No. 96, September, p. 11.

government's disastrous labour relations, strikes, and rolling conflict, for which the unions were significantly responsible.[20]

In contrast with the emerging campaign on the union side, many employers and their representatives were complacent and weak in their response to the potential challenges of union-inspired "industry super". As the industrial campaigns were really beginning to take off in the mid-1980s, David Nolan, then an employer's advocate and Director of the Confederation of Australian Industry Industrial Council, mildly proffered that "[a] scale for vesting of employer-financed benefits should operate with full vesting being available to the member only after ten years' membership in the fund"[21] and that "[p]ortability of both member contributions and vested employer benefits should be encouraged."[22] Seemingly exhausted by the thought of such concessions – time-delayed vesting and the pious encouragement of portability – Nolan pleaded, "[w]e would therefore consider it essential that there be a moratorium on any new superannuation claims until such times as the above issues are resolved."[23] But resolving such issues would never happen without pressing, prodding, and industrial force. For most of their members, the more active union leaders saw that there was nothing to be lost and everything to be gained by pushing the envelope. In 1986 a then-leading metal industry union leader put forward a compelling economic reason for reform: "Tackling superannuation now will speed up the process of greater employee mobility in a rapidly changing workforce, rather than acting as a deterrent to employees changing jobs, not only to the detriment of the employer, but also to the detriment of the employee."[24] This was the kind of argument an economist inspired by the principles of

[20] See Easson, Michael (2013) "Industrial Relations Policy", in Bramston, Troy (2013), editor, *The Whitlam Legacy*, The Federation Press, Leichhardt, pp. 223-34.
[21] Nolan, David (1985) "Superannuation from the Employers' Viewpoint", *Superfunds*, No. 92, September, p. 35.
[22] *Ibid.*
[23] *Ibid.*
[24] Harrison, Greg (1986) "Superannuation – A Union's Viewpoint, *Superfunds*, No. 95, June 1986, p. 14.

"economic liberalism" might be expected to support. Yet the view was being articulated by a unionist marshalling every argument for the cause.

Figure 1: Bob Hawke and Gough Whitlam at the ALP Federal conference at Terrigal, 4 November 1975, photo by Russell McPhedran. Source: Fairfax archives.

Not all employers were so myopic. Bruce Watson of Mount Isa Mines argued that "I have no doubt whatsoever that part of the present interest by unions in superannuation has been brought on as a result of indexation guidelines, and as a means of circumventing those guidelines."[25] He was apparently thinking that as the industrial relations tribunals were then, through wage policy guidelines, clamping down on union-led wage campaigns, superannuation was opened up as a new province of industrial relations disputation. Unlike what

---

[25] Watson, B.D. (1979) "Union Involvement in the Provision of Superannuation", *Superfunds*, No. 69, December, p. 12. Watson was then a director of MIM (Mount Isa Mines) Holdings Limited. MIM was purchased by the mining company Xstrata in 2003.

might have been expected to have been said by most of the cohort of Queensland conservative business knights of the realm – a club he was soon to join – Watson suggested: "I believe union interest is healthy and I believe that the members can have a role as trustees of existing funds and unions can have a role in the provision of accumulation type funds for industries where contact with the union is probably much more consistent than contact with an individual employer."[26] This was both realistic and sympathetic to the practical implications of union involvement. Watson apparently considered that this could also be associated with greater understanding and sympathy for business and "responsible" thinking – perhaps with the view that the unions' anti-business sentiment would be tamed by their engagement in superannuation and investment management.

Figure 2: Bob Hawke addressing ACTU delegates in 1983, Melbourne. Source: Records of Unions NSW.

[26] Watson, B.D. (1979) "Union Involvement in the Provision of Superannuation", *Loc. Cit.*, p. 14.

Stockbroker and NSW Liberal Party grandee, Peter Philips also saw the writing on the wall, suggesting that major adjustments to traditional employer thinking – and knee-jerk rejection of union efforts to invade "familiar territory" – were in order. He wrote: "It was inevitable that unions would, in due course, seek benefits outside the wage indexation guidelines, and superannuation is one such benefit."[27] At the same time he expressed concern that the "deferred pay" issue might cause employees to think they have the right to take their superannuation money as a lump sum and not save for retirement.[28] Philips was contesting a phrase by Storemen and Packers' Union leader Bill Landeryou that superannuation was "deferred pay" and therefore unions had the right and obligation to get involved.[29]

Superannuation became an increasingly significant industrial issue from the mid-1970s to mid-1980s for seven main reasons.

First, unions saw that the existing system was rigged in favour of managerial workers and professionals, to the detriment of many, such as women, low-paid, blue-collar workers, casually employed workers, and part-time workers in industries with high turnover. Bill Kelty characterised superannuation as "the subsidy from essentially lower paid workers with shorter service to higher-paid people with longer service."[30] Generally, the unions argued that:

Existing superannuation schemes, which have grown up in the main on a company-by-company basis, contain many inequities and anomalies. The union movement has been concerned that many

[27] Philips, P.S.M. (1979) "Union Superannuation Funds", *Superfunds*, No. 69, December, p. 24.
[28] *Ibid.*, p. 26.
[29] This is discussed in the next Chapter which discusses the LUCRF super scheme. See: Landeryou, W.A. (1978) "The Union Attitude to Superannuation", *Superfunds*, No. 65, December, p. 31, where he uses the phrase "deferred pay".
[30] Bill Kelty interview, March 2013. The disadvantaged position of women workers with the then contemporary superannuation system was outlined in Owen, Mary (1984) "Superannuation Was Not Meant For Women", *The Australian Quarterly*, Vol. 56, No. 4, Summer, pp. 363-73. Owen was at that time the ACTU Social Welfare Officer.

schemes do not provide adequate information and are insufficiently accountable to members. The *ad hoc* development of superannuation has meant a general lack of security of rights, poor financial returns, and costly and inadequate administration. In some cases companies have used superannuation funds in takeover fights or to provide loanbacks to the company. Of particular concern to the union movement are four dominant/features of existing superannuation provisions; the membership discrimination, the inadequate vesting rights, the lack of portability, and the scant regard given to the preservation of entitlements. Unions are also concerned to ensure that the enforced savings resulting from the expansion of superannuation entitlements provides a local source of investment funding.[31]

In the 1970s, particular campaigns – among stevedores, printers, meat workers, and workers in the skin and hide industry – alerted the union movement of the need to address these issues of inequity. If no national scheme was immediately on offer, then there must instead be campaigns in particular companies and industries. Even in the public sector, it was noted that some 70 per cent of Federal public servants left their superannuation scheme with only their own contributions and the interest that had accrued on them.[32]

For Bill Kelty, "an essential industrial catalyst was Charlie Fitzgibbon [former national secretary of the Waterside Workers Federation] when he decided that among a range of things that he would seek to do for waterside workers was to establish [from the late 1960s onwards] for them industrially as part of a process of adjusting to changing containerisation – using their bargaining power and having a permanent workforce – was to establish superannuation."[33] While President of the ACTU (1969 to 1979), Bob Hawke canvassed

---

[31] Plowman, David & Weavan, Garry (1989) "Unions and Superannuation", in Ford, Bill & Plowman, David (1989), editors, *Australian Unions. An Industrial Relations Perspective*, Second Edition, Macmillan Company of Australia, Crows Nest [Sydney], pp. 253-4.

[32] Weavan, Garry (1985) "Superannuation: The Great Leap Forward", mimeo, ACTU, Melbourne; cited in Plowman, David & Weavan, Garry (1989) "Unions and Superannuation", *Loc. Cit.*, p. 255.

[33] Bill Kelty interview, March 2013.

ideas of setting up union-backed superannuation and insurance entities, but these ideas were never carried through to fruition at that immediate time.[34] The development of broadly-based occupational superannuation was an evolution, particularly driven by the strong strategic focus of Kelty and Keating who, it may now be seen, acted decisively at key moments. Their agenda was to pursue a fairer, well-funded, robust system. If the entire plan for such a system was not clear from the start, as nearly all the main protagonists now recognise, it is still true to say that the need – and the opportunity – to create a significant union-inspired and driven superannuation system was present at the outset.[35]

Second, some unions, with bargaining strength, notably the Waterside Workers, the Pulp and Paper Workers, the Storemen and Packers, and others, aggressively campaigned for "superannuation justice", creating new schemes that became potential models for other unions to emulate. The development of the LUCRF scheme by the FSPU in 1978 in particular was catalytic, causing unions to rethink their roles. Instead of amending and improving inadequate, existing schemes, the demand developed for an entirely new model. This was largely due to dissatisfaction with an apparatus that was widely perceived to be beyond easy amendment. Unions wanted to create a new system.

Third, within the union movement, political realignments and new personnel meant that the ACTU became more influential, as there were also major shifts in power relationships within the ACTU and unions generally. Although ACTU President Bob Hawke was known as a consensus leader,[36] the leadership of some of the major unions, in large swathes, was divided along the legacy of Cold War and other

---

[34] D'Alpuget, Blanche (1982) *Robert J. Hawke. A Biography*, Schwartz in conjunction with Lansdowne Press, Sydney, pp. 178, 240, 243.

[35] Email exchange, Bill Kelty to Mary Easson, 28 November 2013.

[36] Cf. Mills, Stephen (1993) *The Hawke Years. The Story from the Inside*, Viking, Richmond Victoria, pp. 10-12 and throughout. More generally as a consensus-seeking leader throughout his industrial and political life, see: D'Alpuget, Blanche (1982) *Robert J. Hawke. A Biography, Loc. Cit., passim.*

political schisms. As Kelty put matters, he "got on reasonably well with a whole group of people; so we [the ACTU leadership at the time] said, 'why don't we try to harness all sides and actually cause people to work together for a change'. So we are trying to bring them all together. When that happens, you can go straight to the Accord. During the [initial conceptualisation of the] Accord we couldn't get... [to] the level of commitment to have superannuation significantly on the agenda."[37] That was true at first, subject to point seven, below.

Fourth, the personalities of the key players were crucial. Bill Kelty and Garry Weaven had studied economics together at La Trobe University.[38] Crean, Kelty, and Sword were all recruited into the FSPU by union secretary Bill Landeryou. Sword did most of the heavy-duty work of developing and extending the LUCRF scheme across the industries that his union covered. Later, Kelty developed the grand strategy and forced it through the unions. Weaven, whatever his differences with Kelty on the strategy and particular tactics, was a brilliant implementer of the industry superannuation project, particularly in the detailed work associated with the creation of various industry funds. Industry superannuation veteran and CEO of Australian Super, Ian Silk, said of Kelty's drive, "it wasn't just visionary, it was incredibly courageous of Kelty because there were so many people in the union movement that said 'this is a load of bullshit!' and he relentlessly pushed it through."[39]

Fifth, there was an intellectual context to what was unfolding. Kelty has acknowledged that:

At the same time I was at university, I'd been lectured by Professor [Donald] Whitehead[40] and he and I had long discussions about superannuation in terms of wages systems. In fact he wrote a book

---

[37] Bill Kelty interview, March 2013.

[38] They were in the same year and while they did not take every subject together they were close friends for a very long time.

[39] Ian Silk interview, March 2013.

[40] For an assessment of his thinking and an obituary, see Davidson, F.G. (1980) "Donald Whitehead", *The Economic Record*, Vol. 56, Issue 154, September, pp. 281-4.

about wages [*Stagflation and Wages Policy in Australia*, 1973] and he was an advisor to the Liberal Party, an adviser to conservatives. He had a view about superannuation which, I think, in part came from him and part came from me that was part of the industrial works [and] should be out there to be negotiated. He then put forward the view that what the country should do is to make sure that there was superannuation [coverage]. So, intellectually it [i.e., the idea of extending superannuation coverage] had a base and industrially it had a base.[41]

Kelty continued, "so if you're looking for the two catalysts for modern superannuation … the most important is [Charlie] Fitzgibbon getting us started, industrially. [The other is La Trobe University's Economic Department.] The same university had Ian Court[42] and Garry Weaven and Whitehead."[43] Whitehead, hitherto unnoticed in any account of Australian superannuation history, seems to have had a profound impact on Kelty.

In 1977, commenting on a paper by Max Corden, Whitehead advocated a trade-off between reduced direct taxation and little or no increase in nominal wages, contending that the resulting increase in the budget deficit "would not be merely acceptable but positively beneficial *in such a context*."[44] This particular remedy called attention to original ways and means of preventing stagflation. Ironically, given his formative role in the formation of what were to be Kelty's later endeavours in relation to superannuation and wages policy, Whitehead gave evidence for employers at National Wage Case hearings from the mid-1960s onwards. He was a dynamic, engaging, and inspiring intellectual who influenced Kelty's thinking; not in any crude sense of transmission line transfer of ideas, but by encouraging Kelty as

---

[41] Bill Kelty interview, March 2013.
[42] Later an ACTU Industrial Officer.
[43] Bill Kelty interview, March 2013. Dr David Morgan, who went on to become Senior Deputy Secretary of the Australian Treasury, was also an influential, contemporary student presence at the university.
[44] Whitehead, D.H. (1977) 'Comment', *Economic Papers*, Vol. 56, p. 38, emphasis in the original.

a young man to think about the issues. Writing in the early 1970s onwards, Whitehead thought that if Australia faced off-shore price shocks, a bout of inflation comparable or worse than what occurred in the early 1960s, its local institutions, including the industrial tribunals, were poorly equipped to cope. Whitehead advocated wage/tax trade-offs, channelling savings from wage increases to pension plans, labour market planning and training, greater focus on productivity-linked wage increases, price controls, wages policy linked to reducing inflation and improvements to government social programmes.[45] In his unique way, Kelty was to respond to these challenges in the development of the Accords between political and industrial labour, from 1983 to 1996, in the crafting of policy and tactics in response to the challenges of his time.

Also noteworthy in the development of fresh thinking was the publication of *Australia Reconstructed* (1987), a Report by the Mission Members of the ACTU and the Trade Development Council (TDC) to Western Europe the year before.[46] Members of the "mission" – most of whom were leading lights of the union movement, drawn from across the political and industrial spectrum – travelled in 1986 to Sweden, Germany, and the United Kingdom. They looked at the development of what they called "strategic unionism". Their report, "Linking Wage Adjustment Decisions to the Investment Decision", suggested the idea of wage adjustment linked to decisions to invest in particular industries.[47] Although the language of the Report mainly considered government-sponsored investment, the idea of wage restraint in exchange for policy initiatives was firmly planted in the minds of the Australian union leaders. The Report asserted: "Superannuation, as

---

[45] Whitehead, D.H. (1973) *Stagflation and Wages Policy in Australia*, Longmans, Camberwell [Victoria, Australia], supra, but particularly pp. 132-45.

[46] ACTU/TDC Mission to Western Europe (1987) *Australia Reconstructed, A Report by the Mission Members to the ACTU and the TDC*, Australian Government Publishing Service, Canberra. Biographies of those union and associated persons involved in the Australia Reconstructed mission are contained at the end of this book.

[47] In Chapter Two of *Australia Reconstructed*.

a deferred wage, has played a central role in those Mission countries committed to collective capital formation. These funds are channeled into domestic productive activity which creates not only current economic stability but builds on infrastructure capable of supporting a socially adequate standard of living. Bringing superannuation funds back from overseas to Australia is crucial to an improvement in domestic investment …"[48] The significance of superannuation investment for nation-building was emphasised – albeit somewhat naively. The point is that strategic unionism very much envisaged the development of a national system of superannuation. Although the authors of the Report still held to the notion that this might mean one national superannuation scheme, alternatives were canvassed, including some western European, union-employer schemes. Events back home showed that the unions were impatient for reform. By the mid-1980s, individual industry schemes began to proliferate.

Sixth, with the end of full employment, complacency associated with superannuation eroded as the perception grew that the good fortune of the "lucky country" was coming to an end.[49] The decline in agricultural and mining exports in the early 1980s, in particular, jolted many Australians from the stupor of complacency. Demographic pressures meant that Australians were living longer. Fear of being left destitute in retirement was becoming a major community concern. The affordability of the public pension system was questioned. In the early 1970s, in both the United Kingdom (through the activities of UK Labour Politician Richard Crossman) and Australia (with the Whitlam Government's commissioning of the Hancock Review into the need for supplementary savings, possibly through a national superannuation

---

[48] *Ibid.*, p. 93. To state that funds would be brought 'back' to Australia could imply a worldview of a primitive autarky. But the thinking behind the document was fluid and the words represented a compromise between contesting views.
[49] Without debating the concept's utility, Donald Horne (1921-2005) used the phrase as a criticism – Australia was being led by second raters, whose mediocrity was obscured by prosperity due to dumb luck, including mineral discoveries and their exploitation, rather than due to personal exertion or genius. See Horne, Donald (1964) *The Lucky Country*, Angus & Robertson, Sydney.

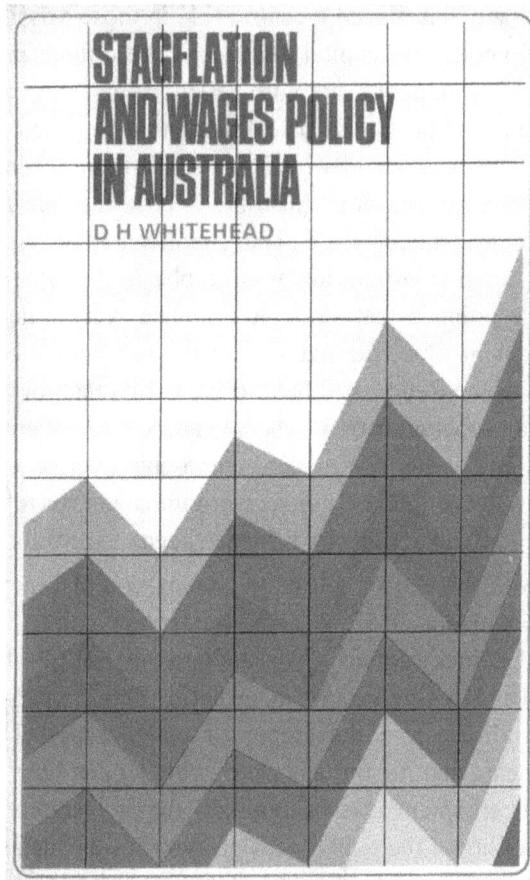

Figure 3: Professor Donald Whitehead's book on *Stagflation*, which influenced a young Bill Kelty while studying economics at La Trobe University. Source: Mary Easson's copy.

scheme), the issue was on the political agenda. Gradually, the idea of union and industry schemes emerged as part of a national system that would transition from retirement welfarism to compulsory self-funded retirement, where wealth would increasingly (but not exclusively) accumulate through long-term investment in the share market and other investment vehicles. It was becoming increasingly obvious that the countries whose economic systems were based on Anglo-

American capitalism had failed to provide adequate social-security benefits, relying instead on workplace pensions and private savings to make up the difference.[50]

Seventh, partly as a response to wage and price pressures and partly as evidence that a constructive relationship between the unions and a Labor government could be effective and transformative for Australia, the unions committed themselves in February 1983 to a Prices and Incomes Accord, effectively a manifesto setting out how an array of policy issues would be developed between the unions and the government. This became a feature of the 1983 election campaign, as Bob Hawke pressed the line about "bringing Australia together" through national reconciliation, national recovery, and national reconstruction.[51] The unions' main concerns were wage indexation, price regulation, and the introduction of a national health scheme, which became Medicare. Superannuation did not feature prominently. Kelty has pointed out that in the Accord Mark I "was an appendage at the end in which we said – Simon [Crean] and I – 'we are pretty keen to act on superannuation so we need to put something in ...we cannot not mention it'."[52] In Kelty's recollection, "Tom [McDonald of the Building Workers' Industrial Union] conceded, Laurie [Carmichael of the Amalgamated Metal Workers Union] conceded and even Ray Gietzelt [leader of the Miscellaneous Workers' Union], who strangely said at the end 'If that's what you want.' So Simon and I, we were the ones that got it into that first Accord."[53] The wording, however, was not so prominent in the first Accord document. It simply read "redress anomalies in the availability of occupational welfare such as

---

[50] Clark, Gordon L. (2012) "From Corporatism to Public Utilities: Workplace Pensions in the 21st Century", *Geographical Research*, Vol. 50, No. 1, February, p. 32.

[51] See Pemberton, Joanne, & Davis, Glyn (1986) "The Rhetoric of Consensus", *Politics, The Australian Journal of Political Science*, Vol. 21, No. 1, pp. 55-62. The article discussed the way Bob Hawke employed the idea and rhetoric of consensus between 1983 and 1985.

[52] Bill Kelty interview, March 2013.

[53] *Ibid.*

superannuation benefits."[54] Yet a couple of years later, Garry Weaven would write: "The ACTU position on superannuation represents a development of the historic decision of February 1983 to support the concepts of a social contract and the social wage."[55] He was emphasising that the unions were vying to be strategic in pursuing wages and social wages policy. Further, he commented that "... the strategy around superannuation does not stand in isolation but forms part of a package of measures designed to achieve the general objectives of improving living standards, creating employment and enhancing the equity of the system."[56]

It is interesting that in this formative period in the development of industry superannuation the key union leaders were keen to spell out their objectives to a wide audience, including members of the established, traditional service providers (from whom some allies and parties capable of implementing the strategy would come). There was a proliferation of articles in the trade journals on the case for change. The most important of the epistles was Weaven's "Superannuation: The Great Leap Forward. An Outline of the ACTU's Strategy for the Establishment of Universal Superannuation Coverage" (1985), published in *Superfunds* magazine, the journal of the Association of Superannuation Funds of Australia (ASFA), which set out the unions' agenda. This is worth referring to in detail.

In a statement that would lie at the heart of the contest between employers and the unions on what could be "afforded", Weaven suggested that "[o]ther things being equal, the advancement of workers' benefits at a pace consistent with the growth of national productivity [should] be neutral with respect to both inflation and overall profitability and hence on the capacity and willingness of

---

[54] ACTU/ALP (1983) *Statement of Accord*, Statement of Accord by the Australian Labor Party and the Australian Council of Trade Unions Regarding Economic Policy, ACTU, Melbourne, p. 12.

[55] Weaven, Garry (1985) "Superannuation: The Great Leap Forward. An Outline of the ACTU's Strategy for the Establishment of Universal Superannuation Coverage", *Superfunds*, No. 92, September, p. 4.

[56] *Ibid.*, p. 5.

business to provide for new investment."[57] In Chapter 5, referencing Dr Don Russell's research, the question as to whether or not this benchmark was achieved is addressed. The proposition that this *ought* be the case was indicative of the economic sophistication of the ACTU. Their leaders knew how to pitch their argument.

Arguments advanced by the ACTU included that "there is great inequity in the current availability of, and participation in, occupational superannuation."[58] This was set out in the table reproduced below which showed that the lower a person's wages, the less likely he or she would be covered by superannuation. Women were significantly less likely to be covered than men. As Weaven emphasised, "[a]lthough women constitute around 38 per cent of the workforce, they are far less likely than men to have superannuation coverage."[59]

He drew a conclusion, "… it would be inconceivable that the union movement would sit idly by if confronted by such inequities in, say, the application of annual leave or long service leave. And so with superannuation. The current problem will not be allowed to stand."[60] Weaven stated that in the development of superannuation policy, the "context is in turn the product of a clearer and developing recognition amongst unions of:

(a) the relative inefficiency of uncontrolled wage push as a means of achieving income distribution objectives;

(b) the importance of competitive Australian industry to longer term job security and living standards;

(c) the importance of government revenue raising and expenditure policies to the social wage and hence to the welfare of trade unionists and their families."[61]

---

[57] *Ibid.* The original had "will" rather than "should" in the sentence. The version here is in the appropriate tense.

[58] Weaven, Garry (1985) "Superannuation: The Great Leap Forward. An Outline of the ACTU's Strategy for the Establishment of Universal Superannuation Coverage", *Loc. Cit.*, p. 5.

[59] *Ibid.*, p. 7.

[60] *Ibid.*, p. 5.

[61] *Ibid.*, p. 4.

Figure 4: Proportion of Employees Covered by Superannuation in 1984			
Proportion of Employees in Receipt of Superannuation by Income and Sex – August 1984[1]			
Income (weekly earnings)	Males per cent	Females per cent	Total per cent
Under $160	9.9	4.8	6.4
$160 and under $200	22.2	18.6	19.9
$200 and under $240	31.0	20.2	25.3
$240 and under $280	37.6	30.7	34.7
$280 and under $320	47.5	39.8	44.8
$320 and under $360	51.4	43.3	49.3
$360 and under $400	57.8	48.9	55.8
$400 and under $440	64.0	46.5	60.4
$440 and over	73.3	52.9	70.2

Source: ABS Cat. No. 6334.0 Employment Benefits, Australia, August 1984. Cited in Weaven, Garry (1985) "Superannuation: The Great Leap Forward. An Outline of the ACTU's Strategy for the Establishment of Universal Superannuation Coverage", Superfunds, No. 92, September, p. 7.

This was very much an agenda requiring the closest cooperation between the industrial and political wings of the labour movement. Such thinking would be hard to contemplate outside of the Accord between both – as is discussed in the next Chapter.

Weaven argued that the problem with superannuation was not coverage alone. It was also the thinking, history, rules, conditions, and biases behind its evolution. Scraping the barnacles off was not enough; a new hull was needed. "Precisely because occupational superannuation has developed in response to the thinking and demands of employers and the Life industry, it is riddled with anomalies and anachronisms from the point of view of ordinary workers."[62]

---

[62] *Ibid.*, p. 7.

In justification, he argued that it was significant that so many in the industry were oblivious to what, from a union perspective, were glaring anomalies:

Consider these three factors:

- a low degree of vesting, and in many schemes no vesting of employer contributions at all;
- a preponderance of individual employer-based schemes;
- the estimate that only a tiny percentage of workers are likely to remain with the same employer throughout their working life.

One is forced to conclude that for the majority of workers the prospects of achieving adequate retirement benefits through traditional occupational superannuation arrangements are very slim indeed.[63]

Vesting was a particular problem: "Lack of vesting is a crucial element in the need for unions to address themselves to superannuation; but there are several reasons, not the least of which is the face that it is extremely rare for employees, in whose interests a scheme is ostensibly established, to have any effective voice in the administration and investment policies."[64] Enough was enough. If the unions had been slow to campaign on superannuation, there would be no more complacency or lethargy in tackling the issues:

> ... the time is right. There is no longer any prospect of dissipating the tide of demand for more and better quality superannuation. Each year sees an increase in the proportion of the workforce covered, and that proportion has now passed through a critical level below which it may have been possible to contain superannuation as a luxury of the privileged few. Moreover, the pioneering efforts of such unions as the Storemen and Packers, the Meat Industry Employees, the Pulp and Paper Workers and more recently the Building and Construction unions in co-operation with the ACTU itself, have set standards of simplicity and attractiveness to workers that simply cannot be ignored.[65]

---

[63] *Ibid.*, pp. 7-8.
[64] *Ibid.*, p. 8.
[65] *Ibid.*

Figure 5: Prime Minister Bob Hawke (right) and Treasurer Paul Keating, pictured at the ALP National Conference in Hobart on 7 June 1988, *Sydney Morning Herald* photo by David Bartho. Source: Fairfax Archives.

The timing was propitious for another reason – the events in 1983-84 which led to the creation of industry superannuation in the building industry:

The point has been made that even in the most difficult of industries (there are currently 5000 separate employers signed to BUSS), superannuation can be made a reality and unions themselves can do it. The only question now is whether the growth continues in a fragmented way or whether it becomes subject to centralised direction and co-ordination having regard to overall economic capacity and a degree of consensus as to the desirable key features of scheme design.[66]

The building industry learnings, discussed in Chapter 3, was pivotal to the unions – and the government – developing the confidence to think beyond the piecemeal and to contemplate creating something massive.

Key Questions

Having sketched the main features of the union campaign for change, some answers are becoming clearer with respect to the questions explored in this book. Broadly, we know the key elements of the system of retirement savings that previously existed in Australia – including, as earlier outlined, privileged access to senior executives in the private sector, poor vesting, woeful portability, discrimination and lack of coverage for large categories of workers. But what were the specific problems that caused particular actors to campaign for superannuation reform and why there was a significant break from past practice, rather than incremental change? It is clear that to fully appreciate what unfolded in the relevant period requires understanding of the personalities and the superannuation issues manifest in particular industries, particularly those that pioneered superannuation policy development in the 1980s. This, in turn, merits consideration of Australia's unique industrial relations system in that period.

A fuller answer lies ahead, in the rest of this book.

In this context, it is important to consider how particular industry funds came into being, the circumstances of their creation. Certainly, not all employers were opposed to the broadening of superannuation

[66] *Ibid.*, p. 9.

within the workforce. This book discusses how some were won over, as well as the significance of the major employer bodies to the debates. It also references the significance of the Australia Reconstructed visit in 1986 to Western Europe for the development of union thinking on superannuation, what the Accord signified, and how it came into prominence on superannuation, as well as the characteristics of the Australian model, including the so-called industry funds.

The story of superannuation policy in Australia emerged around points of influence, tension, and some defining moments of change. What particular actors thought they and others were doing at the time the Australian system was created had a crucial effect on this story, as did the role of experts such as actuaries and asset consultants. The key decision-makers on superannuation between 1977 and the release of Accord Mark 2 in September 1985 are worth examining. It is intriguing to consider whether the early supporters of broad-based superannuation foresaw the impact it would have on the financial sector – including layers of new jobs for consultants, investment managers, and financial advisors and planners – and what they contemplated about the potential consequences.

To explore the questions at the heart of this book, considerable original research was obtained through interviews with key players such as Bill Kelty, Secretary of the ACTU; Garry Weaven, Assistant Secretary of the ACTU and later a founder of Industry Funds Services (IFS) and the "industry fund model"; Greg Sword, one-time Secretary of the Storemen and Packers' Union, later the National Union of Workers, and founder, past Chairman, and former CEO of the Labour Unions Co-operative Retirement Fund; former Prime Ministers Bob Hawke and Paul Keating; former national building and construction union leader Tom McDonald; and others.[67] The interviews explored a range of questions including:

- What did the main proponents think they were achieving? What were their motivations?

---

[67] The full list is in Appendix 1.

- What were the unintended consequences?
- How was policy adapted and changed? Why?
- Could decision-making have been improved?
- Were the circumstances of the Australian experience unique? If so, in what way?
- The Australian system is sometimes described as three pillars comprising the Aged Pension, superannuation and encouragement for private savings. How does superannuation fit into this model?

Interviews were conducted using open-ended questioning to avoid contaminating the subjects' responses with the researcher's own assumptions or concepts. (This method is explained in Appendix 2.)

This book's core hypothesis can be summarised: The modern Australian superannuation system was developed from the creative foresight of its founders, principally those in the unions and the Labor Government.

The system of Australian industrial relations, as it stood in the early days of the development of superannuation, was a vital factor. Superannuation was conservatively considered a non-industrial relations issue until the middle part of the 1980s. Unions were able to exploit a loophole that established the first 3 per cent superannuation schemes and, by 1986-87, the 3 per cent "minimums" in awards. Later this was converted into the basis of the Superannuation Guarantee under the Keating Government in 1992. (Though, to be fair, it had been announced in 1991 by Bob Hawke while still Prime Minister.)

The political and personal dynamics of a few key players were extremely important, especially in the 1980s. This is exceptionally true of Bill Kelty, Paul Keating, and Bob Hawke, and particularly together against the backdrop of the Accord. Although victory has a thousand parents, it is those three – along with others, such as Garry Weaven, Iain Ross, Greg Sword, and Simon Crean – who were the authors of the modern Australian system of superannuation. Significant too was the fact that the ACTU leadership was highly economically literate, capable, and alert to the potential of what they were doing.

No one, however, foresaw how successful the campaign for superannuation justice and the creation of a dynamic part of the Australian savings regime through industry superannuation would become. It is clear, in retrospect, that opponents of industry superannuation, especially in the established retail superannuation institutions and among some employer advocates, were breezily cavalier, and used strategy and tactics that were fundamentally flawed. Some hoped the fuss would dissipate, rather than addressing the legitimate grievances raised by the unions. Their mistakes enabled the unions to establish industry schemes and overcome reservations – not just from industry generally, but even from their own members. After all, it was not obvious when the proponents of occupational superannuation were advocating for change that the industry funds would succeed in the way that later transpired. Unions worldwide, particularly the Teamsters in the United States, did not necessarily have a good record in investing money wisely.[68]

A key feature of the Australian system as it emerged was that the unions and the industry funds co-opted established players – such as actuaries, asset consultants, and fund administrators – to support their initiatives. From the start, the industry funds were notably proper in the exercise of their fiduciary responsibilities and arguably innovative in their approach to asset allocation. In this sense, as one of the founder administrators of industry super said, "the people that really initiated the system – Bill [Kelty] in particular, but others like Garry [Weaven] who worked with him – weren't just introducing a new form of super in the form of industry funds, but they were... I am not sure of the extent to which this was explicit in their minds but they were, in effect, changing the model of the super system that existed at that time."[69] At that formative stage, in the early 1980s, superannuation funds

---

[68] For a brief overview, Holley, William H., Jennings, Kenneth M., & Wolters Roger S. (2011) *The Labor Relations Process*, 10th edition, Cengage Learning, Mason [Ohio, United States], pp. 155f.

[69] Ian Silk interview, March 2013.

and their investments, were by and large run by vertically integrated financial institutions. For example, if a company or individual had their superannuation with the investment and life insurance leviathan AMP, then AMP would usually use AMP investment managers to invest the money, use AMP insurance to provide insurance, have the money invested with AMP and so on. AMP was a vertically integrated provider. Whereas, with industry superannuation, the view was taken by the union founders that "… [because] the organisations that have been involved in super for the last 50 or 60 years, or in AMP's case longer, haven't served our constituents well, our disposition was to not use them. In any event, whoever we use we will pick 'best-of-breed'."[70]

The prudent industry-fund behaviour on investment strategy was in contrast with the more radical aims set out in, say, *Australia Reconstructed* (1987), which had grand ideas of super money "saving" and expanding the manufacturing industry. The development of the Australian system can be said to be the triumph of pragmatism over radical investment strategies. It is an interesting contrast: the ardour associated with the advocacy of a cause and its eventual, tamed outcome. The investment strategies pursued by superannuation funds – prudence caused by a combination of fear of failure, regulatory and market factors – suggest that many funds, despite award entrenchment, faced competition from rival offers. Competition led to calls for reduction in management and administration fees and greater transparency.[71] As for regulation, more focused government oversight and standardised reporting served as a spotlight that shone on all of the parties in the superannuation sector.

Some interesting consequences of superannuation's extension as a near-universal right for employed Australians include the consistent,

---

[70] *Ibid.*

[71] Cf. Bateman, Hazel (2001) "Disclosure of Superannuation Fees and Charges", Discussion Paper for AIST, UNSW Centre for Pensions and Superannuation, August, 43 pp., http://pension.kiev.ua/files/cpsdp200304.pdf; and, Rice, M., & McEwin, I. (2002) "Superannuation Costs and Competition", Investment and Financial Services Association Limited Ltd, Sydney, at www.ifs.com.au.

exponential growth in savings through superannuation. Some nominated likely effects were way off the mark. For example, economist and prominent bureaucrat Vince Fitzgerald and others asserted in the late 1980s to early 1990s, that those promoting a new savings system seemed not to have considered whether a consequence of compulsory superannuation would be a reduction in personal savings and little, if any, increase in net savings. He and a co-author wrote "[i]n contrast to much of the hyperbole in recent public discussion, we conclude that the impact on financial intermediation of government sponsorship of superannuation savings, even in the latest more compulsory form, will not be great."[72] It is clear that compound returns and prudent investment management have proven this prediction wrong. The Fitzgerald critique, made in the early days of the development of the Australian system, highlights that choices were being made in the development of public policy – in part, as to how best to maximise national savings.[73] His fears can be put to rest on two grounds. First, the compound growth in savings, particularly post the Superannuation Guarantee legislation of 1992, has outstripped expectations. Second, the creators of the new environment were interested in ensuring that credible, robust, and enduring superannuation vehicles were created to enable working people to save and to have access to savings in retirement that would otherwise have been denied them.

Rational Policy v Muddling Through

In the development of public policy, it is interesting to see the contrast between those theories characterised by a "rational comprehensive" model (Simon, 1957) and Lindblom's (1957) "incremental" or "muddling through" model. The former, often described as an "economic rational model", assumes that policy development proceeds

---

[72] Fitzgerald, Vince, & Harper, Ian (1992) "Banks, Super Funds and the Future of Financial Intermediation", in Davis, K. and Harper, I. (1992), editors, *Superannuation and the Australian Financial System*, Allen & Unwin, St Leonards, NSW, p. 56.

[73] Events proved them wrong, as discussed later. There *was not* a reduction in personal savings and there was a significant increase in net savings.

logically and neatly, from problem to research, then to solution. This theory is sometimes anecdotally described in Australia as the "Treasury model"[74] but in fact, in the emergence of the Australian system of superannuation, Treasury was on the margins. This is not to say that the policy work and its development was not "rational", but that the process was not neat, tidy, or predictable. It was kinetic and inventive.

Incremental policy-making seems inadequate to describe what happened in the development of Australian superannuation policy. In large measure, policy development happened "on the run". Widely held grievances combined with the right circumstances and interactions among policy actors led to the forging of new policy. The question is: why specifically did this new policy occur in these particular circumstances? In considering conflicting ideas of the development of public policy, Cohen, March and Olsen (1972) refer to the "garbage can model" to explain government behaviour. This is an untidy and slightly misleading phrase. It is more a "drift and stab" model. Issues meander along with the policy players, and where some are more interested than others, they have a stab at a solution and re-set the discussion for everyone else. In this model, preferences are not clearly specified, the processes of organisation are not well understood, and people drift in and out of decision-making roles. The authors describe this as "a collection of choices looking for problems, issues and feelings looking for decision situations in which they might be aired, solutions looking for issues to which they might be the answer, and decision-makers looking for work."[75] At the same time, it is important to recognise that debate and confrontation are often essential to resolve issues, and cannot be entirely subordinated to technical analysis.

The material in this book is based on a "systematic process

---

[74] For an account of Treasury's market-oriented views in the 1980s, see Whitwell, Greg (1986) *The Treasury Line*, Allen & Unwin, Sydney, pp. 236-61.

[75] Cohen, M.D., March, J.G., & and Olsen, J.P. (1972) "Garbage Can Model of Organisational Choice", *Administrative Science Quarterly,* Vol. 17, March, pp. 1-25.

analysis"[76] of the politics of superannuation reform in Australia, which was achieved through a mapping exercise of the retirement incomes policy process. This involved a content analysis of the coverage of policy developments by the main industrial relations and superannuation journals, including the *Journal of Industrial Relations* and *Superfunds* magazine, the publication of the Association of Superannuation Funds of Australia, between January 1983 and December 1996, when many of the major reforms were implemented. The content analysis provided for an assessment of the salience of the retirement incomes and superannuation policy development, which helped to inform the reasons why the Hawke-Keating governments pursued their reforms and to explain how they managed to gain political support to implement them.

Chapter Outline

This first chapter outlines why a superannuation revolution occurred in the mid-1980s in Australia. The industrial relations system was decisively significant. Issues at the time included (among others): portability; different benefit levels to blue- and white- collar workers; coverage of women workers; vesting rules; transferability on termination; adequacy of benefit levels; defined contribution or accumulation schemes versus defined benefit or defined promise schemes; and whether particular benefits were offered at all or to all workers.

Chapter 2 traces the background and development of the Accord, and discusses the emergence of the Australian system of superannuation as largely shaped and inspired by the Accord processes.

Chapter 3 discusses the significance of the building industry as the most important union-inspired breakthrough in securing industry superannuation on a wide scale.

Chapter 4 highlights that without a clear settlement of the legal

---

[76] The phrase is used in: Hall, Peter A. (2008) "Systematic Process Analysis: When and How to Use It", *European Political Science*, Vol. 7, No. 3, pp. 304-17.

questions on superannuation coverage and entitlement, including the relevance of superannuation to the industrial relations system, progress would have been severely limited. Instead, High Court decisions and legislative changes secured opportunities for the unions to pursue extended superannuation coverage from 1986 onwards.

Chapter 5 discusses the significance of the Superannuation Guarantee legislation, which provided a legal framework and platform for extending superannuation coverage beyond the award-regulated workforce. As a consequence, industry superannuation schemes were extended beyond their award and industrial-relations regulated base to cover entire industries. Universality of coverage massively expanded the opportunities for unions to extend their initial, successful forays into industry superannuation. In retrospect, Prime Minister Keating's re-election in 1993 enabled the first phases of the Superannuation Guarantee to be fully phased-in to 9 per cent of earnings by 2002. Further consolidation occurred in 1996, when the incoming Howard government neither reversed the SGC legislation nor, ultimately, sought to restrain the phasing-in of the 9 per cent.[77] One of the interesting questions of Australian political and financial history is what would have happened if Keating had lost the election in 1993, and whether the SGC of 9 per cent of earnings by 2002 would ever have been implemented.

Having largely analysed in previous Chapters the main factors leading to the creation of Australian superannuation, Chapter 6 discusses potential future changes and challenges, particularly in the industry fund sector. Although I had thought the broad features of the system, as developed through the SGC, to be impregnable to large-scale change, now I am not so sure. There are tussles ahead as evidenced by the retail superannuation sector's vociferous endeavours to break into the sphere presently afforded to nominated industry schemes' particular status within modern awards.

Chapter 7 outlines some of the implications and consequences, both

---

[77] A restraining factor, of course, was that the Howard government did not control the Senate at this time.

intended and unintended, in the unfolding of industry superannuation, and its competitive impact. Based on insights offered through the interviews, the chapter also includes suggestions about future challenges.

The final Chapter sums up what has emerged as the distinctive, Australian system of retirement savings, the significance of the Accord, and the key persons involved.

Figure 6: Treasurer Paul Keating (right) and Prime Minister Bob Hawke in June 1988 at the ALP national conference, where the push was on for market-based reforms. *Sydney Morning Herald* picture by David Bartho. Source: Fairfax Archives.

A number of Appendices assist in telling the story. Appendix 1 lists the various persons interviewed. Appendix 2 outlines the kind of questions I asked of all major interviewees. Appendix 3 lists certain key economic indicators and complements Appendix 4 which condenses into a readable, ready reckoner format, the main changes that have occurred in Australian superannuation over forty years. So many "reforms" – it is almost as if, besides ideological differences, that governments of all stripes and their advisers are fickle when it comes to major policy. The summary proves we are living through a dynamic, still evolving public policy. Appendix 5 lists the 20 largest funds. Appendix 6 provides short details on most of the significant industry funds – many of whom emerged in the early and mid-1980s onwards. Appendix 7 lists the major asset consultants, active in advising the industry in Australia. There is a myriad of organisations representing the superannuation industry. The main ones are referenced in Appendix 8. Appendix 9 demystifies some of the key terms used in the superannuation industry. Many outsiders must wonder with so much jargon that some terms might as well be written in hieroglyphs. The Appendix has a glossary of terms. Appendix 10 lists various abbreviations used. I must admit to a tinge of guilt reading various acronyms in the penultimate draft. So I have tried to spell out more frequently what unfamiliar terms and initials mean. Inevitably, in a work like this, there are a lot of abbreviations. Hopefully this Appendix makes it easier for the reader. I very much enjoyed writing the Biographies of Key Persons – with pot shot histories of the main characters. What an interesting lot they mostly were – and are.

In sum, this publication adds to the public knowledge of the emergence of Australia's dynamic financial services industry, offers an unprecedented understanding of the development of the superannuation system, with unique information and insights hitherto hidden, or simply not available. The insights derived from the interviews and research involved in writing the book enable the true history of industry superannuation in Australia to be told for the first time.

2. The Significance of the Accord for Superannuation

The Union Campaign for Superannuation Justice

When a particular service is provided, those who receive it generally have one of three reactions: The first is satisfied loyalty. The second is to voice concerns (without seeking drastic reform) when the quality of services deteriorates and/or they perceive injustice about the services. Third and more radically, they seek an "exit" to set up a competing or significantly different system.[1] In the Australian context, the unions were not satisfied with the status quo concerning superannuation, at least from the time that the matter, as outlined in Chapter 1, was given attention by certain unions. The only loyalists to the existing system were those who benefitted. Working people were generally poorly served by superannuation (if they had access to it at all), so there was no rational reason for unions to be supportive of a system of benefits and entitlements not available to most workers. Effectively, the reforms enacted in superannuation from 1983 onwards were an exit from the previous system and the entire recasting of superannuation policy at a national level.

A very different system might have emerged if more astute heads on the employer side had prevailed and the industry itself seized on the necessary reforms besetting it, including sub-standard arrangements for millions of workers. As noted in Chapter 1, there was nothing inevitable about the union campaigns for superannuation justice – even if more than thirty years later the process might (superficially)

---

[1] Hirschman, Albert O. (1970) *Exit, Voice, Loyalty: Responses to Decline in Firms, Organizations, and States*, Harvard University Press, Cambridge.

look as if it unfolded in that way. One of the more astute employer representatives, George Polites, saw in the early 1980s the potential for the union movement to campaign for changes to the superannuation system. In an article for the Association of Superannuation Funds of Australia (ASFA) journal, he noted: "A number of trade unions are wedded to the pursuit of superannuation coverage for their members and have demonstrated a preparedness to engage in direct action to achieve this end."[2] This was in 1980 – three years before the election of a Labor government that would eventually introduce in tandem with the ACTU sweeping changes.

Polites thought that employers needed to think hard about the potential for unions to aggressively pursue reforms. He noted: "[i]n addition, there is the further development whereby some trade unions either already have or are giving consideration to establishing their own superannuation schemes and are seeking to force employers to contribute to these schemes."[3] Like other business people with an eye on this issue, Polites was interested in the potential financial power of unions, and its implications.[4] But he saw a trend fed by a fight for fairness: "… employers must come to terms with the fact that superannuation benefits can no longer be looked upon as handouts or gratuities."[5] Turning superannuation into an industrial relations contest had its own implications: "Of course the outcome of this sort of approach is without question going to result in a situation whereby those who are well organised and who work in high productivity and profitable areas of industry will fare better in the superannuation race than will those who are in labour intensive and low profit areas."[6] In other words, where bargaining power was strongest the more likely that the superannuation benefits on offer would be more generous.

The hard issues of portability, vesting and, generally, consistency

---

[2] Polites, George (1980) "Superannuation as an Industrial Relations Issue", *Superfunds*, No. 71, June, p. 4.

[3] *Ibid.*

[4] *Ibid.*, pp. 4-5.

[5] *Ibid.*, p. 5.

[6] *Ibid.*

and equity required either that the superannuation industry reached a considered reform view or to effectively delegate to government responsibility to take the necessary decisions to re-regulate the industry. Under the Accord processes, as outlined in this book, the unions struck out with their own schemes which prompted the government to act to address their grievances. Before that gained stampeding momentum, brontosaurus-like sluggishness characterised the industry. It was very slow to act. Yet some industry figures recognised that there was a certain inevitability that change would ensue. One of the State Chapters of ASFA, in an intelligent review of the issues, commented that:

> Portability of superannuation benefits will become an increasingly political issue. If the industry does not take the initiative, pressures will force the government to legislate in the area. In the light of overseas experience, the industry must ask itself if legislation is the solution it desires. If not, then it must come up with a positive approach of its own.[7]

Curing the problems of the industry required leadership and it was difficult to imagine how this might be possible – without external shocks.

Polites saw that "[t]he major factor that generates an interest in National Superannuation is the poor level of coverage for superannuation benefits of the community as a whole."[8] Thus, "[t]he interest of unions in superannuation is fundamentally a logical response to a genuine need – although it can certainly be clouded by some of the issues such as control of investments and vesting which have received so much attention."[9] Regardless of any concern about union involvement in investing decisions and the overall architecture of any new system, Polites said "[w]hether or not trade unions become

---

[7] Western Australian Sub Division of ASFA, Benefits Study Group (1981) "Portability and Vesting–Getting Off the Fence", *Superfunds*, No 77, December 1981, p. 12.
[8] Polites, George (1980) "Superannuation as an Industrial Relations Issue", *Loc. Cit.*, p. 6.
[9] *Ibid*.

more involved it is likely that employees will expect more direct representation than hitherto in the running of funds."[10] He reached a determined conclusion: "Simply put, superannuation can no longer be looked upon as something separate and distinct from the negotiated conditions of employment. It will have to be costed and valued, bartered and argued, as is every other condition of employment."[11] His prognostications largely fell on deaf ears.

Contrary to the interpretation that the unions had to persuade the government of the merits of superannuation, Keating defiantly contended "it fundamentally came even before the trade movement [started their campaign with the building industry scheme in 1983]."[12] Undoubtedly he initiated the first major tax reforms in 1983.[13] His view is that in 1983, while the unions were still unsure about their direction, he initiated a series of reforms, some originally recommended by the Asprey Committee to the Whitlam government in 1975,[14] and that such reforms lay the foundation for the ultimate superannuation package. The development of industry superannuation, with the formation of a series of industry funds, was a prospect only dimly perceived in the early 1980s. In his February 1983 election policy speech, ALP leader, Bob Hawke, stated, "… we are committed to raising over a 3-year period the basic pension rate from 22 per cent of average male earnings to 25 per cent."[15] The party also promised indexation of pensions. The 1984 Federal ALP platform contained several references to national superannuation.[16] But this thinking was still rooted in the majority

---

[10] [anonymous] Editorial (1980) "The 1980s", *Superfunds*, No. 70, March 1980, p. 3.

[11] Polites, George (1980) "Superannuation as an Industrial Relations Issue", *Loc. Cit.*, p. 5.

[12] Paul Keating interview, March 2013.

[13] See Appendix 4 on the major reforms in this period.

[14] *Ibid.*

[15] Cited in Australian Treasury (1984) "Issues and Broad Options Concerning National Superannuation", an Internal Discussion Paper Prepared by the Inter-Departmental Committee on Retirement Incomes, October, typescript, p. 7.

[16] Paul Keating interview, March 2013. The ALP policy is cited in, Australian Treasury (1984) "Issues and Broad Options Concerning National Superannuation", *Ibid.*, p. 8.

position of the Hancock report – national superannuation through taxation.

Early initiatives included the May 1983 statement by Treasurer Keating announcing changes to the tax treatment of lump sums; a joint media release on 15 August 1983 by the Treasurer, the Confederation of Australian Industry (CAI) and the ACTU on reform; and Keating's commissioning of an Inter-Departmental Committee on Issues and Broad Options Concerning National Superannuation, which reported in October 1984.

Policy initiatives in May 1983 included: higher levels of taxation on lump-sum superannuation and related payments; a non-retrospective tax increase on lump sums, excluding non-deductible contributions by individuals from a maximum effective rate of 3 per cent (i.e., 60 per cent on 5 per cent tax) to a maximum rate of 15 per cent for lump sums below $50,000 for recipients aged 55 or over, and 30 per cent for any excess over $50,000. For lump sums received by people under 55, a maximum rate of 30 per cent applied. Lump sums, however, were to be exempt from this tax if rolled over into another superannuation fund, or an annuity or superannuation pension or an approved deposit fund – therefore "assisting portability".[17]

Keating points out: "The pre-'83 position was grandfathered so that all of the 'concessionality' people had up to then was preserved. But after '83 – after that budgetary change in May – we then went to a more rational taxation regime which was on a tax rate of 30 percent. At the same time, I also brought in approved deposit funds (ADFs) and that would allow people, often women, who changed jobs and got a cheque from their employer to have some portable benefit. Remember that the funds were not vested in their name. They were simply money the employer owed you."[18]

A person could leave the workforce and have a family and re-

---

[17] This is Mr Keating's holograph note on a section of Australian Treasury (1984) "Issues and Broad Options Concerning National Superannuation", *Ibid.*, p. 5. He shared the document with me.
[18] Paul Keating interview, March 2013.

enter the workforce and pick up the ADF again. In the meantime the ADF could have been invested and continued to earn. That was done to achieve broader availability of the concessions for the workforce at large. Keating notes that "this was not done with the ACTU's agreement. Bill [Kelty] and I had a – you wouldn't call it a sharp falling out – but a bit of a falling out over it, considering we needed the ACTU then in 1983 with the real wage overhang."[19] Kelty, however, was thinking ahead. Just before the Accord was finalised he said "[a] prices-incomes policy such as that proposed by the labour movement is an attempt to say to this country, and to the unions in this country, that the task before us is to try to reconcile the demands of achieving lower levels of inflation and lower levels of unemployment and avoiding the position where unemployment is forced to increase in order to try and control inflation."[20] Kelty saw that more than wage and price control was needed. He had in mind the "social wage" which he described as "important and concerns the nature of the supportive policies of government". Thus, "[a]s has already been demonstrated in other countries where those supportive policies do not exist a prices and incomes policy will not work."[21] Superannuation was on his agenda, even if some of his colleagues were slow to "pick up".

The tax on lump sums was initially controversial: "The unions in April 1983 or March 1983, would never have agreed to start changing the tax treatment of lump sums. Never … Putting tax up wasn't part of their 'go' and it wasn't one of their issues either."[22] Keating argues that

---

[19] *Ibid.* The "real wage overhang" is a reference to the idea that real wages growth in excess of labour productivity growth created an overhang, which resulted in unemployment. Keating believed that wages explosions over the previous decade, particularly 1980/81 had this effect and was in excess of what the economy could afford. Rebalancing needed to occur. See: Mitchell, William F. (1998) "Macroeconomic Policy in Australia 1983-1996", Centre of Full Employment and Equity, The University of Newcastle, p. 10.

[20] Kelty, Bill (1984) "An Incomes and Prices Policy for Australia", in Aldred, Jenny (1984), editor, *Industrial Confrontation*, Australian Institute of Political Science and Unwin & Allen, North Sydney, p. 43. Although published in 1984, Kelty's piece was written while he was still ACTU Assistant Secretary.

[21] Kelty, Bill (1984) "An Incomes and Prices Policy for Australia", *Loc. Cit.*, p. 45.

[22] Paul Keating interview, March 2013.

he spent hours with Kelty discussing the logic and potential next steps associated with what he was pursuing: "I said to Bill: 'Just think about what this thing offers you. By getting to a rational basis of taxation and superannuation, we have the possibility of extending this as a social thing in the workforce'."[23] Such discussions were part of each of them getting each other's measure, knowing each's motivation and, quickly, the development of trust and rapport.

In August, 1983, in a joint statement with the ACTU on the change of the treatment of lump sums, "... the Treasurer announced that the government had agreed to continue conferring with the ACTU and other interested parties with the objective of considering a national retirement package. Among other things to be canvassed will be the approved deposit funds, portability and vesting ..."[24] This was because "at that stage you [i.e., an employee] didn't own it. It was in a fund belonging to the employer. He might have been obliged to give it to you but it was never yours."[25] This grievance, the iniquities of the then system, aggravated the unions. By the end of the 1970s, the Labour Union Co-operative Retirement Fund (LUCRF) caught the imagination of many in the movement. This is discussed next.

Case Study of LUCRF and Greg Sword

Greg Sword started working for the Federated Storemen and Packers' Union (FSPU) in 1974. Trained as an engineer, he came to the attention of the leadership of the Victorian union movement by impressing the then FSPU State Secretary Bill Landeryou at an ALP Conference. The latter had an eye for attracting able people; he also recruited Bill Kelty and Simon Crean, later ACTU Secretary and President respectively, to the union.

Although he resigned from the Victorian State Electricity Commission just shy of ten years' service to join the FSPU, Sword received nothing in superannuation but his own contributions. That

---

[23] *Ibid.*

[24] Media Release, Treasurer's Office, 15 August 1983. Copy from Mr Keating.

[25] Paul Keating interview, March 2013.

kindled in him a burning desire for superannuation reform. For the FSPU he developed LUCRF, originally set up for the union's officials. In the 1970s, he extended coverage of the fund to workers in the skin and hide industries and retail distribution, and then more generally. In 1984 he was elected national General Secretary of FSPU (later, following amalgamations, the National Union of Workers, or NUW). In leaving his previous employment, he noted that his situation was typical: "People would be in the fund for many years, say 10 to 15 years or whatever, and they'd be terminated or leave or whatever and they would get a return of essentially their own money."[26]

Most of the private sector individual company schemes were run by AMP or National Mutual, not by the employing companies themselves. "When you would ask for the trust deed," Sword notes, "they'd say no … It didn't take you long to appreciate that the way in which the system worked essentially was that it was zero vested, and the only people that actually succeeded in getting something out were those who stayed for 40 years and retired in their 60s."[27]

On the formation of LUCRF, Sword observed that because officials did not stay in the one job for 40 years or so, "we put in place a superannuation fund for the officials and staff, which was an accumulation fund fully vested so that all of the money put in was yours when you left."[28] This prompted him to think of applying the model more generally:

> From that experience, I thought, well, in truth, this is the sort of fund that our members ought to be involved in. Not even a [defined benefit] promise scheme, which promises you the world if you stay in for 40 years, because the people we represent…don't have superannuation. So what we ought to be thinking about was an accumulation fund. And, not only that, the other thing, the other obnoxious thing, from our point of view, was that they had no say in how those funds were operated by the employer.[29]

---

[26] Greg Sword interview, June 2012.

[27] *Ibid.*

[28] *Ibid.*

[29] *Ibid.*

Sword wanted the union movement to think of superannuation as part of a person's wage package. Years later, he seethed, "… what on earth, what sort of thinking leads to saying, 'this is your pay but if you don't stay for 40 years we take it off you'?"[30]

Figure 7: Bill Landeryou *Source*: the ASFA journal *Superfunds*, 1978

At first there was no explicit idea of building something huge. Sword's efforts were localised, aiming to fix the problems of the union members he represented. "The solution was this sort of really aggressive, radical point of view that this was members' money and they should control it, not the employer."[31] As Bill Landeryou put matters, "… the existence of a superannuation fund should be no bar to seeking better or alternative employment. Any scheme that falls short of full portability without loss, is unjust and inadequate."[32] The

---

[30] *Ibid.*

[31] *Ibid.*

[32] Landeryou, W.A. (1978) "The Union Attitude to Superannuation", *Superfunds*, No. 65, December, p. 31.

difference in the approach of LUCRF and other schemes "… was that we didn't want to just amend, we actually wanted to control it."[33] Sword asked Landeryou if he could negotiate inclusion of the LUCRF fund in awards and agreements. Sword wanted to use that vehicle because, in those days, an employee could not join a superannuation fund unless the employer made a contribution to it – "those were the tax rules".[34]

Figure 8: Union Demonstration by the National Union of Workers, Greg Sword in forefront to the right, not dated but *circa* 1989. *Source*: Greg Sword personal collection.

Referring to the skin and hide industry, where in 1978 a dispute broke out on superannuation, he observed, "I mean, the union worked hard for them, but most of them were migrants, most of them… English was their second language. And because it was, and because they weren't good at expressing themselves, I think people thought that they were silly. I didn't find that. I found that they paid much more attention to the detail than the [average] Aussie did."[35] In

---

[33] Greg Sword interview, June 2012.

[34] *Ibid.* For a contemporary account of the superannuation rules, see Knight, E.S. and others (1982) *Superannuation Planning in Australia*, Third Edition, CCH Australia Limited, North Ryde.

[35] Greg Sword interview, June 2012; supplemented by an email exchange, Greg Sword to Mary Easson, 29 October 2013.

response to the union claim, the employers countered with what they thought was an offer too good for the average employee to refuse. "What they did is that they said: 'We will contribute the six bucks to the super fund or the union fund for anyone who chooses to go in it; however, they must make a $2 contribution themselves. Anyone who doesn't want to go into the superfund, we will pay them a tax-free travelling allowance of six bucks.' So, I'd got my offer. So, I said we'd take it back to our members."[36] The members overwhelmingly decided to join LUCRF, rather than taking the travelling allowance. By December 1978, 24 companies in the skin and hide trade had signed up to LUCRF.

The union realised that this could become something big. The union leadership wanted Sword to hone his skills: "The other thing, probably in November, was that they sent me overseas to look at the cooperative sort of insurance industry around the world ... I might have negotiated the agreement with them earlier in '78. I went overseas and I finalised the super fund and the trustee and rules when I came back."[37] In thinking through the issues, Sword said:

What really helped me was the Europeans, the Swedes in particular. I went there and talked to a company called Folksam, which was a cooperative insurance company,[38] and they gave me ideas about the social partnership between unions and employers, and I brought that back too ... how we would approach our trustee; and so we said if we are going to have a trustee company, we are going to have a board to be representative of the employers, because we had the employees of unions on that board, whilst the union would own the company. It gave us a much deeper involvement with the employers and it was a lot more, much more legitimate. If we had only just union people on the board, and we were getting all this money, they could see that claims were going to be made ...[39]

---

[36] Greg Sword interview, June 2012.
[37] *Ibid.*
[38] Folksam is one of Sweden's largest investment managers. See www.folksam.se/english, accessed 23 May 2013.
[39] Greg Sword interview, June 2012.

What I learnt from Sweden and from Europe was the idea of the social partnership between the employer and the unions, and the history, and the good things that they could do cooperatively. So I applied that sort of model to our superannuation. So that's the model we introduced, and we got employers to be representatives on the board. And so by 1 December 1978, contributions started coming in, and we were away ...[40]

It was something that we wanted to solve, the problem for our members, because the superannuation system available to them was essentially not even a myth, and we wanted to put that behind; that was also our view about 'it's your money' and workers should control it; not representatives of capital.[41]

In March 1979 a dispute on superannuation coverage broke out in Melbourne in warehouses owned by Woolworths. Oblivious to the injustices the union was complaining of, conservative stockbroker and NSW Liberal MP Peter Philips lamented in a lengthy 1979 essay on developing union involvement in superannuation: "Woolworths had a perfectly good wages superannuation scheme in existence for 40-odd years prior to the recent dispute, and for this reason alone it is hard to understand why the SPU [i.e., the Storemen and Packers' Union] picked Woolworths so early in its campaign."[42] The complaints Sword fumed about concerning vesting, portability, and the rest were not seriously considered by Philips. "Perfectly good"?! "You would have to be joking!" was the union attitude.

Sword notes that: "At that time, the Chairman of the Board of the retailer Woolworths was on the board of AMP, and there was a fear that what was going to happen [was that the] unions [would be] seeking to take over super, threatening AMP's business model. So Woolworths decided to make a stand and fight ... I somehow think, and I think it is important to say, that it probably wasn't Woolworths, it was their industrial [relations] advice, which was an employer organisation who

---

[40] *Ibid.*

[41] *Ibid.*

[42] Philips, P.S.M. (1979) "Union Superannuation Funds", *Superfunds*, No. 69, December, p. 24.

had a real[ly] fanatical political view."[43] Instead of a localised dispute, perhaps quickly resolved through improvements in the current scheme, it became protracted, with national media coverage and publicity for the union cause.

"That dispute was what created superannuation as an issue, because what happened was because we had Woolworths – we were picketing the stores. It got the publicity, and what was discussed was the polemics; that is, what Woolworths was saying and what the employer's side were saying [was], 'this is socialism. What's going to happen is, they are going to control all the money, they'll have all the shares and then they will be able to start telling companies what to do and we have to stop it. And, not only that, what do these union people know about it? They are either going to lose the money, spend it, [or] steal it'."[44] was Sword's imagining of the arguments on the other side.

The Storeman and Packers Union's revolutionary idea in 1978-79 had been that superannuation belonged to the workers and, through LUCRF, should be controlled by them, fully vested, accumulated, but with joint employer representation on the board. "So that was the difference, it was totally different to what other people were arguing."[45] The next major breakthrough was in 1983 with the building unions' improvement in productivity through superannuation campaigns – which is discussed in the next Chapter.

Interestingly, some in the industry, even among opponents of union-sponsored superannuation, foresaw positive implications. The editorial writer of *Superfunds* magazine, writing in mid-1979, noting the abuses and anomalies in existing superannuation schemes, expressed the conviction that the union campaign could

---

[43] Greg Sword interview, June 2012.

[44] *Ibid.*

[45] *Ibid.* For an overview article on the emergence of LUCRF, see Philips, P.S.M. (1979) "Union Superannuation Funds", *Superfunds*, No. 69, December, pp. 24, 26-9.

lead to worthy, overdue reforms and even the evolution of a national scheme: "If so, the whole superannuation movement may in due course be extremely thankful to the Storemen and Packers' Union."[46] A more typical reaction, however, was to think harder about thwarting union initiatives. Devlin noted that in some industries "… some employers made major improvements to their funds during the negotiating process to counteract the union's demand for an industry or union controlled fund with the result that the union simply dropped the superannuation claim and started chasing a wage increase or some other benefit improvement."[47] This was a smart response by such employers – avoiding industrial conflict with their employees by going part of the way to address grievances. Even here the unions could say that the pressure they had brought to bear produced its own vindication. At the end of the day, the employees were better off than before. One battle, another to follow; the deferment of legitimate superannuation benefits would not be put off forever.

A whole specialist industry seemed to flourish dedicated to advising employers – as well as the life insurance offices, and the industry – on what to do if the unions came knocking. One adviser recommended to his clients:

> To summarise, an employer who wishes to improve wages super-annuation benefits at moderate cost or simply wants to avoid con-tributing to a union fund should:
>
> 1. Introduce a wages superannuation plan if one is not already in existence; 2. Reduce the eligibility period for wages superannuation members to a reasonably short period; 3. Consider the suitability of a uniform integrated benefit structure for his total workforce; 4. Introduce a gradual scale of vesting, preferably including preservation or portability of benefits; and 5. Consider member representation on

---

[46] [anonymous] Editorial (1979) "Who Will the Storemen Send Packing?", *Superfunds*, No. 67, June, p. 2.

[47] Devlin, Michael W. (1986) "Industrial Relations and the Superannuation Industry, Blushing Bride and Reluctant Bridegroom", *Superfunds*, No. 96, September, p. 11.

the trustee and ensure that benefits are effectively communicated to employees.[48]

In addressing the challenge posed by the unions, improvements were incrementally, and in some cases suddenly, being made to some existing schemes – but not enough, in most of them, in the unions' view.

There were some reservations in pockets of the Left of the union movement that union representation would suck the movement into the capitalist system, and that unions would therefore be less independent in making decisions. Sword recalls: "So they were not absolutely opposed, but we were criticised as being right-wingers."[49] But change was afoot. Kelty observed that "you've got others – significant unions like Ray Gietzelt's and others – saying that super is bad. And it was bad for the majority of his members because [it] got converted into payments only for people who stayed on a very long time. This was defined benefits, in which you had thresholds of service, in order to get it."[50] It was the form of superannuation that gave rise to certain objections. The unions were traditionally wary of defined benefit schemes, partly because of the inherent risk of employer failure, partly due to the administrative complexity of creating an industry model.[51] There was also the need to freshly embrace new thinking. "Wally Curran[52] [of the Meat Workers' Union] was not confined by any policy, so he's industrial – nor was Landeryou, and they are starting to think differently from the box that society put them in – but not out of

---

[48] Solomon, D.J. (1979) "Wages Superannuation-Government, Union or Employer?", *Superfunds*, No. 68, September, p. 11.

[49] Greg Sword interview, June 2012.

[50] Bill Kelty interview, March 2013.

[51] It might be noted that the public sector unions mostly loved statute-related defined benefit schemes – and sought to extend their coverage to blue collar workers, women, and the traditionally excluded in the public sector; for many, the old public sector schemes were "rivers of gold" but, equally, golden handcuffs. From the early 1990s onwards, despite significant objection from the public sector unions, most of the defined benefit schemes were closed to new members.

[52] See Appendix 6 for some details of the Australian Meat Industry Superannuation Trust (AMIST) scheme.

their box."[53] The Pulp and Paper Workers' Chris Northover was also a pioneer, whose documentation and experience were drawn upon in the development of LUCRF.[54]

Figure 9: Greg Sword speaking as LUCRF CEO *circa* 2012. Source: From Greg Sword.

Sword summarised that, as radical and innovative as his unions efforts were, the wider extension of superannuation required leadership elsewhere:

> ... ours was the radical beginning of this radical change; there was no other union claiming what we had claimed that provided the underpinning philosophical, policy base. What then happened was if Bill Kelty had done nothing, then all that would have happened is that we would have continued building it, bit by bit ... It was Bill who took what we were doing and turned it into a national cohesive approach to build this everywhere.[55]

He commented elsewhere that "[c]hange did not occur through

---

[53] *Ibid.*

[54] Email exchange, Bill Kelty to Mary Easson, 28 November 2013. Confirmed in Greg Sword interview, June 2012.

[55] Greg Sword interview, June 2012.

evolution, nor through a desire by either industry or the employer to provide a 'better product'. At the forefront of this revolution was the trade union movement and its membership."[56] Kelty thought that the LUCRF experience, and earlier wins in stevedoring by the Waterside Workers Federation, laid the basis for industrial superannuation, "... but you can't get the big breakthroughs because the courts still say you can't do it... You've still got major left-wing unions saying 'we don't want it', like [Laurie] Carmichael. 'We actually do not want this. It's an absorption into the system. It's all right for others but we don't want it'."[57] This thinking was to change, with Carmichael especially, re-evaluating his perspective. But in the late 1970s and early 1980s, many union leaders had reservations about the pursuit of industry super. Despite the seminal importance of LUCRF, it was slow to have a substantial impact. "Although it is true that the ACTU had followed along the experience of the Storemen and Packers from a decade earlier, that had very small numbers,"[58] was building unions' leader Tom McDonald's summation. He went on: "I see this ocean. Then by the '70s I see islands of industry superannuation schemes. I see the beginning of the future ... When I look at the '70s, what happened was several unions, independent of one another decided to make superannuation union business ..."[59]

Reflecting on this, Kelty says, "but then that's how things have changed. Ideas – the catalyst. Simultaneously all those [breakthroughs] are occurring. You've got the Storemen and Packers – I'm in the Storemen and Packers by now and I'm a great supporter of them and superannuation. They've got Landeryou saying this is an industrial thing and it starts to spread: the right to choose your superannuation."[60] Tom McDonald recalls, "injustice was the big issue. Blue-collar

[56] Sword, Greg (1992) "Superannuation as a Recruitment Tool", in Crosby, Michael, & Easson, Michael (1992), editors, *What Should Unions Do?*, Pluto Press in conjunction with the Lloyd Ross Forum, Leichhardt, p. 225.
[57] Bill Kelty interview, March 2013.
[58] Garry Weaven interview, March 2013.
[59] Tom McDonald interview, August 2012.
[60] Bill Kelty interview, March 2013.

workers were being discriminated against. You had company schemes in cases where it would apply in the salary area, but not to blue-collar [workers] … I've talked to Greg Sword and others and largely it was about injustice. It was largely about giving workers a decent income in retirement. I don't think they saw it [at first] as part of the big picture, about increasing domestic savings."[61]

The Industrial-Relations System and the Emergence of the Australian System

In early 1983, with the first Accord in draft form, then ACTU Vice President Simon Crean recalls that "the [draft] version of the Accord didn't have superannuation at all mentioned. And we added '… and superannuation'."[62] Along with ACTU Secretary Kelty, Crean was thinking strategically about the perils and opportunities for a future Labor government in Australia. "At that stage we were looking for all sorts of avenues because we had just carried, at the [1982] Labor Party [Conference], automatic quarterly cost of living adjustments… This was the big fallout at the conference … The left was opposed to a prices-incomes policy – a wages policy – because Callaghan had been defeated in the UK in 1979."[63] The ALP called for a "catch-up" in wages, as the Fraser government had imposed a wage freeze.[64] The UK experience was of deep interest to Australian observers. There had to be experiences to understand there, including mistakes to be

---

[61] Tom McDonald interview, August 2012.

[62] Simon Crean interview, May 2013.

[63] *Ibid.* The UK economy was in deep trouble in the late 1970s, with an IMF bailout and, from 1978, deep public spending cuts that led to a wave of strikes (the "winter of discontent") and the defeat of the UK Labour government at the 1979 General Election. See Artis, Michael John, & Cobham, David P. (1991), editors, *Labour's Economic Policies 1974-1979*, Manchester University Press, Manchester, pp. 273-7; and Dorey, Peter (2001) *Wage Politics in Britain: The Rise and Fall of Incomes Policies Since 1945*, Sussex Academic Press, Brighton [UK], pp. 201-25.

[64] For background see Dabscheck, Braham (1989) *Australian Industrial Relations in the 1980s*, Oxford University Press Australia, Melbourne & Oxford, pp. 26-41.

avoided and applied to Australia. Kelty thought "[a] country which is devoid of any solution other than to increase unemployment in order to come to terms with economic problems is a country which, in effect, is abdicating its basic responsibilities and conceding defeat."[65]

Crean had undertaken a study tour concerning the British experience of wages and prices policy. Conventional wisdom arising from the UK's travails was that income policies were too inflexible to control the economy. Discussing the Accord, former Hawke Government Industrial Relations Minister Peter Cook commented on the UK experiment that "Denis Healey[66] once said that adopting an incomes policy was like jumping out of a second-storey window: nobody in their right mind would do it unless the stairs were on fire."[67] Crean thought otherwise: "I looked at the Callaghan period[68] and I was part of the conference that really saw [that] this [was] something the Labor Party should be evolving to, but it was blocked by the Left. I went on this study tour ... and I went up to Oxford. I met with the people that had been involved with the prices-incomes policy in the UK. I saw how the thing had collapsed because there was this silly argument about wages – wages alone – and I came to the view that we couldn't allow the focus to be so narrow. We really had to find ways in which we addressed aspirations or improved benefits for our members other than just through money wages."[69] "Wages alone" would doom a prices and incomes policy; more was needed. Political and industrial labour needed to imagine what might be possible – with the social wage, for example.

---

[65] Kelty, Bill (1984) "An Incomes and Prices Policy for Australia", *Loc. Cit.*, p. 43.

[66] Healey was Chancellor under the Callaghan government and responsible for economic policy.

[67] Cook, Peter (1991) "The Accord: An Economic and Social Success Story", address given to the LSE in June 1991, reprinted in Crosby, Michael, & Easson, Michael (1992), editors, *What Should Unions Do?*, Pluto Press in conjunction with the Lloyd Ross Forum, Leichhardt, p. 152.

[68] Prime Minister "Sunny Jim" Callaghan's disposition turned dark during the strikes of 1978-79 that helped usher in the Thatcher government and 18 years of Conservative party rule in Great Britain.

[69] Simon Crean interview, May 2013.

Crean continued, "that was a lasting consequence for me, and that is why I came back and said '… and superannuation'. We had everything else in it."[70] Bill Kelty had only become Secretary of the ACTU in February 1983,[71] following the surprise resignation of Peter Nolan. ACTU President Cliff Dolan left much of the policy and strategic work to the two young, dynamic ex-Storemen and Packers officials, Kelty and Crean.[72] They were bold in seeking to effect industrial relations reform, within the context of responsible economic change, while striving for superannuation equity. Kelty thought that the key test was whether unions were capable of showing the discipline and responsibility needed to make an Accord work: "The basic impact will be that unions will no longer be able to hide behind industrial tribunals: as a trade union movement you have got to be involved, you have got to take responsibility."[73] This had never been attempted before in Australia.

The first Prices and Incomes Accord was an agreement between the ACTU and the ALP in February 1983, on the eve of the March 1983 Federal elections. It set out an agenda for political and industrial change by a Labor government. Eight Accords were developed through the life of the Hawke and Keating governments, from 1983 to 1996. An understanding of the development of the Australian system of superannuation requires an understanding of those documents, because so much of the bargain on superannuation between political and industrial labour is encapsulated within them.[74]

There eight iterations of the Accord are now discussed.

---

[70] *Ibid.*

[71] [anonymous] "ACTU Secretary", *Canberra Times*, 12 February, p. 3.

[72] Crean succeeded Cliff Dolan as full-time ACTU President in 1985. Immediately before, he was national Secretary of the Storemen and Packers Union and simultaneously a senior ACTU Vice President.

[73] Kelty, Bill (1984) "An Incomes and Prices Policy for Australia", *Loc. Cit.*, p. 47.

[74] The information here is based on ACTU documents on the Accord as well as personal understanding. See: Cook, Peter, *Loc. Cit.*; Dabscheck, Braham, *Loc. Cit.*; and, ACTU (2005) History of Super. Melbourne: Australian Council of Trade Unions, http://www.actu.asn.au/super/about/super_history.html, accessed 5 April 2013.

Accord Mark I (February 1983)

The original Accord was a strategic and political document designed to demonstrate to the Australian public that the ALP was "ready" to govern in tandem with a responsible trade union movement. In contrast with the Whitlam years, the agreement between political and industrial labour was evidence of a coherent analysis of, and remedy for tackling, a stagnant economy and reducing the number of industrial disputes. The Accord proposed half-yearly wage increases indexed to the CPI and supported the introduction of compulsory medical insurance, Medicare. Implicit with the latter was the possibility that if actual health-insurance costs were reduced because of a tax-levied national medical insurance scheme, the CPI would fall meaning that any wage claim would be discounted. In that respect, workers would pay for Medicare should they forego such wage increases.

Figure 10: Bob Hawke addressing ACTU delegates in 1983, Melbourne. Behind him, from left to right are Bill Mansfield, then Federal Secretary of the Australian Telecommunications Employees' Association; Paul Munro, National Secretary, Australian Clerical Officers Association; Ray Gietzelt (obscured), National Secretary, Federated Miscellaneous Workers' Union of Australia; and John MacBean, Secretary of the Labor Council of NSW. Source: Records of Unions NSW.

Kelty reflected, "it is because the health care costs implemented reduced the CPI. We had to accept the modified CPI. We effectively had to pay another 2 per cent so we accepted it – 4.5 per cent for a national healthcare system. We chose to accept it. People thought that might be hard for them. But that was easy because the entire union movement wanted a national healthcare system and they were prepared to pay for it. If it was 2.5 per cent or 3 per cent or 4 per cent, it didn't really matter."[75] He goes on to say, "it was important just to get it. It wasn't very hard to get at all because there was no bargain about it. You didn't have to go to Carmichael and say, 'look, please agree to it,' [as if] he wouldn't want to. So that wasn't hard."[76] Strategically, the key unions across the political spectrum saw Medicare as an essential reform, literally worth paying for.

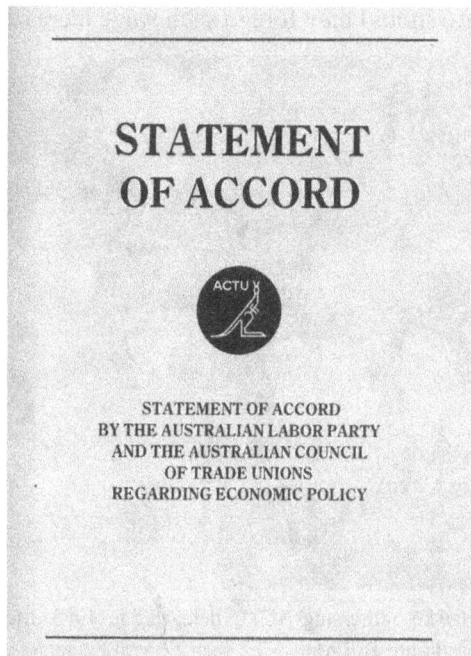

Figure 11: The Statement of Accord, adopted in February 1983

---

[75] Bill Kelty interview, March 2013.
[76] *Ibid.*

Left unresolved was the promise of "catch-up" after the wage freezes of the last years of the Fraser government. This promise was enshrined in the 1982 ALP platform and reinforced in fiery speeches given at union rallies prior to the March 1983 election. The new Prime Minister, Bob Hawke, described the Accord as a centralised system of wage fixation for the purpose of economic recovery. At the same time, he felt that he needed to share the Government's challenges and forge a wider consensus by convening an economic summit of unions, employers, welfare, and political leaders. He stated at the summit held soon after his election:

> As far as wages are concerned, the Government will participate in the conference on wage fixation scheduled to be held in the Conciliation and Arbitration Commission. We will base our approach to that Conference on the conclusions of the Summit and on the prices and incomes Accord. In that context, I would point out again that all at the Summit agreed that if a centralised system of wage fixing is to work, there must be an abstention from sectional claims except in special and extraordinary circumstances. Let me say that my Government's interpretation of what constitutes such circumstances is the common sense interpretation and leaves no room for selfish claims from maverick sections of the trade union movement. Participants at the Summit Conference recognised that if restraint in incomes is to be exercised, then it should be exercised universally. In that spirit of equitable sharing of the burdens of recovery the Summit also stressed the need for restraint in non-wage incomes such as dividends, professional fees and the like.[77]

Part of that restraint entailed trade-offs such as agreeing to lesser wage demands in exchange for social wage benefits, like comprehensive medical cover. But Hawke and the unions wanted restraint all round, including from business. Thus a number of consultative bodies were established, such as the Economic Planning

---

[77] Hawke, Hon. R.J.L. (1983) "Statement to the National Economic Summit", House of Representatives *Hansard* (Parliament of Australia) 3 May.

Figure 12: ACTU Secretary Bill Kelty speaking to ACTU Industrial Officer Jan Marsh outside of the ACTU Congress, September 1983, Melbourne. Source: Records of Unions NSW.

Advisory Council (EPAC) in 1983 and the Prices Surveillance Authority (PSA) in 1984.[78]

Hawke was to reflect that, "we started right off at the summit and it went on from there. One of my favourite sayings is 'ignorance is the enemy of good policy'."[79] He wanted all stakeholders to think through the consequences of their actions and to constructively decide policy mindful of wider impacts. On the employer side, many CEOs felt inadequate to properly engage in the discussions at hand. Large company representatives felt "outflanked, disorganised, even

---

[78] On the summit, see Kemp, D.A. (1983) "The National Economic Summit: Authority, Persuasion and Exchange", *The Economic Record*, Vol. 59, Issue 3, September, pp. 209-19, which refers to the creation of the PSA. More generally, see Fallick, Leslie (1990) "The Accord: An Assessment", *The Economic and Labour Relations Review*, Vol. 1, No. 1, June, pp. 93-106.

[79] Bob Hawke interview, December 2012.

traumatised by the summit meeting."[80] This led to the formation of the Business Council of Australia (BCA).[81] Kelty recalled: "we sit there and we then have an Accord and we have to then decide where it fits. It is essentially about a limited range of things. Essentially, about legitimacy of a cooperative approach which is 'rhetorical' but also real. Strategically, it's about consolidating the concession made by the unions to pay for Medicare. We've got to pay for it in two ways. We've got to pay for it in a levy, which we were prepared to do, but we also had to concede a wage increase."[82] Not everyone was enthusiastic. Employers were wary, thinking that the wage restraint under the Accord was just a lull before another industrial storm. Metal industry employers' advocate Bert Evans said "we opposed the first Accord, but then people said to us, 'what are you bloody doing? This is too good to be true. We have got industrial stability, we know what our costs are going to be, we have got unions' cooperation, we were restructuring the award, and we got rid of 380 classifications. It was restructured down to 14 so all the things enabled us to do all of that while the Accord was developed."[83] Such thinking marked a radical departure from the experience under the Fraser government, and indicated a new-found flexibility from the unions. One contemporary observer commented that "1984 will be remembered as the year that wage increases almost went out of fashion. Into fashion instead came superannuation packages, tax reductions, shorter working hours and improved long service leave."[84]

On 23 September 1983 the Conciliation and Arbitration Commission established a system of principles for fixing wages and

---

[80] Allen, Geoff (2012) "Business Council of Australia. Its Origins and Early Years", in Sheehan, Mark & Sekuless, Peter (2012), editors, *The Influence Seekers: Political Lobbying in Australia*, Australian Scholarly Press, p. 82.

[81] Formed in 1983, the BCA comprises the CEOs of Australia's biggest corporations. Originally, it was of the top 100; now it is the top 121 CEOs.

[82] Bill Kelty interview, March 2013.

[83] Bert Evans interview, May 2013. The last points reflected later iterations of the Accord, but Evans is recalling what for him was a new, surprising spirit in industrial relations.

[84] Mulvey, Charles (1985) "Wage Policy and Wage Determination in 1984", *Journal of Industrial Relations*, Vol. 27, No. 1, March, p. 68.

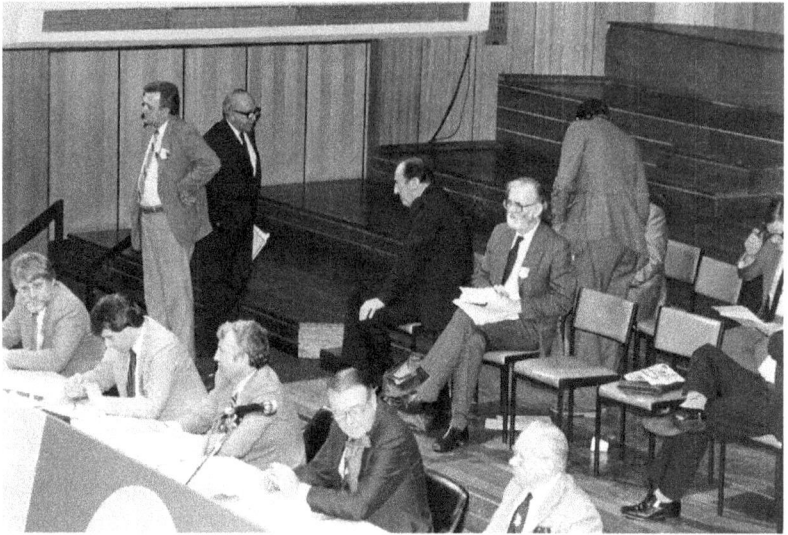

Figure 13: ACTU Congress in Melbourne, September 1983. Standing to the left at the back, John Maynes speaking to George Slater, federal secretary of the Postal workers' Union; seated is Paul Munro Secretary of the Australian Clerical Officers Association; behind him to the right is Jim Maher, reading his papers. On the stage, from right to left, are Charlie Fitzgibbon, Waterside Workers Federation and Senior Vice President of the ACTU; Cliff Dolan, ACTU President; Bill Kelty, ACTU Secretary; Simon Crean, ACTU Senior Vice President; and Bob Gradwell, joint Assistant Secretary. Standing behind them on the stage is Bill Richardson, ACTU joint Assistant Secretary. Source: Records of Unions NSW.

working conditions for a two year period. This provided for CPI adjustments to award wages in each six month period, subject to the state of the economy, and a hearing in 1985 to determine the distribution, if any, of productivity growth in the period. Wages increased by zero in the period to June 1984, due to the 0.2 per cent drop in the CPI for the March and June quarters of 1984 (associated with a drop in medical costs occasioned by the introduction of Medicare). The following six months, also affected by the depressive impact on the CPI of reduced medical costs, saw inflation-linked wage adjustments of 2.6 per cent awarded by the Commission in April 1985. Associated with wage restraint was a gradual improvement in the economy: 5 per cent GDP growth in 1984-85, recovery of profits, fall in unemployment to 8.1 per cent (down from 10 per cent in 1983) and the reduction in underlying inflation to 6.7 per cent.[85]

Crean remembers that in early 1983, "we then get to a position where we are going to the election with the Accord that says, 'we will revert to quarterly cost of living adjustments. There will be a claim for catch-up ...', and that's what got into the Accord, and it was an Accord that had been re-written to include super. Then what happened with the economic summit – because they introduce Medicare initially – the effect of introducing the Medicare levy is to reduce the cost of health, which had been a huge thing in the CPI. So the CPI was negative. Negative!"[86] Moreover, he notes, "it carried over for two quarters. So, effectively we got into office and for another six months there was no wage increase, but it was all consistent with our policy prescription. We still kept saying that there would be catch-up."[87] But Kelty and Crean argued that catch-up need not be entirely by wages. They were positioning the unions to be more strategic in pursuit of their goals. As Crean notes, "the other way you take pressure off wages is to do family payments, social wage ... So we started building a credibility of delivering that, which kept giving wages relief."[88]

Crean insists that superannuation was high on the agenda, because, as a means of catching up, "it would stop inflation ... We said it would help with the inflation because if you got a 3 per cent wage increase then the on-costs would inflate that figure. The on-costs on a wage increase were another third. So 3 per cent becomes 4 per cent." Working through this policy position, however, was controversial and contested within the unions. The debate over securing increases in minimum rates, without blowing the economy apart by unleashing inflation, was a case in point. Crean says:

---

[85] Dabscheck, *Loc. Cit.*, p. 97.
[86] Simon Crean interview, May 2013.
[87] *Ibid.*
[88] *Ibid.*

With the partnership that Bill [Kelty] and I forged in the lead-up to the 1983 election, … when I [ran] the big wages campaign for the Storemen and Packers, we accepted the principle of absorption. The Metal Workers on the Left would never accept it … I knew it was the legacy of that trip to the UK and how things can break down, but I knew that what we had to do if indexation was to work, you had to lift the minimum rates. Our minimum rates were depressed. We ran the campaign for a $30 increase in the minimum but a $10 absorption, so if people were $10 or more over the award they [i.e., employers] didn't have to pay the full $30. The Metal Workers went berserk about that but I did it anyway. We won it in Victoria. I went up to New South Wales because [local FSPU Secretary] Frank Belan asked us to come up. Alan Jones was the head of the Employers' Federation, and I had used the tactic in Victoria successfully that said, 'we will exempt you from the dispute if you sign up.' But I had to get the approval of the members for that because this [was], potentially, a breach in solidarity with the Metal Workers.[89]

The tactic worked in Victoria. Crean remembers that in NSW, however, Alan Jones stormed in to one meeting with his deputy Garry Brack in tow. Crean recalls Jones saying in quivering tones: "'I will just tell you this, Mr Crean. They are a weak pack of bastards in Victoria, but you won't find that here. There is no way that you are going to come up here and use those bully tactics in the same way with our employers'."[90] Crean recalls responding, "'Alan, if I can call you that, just come over and look out the window'. He said, 'what is this for?' I said, 'see all those cars down there?' I said, 'they are all signing up'. I said, 'there is the pile of letters'. I said, 'Alan, I believe at this moment that I represent more of your members than you do'. And I said, 'by the way, we are going to be pursuing superannuation as well'."[91]

Interestingly, Crean recalls "[Jones said,] 'I believe people should have superannuation.' He was actually an early advocate which, in its own way, is a reason why I was convinced that we had to push for

---

[89] *Ibid.*
[90] *Ibid.*
[91] *Ibid.*

superannuation … What I then got was the $30 wage increase. This [was] the wages breakout the Fraser government could not contain. In the oil industry, along with the Metal Workers, we got the 38-hour week. So, what we had was a solid foundation on which to go. What Fraser wanted to stop... he wanted to engineer a dispute in the oil industry. He did. But anyway, [he] lost the election."[92]

At the economic summit of May 1983, Kelty and Crean privately canvassed superannuation options with employers. "We had spoken to the employers as part of the Business Council discussions and the Economic Planning Advisory Council (EPAC), which came out of that economic summit. We said to them, 'there is merit in this. As a nation we have to come to grips with it. It is less of a cost to employers if we can get the trade-off. Let's have the Commission determine it'."[93]

Crean says, "it came back to the fairly fundamental precept that says, 'unions are about distribution, but you can't influence distribution effectively unless you are growing the show,' and you can't just keep indexing if there is not the capacity to pay – as much as we would fight the capacity-to-pay argument. So, we had to be part of the wealth-creation thrust. That's what they needed us for, and in the end... they had confidence in what we were trying to do on the remuneration or disposable income front and do the trade-offs in taxes …"[94]

Kelty recalls putting matters into the context of breaking the cycle of spiralling inflation: "… we said, 'we've got an exit strategy in terms of this cycle, and our exit strategy will make sure that the industrial system doesn't do the same damage it did in the past. What happens is, if metal workers or building workers seriously got a big wage increase, that would [then flow] to the transport workers, and then would go to everybody. So we said, 'what we are going to do this time is have a discussion with [Federal Treasurer] Keating before the summit.' And I said, 'I would like to transfer the wages pressure into

---

[92] *Ibid.*

[93] *Ibid.*

[94] *Ibid.*

superannuation pressure'."[95] Kelty remembers, "... the only people who were prepared, at this point – who knew what we wanted to do – were Simon Crean, Laurie Carmichael and me. Only three people in a country who said that's what we intended to do."[96] Carmichael had acknowledged that the last recession had really hurt. The early 1980s recession induced a spectre of thousands of metal-workers losing their jobs after 20 years' service. Kelty argued, "'Laurie, you can never let that happen again!' and he said, 'all right, but it's got to be our super'."[97] Kelty goes on, recalling his conversation with Carmichael, "'we can't put money into defined benefits.' He said, 'I will think about it.' Intellectually he then became committed. Strategically this was very important. Because if he said 'No' you'd have lots of trouble because, one, his is a great intellect; [and] two, he did understand the significance. They were the only people that knew. That's what we had in mind to try to achieve."[98] From Crean's perspective, "I think it was because there was a level of trust and a genuine recognition on our part that we wanted to be active participants in the big social change. Here was the opportunity to present the labour movement for the first time in its history as the two wings working in-sync with economic advancement."[99]

After 1983, occupational superannuation was extended to most workers through the industrial-relations processes using the dispositional power flowing from the Accord between the ACTU and the Federal Labor government. With the passing of the Superannuation Guarantee Charge legislation in 1992, superannuation moved more to the political rather than the industrial-relations sphere, although every inch of the journey continued to have implications for industrial relations. But that is to jump ahead of the narrative, because Accord Mark II, discussed next, is vital to the story.

---

[95] Bill Kelty interview, March 2013.

[96] *Ibid.*

[97] *Ibid.*

[98] *Ibid.*

[99] Simon Crean interview, May 2013.

Accord Mark II (September 1985)

Accord Mark II was a reaction to the falling Australian dollar, the decline in the terms of trade, and to inflation caused by higher-priced imports. The agreement, a wage-tax-superannuation deal, was struck in September 1985, with the ACTU committing to an effective 2 per cent wage cut and government support for 3 per cent employer contributions to superannuation through industry funds. Dabscheck summarised the agreement, saying, "… in the 1986 national wage case, the ACTU and the Hawke government would agree to discount the six-monthly CPI adjustment for the price effects of the devaluation of the Australian dollar to a maximum of 2 per cent; wage and salary earners would be compensated for this loss by a reduction in the level of personal income tax, to take effect from 1 September 1986; and the productivity case would be converted into a claim for extending and improving superannuation entitlements of Australian workers, to be based on a 3 per cent wage equivalent …"[100] Under the second version of the Accord (1985-87), wage indexation was again "discounted"; this time in return for a promise to consider tax reform, including personal tax cuts, and improved superannuation rights for workers.

A contemporary observed: "The renegotiation of the Accord brought forth a new series of trade-offs between the ACTU and the Federal government. The ACTU eventually retreated from its commitment to full wage indexation, in every instance, in the face of pressure over the inflationary effects of this in company with devaluation of the dollar. Instead, it accepted discounting for 1986 in return for an average $5 a week tax cut."[101] The 1985 biennial ACTU Congress was marked by near-unanimous acceptance of the new trade-offs, despite the initial reservations expressed by the Australian Workers Union (AWU), the Federated Clerks' Union (FCU), the Shop Distributive and Allied Employees' Association (SDA) and the Clothing and Allied Trades Union about giving up the productivity claim and the problems for

---

[100] Dabscheck, Braham (1989), *Loc. Cit.*, pp. 98-9.
[101] Gardner, Margaret (1986) "Australian Trade Unionism in 1985", *Journal of Industrial Relations*, Vol. 28, No. 1, March, pp. 133-4.

white-collar and public-sector unions in ensuring that their members would benefit from the 3 per cent. Gardner notes, "[t]his endorsement seems to have been achieved by using a broadly based negotiating team that ensured the commitment of factional and regional groups in the trade union movement."[102] But this is not to say that even with relative unity between the unions, and with government support, that the processing of the unions' claims was straightforward, as "[d]evelopments in the Australian economy during 1986 pointed to the need for a dynamic and adaptable wages policy."[103]

The last three-quarters of the fiscal year 1985-86 had yielded declines in seasonally adjusted real gross domestic product, accompanied by higher inflation, a marked slowdown in the growth of employment, and the first rises in unemployment for over two years. A continuation of the tight monetary and high interest-rate policies that had been instituted in 1985 failed to keep the terms of trade – which were associated with then-record deficits on the current account and record lows in the trade-weighted index of the dollar against other major currencies – from worsening.

The drawn-out nature of the first national wage case of 1983, earlier referenced, played a major part in moderating wage pressures. Beyond that, the second national wage case was not finalised by the end of 1984. The maintenance of real wages in the original Accord as an objective over time had already taken a beating. According to the Treasury, real earnings declined by 2.4 per cent in 1985-86, following negligible increases in the preceding two years.[104] The earnings data for public sector employees showed that their wage increases had lagged behind those of private sector employees by up to 4.0 per cent in the year to August 1986. Postponed tax-rate reductions, government expenditure cuts affecting the "social wage", and very few productivity-funded superannuation agreements also pointed to intense pressures on the continued viability of the Accord model.

---

[102] *Ibid.*, p. 134.
[103] Petridis, A. (1987) "Wage Policy and Wage Determination 1986", *Journal of Industrial Relations*, Vol. 29, No. 1, March, p. 75.
[104] Budget Statements 1986-87, p. 26.

Industrial disputes associated with productivity-linked superannuation claims in the transport industry and similar "extra claims" in the coal industry threatened the national wage case even before it had begun. The Conciliation and Arbitration Commission began hearings on 11 February 1986, but adjourned sittings twice in the first few days, and again in early March, because of bans imposed by unions in the transport industry. Eventually the wage case was resumed as the bans were lifted under pressure from the ACTU, the government and the Commission, which had threatened to delay the rest of the wage case and hear the transport union's superannuation case first.

Recalling 1986, Kelty says, "there were two things happening in terms of superannuation. 1) The Treasury convinced Paul Keating the government should tax super, but he never talks to us. This is taxing the people who have got super … [and] he never talks to us. So, he produces, unexpectedly for us, this industrial campaign about super. I've got to be honest, it wasn't really on the cards for us, looking after the high-paid in super, but you never let an opportunity like that go. So now you've got a campaign called superannuation – industrially and politically. For those who were getting it [i.e., associated with the union campaign for superannuation coverage] and those who were losing it [i.e., those who were losing some of their benefits due to proposed government taxation]."[105] In Keating's recollection as Treasurer, the government had laid down rules on preservation, vesting, portability, and the security of superannuation funds, all tied to the incentive of compliance, thereby earning the right to tax concessions. Years later, Keating noted: "We changed the tax concessions themselves to give greater preference to annuities over lump sums, and to genuine retirement provision as opposed to deferred pay schemes. A change that met stiff opposition including, and especially, by unions."[106]

Kelty saw a tactical opportunity for the unions: "Everything was falling into place for us. Nobody meant it, but you couldn't have done

---

[105] Bill Kelty interview, March 2013.
[106] Keating, Paul (1991) "A Retirement Incomes Policy", address to the Australian Graduate School of Management, July 25, typescript, p. 3.

it better. To do something as a catalyst for all the other people not covered. So suddenly 'super' is on the agenda. Then what happens is that the terms of trade collapsed, so they [the government] have got to come to us and ask for a delay in the wage increase. They've got to delay... Instead of getting a 4 per cent wage increase, they want us to accept something else. So they see us and I say, 'No. I've given enough. No! Not interested'."[107] This was an unnerving position for the government to hear.

Kelty saw the window of opportunity: "I say: 'You've got one chance. I'll do one thing. Trade off the wage increase for superannuation'. Bob [Hawke] said, 'you're mad'; he said, 'that's a crazy idea'. The terms of trade collapsed and we're deferring people's income and trading off super. I said, 'I don't care'. It was a very hostile meeting – not personally, but tough."[108] Hawke queried whether Kelty could actually deliver an agreement from the unions. As a former ACTU President he was well-placed to express uncertainty as to the risk that a deal between the ACTU and the government would unravel. This would leave both of them weakened, the government potentially fatally so. On one occasion they went to the Lodge and talked for two hours. Kelty said to Hawke: "There is one deal – just one. You are not getting me ever to agree to any further concession unless you can do the reverse [in support of superannuation]. You've not even done the reverse. No more superannuation campaign. You give it to us."[109] In Kelty's recollection, Hawke appeared unhappy. "I walked out of the Lodge that night and Paul Keating comes up to me and [says], 'Bill, I've been thinking about it.' He said, 'I think you've got me'. He said '… we are in this. We actually are in this for Labor'."[110] Keating, for his part, recalls, "I always wished to extend the superannuation concessions to the great body of the workforce. What happened was this. It was such a glaring anomaly. In those days superannuation was

---

[107] Bill Kelty interview, March 2013.
[108] *Ibid.*
[109] *Ibid.*
[110] *Ibid.*

a preserve of people in public sector schemes or at the top end of industry. It was not for ordinary working people. They had no access to it, effectively. It was so generous, and what's more, there was nothing to produce a retirement income. It was just a tax concession; [people] accumulated a lump, paid no tax on it and left."[111]

There was considerable concern over whether a deal could be delivered. In Kelty's words, "I said, 'fine. I'll get the unions together – the key unions – the bargaining unions'. And I said [to Hawke], 'I'm not going to hurt you. I'm not going to close on your position, where you go out and accept something that we can't sell because that would be too much to ask'. We got the unions at the ACTU wages negotiating committee, and we said, 'we've got the chance in history. This is your great chance. This is a night I think you'll remember. This is the night that we are going to create national superannuation for everybody'. And a couple said, 'no'. And all the really tough unions that Carmichael set the course for, every real bargaining union, said 'of course'."[112]

The 1986 national wage case reviewed the wage-fixing guidelines and determined the merits of a national 3 per cent productivity claim as well the flow-on consequences of any CPI increases. The ACTU regarded the three matters now as a single package that had been agreed to between the government and the ACTU as part of Accord Mark II. Despite this, the employers argued before the Commission about the various elements of the package, employing protracted legal arguments to slow the progress of the case. The ACTU opened proceedings before the national wage bench with a claim for a 3 per cent productivity increase in the form of superannuation and a 2.5 per cent CPI increase, which included discounting by 1.7 per cent for the effects of the depreciating dollar in the September and December quarters of 1985. The employers, through the Confederation of Australian Industry advocate, immediately challenged the jurisdiction of the Commission over productivity-financed superannuation on

[111] Paul Keating interview, March 2013.
[112] Bill Kelty interview, March 2013.

the grounds that superannuation was not an industrial matter, that payments by employers to third parties for superannuation were not an industrial matter, and that the Commission could not use its jurisdiction over wages to influence superannuation, which was outside its jurisdiction. The employers' discontent on superannuation reflected their belief that the agreement between the ACTU and the government was an unconstitutional method of obtaining *fait accompli* Commission approval. The bench, however, decided to continue hearing submissions to the national wage case while it deliberated on the jurisdictional challenge.

On 27 March 1986, the full bench of the Commission made a ruling to continue hearing all aspects of the unions' claims. This was an invitation to the employers to take the matter to the High Court, which they promptly did (this is discussed in more detail in Chapter 4). In May 1986 the High Court ruled that superannuation payments and benefits constituted one of the conditions of employment over which it was possible to have an industrial dispute; the matter fell under the jurisdiction of the then industrial relations statute.

With the national wage case lasting an unusually long 50 sitting days, economic events began to overtake the government and the ACTU, while the delays were a godsend to the employers. From their viewpoint, fresh adverse economic data might unnerve the national wage bench, while each month's delay was estimated to be keeping the annual wage bill down between $250 million-$400 million. Some unions called on the bench to backdate any increases. On 28 May 1986, the ACTU wages committee organised a day of protest at the delays. The national wage bench responded by not sitting for one day. Before the bench had concluded hearing submissions, a string of unfavourable statistics indicated that the balance on current account was still deteriorating, and that Australia's relative inflation rate was running at more than double the Organisation for Economic Cooperation and Development (OECD) average. The Australian dollar further depreciated. There were signs of alarm in the government's response to the economic data, as a proposed mini-summit was converted into an address to the nation by the prime minister.

The government had therefore begun to discuss further discounting CPI increases. At first the ACTU held firm, claiming that, despite the achievement of higher profits as a share of GDP and declines in real unit labour costs, the major problem in the economy was the failure of business to increase investment in new plant and equipment, and so on. The ACTU emphasised this argument in a special statement on the economy a few days before the Prime Minister's address to the nation on 11 June. That speech heralded another major adaptation of wages policy, as the government called for a real wage cut to match the 3 per cent reduction in GDP in response to the deteriorating terms of trade: the only wage increase in 1986 should be the one then under consideration by the national wage bench. Moreover, there should be discounting of up to 3 per cent in the next wage case, further cuts in government expenditure, probable postponement of the Accord Mark II tax rate reductions until December 1986 and the gradual implementation of any productivity/superannuation decision over two years.[113]

The ACTU's opposition to the government's proposals was muted, and appeared to be deliberately ambivalent, and it became obvious that it was prepared to accept further wage discounting, but only as part of a package deal. The ACTU leadership saw an opportunity to contribute to the development of a new policy, and superannuation was at the forefront of their thinking. Clearly, they accepted the reality of Australia's economic circumstances and were anxious to preserve the Accord and the centralised nature of wage determination, which gave them influence.

The prime minister's address to the nation and accompanying documents were sent to the national wage bench, which then invited all represented parties to make written responses, which further delayed the case. Employer bodies emphasised the stark contrast regarding

---

[113] Cf. Bramston, Troy (2016) *Paul Keating. The Big-Picture Leader*, Scribe Publications, Brunswick [Australia], p. 257.

Figure 14: ACTU Special Unions Conference, 6 November 1986 held in the Victorian Trades Hall, Melbourne. Source: Records of Unions NSW.

the state of the economy presented by the prime minister compared to the government's earlier, more optimistic submissions in the wage case. The Confederation of Australian Industry asked the bench to reject the claim for any wage increase as well as the principle of wage indexation, to further delay national wage cases until September 1987 and to reject the principle of separate productivity adjustments and superannuation. In contrast to the other employers' organisations, the Australian Chamber of Commerce and Industry indicated that it was prepared to accept a suitably discounted indexation wage increase as long as it was within an employer's capacity to pay on a company-by-company basis.

In the end, the national wage bench granted a wage increase of 2.3 per cent – a 2 per cent discount on what might be justified by indexation alone – to be paid on or after 1 July 1986, and ensured it was the only increase in 1986 by stating that the next wage adjustment would take effect on or after 1 January 1987, with a review at the end of 1986. Payment of the increase would be subject to a "no further claims" undertaking by the unions. The way was cleared for employer-union bargaining for occupational superannuation, subject to a number of conditions; the most important of these was that superannuation payments should not exceed the equivalent of 3 per cent of ordinary-time earnings and that agreements would generally be phased-in on or after 1 January 1987.[114] Regulation and implementation of agreements and consent awards would be left to the Commission, which stated that it had made only minor amendments to the principles of the previous package of wage fixation. Despite the Commission's conclusion, two amendments stood out. First, wage-indexation adjustments would be much more explicitly subject to review because of economic conditions; and second, the new Accord would allow opposition to wage increases "on the grounds of very serious or extreme economic adversity".

When the national wage case re-opened in November, the ACTU advocate presented a claim, based on the CPI increases for the March, June and September quarters of 1986, for a 6.7 per cent wage increase. As this was an unlikely outcome, the proposal for a new two-tiered wage system was presented. The first tier was to deliver two flat wage increases for all workers in 1987, with bargaining up to a maximum amount being allowed under the second tier. Negotiations between the parties would determine the size of the first-tier wage increase. By contrast, the government submission argued for a single wage increase of $10 per week to be paid in March 1987, a ceiling of 3 per cent to be placed on the second tier and an end to the superannuation campaign. The submissions of the major employer bodies substantially agreed in calling for a modified two-tier system. But they argued that only one wage rise should be granted in 1987 based on capacity to pay, rather than on movements in the CPI. The total movement in wages should

---

[114] Petridis, A. (1987), "Wage Policy and Wage Determination 1986", *Journal of Industrial Relations*, Vol. 29, No. 1, March, p. 79.

be determined by the national wage bench on the basis of capacity to pay, and enterprise bargaining would then determine actual increases in the second tier. To prevent flow-ons and leapfrogging, the principle of comparative wage justice should be explicitly expunged from the wage system.[115]

On 23 December, the Commission's full bench brought down a decision effectively ending three years of a wage-indexation regime and proposing moving in principle to a two-tiered system, with an emphasis on low-income earners in the first tier. The way was left open for further negotiations over superannuation. Similarly, the size and timing of wage rises in the first tier and the criteria for the second tier were also to be resolved in conferences involving all parties in January.

A contemporary posited:

> There is no doubt that the new two tier system is a sincere attempt to protect the living standards of low-wage earners, and to make the system more flexible, while still preserving a role for the Arbitration Commission through the national wage cases. Nevertheless, these wage cases will now take on a diminished significance. From the employers' point of view there is an initial promise of lower wage outcomes and flexibility in enterprise or industry bargaining. Of course, the extent to which wage outcomes are now more consistent with efficiency criteria will largely depend on whether the distribution and exercise of bargaining power in enterprises corresponds with efficiency in the same enterprises. Whether the ACTU can avoid a rank and file revolt in the face of further falls in real wages is crucial.[116]

Other union leaders understood the wider agenda. Anna Booth, then of the Clothing and Allied Trades Union, says:

> I seem to recall that our thinking around the 3 per cent [level] in the second Accord was also about – understanding, of course, that the 3

---

[115] Cf. Green, Roy (1996) "The 'Death' of Comparative Wage Justice in Australia", Research Paper Issue 27, Employment Studies Centre, University of Newcastle [Australia], 27pp.

[116] Petridis, A. (1987) "Wage Policy and Wage Determination 1986", *Journal of Industrial Relations*, Vol. 29, No. 1, March, p. 83.

per cent would come from employers – but understanding how you could try to minimise the transmission of the impact into the macro-economy, and how you could harness it to build the national savings nation. So, as much as it was about dignity in retirement for ordinary working people and the inequity of the employers and public-sector workers getting a retirement benefit and others not getting it, there was also this bigger agenda.[117]

This bigger agenda is further explored later in the book.

In summary, by the end of 1986, the Australian Industrial Relations Commission arbitrated on an ACTU claim that all workers covered by an industrial award should be provided with 3 per cent superannuation – that is, 3 per cent of their ordinary time earnings (that is, the employees usual, gross weekly or fortnightly wage or salary, including loadings). This led to the establishment of multi-employer industry funds that covered most industries, as well as some State-based funds. But, as not all workers were covered by awards, not all employers complied.

In the course of considering this matter, the High Court ruled that the Federal industrial tribunal had the power to make awards and determinations on superannuation (this is examined in greater detail in Chapter 4). Previously, it had been widely assumed that superannuation was a non-industrial matter and therefore could not be arbitrated by the Federal Commission.

Accord Mark III (March 1987)

In 1987 the ACTU and the Labor government formally agreed on Accord Mark III which defined how the two-tier wages system would work. The first tier was an across-the-board $10 a week pay rise and the second tier was for a 4 per cent wage increase in return for lifting certain alleged "restrictive work practices". This did not catch-up for inflation and represented a further discounting of wage compensation, albeit workers could trade-off what some considered as being overly restrictive classifications, and introduce more flexibility and multi-skilling in awards so as to gain the second tier increase.

---

[117] Anna Booth interview, August 2012.

Figure 15: Keating "bringing home the bacon" – speaking after delivering the 1988/89 Budget. Source: The National Archives.

Accord Mark III signalled the end of formal indexation and facilitated a move from formally indexed wage rises to a two-tier system of wage fixation that required efficiency offsets in exchange for wage increases.[118] Industrial Relations Minister Peter Cook noted, "[i]t became generally accepted that productivity promotion was a vital element in the recovery of Australian living standards and this led involved parties to look for ways of securing the necessary degree of labour market flexibility in the wage fixing system, in order to obtain improved productivity, and thus international competitiveness."[119] Through the Restructuring and Efficiency Principle of the AIRC wage guidelines, this involved a minimum-tier wage increase to a set level of income. Any increases above this limit would be according to productivity and other circumstances. An ugly phrase, which

[118] At the time, it was contended many of these offsets were artificial; and it was extraordinarily difficult to quantify the financial value component in every contested case.

[119] Cook, Peter, *Loc. Cit.*, p. 164.

particularly sounds unfamiliar 30 years later, the "restructuring and efficiency principle" required recognition that different industries had different capacities for generating and proving gains in efficiency. The concept had the merit of encouraging all parties to concentrate on productivity improvement in every industry.

Accord Mark IV (1988)

In the next year, 1988, Accord Mark IV introduced a new two-tier system. The first tier was for a 3 per cent wage rise but this would only be granted if unions agreed to comprehensively review the awards under which their wages and conditions were determined. The second tier was a flat $10 a week increase but only payable six months later. Again, this entailed a real wage lag.

Accord Mark IV was significant for popularising the idea that any future wage increases had to be justified on the basis on improvements to the "structural efficiency" of particular industries.[120]

Accord Mark IV stressed the structural-efficiency principle. It encouraged employers to adopt new ideas such as the establishment of career paths, broad-banding (that is, classifying a position across two or more job levels), multi-skilling within specified work patterns (meaning, breaking down strict rules limiting the range of work that might be performed at a particular job level – award classifications in many cases, particularly in manufacturing industry, were highly prescriptive, and needed to change), and other arrangements aimed at "modernising awards". It also encouraged a focus on productivity in award adjustments and commensurate wage increases – based on real, achieved improvements in efficiency and productivity.

Under the wage system established by the AIRC, increases were available to unions that made a commitment to a fundamental review of awards that would determine measures to improve efficiency and provide workers with access to more varied jobs. "The aim was to

---

[120] For a critical discussion, see: Costa, Michael, & Duffy, Mark (1991) *Labor, Prosperity and the Nineties. Beyond the Bonsai Economy.* The Federation Press, Leichhardt, NSW, pp. 140-56.

reform the highly specialised award regulation of the work process to encourage multi-skilling and to try to minimise demarcation disputes. This became known as award restructuring."[121]

Accord Mark V (1989)

Accord Mark V built on Mark IV, with wage increases based on the implementation of changed award wages. Cook comments, "[t] he Accord Mark V agreement in 1989 was intended to secure wage restraint while providing improvements in real disposable income. It was based on a combination of moderate wage increases, substantial cuts in personal income tax and improvements in the social wage (including increases in the Dependent Spouse Rebate, Family Allowance and Family Allowance Supplements)."[122] The latter won vital support from the right wing of the trade union movement, which had long campaigned for such measures.

Accord Mark VI (February 1990, revised November 1990)

Accord Mark VI was negotiated in 1990, on the eve of a recession associated with sharp rises in interest rates, following a blow-out in the balance of payments and a dramatic rise in foreign debt.

The new Accord imposed a 14-month freeze on general wage increases in return for promises of tax cuts and improved superannuation. It also announced the shift away from centralised wage fixing to "enterprise bargaining". Hitherto, enterprise bargaining, which was often painted by some unions as one of the "nasty" policies of the New Right when the Accord was first introduced, meant the negotiation of wages and conditions on an enterprise-by-enterprise basis.[123] The ACTU was willing to accept enterprise bargaining as

---

[121] Cook, Peter, *Loc. Cit.*, p. 164.

[122] *Ibid.*, p. 165.

[123] It is interesting to observe, however, that within the NSW jurisdiction under State law, for example, there had been a long history of what were known as s.11 agreements which were separate from awards and were effectively, in modern parlance, enterprise agreements.

long as one of its affiliates or the ACTU itself was guaranteed a role in its negotiation.[124] Not that this was an entirely smooth process. In some industries a new round of inter-union rivalry was sparked off as unions fought to attain sole coverage of workers under enterprise deals for new projects.

As the Australian economy retracted due to a recession in 1989-90, the government and the ACTU, the parties to the Accord, agreed that during 1990-91, through a combination of wage increases, tax reductions, and improvements in the social wage that this would provide for an increase in disposable income and living conditions while achieving a sustainable reduction in inflation and interest rates. Mark VI incorporated a wage-tax-superannuation trade-off, a claim for a $12 a week wage increase to apply from May 1991 and further improvements in employer-funded superannuation.[125]

Point 12 of the Accord VI agreement stated:

Additional superannuation equivalent to 3 per cent of ordinary time earnings shall be available from May 1st 1991 and shall be paid no later than May 1st 1993. The superannuation increases shall be phased, in aggregate, over a three year period in a manner negotiated by the Award parties. Failing agreement, Industrial Tribunals may determine the dates of implementation provided the first increase shall be no later than the 1st May 1992 and the balance be implemented no later than 1st May 1993.

In Keating's summation, "Accord Mark VI provided for the second 3 per cent of superannuation to be paid on a phased basis flowing from the wage restraint of the past few years."[126] But, as discussed below, this proposal proved controversial and the Commission rejected it. In April 1991, the AIRC, instead of agreeing to lift superannuation from 3 to 6 per cent as part of the next National Wage Case, agreed with employer organisation representations in rejecting the claim as

---

[124] Cf. Costa, Michael, & Duffy, Mark (1991) *Labor, Prosperity and the Nineties. Beyond the Bonsai Economy*, Loc. Cit., pp. 75f.

[125] Cook, Peter, *Loc. Cit.*, p. 165.

[126] Keating, Paul (1991) "A Retirement Incomes Policy", address to the Australian Graduate School of Management, July 25, typescript, p. 9.

"premature" considering the economic circumstances at the time. Australia was then in the midst of a recession. This triggered the government's consideration of legislation to achieve similar ends. On the eve of the 1991 Federal Budget, Prime Minister Hawke, under intense pressure from the ACTU leadership and former Treasurer Paul Keating,[127] agreed to the Superannuation Guarantee. One contemporary historian of this event later wrote: "Employers would be required to make contributions on behalf of their employees, making the system near universal. It was a political fix. There was no policy analysis, no Treasury White Paper that might be expected of such a sweeping compulsory measure."[128]

Accord Mark VII (October 1991)

In 1991 the *Australian Financial Review* published a fond "obituary" to the Accord process:

> The prices and incomes Accord has enjoyed surprising longevity. Labor politicians boast of its unique place in the history of such world phenomena, a once-off hybrid like so much in Australian industrial relations, a sort of social contract platypus which has, miraculously, survived.
>
> The fact is the "state of mind" among the small coterie who formulated the original idea has spread, evolved and matured. Acceptance of the need for continuous change in working habits and relationships has penetrated into the consciousness of the union movement ...
>
> Strata upon strata of union officialdom now are faced daily with the disciplines exerted by the market and the implications of their own decision making on a wide range of macro-economic outcomes in a way unheard of just a decade ago.
>
> If its benefits seem so tangible, why should the Accord now be buried? The short answer is that it has delivered its two major achievements

---

[127] Keating had challenged Hawke in an internal Caucus ballot in June 1991 and retired to the back bench, to then successfully challenge Hawke again for the leadership in December 1991.

[128] Kelly, Paul (2011) *The March of Patriots, The Struggle for Modern Australia*, Melbourne University Press, Carlton (first published in 2009, updated in 2011), p. 146.

– an attitudinal shift among union officialdom and a moderation in aggregate wage outcomes through the 1980s …[129]

On the contrary, the platypus still had life. Abandoning the Accord at this time might have tempted some in the unions to revert to bad, old ways. Though, undoubtedly, there were tensions within the labour movement as to how long the Accord processes could continue to be creatively recast, renewed, and prove useful. For completeness, whether right or wrong, the Accord process (and, on one view of it, its neutering effect) was contentious among some quite respectable unions and commentators. Eminently reasonable minds differed about whether the Accords (and all the associated trade-offs and concessions) were beneficial overall to workers. This was also occurring around the time of the ACTU's desire for the super-unions and the concentration of its agenda on limiting the role of State-based unions and the like.[130] One significant reason for the continuation of the Accord processes, including a mostly benign approach to wage restrain by the unions, was that many of the key industrial unions thought that consolidation and extension of the industry superannuation schemes made the bargain worthwhile.

To promote greater levels of flexibility and wage adjustment, Mark VII continued the development of enterprise bargaining. In 1992 the government introduced the Superannuation Guarantee (SG), following a refusal by the AIRC to increase the level of contributions under awards. All workers had to receive a level of superannuation during their employment, as long as they earned more than $450 a month. Super contributions were to be increased progressively from 3 per cent in 1992 to 9 per cent in 2002.

Accord Mark VIII (June 1995)

Though the Accord Mark VIII, an agreement reached on 21 June, 1995, was never implemented, it was intended to support and strengthen

---

[129] Editorial (1991) *Australian Financial Review*, 15 August.
[130] Cf. Costa, Michael, & Duffy, Mark (1991) 'The Decline of Trade Unions and the Amalgamation Quick Fix', *Labor, Prosperity and the Nineties. Beyond the Bonsai Economy*, Loc. Cit., pp. 100-32.

the government's Budget strategy, recognising the need to address retirement income imperatives and the national savings shortfall. Clause 6 of the document stated:

6.1 Under the Accord, occupational superannuation has moved from being a benefit enjoyed by a privileged few to being a central plank in providing all Australians with a better retirement income, and increasing national savings.

6.2 The Governments' Superannuation Guarantee legislation made provision for the phased implementation of a minimum employer-funded superannuation contribution for all employees. The further initiatives announced in the recent Budget will facilitate the introduction of employee contributions. These measures will mean a significant improvement in retirement incomes for workers – lifting the superannuation savings of a worker around average earnings to a minimum of 15 per cent of their wage, and up to 19 per cent for very low earners.

6.3 There are other benefits to Australia from the superannuation changes. It is understood that to maintain healthy growth in production and employment, Australia's businesses need additional investment in up to-date plant and equipment for their enterprises.

6.4 The capacity of the Australian economy to support investment growth is enhanced through the existence of an increased flow of domestic savings generated by superannuation and from a decreased reliance on the international financial community and foreign debt.

6.5 Consistent with the Budget Statement, the Accord parties support the phased introduction through industrial agreements and awards, where benefits are improved, of a requirement for employees to contribute 3 per cent of their earnings to superannuation by the year 2000. In recognition of the need to improve the retirement savings for working people, and specifically the low paid, the Government will make means-tested superannuation contributions matched to those made by employees.

6.6 The Accord parties support an approach whereby the introduction of employee contributions through awards is timed to coincide with the Safety Net Adjustments. This is to avoid any decrease in employees' existing disposable incomes.

6.7 Under this plan, awards will require employee contributions of 1 per cent, 2 per cent and 3 per cent from 1 July 1997, 1 July 1998 and 1 July 1999 respectively, with the matched Government contributions being provided on the same basis in the year following.

6.8 The introduction of total superannuation contemplated by these arrangements will be in accordance with the following table:

Circumstances, however, worked against the Government implementing the superannuation features of Mark VIII. In 1996, the Keating government was defeated at the elections. The Howard government declined to extend superannuation beyond the 9 per cent minimum (then due to be phased in by 2002).

Looking back is to discover that "the past is a foreign *country*: they do things differently there."[131] Many employment and industrial relations concepts and terms of the Hawke-Keating period are now alien – the two-tier wage system, the "structural efficiency principle", "award restructuring", linkages in the mid-1990s of most awards to the minimum wage set in the Metal Industry award, and so forth. The emphasis by the ACTU leadership at the time on amalgamation of unions, reducing demarcation disputes, creating flexibility in work rules, indicates that everything was in thrall to a world in flux, where what once made sense needed to change after the Australian economy

---

[131] The phrase belongs to Leslie Poles Hartley (1895-1972) from the opening line of his 1953 novel *The Go-Between*, Hamish Hamilton, London.

Figure 16: Proposed Superannuation Contributions Under Accord VIII

Financial Year	Payroll up to $1 million, per cent	Payroll - $1 million of more, per cent	Employee Contribution	Government Contribution	Total
1992-93	3.0	4/5	-	-	3-4-5
1993-94	3.0	5.0	-	-	3-5
1994-95	4.0	5.0	-	-	4-5
1995-96	5.0	6.0	-	-	5-6
1996-97	6.0	6.0	-	-	6.0
1997-98	6.0	6.0	1.0	-	7.0
1998-99	7.0	7.0	2.0	1.0	10.0
1999-2000	7.0	7.0	3.0	2.0	12.0
2000-01	8.0	8.0	3.0	3.0	14.0
2001-02	8.0	8.0	3.0	3.0	14.0
2002-03	9.0	9.0	3.0	3.0	15.0

*Minimum Government Contribution capped at prescribed percentage of Full-Time Adult Average Weekly Ordinary Time Earnings (AWOTE) and phased out at twice AWOTE. A footnote to the table read: "The Government has taken substantial steps and will continue the process of consolidation of superannuation funds in low balance accounts to ensure that these funds are not eroded by fees, in recognition of the special needs of casual, part-time and women workers." This idea was part of the origin of the AGEST scheme, as the default scheme for Commonwealth public servants. AGEST eventually merged with AustralianSuper.

became more open from the early 1980s onwards. Bill Kelty and his colleagues drove hard the proposition that unions needed to transform, amalgamate, "modernise".[132] In some workplaces there were twenty or more unions each defending their patch with a litigious culture and rigid work rules defining exactly what work could be done by what

---

[132] At the time there was a plethora of articles and books discussing strategic unionism – union activity that went beyond resolving everyday disputes and, instead looked at bigger picture issues, including superannuation – and the challenges of what unions might best focus on. For a representative sample, see the essays in Crosby, Michael & Easson, Michael (1992), editors, *What Should Unions Do?*, Pluto Press for the Lloyd Ross Forum, Leichhardt, NSW, Australia.

skill grade of worker. It all had to change – though not necessarily along the route promoted by the ACTU leadership. They proposed amalgamation of unions to form twenty conglomerates. It made a good deal of sense in the manufacturing, transport, building and construction industries. But elsewhere, in the wider economy, many unionists and organisations shrugged their shoulders and wondered "why?" Likewise, on the discrete issue of award recalibration, many tried to imagine what "structural efficiency" actually meant for them. But the big focus concentrated minds on finding productivity changes. As untidy as all this now seems, the changes wrought in the late 1980s onwards transformed the Australian economy and made it more productive and, in the process, broke the back of inflation. Changes to and the universalisation of superannuation entitlements was one incentive to powerful economic agents – the unions – to support this transformation. This was part of what Argy calls "the program of bold economic reform" combined with "distributional equity" that "has helped produce a remarkable economic renaissance over the last decade" – being the 1990s.[133]

In sum, a number of industries' unions had started superannuation campaigns, some successfully. Kelty saw that from the Maritime Workers and the Meat Workers, many of the left-wing unions had won benefits for their members through particular industry schemes. These agreements were typically a bargain in exchange for industrial reform – containerisation in stevedoring, for example. On a wider scale, in the latter part of the 1970s, the Storemen and Packers union started to secure superannuation coverage in certain industry sectors. They drove the idea hard that superannuation was not just a special bonus, but an integral part of an employee's wage package, part of their total remuneration.

When the Hawke Labor Government came to office in 1983, it adopted an Accord with the trade union movement in which wage increases were restricted to movements in the CPI. When the Accord was renegotiated in 1985, superannuation was identified as a key

---

[133] Argy, Fred (2003) *Where to From Here? Australian Egalitarianism Under Threat*, Allen & Unwin, Crows Nest, NSW, Australia, p. 48.

issue. In 1984 "BUSS", the union-sponsored superannuation scheme for the building industry was created with the funds controlled by a board comprising equal representation from employers and employees (the latter of whom could be union representatives). As Gardner notes, "[t]he other issue to be resolved concerning superannuation – the composition of boards of trustees for the schemes – seems to have been settled with ACTU agreement to equal employer and union representation."[134] In Sword's summation, "... they used our model. In all the accumulation funds, they all have 50/50 employer/ union representatives on the board."[135] Similar funding schemes to the building-industry scheme were established in the following years. These were called industry funds.

The unique nature of the superannuation scheme model that was finally adopted by the Labor government was that it was paid for by employees through their employer deducting contributions, rather than paid for by the government. In effect it was partly a wage increase off-set in the form of compulsory retirement savings (whereas many commentators said employees would prefer to have the wage increase in their pockets and spend or invest it as they chose rather than having this unilaterally determined). It was paid for by employees, albeit the administrative mechanism was through the employer's payroll system – by making specified contributions to superannuation funds rather than contemporaneous increases in take-home pay. In practical terms, a percentage of the employee's wages is typically paid in superannuation contributions.

Commentators also noted that superannuation would likely be used by the government, in due course, to reduce or avoid paying age pensions to retirees – and this, at least to some extent, has come to pass or could come to pass. Crucially, superannuation became totally portable – as people changed jobs, they did not lose their savings – with the transferred benefit from defined contributions and interest, not defined benefit schemes which have nearly all been shut to new contributors.

---

[134] Gardner, Margaret (1986) "Australian Trade Unionism in 1985", *Journal of Industrial Relations*, Vol. 28, No. 1, March, p. 136.
[135] Greg Sword interview, June 2012.

Universal and compulsory superannuation – where every worker has the right to their own superannuation account – would not exist had it not been for the campaigns fought by union members from the 1970s accelerating into the early 1980s onwards. In 1985 only 39 per cent of the workforce had super, and access to it largely depended on age, gender, occupation, occupational status, whether you were full or part time, permanent or casual, or a contractor. Access to superannuation was deeply inequitable: only 24 per cent of women had superannuation, compared to 50 per cent of men. Higher-income earners, such as permanent public servants and full-time, white-collar, private-sector employees, were more likely to have access to superannuation. Women and blue-collar workers were the least likely.

Over time, the regulation and structure of superannuation became controversial. Some companies treated the superannuation fund as a company asset, and its use as a means to make loans to companies was not uncommon. In the early 1980s, most funds were under "defined benefit" terms, which disadvantaged people who changed jobs throughout their working lives and advantaged those who stayed in one job for 20 or more years, especially those who retired on high salaries. There were reasons why, in the alternative, accumulation type funds would be favoured. In the evolution of the building scheme, BUSS, as we see in the next Chapter, thought was given to amending the then-existing defined benefit funds. But the tortuous effort was like an un-clickable Rubik's cube. ACTU Assistant Secretary Garry Weaven, writing in 1986 on union strategies, noted that:

> Success of the ACTU strategy will certainly lead to an upsurge in accumulation type funds. The main reason for this is of course that a high degree of vesting will make it quite costly to promise additional benefits upon retirement. Also, because many employers will be required for the first time to provide a certain percentage of wages for superannuation, they will be unlikely to do more than this. Further, as superannuation changes from a unilaterally provided benefit to a collectively bargained condition of employment, there

will be a tendency for both parties to want to be able to precisely fix the cost.[136]

A reason for the bedeviling complexity is that, as Drew and Stanford dryly noted in 2003, in the context of a study of private sector defined benefit schemes, "[t]hat other schemes may have been unfunded was not a problem in the face of poor preservation and vesting requirements."[137] Reforming vesting and preservation standards entailed unravelling the actuarial viability of such schemes.

In the early 1980s the ACTU developed strategies that would address Australia's ageing population. Research demonstrated that there would be insufficient taxpayers to sustainably meet the cost of pensions for retiring baby-boomers.

The first industry funds of the type common today were established in the late 1970s. These funds had developed from unions' industrial demands on employers; in some cases, vigorous campaigning, including strike action, was required to persuade employers to contribute.

The main objective of the ACTU and the unions was to achieve a universal system of compulsory superannuation, which had the following characteristics:

- Superannuation for all workers, irrespective of age, gender, occupation, industry or work pattern.

- Vesting: superannuation would belong to workers rather than employers, so that workers kept their entitlement even if they left their job before retirement.

- Portability: when workers changed jobs they took their superannuation benefits with them – assuming they

---

[136] Weaven, Garry (1985) "Superannuation: The Great Leap Forward. An Outline of the ACTU's Strategy for the Establishment of Universal Superannuation Coverage", *Superfunds*, No. 92, September, p. 11.

[137] Drew, Michael, & Stanford, Jon (2003b) "A Review of Australia's Compulsory Superannuation Scheme After a Decade", Discussion Paper No. 322, University of Queensland, March, p. 2.

worked within the same industry, it would be with the same superannuation fund; thus the term "industry funds". (Most industry funds are now "public offer" meaning that workers can join any industry fund regardless of the industry they work in.)

- Preservation: the purpose of superannuation is to provide an income for retirement. Unless there are special circumstances (financial hardship and/or permanent disability), employer contributions should be preserved until retirement.

- Equal representation: in accordance with union demands, representatives of employees as well as employers – not just of employers – act as trustees of industry superannuation funds.

- Insurance: unions also sought insurance provisions, including death and disability cover, for workers through their superannuation fund.

The provision of superannuation came about through union-employer negotiations, and was provided by employers instead of pay rises. Superannuation was therefore regarded as "deferred pay" that rightfully belonged to workers.

The Liberal and National parties continued to oppose government mandated compulsory superannuation until late 1995, just before the 1996 election which they won on 2 March. The superannuation reforms, which had taken over a decade to secure, were now more secure – with even the conservative parties formally supporting the phasing-in of 9 per cent compulsory savings. Though there were skirmishes ahead – as described in the following Chapters.

By 2008, the industry funds, covering more than 4.7 million members, began to aggressively campaign on their not-for-profit orientation, relatively strong investment performance and low fees. Nineteen industry funds combined to promote the "Compare the Pair" advertising campaign, which compared two members in different super funds and their performance.[138] As Weaven explained, "we put in the first index for super ratings and first drew attention that there is only one true measure which is net benefit to the member over a proper period of time."[139] Since 2008, the ACTU has campaigned for better retirement incomes through a lift in employer superannuation contributions from the minimum of 9 per cent – where it had remained since 2002 – to 12 per cent, and then a further lift to 15 per cent. At the time of writing it is at 9.5% with a phase-in to 12% by 2025/26. The building industry was the unlikely place where the superannuation revolution of the 1980s would begin. The next Chapter examines that phenomenon.

---

[138] Cf. Taylor, Mike (2010) "Industry Super Funds Stumble on the Secret of Success", *Money Management*, 18 October, http://www.moneymanagement. com.au/opinion/superannuation/archive/industry-super-funds-stumble-on-to-the-secret-of-s, accessed, September 2013.

[139] Garry Weaven interview, March 2013.

3. THE BUILDING INDUSTRY BREAKTHROUGH

By September 1983 the arbitration system had set down new wage-indexation guidelines. The employers' advocate Colin Polites summarises that year's National Wage case: "In substance, the full bench has returned to a structured, centralised form of wage indexation, adjustments for productivity improvement, and severe constraints on labour cost increases outside those areas."[1] Within the building industry, however, there was tension caused by a tradition of militancy and a keen desire to "catch up" on previous wage-restraint outcomes. Just prior to the Accord's adoption by unions in February 1983, the building unions had reached an in-principle agreement for a $7.00 a week allowance with several major employers.[2] This had not quite been finalised, but the unions expected a Labor government to allow its eventual ratification.

Weaven recalls, "one of the jobs I had picked up when I came into the Australian Council of Trade Unions [ACTU] was to try and get some collective position out of the building unions. Not in respect of super but in respect to their industrial arrangements because there were many, many separate unions, lots of demarcation fights between them... and one fairly rogue union called the BLF ... when Labor came to power in 1983, really they wanted to find a way to get peace in the

---

[1] Polites, Colin G. (1984) "Major Tribunal Decisions 1983", *Journal of Industrial Relations*, Vol. 26, No. 1, p. 109. See Appendix 4 for a reference to the development of national wage guidelines.
[2] Weaven, Garry (2016) 'Workers' Capital: The story of Industry Funds and Australia's Superannuation Revolution', Foenander Lecture at the University of Melbourne, 15 November 2016, pp. 4-9.

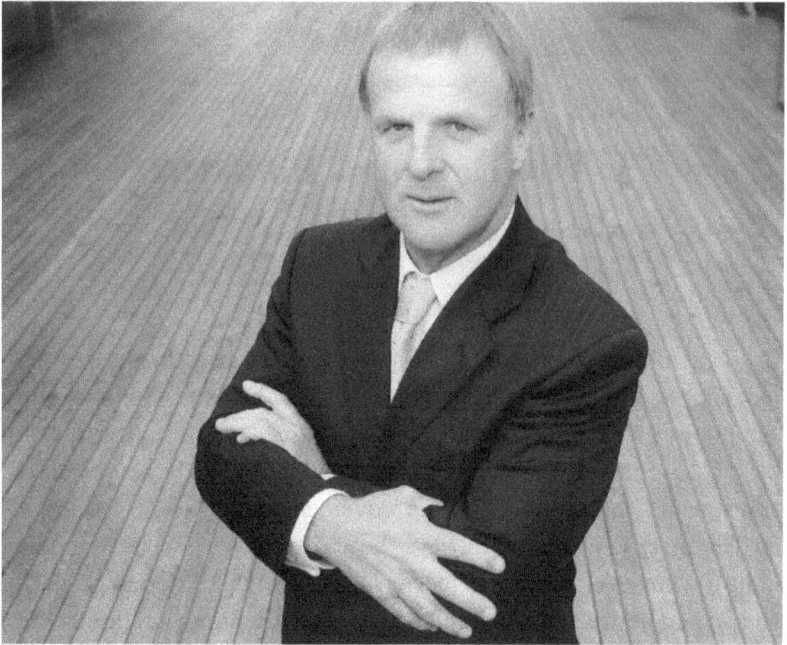

Figure 17: Garry Weaven, chairman of Industry Funds Services, 10 August 2005, photograph by *The Age* by Michael Clayton-Jones. Source: Fairfax Archives.

building industry so they could stop the deregistration proceedings.[3] I was assigned that industry and assigned the job of convening the building unions together – to try and get a peace agreement."[4]

Retired former Commissioner Allan Vosti was appointed to chair a series of conferences (the first of which was held on 26 April 1983) involving the Builders' Labourers' Federation (BLF),[5] the Building Workers' Industrial Union (BWIU),[6] the ACTU, other building unions, and the Master Builders Federation of Australia (MBFA), as well as

---

[3] Such deregistration proceedings against the BLF had already been initiated by the Fraser government.

[4] Garry Weaven interview, March 2013.

[5] The BLF tended to cover unskilled and non-tradesmen in the industry.

[6] In those days, the BWIU covered tradesmen and semi-skilled workers. There were sometimes bitter disputes between the two major building unions for coverage.

the Industrial Secretariat the MBFA had established in conjunction with the Australian Federation of Construction Contractors (AFCC). Weaven said, "just getting them in the same room was often a bit of a task, which led ultimately to a somewhat artificially forced industry-wide agreement. On one hand you are threatening to deregister the BLs [i.e., Builders' Labourers' Federation], and we came to an industry-wide agreement that Allan Vosti had put some sort of a seal on and … it was all subject to it being approved by the bench of the Commission."[7] The building unions did not seem greatly excited by superannuation in those negotiations: "It had superannuation as claim number 25 [in the log of claims], which didn't get addressed … but it did include a special allowance in [the agreement], which was the amount that was to keep the peace. In particular, the BLs and the plumbers were pushing to break outside of what was being negotiated in the metal industry and so on."[8] For the ACTU, Weaven negotiated a new protocol with the unions and the employers in the industry; it proposed that employers pay a $9.00 allowance to each employee, called the Building Industry Recovery Procedures (BIRP) allowance, in exchange for adherence to the new dispute-resolution arrangements. The Memorandum of Understanding that resulted from those conferences addressed various award claims, provided a process for resolving disputes with the BLF and its state branches and enabled the Hawke government to withdraw the application to deregister the BLF.

The Commission's rejection of the building industry agreement in November 1983, on the grounds that it involved increases in pay in excess of the 4.3 per cent in the national wage case, left all parties dissatisfied. One observer noted, "Justice Ludeke made it plain that the Commission's first priority was to safeguard the new wage indexation principles …"[9] This was to emphasise that other employers and the Federal government feared that other industries would also demand similar allowances, and that the resulting spiralling increases

---

[7] Garry Weaven interview, March 2013.

[8] *Ibid.*

[9] Burgmann, Meredith (1984) "Australian Trade Unionism in 1983", *Journal of Industrial Relations*, Vol. 26, No. 1, August, p. 92.

Figure 18: (L-R) Pat Clancy of the Building Workers' Industrial Union; Dick Dusseldorp of Lend Lease and Jack Mundey of the NSW Builders' Labourers Federation at a Lend Lease meeting at Sydney Town Hall on 31 October 1972. Dusseldorp and Lend Lease were masters at focusing on cooperative industrial relations, employee training, and occupational health and safety. Even ideological and industrial relations enemies in Clancy and Mundey were able to share a beer and jointly agree on an "orderly" industrial relations agreement with the company. Photo by News Ltd/Newspix.

across industries would break down the principle of orderly wage indexation. But building employers, unions, and the Commonwealth had all supported the deal and were anxious to find ways it could be reincarnated in a form acceptable to the Commission.

Oblivious to the developing implications, Mulvey, in a review of major tribunal decisions for 1983, asserted: "[r]ejection of the building industry agreement signalled the determination of the Commission to protect the national wage case decision … the Commission asserted its independence and also assumed the role of guardian of the wages side of the prices and incomes policy. It was business as usual."[10] A

---

[10] Mulvey, Charles (1984) "Wage Policy and Wage Determination in 1983", *Journal of Industrial Relations*, Vol. 26, No. 1, August, pp. 118-9.

Figure 19: Tom MacDonald, national secretary of the Building Workers Industrial Union, speaking at a mass meeting outside of the NSW Parliament House, *circa* early 1990. Source: personal collection of Tom and Audrey MacDonald.

factor in the building industry, as one observer described matters, was "the [Builders' Labourers' Federation's] propensity for squabbling with every other building union."[11] The tensions and rivalries between unions, and the brinkmanship between them, were factors

---

[11] Burgmann, Meredith (1984) "Australian Trade Unionism in 1983", *Loc. Cit.*, p. 93.

that should not be underestimated. The BLF set the ball rolling with a straightforward claim for a $9.00 a week (instead of $7.00 a week, as previously agreed with other unions) immediate wage increase in February 1984. This approach lacked subtlety, since it involved a blatant "extra claim" in breach of the national wage-fixing principles. But their tactic had the merit of concentrating the minds of everybody else. This led to a minor crisis amongst the building unions, particularly as the BLF and BWIU tended to compete with each other as to which was the most militant.

With the BLF's renewal of its campaign to fight for a flat $9.00 a week wage increase, some of the unions were not sanguine about the chances of success. Tom McDonald recalls, "… the Labor government would oppose us because they were worried that we were going to bust open the Accord and wage restraint. The ACTU was opposed to us. Every bastard is opposed to us, so the ACTU came forward with the view 'why don't we put it into a superannuation fund?'"[12]

Indeed, Kelty proposed that the demand be converted into a claim for a superannuation allowance. He said that initially, "I talked to Norm Gallagher [head of the BLF]. He's [just] got out of jail.[13] I've gone to the footy with him, set him aside. I am actually close to Norm Gallagher. I've got to be honest. That's closer to Norm Gallagher than I was with Pat Clancy [head of the BWIU]. I said, 'Norm, I think it's actually a great thing to do with super and I would like you to support it.' And he said, 'I am thinking about it, and thinking about it.'"[14] Kelty remembers, "[a]t *no* stage did I ever let Garry Weaven or Tom McDonald believe that BIRP could be taken as wages. It was always to be superannuation, hence their phone calls to tell me that it could not be delivered."[15] A problem was that the BLF came to believe – and argued for the position – that superannuation would be far harder

---

[12] Tom McDonald interview, August 2012.
[13] Gallagher had been released on appeal, as the Court had set aside his conviction for allegedly taking secret commissions.
[14] Bill Kelty interview, March 2013.
[15] Email exchange, Bill Kelty to Mary Easson, 28 November 2013. Emphasis in the original.

to sell to its members than cash in hand. Gallagher asserted that his members at building sites were saying, "we don't want it. We don't want it in super, we want the money!" He rejected Kelty's proposed solution. "The builders' labourers are saying 'stuff that!' They say, 'superannuation is … a pie in the sky',"[16] Tom McDonald recalled.

This unsettled the other building unions, with the BWIU considering whether to cave in, accepting the BLF militant position demanding money now "in the hand", rather than appear weak in comparison to its arch rival. McDonald, then the national Assistant Secretary of the BWIU, went to the ACTU to discuss the alternatives. In Kelty's recollection, McDonald said, "we want the money too". He received a roaring response:

> And I said, 'stuff you! You're not getting the money.' And I said, 'I will do my utmost to make sure you are not getting the money.' And I went to Ludeke and said, 'in no way is the BIRP allowance going to flow through the industrial system's wages. I will just tell you that. I will tell you that plainly and honestly.' And I said, 'I don't want you to give it. I want you to reject it. I don't give a care what you say, but you've got to reject it because it is just impossible. We will transfer this into superannuation.'"[17]

Weaven recalls, "Bill said to me, 'look, this is not really going to fly.' He didn't tell me that he made sure it didn't fly, but it didn't get approved by the bench. It was Terry Ludeke [who] was the Deputy President of the bench, and they approved the package other than that allowance. The BLs [builders' labourers] immediately seized on that as a reason to go out and campaign for an extra wage payment, but Bill convinced me, and also Tom McDonald and Pat Clancy, that it could be converted to a superannuation claim, and pursued as a super claim."[18]

In Kelty's recollection, McDonald appeared mellow in his reaction to the game plan. Kelty pressed his point, saying, "we've got one

---

[16] Tom McDonald interview, August 2012.
[17] Bill Kelty interview, March 2013.
[18] Garry Weaven interview, March 2013.

Figure 20: Tom MacDonald speaking at a union public meeting, *circa* late 1980s. Source: personal collection of Tom and Audrey MacDonald.

chance in history – and [we're] not letting it go."[19] Interestingly, Kelty never got on particularly well with Pat Clancy, the crusty leader of the BWIU, who was by the middle 1980s nearly completely blind, but

---

[19] Bill Kelty interview, March 2013.

still astonishingly authoritative within his union, still its undisputed master strategist. Clancy saw an opportunity for his members, and simultaneously a way to weaken his arch rival in the building unions. Kelty argued with him about the historic opportunity, reasoning that the Commission would reject the allowance anyway:

> If they reject the decision on Wednesday morning, if you say on Wednesday afternoon that we have negotiated an entire agreement that has to be met in another way, then we will look at other ways to meet an entitlement, but we will not give up your entitlements … If that happens to be superannuation, that claim will be pressed [strongly by the ACTU].[20]

Kelty remembers that to his surprise, McDonald, with Clancy's support, said, "'well, we're in if that happens'. They did it and they did it precisely in those steps. They got it right and from that moment on – once they said that, then that didn't mean you were going to have a fight, because that only came with Gallagher."[21]

Weaven says, "so, Tommy [McDonald] came back to me and said, 'look, he's been very persuasive and I think we can do that'; and so that was momentous. Then we set about, first of all, the politics of how we out-do the BLF. We decided to take the claim of $9 and to add a couple of more dollars to it so that it was more than $9. Present[ed] it to the workers as a more militant position. At that point, I drew up the [superannuation] scheme, how it should look and so on, and we tendered it out and we got the unions on board."[22]

Tragically for the BLF, the superannuation campaign was part of its ultimate divorce from the wider union movement. It could have been a great victory for Gallagher, but instead he saw it as a chance to separate for political purposes. He lost. On 30 October 1984, the NSW Parliament passed the *NSW Industrial Arbitration (Special Provisions), 1984*, which enabled the cancellation of the NSW BLF's registration as an industrial union under the *NSW Industrial*

---

[20] *Ibid.*
[21] *Ibid.*
[22] Garry Weaven interview, March 2013.

Arbitration Act, 1940. The deregistration was gazetted on 11 January 1985. The Victorian Government similarly cancelled the Victorian State registration of the Victorian branch with the *Builders Labourers' Federation (Derecognition) Act, 1985*, which received Royal Assent on 30 July 1985. On 14 April 1986, Royal Assent was received for the Federal Parliament's *Builders Labourers' Federation (Cancellation of Registration) Act, 1986*. The Federal Government also successfully introduced the *Builders Labourers' Federation (Cancellation of Registration – Consequential Provisions) Act, 1986*, which allocated the work formerly covered by the BLF to the BWIU, the Federated Engine Drivers & Firemen's Association of Australia (FEDFA) and the Plumbers and Gasfitters Employees Union of Australia (PGEU).[23]

Kelty recalls, "now once the decision was made, Garry Weaven was superb and Tom McDonald [was] just superb... You could not have questioned their capacity or their ability. They were superb in putting [the creation and development of the building-industry fund] together."[24] Effectively, at that time, a union official had two main choices: to try to negotiate, say, a $9 a week per employee wage increase and fail, because it would breach the National Wage guidelines imposed by the Commission, or to pursue the opportunity to negotiate an equivalent superannuation claim. "Well, what do you go for? You'd go for superannuation because you will get it,"[25] Kelty muses.

The building superannuation claim provided the very precedent that the Commission and employers had wanted to avoid: the extension of a claim in one industry to the rest of the economy. The ACTU argued several counter-points. First, awarding money for superannuation added to the capital base of the nation. It was not immediately inflationary, as it added to overall investment capacity. Perhaps more

---

[23] See Elder, John Richard (1994) "The Australian Building Construction Employees & Builders Labourers Federation and the NSW Building Industry", Thesis for Master of Industrial Relations, University of Sydney, pp. 151f.
[24] Bill Kelty interview, March 2013.
[25] *Ibid.*

relevantly, whereas wage increases were typically linked to award and industry allowances, going up proportionately. A 3 per cent increase in wages, when also applied to such allowances, would have further increased wage inflation. In contrast, with superannuation, an increase limited to the base award rate reduced the inflationary impact. The main justification was that the unions saw this as responsible catch-up, given that wages had significantly fallen in real terms over the late 1970s and early 1980s.

A question the parties were required to address was, "when is an extra claim not an extra claim?" One answer was when it concerned an issue that was not an "industrial matter". A superannuation scheme appeared to fit this bill. Although not a new idea, it became the central theme of negotiations in the building industry in March 1984. The negotiations were troubled from the outset. The $9 a week wage claim translated first into a superannuation claim worth $10 a week (the extra $1 was for administration costs), and later $11 a week (including an extra $1 for death and disability insurance cover). The employers resisted, intervening in the national wage case to argue that the unions' claim was an extra claim, and therefore inconsistent with the wage-fixing principles. The Commission declined to abandon the wage-fixing principles as a result of the situation in the building industry, suggesting instead that the employers pursue the matter with the appropriate industry panel. In the meantime, however, the National Industrial Construction Council, representing large contractors and the states' Master Builders Associations, reopened negotiations with the unions on the superannuation scheme. Agreement in principle was reached when, in late April 1984, Justice Alley delayed payment of the 4.1 per cent wage increase to building workers covered by Federal awards. This created major anomalies, since the 4.1 per cent had already flowed to building workers covered by state awards in all states except Victoria, where the BLF was strongest. The case revealed that the employers were hopelessly split on the issue, with the Confederation of Australian Industry, the Metal Trades Industry Association, some state employers' associations, and several contractors' organisations

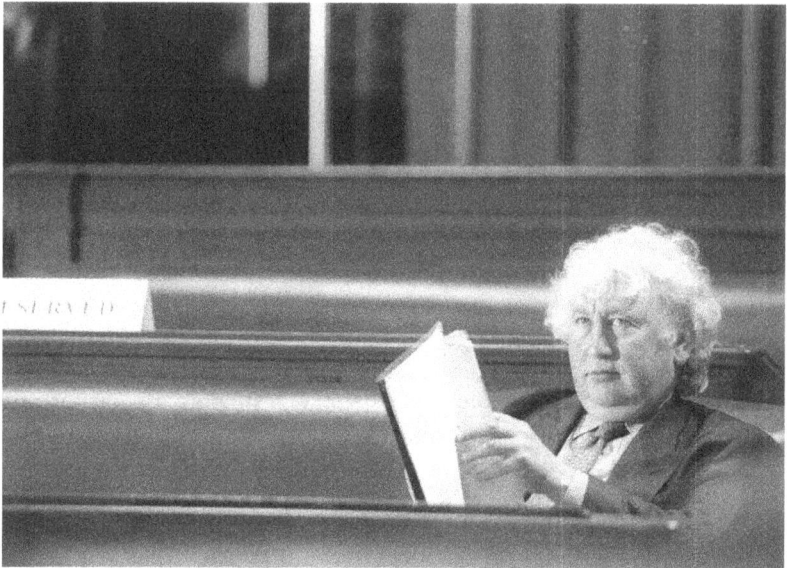

Figure 21: Pioneer of "industry super", the ACTU Secretary Bill Kelty after addressing the 1996 MTIA (Metal Trades Industry Association) National Conference in the Senate Chamber of old Parliament House. Photographer: Mike Bowers. Source: Fairfax Archives.

opposing the superannuation scheme, while the National Industrial Construction Council supported the deal with the unions.

On 11 May 1984, before the full bench, the Commonwealth joined the ACTU, the building unions and the National Industrial Construction Council to support the extension of the national wage case pay rise to Federal building awards. The application was opposed by the Confederation of Australian Industry, the Metal Trades Industry Association, and other employer groups. In the building industry, "… the employers started being beaten up – site by site – and falling in one at a time."[26] With some reluctance, in mid-June the Commission handed down a decision in favour of the unions, and implicitly gave the nod to the superannuation deal. In declining to prevent the wage increase flowing on into Federal building awards, the Commission was critical of

---

[26] Garry Weaven interview, March 2013.

the parties to the superannuation agreement, as a blatant attempt to escape the overall wage guidelines on "no extra claims", and it warned against a general flow-on of such a scheme to other industries.

One contemporary account summarised the drama: "It was some time – and some trouble – before the building industry superannuation scheme was in operation. Although an agreement between the National Industrial Construction Council and a number of building unions was signed in July [1984], some employers continued to resist the scheme, and two unions refused to sign the agreement. The Plumbers and Gasfitters Employees Union of Australia declined to sign the agreement and engaged in industrial action in pursuit of a revised agreement and a 36-hour week, nine-day fortnight. The Builders Labourers Federation also declined to sign the agreement, but for reasons that were never made clear. Great pressure was brought to bear on these two unions. The Plumbers and Gasfitters had a penal clause inserted in its awards in Victoria and New South Wales, and the BLF was threatened with draconian legislation from the Federal and Victorian governments and with expulsion from the ACTU. In early October, the pressure bore fruit, and the building industry agreement was finally signed by all concerned, to the great relief of the Federal government."[27]

The finalisation of the building industry agreement was of significance in two main respects. First, it brought to an end a potential threat to the Accord. The importance of the agreement to the Federal government in the run-up to an election,[28] with its entire economic strategy dependent on the survival of the Accord, was hard to overstate. To have survived a storm from the building industry was an indication that the Accord was robust enough. Second, the building industry agreement signalled that although wage increases outside national wage cases were disallowable, the scope for agreements including non-award matters was considerable. This promised to be of even greater significance in the future, as wage policies continued to constrain union action for higher wages.

---

27 Mulvey, Charles (1985) "Wage Policy and Wage Determination in 1984", *Journal of Industrial Relations*, Vol. 27, No. 1, March, p. 71.
28 Won by the ALP on 1 December, 1984.

For the union leaders in the building sector, "winning" superannuation was just the beginning of a challenge for which they had little preparation: how to run a big, complicated, new scheme. In Weaven's summation, "what it mainly took was not being too steeped in the super industry. You start with a blank sheet of paper ... a lot of it was making up the rules as you go, and ignoring a lot of the additional rubbish that went into superannuation."[29]

The casualisation of the industry's workforce and the multiplicity of small employers, posed significant administrative hurdles. As McDonald said, "in the building industry, all that some of the employers offer is the glove box of their ute. How do you make it work in a casual industry like the building industry?"[30] Indeed, there was not only fierce opposition to union superannuation, but also suspicion that it would all unravel because the unions would be incapable of implementing the very schemes that they had proposed.

Some of McDonald's colleagues asked, "how the bloody hell do you do it?"[31] McDonald noted that all the pieces of the puzzle were there. One was the technology that now existed for sophisticated record-keeping and tracking of members in the system. The second was the model similar to what became the BUS scheme for long-service leave. This had been created legislatively in NSW and other States years earlier.[32] "I strongly pressed [that] this was not just a challenge to set up a scheme, this was a challenge to make a scheme work. It would be a disaster if we had set up a scheme and it collapsed. For the building unions, it would be a great disaster. The key to it being successful was simplicity of design and this was our secret,"[33] McDonald claimed. He said, "we designed the scheme so that it was not based, like other schemes, on the hours worked. It was not based on salary or a percentage of salary. It was a flat amount. Everyone,

---

[29] Garry Weaven interview, March 2013.

[30] Tom McDonald interview, August 2012.

[31] *Ibid.*

[32] Arising from legislation introduced in 1975 and later amended to the NSW *Building & Construction Industry Long Service Payments Act,* 1986.

[33] Tom McDonald interview, August 2012.

the employer paid the same. It was based on time employed, not time worked. This we had learnt from the [complexities of the] building industry long-service leave scheme."[34] Simplicity, as everyone knows in data management systems, especially thirty years ago, is everything.

Thus, "when it came to ensuring that proper payments were made by employers, it went like this. The scheme finished up being $11: $9 super, $1 for life insurance and $1 for administration. We said to the employer 'We want you to pay the administration', therefore deliberately so that the employers would want to have an efficiently administered scheme – because if it was inefficient, they would be paying extra. We wanted it to be efficient, so workers wouldn't get all confused with division and uncertainty. It was $11 per week employed, not days worked."[35]

As for the argument that unions were "giving away" wages for superannuation, there was a contrary explanation: "In '85 we [were] still recovering from the crisis of stagflation. If we had gone to the commission with a 3 per cent increase in wages, we would have got bugger all. We wouldn't have got it in the economic circumstances. The reason why we got it in super was because we were able to prove that it is non-inflationary. We could not prove that a wage increase was non-inflationary... We sacrificed the right to seek it. We never sacrificed 3 per cent because we would never have got the bloody thing."[36]

The ACTU had decided that universal superannuation was going to be pursued through the award system generally. The ACTU made the application and got the Federal Government to support it. In the documentation, the ACTU argued that universal superannuation was not inflationary because the 3 per cent would not feed into wages, and thus would not then feed into demand. It would instead go into investment capital, and therefore would stimulate the economy.

---

[34] *Ibid.*

[35] *Ibid.* This meant that, for example, a casual worker working for, say, three days in the week got $11, rather than a percentage.

[36] Tom McDonald interview, August 2012.

Figure 22: Mavis Robertson, a pioneer of the building unions' superannuation schemes, at a meeting of members of the Retirement Futures Forum, held at the CBUS Board Room, Melbourne, 19 March 2001. Source: Fairfax Archives.

It would not have the same inflationary effects as a wage increase, because it would not be changing consumption demands. Whether such economic analysis is strictly correct (any cost increase is surely a pressure to increase prices), this thinking characterised the arguments of the time, and filled the union leaders with righteous vigour in pursuit of their objective. Kelty and others saw the outcome as less inflationary than the possible alternatives, and enabled the pursuit of an important political and social objective with overwhelmingly long-term positive economic benefits, through a national system of superannuation via a proliferation of industry schemes.

The achievement of the building scheme created a potent precedent for others to follow. Simplicity and focus were important. Cyril Twomey, a professional appointed by BUSS from the fund administration industry, wrote that: "During 1985 interest in superannuation will continue. Unions will be seeking:- 1. Coverage for all workers 2. Vesting 3. Portability 4. A say in the running of the schemes."[37] He argued that the rigidity of many existing funds, particularly defined benefit types, would be nigh impossible to amend efficiently. He argued that "[i]t is my opinion that existing defined benefit or benefit promise schemes will *not* be able to cope with these issues."[38] He went on to comment: "I recently saw an attempt to change a defined benefit scheme to cope with vesting/portability plus allowing for viable contributions. Theoretically the formulae used may have been correct but I would hate to try to explain the benefits to workers on a construction site."[39] He could not and would not. An accumulation plan was much easier to explain and manage, and so the BUSS and all the industry funds that followed were of that type. Additionally, the inclusion of $1.00 a week for death and disability cover insurance was a masterstroke in the building industry. Many workers found it difficult to obtain cover, many more did not bother to apply. Through mass coverage, the numbers covered was broadened, overall premiums reduced, and an important social aim achieved. It was an unalloyed good.

---

[37] Twomey, Cyril (1985) "Building Unions Superannuation", *Superfunds*, No. 90, March, p. 19. The author of the article was the then Victorian State Director of Jacques Martin Pty Ltd., the fund administrator at the time.

[38] Twomey, Cyril (1985) "Building Unions Superannuation", *Loc. Cit.*, p. 19, emphasis in the original.

[39] *Ibid.*

As Weaven put it, "the way that it took off in the building industry was a big wakeup call because the building industry is very 'casualised'. There were very few long-term, employer-employee relationships. The point being, if you could run it there – and mind you, there were tremendous stuff-ups – the belief was that you could run it anywhere."[40] In McDonald's words, "we decided that it had to be started quickly and therefore ... we developed a plan ... I remember going to the secretary – I was the assistant national secretary – going to the [national] secretary [Clancy] and saying, 'They can't very well renege on the position they have made, particularly if we put it in super. We have got the support of the Federal Labor Government, and if we are ever going to get super, it's now. This is our moment.'"[41]

Implementation meant moving extraordinarily quickly, with McDonald and Weaven driving the process. "Garry was very clear and had a massive input into it. It couldn't have been done without him and the ACTU. We called on the employers to join the scheme."[42] But they were divided, and the big builders wanted two things: first, clarity and administrative simplicity on employees' payments; and second, equal representation on the board. Even so, the employers were all over the place: "There was an appeal for employer class solidarity. They were under enormous pressure. The workers had them under pressure. The ACTU had them under pressure, so they were all over the place. Some of them, however, saw superannuation as inevitable so they thought, 'we might as well support and get our foot in the door and have some say about how it's run'."[43] McDonald recalls.

Fearing a loss of momentum, the unions set up a union board of trustees as an interim-board, and from there they designed the

[40] Garry Weaven interview, March 2013.
[41] Tom McDonald interview, August 2012. See also McDonald, Tom "CBUS and the Superannuation Revolution", in McDonald, Audrey & Tom (2016) *Dare to Dream. Stories of Struggle and Hope*, self-published, Sydney, pp. 217-22.
[42] Tom McDonald interview, August 2012.
[43] *Ibid.*

scheme. The unions tendered out the management of the scheme, seeking tenders from AMP and others. AMP, however, declined to submit because of concerns about upsetting some of their clients, who were in the company schemes that they managed. National Mutual and Colonial Mutual were the two main applicants, and Colonial won the bid through its subsidiary, Jacques Martin.[44] Its then CEO, Sandy Grant, came to play an extremely important strategic role, beginning as the head of an administrative service provider to the industry funds. McDonald remembers "the thing about Jacques Martin is [that] they listened to us. They didn't come along as the experts and tell us, 'this is how it should be'."[45]

There was much anticipation of failure. Some employers thought that entrusting unions to manage super, or to take a major role in inventing a new system, was as absurd as giving bicycles to kangaroos.[46] One consultant to the corporate funds, when the unions were just beginning to run campaigns in the late 1970s on superannuation, wrote that: "Thus far a small number of unions have shown that they are well informed and capable of arranging superannuation plans of their own."[47] David Nolan, an advocate for the Confederation of Australian Industry in a speech in 1985, referred to the "infamous BUS scheme".[48] A reason for his scoffing was due to supreme confidence that the fund would come unstuck, messed up by inexperienced, poorly qualified amateurs. There had been little contact between the professionals in the superannuation industry and the leaders of the unions. As one of the former wrote in the mid-1980s, "[t]o date, the involvement of the superannuation industry in

---

[44] *Ibid.*

[45] *Ibid.*

[46] The phrase is appropriated from an expression I first heard – in a different context – by the late political philosopher Frank Knopfelmacher (1923-1995).

[47] Solomon, D.J. (1979) "Wages Superannuation – Government, Union or Employer?", *Superfunds*, No. 68, September, p. 11.

[48] Nolan, David (1985) "Superannuation from the Employers' Viewpoint", *Superfunds*, No. 92, September, p. 33.

the industrial relations sphere has been, with a few notable exceptions, minimal."[49] But this was soon to change.

Fear of failure was a discipline on the union and BUSS side too. Getting the systems and administrative details right meant a delay in implementation. Partly as a way of mollifying employer resistance, the building unions agreed not to push for "retrospectivity",[50] but with a proviso: employers needed to put up $11 a week. As part of that deal, the unions agreed that the scheme would start in two stages. Stage one, from 1 July 1984, would only include the direct employees of principal contractors – not the employees of all their sub-contractors. McDonald recalls, "they [critics and the employers] thought people like me were going soft, but there was a method in the madness. We realised it was going to be a tremendous job to get it right, and we had to get it right from day one. We couldn't stuff up and then six months later say, 'let's correct it'. It would be too late."[51]

The aim was that the first group would be four or five thousand workers. These were employees from the big contractors who had sophisticated, computerised record systems. Any bugs, in the sense of enrolment and processing, would be identified there. There would be the opportunity to correct them, so that when all the sub-contractors' employees came in from 1 January 1985, there would already have been a trial run and the administration would be better equipped to manage things.

The fundamental difference between BUSS and the "island" schemes of the 1970s was in scale and depth of coverage. For example, while LUCRF had over a period of the 1970s and early 1980s recruited three or four thousand members, by the end of 1985, one year after the big bulk of members started to come in, the building scheme had

---

[49] Devlin, Michael W. (1986) "Industrial Relations and the Superannuation Industry, Blushing Bride and Reluctant Bridegroom", *Superfunds*, No. 96, September, p. 11.

[50] In other words, in this instance, pursuing a catch up on superannuation payments before BUSS was set up properly.

[51] Tom McDonald interview, August 2012.

enrolled 54,969 members. "Who has ever set up a business with 500 customers to 55 or 56 thousand in a year? Grace Brothers grew from a little store. Here we were going from nothing to a giant within a year,"[52] McDonald states.

As a start-up scheme, the simplicity of the system and getting it right in the first place was a significant administrative achievement. The scheme had to be capable of reaching 57,000 employers in the industry, scattered all over Australia. Within a year it had doubled to over 108,000 member accounts at the end of 1986. Today it is 750,000 – which is to say, too many (for reasons discussed in Chapter 6. There are too many member accounts.)

The building scheme was a pivotal stage in the development of a national superannuation scheme, and other industry funds adapted the BUSS model. BUSS covered not only the building industry, but the larger construction sector; it became the model for all the schemes. The ACTU played a crucial role in designing every one of the model's fundamental points. It was never a case of just the building unions inventing their scheme. Almost overnight, widespread industry superannuation emerged from nothing to become a colossus – the corporate model was being replaced by the union-inspired model, with all its flow-on effects. An amused McDonald notes:

We're about 1985. There is the Hilton. There is this big ballroom – a big conference room in there, where it holds 300 or 400 or whatever. 'Big-shots' in the area of retail superannuation. They have this global world authority doing an analysis of the building industry's superannuation scheme. But the person doing the analysis didn't know that there was one person from the union that was sitting in that meeting – and it was me. He went off about 'this is the back door to socialism',[53] and I thought, 'I can claim some of the credit. As far as I can recall Lenin

---

[52] *Ibid.*

[53] Perhaps the visiting speaker was responding alarmingly to the provocative, though benign prognostications expressed by Peter Drucker about "superannuation socialism". See Drucker, Peter (1976) *The Unseen Revolution: How Pension Fund Socialism Came to America*, Harper & Row, New York.

never thought about super-socialism. He only thought about scientific socialism,' just as a joke. Anyway, he goes off and he criticised it and I got up and asked a question. My question was a tactic of saying something provocative. And the reporter from the *Financial Review* was there, and when the report came out on the conference it's about this episode … I was a delegate of Jacques Martin, [which] was our administrative manager.[54]

After BUSS's $11 a week scheme was up and running, the unions eventually sought another 3 per cent, equivalent to $13.50, and it later became $24.50. And the amount rose commensurately as time went on.[55]

Weaven, reflecting on the events and arguments of his time that had led to industry superannuation, states: "I think we were a bit ambivalent, almost two-faced. One face was saying to the employers, the government and the world at large, 'this is in lieu of wages. We've forgone this and we are entitled to this in lieu of wages.' Because what happened once the building industry campaign got under way, the ACTU then took the position that we could spread this out from the building industry. And so we started encouraging similar funds to be set up. We had two funds in the building industry, BUSS and the Allied Unions Superannuation Trust (AUST) at first, which came together – but there were two at the start."[56]

Gardner notes that by 1985:

Superannuation seems to be the issue proving the exception to the restrictions imposed by the Accord on direct negotiation and industrial action. ACTU support for industrial action on this issue suggests that it is prepared to graft the decentralised strategy of hours' struggles and pre-Accord days onto the present centralised negotiating framework. This seems to be, to some extent, a response to the superannuation push already under way in many industries, with BUSS in building,

---

[54] Tom McDonald interview, August 2012. See Munton, Joel Len (1985) "'Intruder' Upsets ASFA Talk on Builders' Scheme", *Australian Financial Review*, 20 February.

[55] That is to say, to 9 per cent, though many building industry agreements provided for higher payments than the Superannuation Guarantee minimum.

[56] Garry Weaven interview, March 2013. The two came together in 1992.

MUST in metals and the TWU [Transport Workers' Union] well under way with a 4 per cent superannuation claim before the deal. Laurie Carmichael is credited with developing the notion of the trade-off with the productivity increase, which breathed renewed life into action over this issue in the latter months of the year. Although superannuation deals were supposed to wait for the July 1986 deadline, the TWU concluded negotiations with major employers, such as Brambles, making themselves the main exemption to the deal. The paint industry dispute in November exemplified union preference for industry-based schemes. Action by FSPU members in this industry and intervention by the ACTU and Federal government after the resulting stand-downs in the vehicle industry moved the issue from choice of superannuation scheme to an agreement that the employers would contribute to the industry-based scheme. In December, an agreement was signed between the ACTU and the ACM [Australian Chamber of Manufactures employer group] for a joint superannuation scheme to cover manufacturing.[57]

Weaven recalls "we used to hold those meetings simultaneously. We would have all the ETU [Electrical Trades Union] and the plumbers and iron workers down one side and the BLF, BWIU and the carpenters were joined down the other side, and 99 per cent of the agenda was identical. And when there was an issue of difference we would minute that and it was nice to chair both at the same time. It was pretty good fun, but then we set up a similar thing in the metal [industry] or manufacturing called MUST – Manufacturing Unions' Superannuation Trust, which then became [the] Manufacturing Unions Super Trust – which then, considerably later when the employer group came in later in the '80s, became the Superannuation Trust of Australia. And later it amalgamated with Australian Retirement Fund, which was the other employer group, to become now the biggest fund in Australian superannuation."[58]

---

[57] Gardner, Margaret (1986) "Australian Trade Unionism in 1985", *Journal of Industrial Relations*, Vol. 28, No. 1, March, p. 135. The manufacturing scheme became the Superannuation Trust of Australia (STA) in 1988.

[58] Garry Weaven interview, March 2013. Weaven is referring to Aus-tralianSuper, formed from the merger in 2006 of the Australian Retirement

Weaven notes "that was the genesis. The early success in the building industry – site by site – and taking the employer-by-employer thing out, the TWU launched a campaign at the same time with some success. The metal unions, co-ordinated by the ACTU under this MUST scheme, had quite a lot of success, and we then emulated it everywhere that we could. Sometimes, the unions just did it off their own bat, sometimes with the ACTU cajoling."[59]

The immediate opportunity resided on the exploitation of a myth. As argued in the next chapter, conventional wisdom was that superannuation was a non-industrial matter that could not be legally considered under Federal law by a Commonwealth industrial tribunal. Therefore the industrial tribunal was powerless to consider a dispute at the Federal level over a superannuation claim. This matter was only conclusively resolved when, in 1986, the High Court clarified that superannuation, in fact, could be considered by a Federal industrial relations tribunal.

Gardner notes that there were difficulties in maintaining discipline while retaining the capacity to mobilise so that the ACTU could have a strong, credible bargaining position. "These [difficulties] have been resolved in 1985 by a skillful mixture of cajolery and balancing of factions, isolation of 'mavericks', and nurturing of the campaign for industry-based superannuation schemes."[60]

In 1983, the aspirational vision for widespread superannuation coverage had been hesitatingly expressed. In 1985, the strategy unfolded into a campaign for industry-by-industry superannuation. In between, a unique situation had developed in the building industry. Later, even with such a significant outcome, and the eventual rolling out of superannuation across the award system following the 1986 wage case, says Tom McDonald, the ACTU went to the government and said in his summary, "superannuation is going to wither on the

---

Fund (ARF) and the Superannuation Trust of Australia (STA).

[59] Garry Weaven interview, March 2013.

[60] Gardner, Margaret (1986) "Australian Trade Unionism in 1985", *Loc. Cit.*, p. 134.

vine if it stays at 3 per cent because at that level it could not deliver to anyone a decent retirement income. So, why have a scheme that cannot deliver? It has to blossom or die."[61]

All these issues came to a head, leading to a crisis. Keating, on the basis of an ACTU proposal, agreed to support 9 per cent, phased-in. On the union side, the architect of that idea was the ACTU's legal officer at the time, Iain Ross.

In the so-called unloseable 1993 election, Opposition Leader Dr John Hewson agreed with his industrial relations spokesman, John Howard, to freeze the phasing in of the 9 per cent. The Superannuation Guarantee rate was then at 4 per cent of earnings. Had the Liberals won, it could have been the downfall of industry superannuation. Keating's surprising win in 1993 ensured that by the time the Coalition won the next election in 1996, with legislation on the statute books that phased-in superannuation to 9 per cent of salaries by 2002, it looked like industry superannuation was irreversible. The explication of that story lies ahead. A key question was what role, if any, the Australian Industrial Relations Commission could play in disputes over superannuation. The issue turned on what matters the Commission could consider. Far from an arcane question of law, the answer had huge implications. This subject is addressed in the next Chapter.

---

[61] Tom McDonald interview, August 2012.

4. Industry Super on a National Footing

A critical issue in the development of the modern Australian superannuation system was the evolving definition of "industrial dispute" within the meaning of Federal industrial law. Until the mid-1980s, "... employers tended to argue that superannuation was not an 'industrial' matter for the purpose of the Conciliation and Arbitration Act and the Conciliation and Arbitration Commission (the Commission) and unions themselves were afraid to risk a High Court challenge."[1] Despite the law determining what could be considered within the jurisdiction of the Federal industrial tribunals, "[t]his does not prevent agreements being concluded between trade unions and employers on superannuation; such agreements would be outside of the jurisdiction of the Federal Commission."[2] Additionally, awards and agreements that might be put to the States' tribunals would be untrammelled by constitutional issues of what was an appropriate matter to come before them. But, as is examined in this Chapter, there was a mindset by the unions that precluded the pursuit of superannuation before the industrial tribunals.

When the building industry superannuation campaign emerged in 1983-84, ACTU Secretary Kelty's position was simple: "... we do not accept the narrow-constrained argument that it's not part of the 'industrial relations' [system]."[3] As the unions sought a 3 per cent

---

[1] Plowman, David & Weavan, Garry (1989) "Unions and Superannuation", in Ford, Bill & Plowman, David (1989), editors, *Australian Unions. An Industrial Relations Perspective*, Second Edition, Macmillan Company of Australia, Crows Nest [Sydney], p. 251.

[2] Gill, Howard (1979) "Industrial Relations and Superannuation", *Superfunds*, No. 69, December, p. 6.

[3] Bill Kelty interview, March 2013.

wage increase allocated to superannuation in the 1986 national wage case, Kelty's position became strident: "The High Court can't tell us it's not part of an industrial [dispute]. [Superannuation is] a right. They can say whatever they like, but we want it."[4]

On the surface, it might now seem obvious that disputes about superannuation are clearly matters pertaining to the employer-employee relationship, but the law, as it had been interpreted to the mid-1980s, suggested otherwise. A brief excursion explaining the significance of this interpretation is crucial to appreciate how the unions exploited a loophole and, having created some momentum with the ALP government for industry superannuation, changed the law and decisively influenced the interpretation of the law to suit their purposes.

The then prevailing interpretation of the limits of Commonwealth power highlighted that the Australian Constitution, under s.51(xxxv), conferred powers to the Commonwealth in the conciliation and arbitration of industrial disputes. This states:

> The Parliament shall, subject to this Constitution, have the power to make laws for the peace, order and good government of the Commonwealth with respect to … Conciliation and Arbitration for the prevention and settlement of industrial disputes extending beyond the limits of any one State.

Read in conjunction with s.51(i) of the Constitution, which conferred powers to the Commonwealth to regulate trade and commerce with other countries and among the States, suggested a narrow scope. Much turned on the interpretation of "industrial" and whether a dispute that did not extend beyond the borders of one State could obtain sufficient standing to be considered a Federal dispute. These issues were explicated in the "Engineers Case" of 1920.[5] In

---

[4] *Ibid.*

[5] *Amalgamated Society of Engineers v Adelaide Steamship Company Limited and Ors.*, (the "Engineers' Case") *CLR* (1920-21), Vol. 28, pp. 129f. See also *Federal Clothing Trades of the Commonwealth of Australia v Archer and Ors.*, (1919-20) CLR, Vol. 27, pp. 207f.; *R v Portus and Ors; Ex parte Transport Workers' Union*, (1978-79), *CLR*, Vol. 141, p. 1.

this matter, the Amalgamated Society of Engineers had served a log of claims on the Adelaide Steamship Company and over 800 other Australian employers. On 23 August 1920 a compulsory conference was held before Justice Higgins in the Commonwealth Court of Conciliation and Arbitration, but no agreement was reached. The Western Australian Minister for Trading Concerns, representing one of the employers served with the log of claims, claimed the Court had no jurisdiction over the State Government employers, as there could be no inter-State industrial dispute within governmental concerns. The Court, however, held that:

> ... the Parliament of the Commonwealth has power, under s.51(xxxv) of the Constitution, to make laws binding on the States with respect to conciliation and arbitration for the prevention and settlement of industrial disputes extending beyond the limits of one State; that a dispute between an organisation of employees and a Minister of the Crown for a State acting under the authority of a statute of that State as an employer ... is such an 'industrial dispute'.

Even so, in this case, the High Court recognised limitations on the power of the Commonwealth over certain State employees that had until that moment been only implied. Under this doctrine, the general powers of the Commonwealth in s.51 of the Constitution could not be used to regulate governmental functions of the States, or the activities of state instrumentalities and statutory authorities. Therefore the power in s.51(xxxv) did not allow the then Commonwealth Court of Conciliation and Arbitration to make an award to settle disputes between state instrumentalities or departments and their employees. In addition, and more significantly, the High Court read "industrial" as designating a dispute in an industry; this was narrowly read to mean a business in commerce, which omitted ordinary government enterprise. This had the effect of excluding significant groups of State Government employees from the jurisdiction of the Federal tribunal, including railway employees, school teachers, academics, administrative employees, and fire fighters.

Without exhaustively canvassing the constitutional merits

of Australian industrial laws, such background is relevant to a prominent, defining (that is, binding for 30 years) decision on superannuation jurisdiction, namely the "Hamilton Knight Case".[6] In this 1952 decision, a claim that pensions be paid by employers to retired employees was held not to be about an "industrial matter", and therefore could not be dealt with by the industrial tribunal.

But as noted above, in the Manufacturing Grocers' Case in 1986,[7] the High Court permitted the Federal industrial tribunal to make any award dealing with superannuation, finding that a dispute about whether an employer should pay contributions to a superannuation fund for its current employees as part of their remuneration came within the statutory and constitutional sense of an "industrial dispute".[8]

Weaven recalls, "one of the fascinating things in the lead-up to that High Court case was that there had been an earlier High Court case called the Hamilton Knight case, which was a case that rejected the handling of a dispute about super involving the Seamen's Union in the arbitration Commission on the grounds that super wasn't an industrial matter. Every time, up until '86, each time an actual dispute had occurred and the union tried to use the Conciliation and Arbitration Commission, the matter went nowhere or was avoided."[9]

Weaven remembers feeling frustrated. "The commissioners would say, 'the Hamilton and Knight Case was not an industrial matter'. I honestly think I was the only person in the labour movement who had actually read the Hamilton Knight case.[10] It never said that. What it

---

[6] *R v Hamilton Knight and Ors; Ex parte the Commonwealth Steamship Owners Association,* (1952-53), *CLR,* Vol. 86, pp. 283f.

[7] Named after the union (eventually absorbed into the NUW) in whose name the ACTU conducted the case.

[8] In *Re Manufacturing Grocers' Employees Federation of Australia; ex parte Australian Chamber of Manufactures* (1986) 160 CLR 341 (hereafter the "Manufacturing Grocers' Case").

[9] Garry Weaven interview, March 2013.

[10] But surely not; Iain Ross, the then ACTU Legal Officer, read everything. In fairness, Weaven was speaking rhetorically. Unfortunately, due to time constraints as President of Fair Work Australia, I was unable to interview or communicate with His Honour Mr Justice Ross for this book.

said was that a dispute about a pension payment can't be an industrial matter because this person is no longer employed. The person in that case was on a pension. There is no employee-employer relationship; therefore there was the rejection of the union's claim ... It became a matter of convenience to say that super is not an industrial matter. To such an extent, that [in the 1986 national wage case] the Confederation of Australian Industry (CAI) said, 'we will win this. Super is not an industrial matter!'"[11]

The issue was finally clarified in a series of decisions by the High Court. During the 1986 national wage case, the ACTU had to overcome a challenge mounted by certain employers groups to the jurisdiction of the Commission in relation to superannuation. In its May 1986 decision, the High Court upheld the jurisdiction of the Commission to deal with disputes concerning superannuation. By so doing it clarified and effectively changed the law as stated in Hamilton Knight, in which the Court had decided that a claim for employers to pay regular pensions to ex-employees, who had retired, was not within jurisdiction.

In 1986, the employers argued that the union claim for award superannuation did not have a sufficient connection with the employer-employee relationship, as payments were required to be made to a third party – the trustees of superannuation funds. The High Court, however, held that these payments were still for the benefit of employees and directly arose out of the employment relationship. As researcher Graham Harbord asserted, "[s]uperannuation has finally come into its own in 1986 as a major industrial relations issue. Although the ACTU did not succeed in their claim for a productivity increase in the April 1986 national wage case, the commission did leave the way open for ratification of agreements on superannuation. As a result, it has been high on the bargaining agenda throughout the year."[12]

In *Re Amalgamated Metal Workers Union of Australia; ex parte*

---

[11] Garry Weaven interview, March 2013.
[12] Harbord, Graham (1987) "Major Tribunal Decisions in 1986", *Journal of Industrial Relations*, Vol. 29, No. 1, March, pp. 67-8.

The Shell Company of Australia Ltd, the High Court was asked to further consider the scope of the jurisdiction of the Commission over disputes about superannuation. The Shell Case gave the High Court the opportunity to consider the effect of the redrafting of the industrial legislation in 1988. The *Industrial Relations Act 1988*, which had replaced the *Conciliation and Arbitration Act 1904*, relied on the constitutional validity of the Commonwealth ratifying ILO Conventions and then applying such conventions to Australian law.[13]

The Shell group of companies had arranged for the establishment of a pension fund in 1947. Employees made compulsory contributions to the fund and employer companies made further contributions sufficient to meet the fund's obligation to pay defined benefits to the employees on retirement. A considerable surplus accumulated in the fund, but the trust deed made no provisions for its disposition. The deed, however, did contain a prohibition on any amendment to the trust deed that would result in payments from the fund to any of the member companies. Motivated in part by a desire to gain access to the surplus in the pension fund, Shell arranged for the establishment of a new superannuation fund in 1990, and for the amendment of the trust deed of the pension fund to allow transfer of employee entitlements (including a pro rata share of the surplus) to the new fund. The superannuation fund trust deed, in contrast with the old pension fund, made provision for dealing with any surplus, and expressly permitted distribution to the Shell group of companies.

Trade unions covering Shell employees initiated a dispute by demanding that the companies appoint actuaries to ascertain the extent of any surplus. If there was a surplus, they insisted that the companies use their best endeavours to procure amendments to the trust deed so as to give the employees a 50 per cent share and that the Shell trustees not act unilaterally in favour of Shell in the distribution of any surplus

---

[13] Cf. Landau, C.E. (1987) "The Influence of ILO Standards on Australian Labour Law and Practice", *International Labour Review*, Vol. 126, No. 6, November-December, pp. 669-90; Easson, Michael (1995) "ILO to the Rescue?", *Economic and Labour Relations Review*, Vol. 6, No. 1 June, pp. 149-57.

in the fund. The Shell companies refused to accede to the demands, and the question for the AIRC and the High Court was whether there was an industrial dispute that could be arbitrated by the industrial tribunal. A 4-3 majority in the High Court confirmed the view of the 2-1 majority in the full bench of the AIRC that the tribunal did have jurisdiction over the dispute, at least as to key aspects.

The High Court majority addressed two substantial arguments against the Commission's jurisdiction. The first was that in essence the unions were demanding amendment of the trust deed of the pension fund and payment of the surplus to the employees – matters that were beyond the power of the employer companies, and that lay within the control of the trustees, who were governed by the terms of the trust deed. This argument invoked authority that a demand "which ... employers themselves... have no power to grant" could not "give rise to an industrial dispute within the [Conciliation and Arbitration] Act or within s 51(xxxv) of the Constitution", because "assent or dissent ...[was] completely irrelevant to the thing demanded". The second and related argument against jurisdiction, drawing on the authority of Manufacturing Grocers' Case and other precedents, was that for a matter to be "industrial", the dispute "must be connected with the relationship between an employer in his capacity as an employer and an employee in his capacity as an employee in a way which is direct and not merely consequential."[14]

The High Court, by majority, endorsed a broad approach to the tribunal's jurisdiction about superannuation. In 1986 the Court had held that "entitlement to participate in a superannuation scheme and the means by which that scheme is to be funded" were "industrial matters" as defined in the *Conciliation and Arbitration Act, 1904* and that entitlement to participate in a superannuation scheme lacked substance unless viewed in the context of the nature and level of the

---

[14] "Manufacturing Grocers" (1986) *CLR*, Vol. 160, p. 353. See discussion in McCallum, Ron, & Wood, Karen J. (1995) "Crafting the Law: The High Court and Superannuation as an Industrial Matter", *Australian Journal of Labour Law*, Vol. 8, No. 2, August, pp. 121-36.

superannuation benefits and the circumstances in which the benefits would be paid. As a result, the majority concluded that a dispute about the form of a superannuation scheme was within the tribunal's jurisdiction.[15]

Further, the majority relied on the recasting of the statutory concept of "industrial dispute" in the *Industrial Relations Act 1988*. Whereas the *Conciliation and Arbitration Act 1904* had defined "industrial dispute" in terms of a "dispute as to industrial matters" (and in turn defined "industrial matters" as "matters pertaining to the relations of employers and employees"), the 1988 Act defined "industrial dispute" as "a dispute ... about matters pertaining to the relationship between employers and employees". According to the majority, the formulation of "about" was satisfied by "a less direct relationship than might be necessary in the case of a requirement that a dispute be as to an industrial matter". Therefore, a dispute between unions and employers as to whether the employers should endeavour to influence third parties who have the power to provide the desired superannuation benefits, concluded researcher Phillipa Weeks, "can fairly be described as a dispute about superannuation benefits."[16]

The Shell decision confirmed that the AIRC could deal with aspects of superannuation beyond the employer's obligation to make contributions to a fund. The majority found that the change of statutory language in 1988 displayed a parliamentary intention to broaden the concept of "industrial dispute", and specifically to allow for a less "direct" connection between a dispute and the relationship of employees and employers.[17] Therefore, any doubt about the standing before the tribunals, whether superannuation claims put forward by unions could be considered, had dissipated.

That settled, the unions embarked on an ambitious campaign to

---

[15] Colvin, John, & McCarry, Greg (1986) "Superannuation and Industrial Law", *Australian Law Journal*, Vol. 60, p. 503.

[16] Weeks, Phillipa (1993) "Major Tribunal Decisions in 1992", *Journal of Industrial Relations,* Vol. 35, No. 1, p. 100, drawing a quote from the majority decision.

[17] *Ibid.*, pp. 101-2

extend industry superannuation coverage. Crean recalls "we made a conscious decision with the 3 per cent that it all had to be accumulated. That was what the trade union movement was united on. That it had to be an accumulation account because the defined benefits' schemes were just too hard."[18] Besides, there was concern about the long-term viability of defined-benefit schemes: "... every single trustee that I have looked at, they usually say, 'These are the benefits we promise, provided the employer has the economic capacity to deliver these agreements.' So, you can say they are promised, but they are not, because there's a good chance the company won't be there in 40 years."[19]

Sword says that there was "audacity" in Kelty's positioning of the unions in support of superannuation. Sword adds: "He thought that it would make it easier for the government to agree to as well. When we came back to the ACTU executive – Bill was brought into the ACTU executive – so Bill said, 'great news – the government is going to support the 3 per cent wage increase; however, they will only agree to it if we agree that it goes into super'."[20] This was to be adept with – and strategic about – the exact truth – "economical with the actualité", to use an expression a UK politician once used about a particularly vexed matter.[21] What Kelty advised the Executive was a venturously clever, but not entirely accurate representation of the precise position of the government. Kelty wanted the payment to go to superannuation. The government wanted to see if he could deliver, keeping its options open.

"Now, there [were] going to be arguments because employers said, 'we'll just put the extra 3 per cent into our funds,' and unions said, 'no, we want the 3 per cent to go into this fund that we are setting up.' So, essentially, the argument was over which fund. The other thing that happened is that clauses went into Awards and State Awards [that] stated what fund the 3 per cent would go into. For example, with LUCRF, we had Common Rule Awards in Victoria and New South

[18] Simon Crean interview, May 2013.
[19] Greg Sword interview, June 2012.
[20] *Ibid.*
[21] That is, the UK politician Alan Clark (1928-1999).

Wales, and their clause was that 3 per cent had to go into LUCRF. That spread ... and then [the] SG [Superannuation Guarantee] came along and that increased it. That's why it was really significant and important to have your fund in the Award; it's no longer in the Award.[22] ... What I would say about our role is that it was a very localised role, and it was very radical and we backed it up with industrial muscle."[23]

Kelty recalls that there was a lot of resistance from various quarters, including some unions, to the specific superannuation campaigns in the mid-1980s. Some officials, for example, wanted money in individuals' pay packets rather than into a superannuation account. Kelty wanted to tame opposition by galvanising the unions in an industrial campaign, with the $8 a week general wage claim campaign and the 3 per cent super claim added to it. "We've got two campaigns going in the universe and we do know they are going to morph into one, and we had to accelerate that plan and bring it to a head to get the 3 per cent for everybody."[24] Some unions only wanted a wage increase; for them, superannuation was a lower priority. But it did not need to be an either/ or choice. It could be a bit of both. The ACTU Wages Committee backed the campaign. Kelty went to see Keating at the Australian government ministers' offices at Treasury Place, Melbourne, and told him that he was confident of unanimous support from his colleagues. "Keating said, 'just as a matter of historical interest, here's the advice of the Treasury. It said that there had been many silly ideas the officer has seen in six years; this is one of the silliest.' He added, 'here is the advice from the Department of Industrial Relations. Even if you wanted to do it, you can't do it because it is unconstitutional.' I said, 'that's one hurdle'."[25] Kelty asked Keating what his response would be to such sage advice. He recalls the reaction: "Keating said, 'don't

---

[22] The Howard government, in its "simplification" of matters that could be included in an industrial award, excluded superannuation entitlements. But by then, the union-backed industry funds were sufficiently well-established to consolidate and to grow.

[23] Greg Sword interview, June 2012.

[24] Bill Kelty interview, March 2013.

[25] *Ibid.*

worry about it. I'm supporting you.' He said, 'Bill, we'll learn. Once I go in to bat for you, I don't care what these people say.'"[26] As for the matter needing to qualify as an industrial issue, Kelty insisted, "but it was. There was already an industrial campaign for it."[27]

There was protracted opposition. The Business Council of Australia (BCA) opposed the superannuation campaign, but the unions signed-up 28 big BCA-member companies. It was decided that "we'll target them and see whether they agree. It only takes two weeks. Everyone's agreed and they say, 'Don't pick on us.' They all agree. 'You sit here and everything that you planned for – because you do plan strategically and try to say, if you do that, what's the likely outcome?', and nearly every occasion they did the thing we really wanted them to do."[28] Thus the extent of the achievement was becoming clearer: "So, we're established now as the universal industrial benefit, but on our terms – but [from] their wages. It was wages, had to be wages foregone... We are not inventing this. We actually got real wage reduction in all of this. This is not some story. Once it becomes their wages, then you are at least entitled to have a say in the control."[29] In other words, workers were persuaded to forego some of the wage increases, in the hand, that they would otherwise achieve, through superannuation payments into their individual accounts in the burgeoning industry and other funds.

Case Study: The Metal Industry

An interesting case study is the metal industry, which had long been a hotbed of rampant industrial conflict and protectionism (including government-imposed tariffs). It was "warfare by other means".[30]

---

[26] *Ibid.*

[27] *Ibid.*

[28] *Ibid.*

[29] *Ibid.*

[30] Count Carl von Clausewitz once quipped that war is the continuation of politics by other means. Arguments before the tribunals concerning industrial relations in the metal sector seemed a continuation of the war on the field. Clausewitz, Carl von (1832, 1984) *On War,* Howard, Michael, & Paret, Peter, editors, Princeton University Press, New Jersey, p. 87

The emergence of industry superannuation reflected a structural and cultural shift in the organisation of industrial relations in that sector of the economy.

From the 1950s onwards, typically industrial relations in the metal industry had been conducted through strikes, secondary boycotts, and bitter disputes, though usually of short duration. Labour historian Tom Sheridan described the Amalgamated Metal Workers Union (AMWU) as "mindful militants".[31] Metal employers' advocate Bert Evans recalls, "when I joined [the Metal Trades Industry Association or MTIA] in 1958 there was a 6 month strike at Metters – a big bath plant – 6 months long. This is what I was introduced to … It was mad. Beer strikes every Christmas, transport strikes, petrol strikes"[32] – a comment that applied to industrial relations experiences generally in this period.

Measured by days lost per employee, in the 1960s Australia had had one of the worst industrial-relations systems in the world.[33] It was marked by frequent factory strikes and enterprise bargaining styled as over-award payment claims.[34] An over-award payment claim was made on a factory-by-factory basis and the unions would

---

[31] Sheridan, Thomas (1975) *Mindful Militants. The Amalgamated Engineering Union in Australia, 1920-1972*, Cambridge University Press, Cambridge. The union until 1972 was part of the UK Amalgamated Engineering Union. Following various amalgamations, the union is now known as the Australian Manufacturing Workers Union, or more fully, the Automotive, Food, Metals, Engineering, Printing and Kindred Industries Union (AMWU) (the "metalworkers'" or "manufacturing workers'" union.)

[32] Bert Evans interview, May 2013.

[33] This summary might be contested. The era experienced an industrial relations system which had delivered workers (admittedly male, mostly) decent basic wages and conditions which were the envy of many industrialised countries. The industrial tribunals (State and Federal) could arbitrate outcomes – which were typically accepted by industrial parties, even if they were dissatisfied with particular outcomes. But the metal industry was a law unto itself. As Australia modernised in the 1980s, so too did industrial relations need to change.

[34] Cf. Foenander, Orwell de R. (1959) *Industrial Conciliation and Arbitration in Australia*, Law Book Company, Sydney.

Figure 23: Bert Evans, circa early 1990s, photographer Josh Robenstone, Fairfax Archives.

stake a claim, slightly localised for the particular target. The MTIA had a team of what Evans describes as "strike settlers" – employees seeking to mediate and broker industrial relations peace. "That was all we did – settle strikes. We would always sign an agreement for twelve months. Then they made a claim and this just went on and on."[35] The Australian industrial-relations system, the new province of law and order in Higgins' phrase, was supposed to minimise industrial action through comprehensive conciliation and arbitration, with legal remedies for breaches of awards or agreements, including for employers to seek fines on unions for illegal strike activity. Reality in militant industries bore little resemblance to the industrial relations equilibrium of Higgins' imagination.[36]

Expostulating on bargaining in the Australian industrial-relations system of the 1970s, Whitehead stated that "there seems no solution which is institutionally practicable … in the near future."[37] There was a bans clause in the metal industry award that said there should be no strikes during the life of the agreement or an Award. The employer organisations regularly applied to the Commonwealth Industrial Court for an order to terminate a strike, and the Court would regularly order cessation of industrial action because of the evidence presented on the strike. This, on its own, would show that there had been a breach of the award and agreements the unions had assented to. The unions would sometimes argue that the action had been spontaneous, that they had not coerced or encouraged militant activity, such as a strike in a factory. The Court would make an order for the strike to cease. Unions were often fined, not for the strike but for contempt of court. Evans recalls "there [were] something like 400 to 500 strikes in the metal industry in New South Wales a year."[38] Sometimes the unions

---

[35] Bert Evans interview, May 2013.

[36] Cf. Higgins, H.B. (1922) *A New Province for Law and Order*, Constable, London (the book collecting articles originally published in 1915 in the *Harvard Law Review*). For a commentary on Higgins' idealist account of the potential, peaceful implications of conciliation and arbitration, see: Callaghan, P.S. (1983) "Idealism and Arbitration in H.B. Higgins' *New Province for Law and Order*", *Journal of Australian Studies*, Vol. 7, No. 13, pp. 55-66; and Dabscheck, Braham (1990) "Enterprise Bargaining: A New Province for Law and Order?", *The Australian Quarterly*, Vol. 62, No. 3, Spring, pp. 240-55.

[37] Donald Henry Whitehead (1973) *Stagflation and Wages Policy in Australia*, Longman, Camberwell [Melbourne, Victoria], p. 105.

[38] Bert Evans interview, May 2013.

would say "we are not going to pay the fines." Evans had a stock response: "That's fine. I hope you enjoy walking to work and writing your stuff out in longhand because you will have no typewriters and you will have no cars. We will be over tomorrow with the Sheriff and we will collect your goods."[39] The MTIA became specialists in resolving disputes and playing hardball, collecting every penny of costs. This is another side to what Henderson has perhaps aptly coined the "industrial relations club",[40] perceived as the cosy coterie of employers, unionists, and tribunal members, living in their own industrial relations cocoon. Given the perpetual pattern of conflicts that seemed to exist in this period, one might say "some club". In the metal industry, it was far from genteel and convivial in this period.

Evans remembers that in the 1970s the metal industry had been the battleground for over-award payments and "the going rate". There was a going rate in Parramatta, in Springvale, in every pocket of industry. Whatever was the going rate was the subject of a flow-on claim. Until the mid-1970s, labour was in short supply. The going rate would go up and mostly everybody paid up. If the unions got a breakthrough with one employer, meaning an over-award payment, they sought to achieve that rate everywhere else. "It got so bad that in the end we stopped doing surveys because everybody wanted to know what the going rate was. Without being asked they were going up. We had the sheet-metal section and a foundry section and the Bankstown section, the Springvale section and all over Australia, there were different sections. About 8 in New South Wales and about 7 in Melbourne, 4 in Queensland and 3 in South Australia," he remembers.[41]

Evans claims that the MTIA eventually supported automatic index-ation in Accord Mark I because it was better than the over-award payment chaos; with the unions, in Evans' then view, the idea of honouring an agreement meant nothing. With the AMWU and its predecessors,

---

[39] *Ibid.*

[40] Henderson, Gerard (1983) "The Industrial Relations Club", *Quadrant*, Vol. 27, No. 9, September, pp. 21-9.

[41] Bert Evans interview, May 2013.

"nearly all 'comms' [i.e, a Communist Party member or fellow traveller] they caused a lot of strikes over wages. Over-award payments were the norm. That was it. We had these over-award payments and strikes impossible to settle. A real smarty, a good mate of mine, Wally Buckley, a great bloke, I used to ring him up and I would say, 'listen Wally. I am trying to settle some strike at ABC Engineering.' And he said to me one day, 'Don't waste your time, mate. The [Communist Party of Australia] has got a hold of [the dispute]',"42 would be a response. "From then on, I would ring up and he would say, 'it's fine,' or 'it's wet,' or 'the dogs are on tonight. Do you want to come to the dogs?' He wouldn't ever talk about the strike. If the Party had hold of it, he would talk about something else. If he wanted to settle it, if he could settle it, he would talk about it. That was our code."42

In 1981 there were numerous disputes about claims for a reduced 35-hour working week. "These were bitter strikes – really long six-month, five-month strikes. Never [just] overtime bans, [the union pursued] guerrilla tactics. We did all sorts of things during that time but in the end we were still opposing it. Everybody else had given in, so I decided that I would take a case to the full bench. I will never forget this. I had to create a dispute. I said to my solicitor bloke, 'I think that if I file a claim that hours should remain at 40 for five years that will create a dispute,' which is what we did."43

The MTIA went through the latter period of the Fraser government embracing automatic indexation, which had been anathema before, but the members said, "it was better than what we've got now. At least we all know what is going to happen." That functioned well for a time, but eventually fell apart.44 Evans remembers that one day he was on

---

42 *Ibid.* For an account of the politics, personalities and rivalries within the then Amalgamated Metal Workers and Shipwrights' Union, later the AMWU, circa the late 1970s, see Huntley, Pat (1978) *Inside Australia's Largest Trade Union*, Ian Huntley Pty. Ltd., Braddon [ACT].

43 *Ibid.*

44 See Appendix 4.

an ABC radio broadcast with Carmichael. "I said, 'I am prepared to talk to you but I can't really in good faith talk to you because you have never honoured an agreement. Your mob has never honoured one agreement ever.' I have been there 23 years now and I am a strike settler. I have handled more strikes in Australia than everybody else put together. That is my record. I said, 'I can't do it. You would have to give me a no-strike clause'." A surprising response arrived: "He [Carmichael] said, 'I can't give you a no-strike clause, but I can give you a no-extra-claims clause.' He said, 'if we can't make claims, we can't go on strike'. So, I said, 'okay.' We have all our discussions. It was me and Carmichael only, and I go back to the meetings of MTIA member company representatives, and I say, 'this is the position.' They say, 'how can you trust Carmichael?' I say, 'I don't have to trust him. I have never been able to trust any of the others, but he has given me his word that he will do it. He has given it to the Commission that he will do it.' They said, 'we have got no bloody choice, have we?'"[45]

By then the building industry employers had conceded a 35-hour week. The MTIA fought to get it back to 38-hours and resist flow-on to the metal industry. Evans recalls:

I get the mandate and it was near Christmas Eve and I remember going to the American Club and I got a big clap. I settled these strikes. I waited about three days and there hadn't been a strike, and about another 10 days and there hadn't been any strikes. Of course, we had this national-disputes procedure to set up, if ever there was a dispute to go through.

I got back to work after about 10 to 12 days, maybe 14 days, and there were three claims or four claims. I rang Carmichael and I said, 'you had better convene this disputes panel because we have got three or four claims.' He said, 'no, I am not going to just do that, mate.' He said, 'you can forget it.' I never had a strike. He stuck to his word. He went out. He said [to his members], 'you bastards voted for this. You are going to do it. Drop it.' That then became the basis of the Accord. Hawke told me that he wouldn't have entertained the idea of the Accord if the metal unions hadn't proved they could be trusted.[46]

[45] Bert Evans interview, May 2013.
[46] *Ibid.*

By the time of Accord Mark VIII, the MTIA was not involved directly in the negotiation of its terms, but was openly supportive. Evans remembers saying to Keating and Kelty, "'we have got to put here something about exports. We've have got to put in R&D. We got to be into innovation. We have got to put all these things in.' Kelty said, 'we can't put these things in an Accord. We are a union.' Keating said, 'give him what he wants. Whatever he wants is going in.' But then, of course, they lost the election and the Accord fell over."[47]

In 15 months during 1984 and 1985, however, there were protracted superannuation disputes and strikes. Metal union leader Greg Harrison became enthusiastic for the Manufacturing Unions Superannuation Trust (MUST), the scheme the AMWU wanted to see applied across manufacturing industry. "The Accord is more than just a wages agreement. The Accord opens up opportunities for unions to become involved in broader social issues; superannuation is such an issue,"[48] he observed. In contrast, Evans was alarmed: "In every state – 15 months ..."[49] [the superannuation [campaign] had this real bitterness and I just wouldn't budge ..."[50] In the middle of one heated phone debate [with Greg Harrison, who was leading the union campaigns for the MUST fund], it was over the phone, I said, 'nobody in their right mind would invest money controlled by unions.' Two days later I get a defamation writ. I said, 'Harrison! You little shit.' He had issued it. You didn't need to be a ruddy Rhodes Scholar to work out who was the driving force behind it. I thought 'you bastards! You bastards!'"[51]

Evans saw Tom Hughes QC, whose opinion was, 'if you have said it, you have said it. You are indemnified.' Then the national wage case came on. The writ was hanging over Evans' head: "The union suddenly panicked because they thought I was going to turn up and

---

[47] Ibid.
[48] Harrison, Greg (1986) "Superannuation – A Union's Viewpoint, *Superfunds*, No. 95, June 1986, p. 12.
[49] Bert Evans interview, May 2013.
[50] Ibid.
[51] Ibid.

NAME: **GREGORY JAMES HARRISON**

DATE OF BIRTH:
26 / 08 / 47

DATE JOINED:
26 / 02 / 87

MEMBERSHIP NUMBER:
41191404

MANUFACTURING UNIONS
SUPERANNUATION TRUST

Figure 24: Greg Harrison's MUST Card. Source: From Greg Harrison

argue that the case couldn't proceed because I had a defamation action against me."[52]

The disputes continued into 1986, with the MTIA objecting that the MUST trust deed gave unions ownership and control which then gave them power to exercise discriminatory power against employers.[53] But a new window was opening.

Weaven recalls that around 1988, "I think the next thing was some of the employer associations actually came on board and negotiated – the key one being the Metal Trades Industry Association.[54] They had a long negotiation with us. Instead of being a big, negative, wet blanket on their members, they became mildly positive. A lot of 'un-unionised' sites then began to come in."[55] Kelty saw the MTIA's Barry Watchorn as "a key figure in superannuation, supporting the

---

[52] *Ibid.*
[53] See arguments in the report by Robinson, Paul (1986) "Employers Warn on Metal Unions' Super Scheme", *The Age* (Melbourne), 24 March, p. 3.
[54] Now the Australian Industry Group (AiG).
[55] Garry Weaven interview, March 2013.

strategy from the employer's viewpoint and being a person who would take an independent and supporting view in supporting independent asset-allocation strategy and establishment of organisations such as Member's Equity (ME) bank, Industry Funds Services (IFS), Industry Superannuation Property Trust (ISPT), etc."[56]

Figure 25: On 28 May 1986 metal workers' leader Greg Harrison addressesa mass meeting of workers at Parramatta Stadium on the Manufacturing Unions' Superannuation Trust scheme. Source: From Greg Harrison

The MTIA decided, 'okay, we're joining in'." The AMWU presented the MTIA with the trust deed. Part of the solution was to extinguish the defamation case. The MTIA insisted on rewriting the trust deed, with a reformed board of five-a-side. "We had myself, and Roger Boland[57] was one of the Directors. Then we had Grahame Willis, our financial secretary, who was invaluable. Willis would go over the agenda and go over the minutes and the signatures. He is still there.[58] He is still working for AustralianSuper after all these years. He played no role in policy but a huge role in policing the corporate governance

---

[56] Email exchange, Bill Kelty to Mary Easson, 28 November 2013
[57] Later Judge Boland, President of the NSW Industrial Commission.
[58] Indeed, Willis is still on the board of AustralianSuper in 2016.

of it. He deserves enormous credit for getting the governance right. Then we had the Managing Director of General Motors and the Managing Director of one of the big component companies. We were the five," Evans recalls. This was how the Manufacturing Unions Superannuation Trust (MUST) became the Superannuation Trust of Australia (STA), with a bi-partite board drawn from nominees of the unions and employers.

This story is also part of the radical transformation of industrial relations in the traditionally militant metal industry and an example of a wider campaign. As Weaven was to reflect, "the industrial campaign, company by company, sector by sector, from 1984... established the basis for sweeping reform and the success of the industry-fund model in disarming opponents."[59]

The spread of industry superannuation proceeded apace, even in weakly-organised industries such as retail – which is now examined.

Case Study: The Retail Industry

Industry superannuation in the retail sector took shape with the employers taking the lead on the creation of the main superannuation fund. The key retail union, the Shop Distributive and Allied Employees' Association (SDA), was a reluctant convert to the idea of deferred pay through superannuation, rather than cash in hand. The then-secretary, i.e., head of the key retail union, Joe de Bruyn, frankly states, "I can say 'I was not an architect of superannuation' because when the proposition was put to the union movement, sometime in the '80s, there was a 3 per cent productivity increase that was going to be available to working people, and the proposition was 'should we take this as superannuation or as a wage increase?'..Jim Maher [then national President of the SDA] and I preferred the wage increase."[60] This was primarily because retail workers were typically low-income workers. "We thought that the superannuation was very nice, but at this time we preferred to get the money in our pockets. We also felt if

---

[59] Email correspondence, Garry Weaven to Mary Easson, 7 November 2013.
[60] Joe de Bruyn interview, March 2013.

we went out and asked people, 'would you like this as superannuation which you get at retirement or do you want it now?', they would take it now.'[61]

Figure 26: ACTU Congress showing the Clerks and the Shop Assistant Union delegates, September 1983, Melbourne. Source: Records of Unions NSW.

The union, however, saw merit in the government's actions in cutting taxes for lower-paid workers, support for a wage system geared to helping lower-paid workers and boosts to family allowances (a long-time policy goal of the SDA). They therefore went along with the ACTU superannuation campaign. "That was our view. I remember I had discussed it with Jim Maher and I had said to him, 'look, the money is better for our members.' And Jim agreed. But anyway Kelty had a different plan and so we had to fall in line."[62]

Then there was the challenge of creating a fund that would cover

---

[61] *Ibid.*

[62] *Ibid.* In passing, it is unclear and interesting given the power of the SDA why deBruyn states they had to fall in line. There have been matters where, of course, he and the union vigorously pursued an independent line. In this case, as now seems clear, the SDA leadership wanted to see how matters would develop and to give Kelty the benefit of the doubt. There was a feeling that it was either superannuation or nothing.

the whole, or as much as possible, of the retail industry. The Retail Employees' Superannuation Trust (REST) became the retail industry fund, over the initial objections of the retail union. The SDA leadership had initially agreed with John Maynes, Federal President of the Clerks Union, which then covered administrative and clerical workers in the retail sector, that both would be in CARE, a joint fund between the two unions. Maynes's idea was to have two right-wing unions form a joint superannuation scheme. At the time both unions shared the ownership of their mutual head office building in Queen Street, Melbourne.[63] "The big fight for us around Australia in every jurisdiction was to get an industry fund up. John Maynes' proposal to the SDA was, 'let us set up a fund for both clerical and retail employees' – which is CARE, which is still there, and at that time was supposed to stand for Clerical, Administrative and Retail Employees. Jim [Maher] and I became two of the four Directors on there, and John Maynes was there and somebody else from the Clerks Union, and so what we conceived was that this would be the fund for the retail industry. However, Kelty didn't agree. I don't know why, but he didn't. The retailers didn't agree. They said, 'There should be a fund for the retail industry only and not for the clerical people,' which goes wider across a whole diversity of industries."[64]

de Bruyn recalls that "the definitive argument took place in the Victorian State Industrial Commission, where you had Keith Marshall, who was the previous industrial registrar and who had become the President of the Victorian Industrial Relations Commission, presiding. And we argued that for Victoria – because our awards at that time were all state-by-state – we said, 'in Victoria the fund should be CARE,' and the retailers said, 'no, we want a different fund. We have a fund that

---

[63] Joe de Bruyn interview, March 2013. In this period, politically, the unions were closely aligned, with the Victorian leadership and national officers recently reconciled with the ALP. The Victorian branches of the FCU and the SDA rejoined the Victorian Branch of the ALP in 1985.

[64] Joe de Bruyn interview, March 2013. See also Weaven, Garry (2016) 'Workers' Capital: The story of Industry Funds and Australia's Superannuation Revolution', Foenander Lecture at the University of Melbourne, 15 November 2016, p. 11.

we call REST.' This was a shelf company that the retailers in Sydney had and they used that to become the trustee of a potential fund."[65]

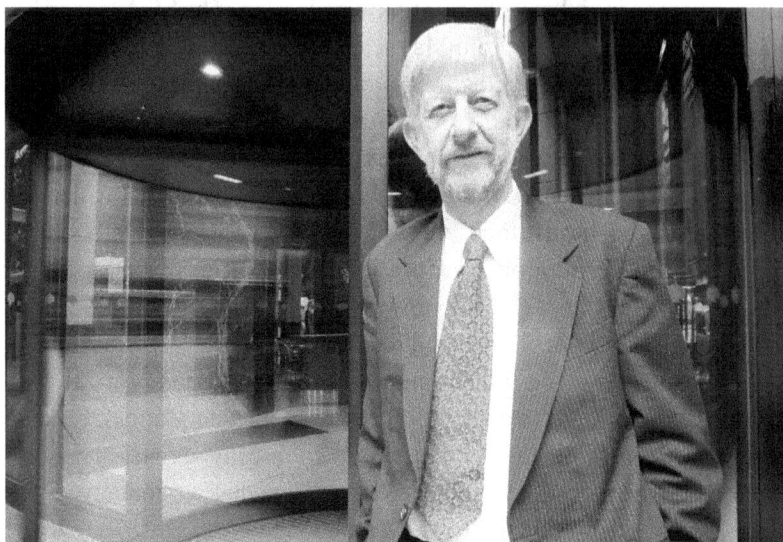

Figure 27: Joe de Bruyn in Sydney on 22 August 2007. Source: News Limited, photo by Vanessa Hunter.

The retailers put up the argument that it should be a fund for the retail industry only. de Bruyn speculates, "I don't know if Kelty was directly involved in making any submissions, but his view was very clear to us and he possibly made that view widely known. When Keith Marshall made his decision, he said, 'there should be a fund for the retail industry. It should not be CARE. It should be REST'."[66] Once that decision was given, the SDA had to revisit its entire strategy, including in Western Australia, where the industrial tribunal there had decided that CARE should be the preferred retail industry fund. Mark Bishop was the WA secretary. The case was re-opened, arguments were put forward and REST became the approved fund. That became the pattern around Australia. "The retailers then invited us on, and

---

65 Joe de Bruyn interview, March 2013. But Kelty's direct involvement in this way seems unlikely.
66 Joe de Bruyn interview, March 2013.

we had four of the eight Directors. Jim Maher, myself and – I can't remember who else, but in about December of 1988, that is when we went on."[67]

Some of the companies wanted their own individual company funds. At that time Coles and Myer were in one company called Coles Myer, and they set up a Coles Myer fund. In contrast, Woolworths was happy to be in REST. Franklins, which was a big NSW company, was also content to be in REST. David Jones wanted its own fund, and so on. Each company made up its own mind, according to de Bruyn's recollection.

In Tasmania, the local SDA branch secretary was persuasive in proposing Tasplan, a State-wide industry fund, as a default scheme in that State for retail workers. It became the fund that Woolworths went into there because the State Manager of Woolworths was one of the Directors of Tasplan. The thinking was that all the Tasmanian money should be in one Tasmanian fund, so that it could be invested predominantly in Tasmania.

In Queensland, the State Commission said that the funds appropriate for the 3 per cent superannuation should include REST, some other industry funds like SunSuper and another set up by the Queensland Retail Traders and Shopkeepers Association (although that fund never eventuated). The Queensland Commission allowed any company fund that, at the time of its decision, had already been established, but refused to recognise any new company funds. The Coles Myer fund was already in existence at the time, and became a fund for Queensland. Eventually, when Coles Myer found that throughout the rest of the country everybody had to be in REST, the company ultimately closed its Queensland fund and put all its employees into REST.

Rapidly, REST grew in membership, particularly with favourable recognition in the retail awards – as the default fund for most of the industry – and still further after the SG legislation was passed.[68] The

---

[67] *Ibid.*

[68] Way, Nicholas (1994b) "Retail Sector Soars in Award Super Stakes", *Superfunds*, No. 174, August, p. 7.

SDA, with around 215,000 members,[69] continues to be influential in the identity and continuation of the REST scheme as does the Australian Retailers Association, the principal retailers' employer body.[70] REST today has 1.2 million members for occupational superannuation contributions, and another 750,000 who formerly have been employed in the industry. The fund is now one of the bigger industry funds, with over $40 billion in assets. de Bruyn insists that merger with another industry fund, substantially unconnected to the retail industry, is not a realistic option: "Merger would mean that you would lose one of your unique marketing opportunities, which is that we are the fund for the retail industry. If we merge with somebody else you can no longer say that we are the fund for the retail industry because you will be the fund for other things as well."[71]

In this instance, the union leadership of the SDA was, despite initial reservations about the merits of superannuation rather than immediate pay increases, persuaded in the end by arguments of the type advanced by Kelty and its support for social-wage improvements (such as family allowances and tax cuts for the lower-paid) and for the wage system, including safeguarding and improving minimum award standards, to ultimately support retail-industry super. Kelty supported the merits of the retail-focused scheme, REST, rather than something more political in its origin, which is how he first saw CARE in its first manifestation.[72] His role was decisive in the retail sector. There was merit too in shepherding the employers along the path leading to the

---

[69] Joe de Bruyn interview, March 2013.

[70] Previously known as the Retail Traders' Association of Australia prior to 1991, and the Retail Council of Australia to 1998, until thereafter adopting the name Australian Retailers Association.

[71] Joe de Bruyn interview, March 2013.

[72] The clerical industry was a dying sector of unionism. Moreover, the union was besieged with political challenges and contests. In the middle and latter part of the 1980s, the FCU Victorian leadership fell to the left, led by Lindsay Tanner. The SDA, in retrospect, was glad not to be tied to their boat. For an account of the internecine warfare within the FCU, told from the side of the new leadership, see Tanner, Lindsay (1996) *The Last Battle*, Kokkinos Press, Carlton.

joint formation with the unions of the industry funds. Kelty understood that the viability of the industry fund model required buy-in from the employers. With the appointment of competent, independently-minded management, the REST scheme developed a reputation as one of the most effective in the country.[73]

The development of many of the industry funds was off to a promising start. But their continuing existence remained perilous. Much more was needed to ensure they were entrenched. And more was required to be done to guarantee that improved superannuation entitlements, superannuation rights generally, were entrenched. The next Chapter addresses how that was done with the Superannuation Guarantee legislation and associated reform.

---

[73] Cf. [anonymous] (1994) "REST Assured – It's Bigger and Busier", *Superfunds*, No. 173, August, pp. 14-16 – an article that highlights management's relentless focus on fee reduction from service providers.

5. LEGISLATING FOR PERMANENCY

There were three main phases of the Australian labour movement's consideration of legislative provisions for superannuation. First was the Hancock Review under the Whitlam government in the 1970s. Second was providing support for the fledgling industry funds in the mid-1980s, and related reforms in superannuation legislation to extend rights and obligations and benefits to all. Third was to give legislative effect to support minimum standards, not only with award superannuation, but to all employees in the early 1990s. Having largely discussed the second phase in previous Chapters, this Chapter examines the first and third phases.

In the early 1970s, when Gough Whitlam was Leader of the Opposition, his chief of staff, Race Mathews, was attracted to the writings of UK Labour politician Richard Crossman, including his advocacy of a national system of superannuation.[1] Whitlam wanted his staff and the party to draw on overseas experience as potentially relevant to Australia. Mathews recalls that "… we looked at what was going on in England and we thought, 'oh, that sounds good. Let's consider that'."[2] Inauspicious though this comment now seems, more particularly considering what was to eventuate in Australian superannuation developments in the decades that followed, this was the formation of the thinking that led to the Whitlam government's commissioning of the Hancock Inquiry into retirement savings in Australia. Crossman had in turn been influenced by the social theorist and public-policy academic Richard Titmuss. When asked "where

---

[1] Cf. Crossman, R.H.S. (1972) "The Politics of Pensions", *The Eleanor Rathbone Memorial Lecture,* Liverpool.

[2] Race Mathews interview, June 2012.

147

did the policy originally come from to look at retirement incomes?",
Mathews responded: "To be honest, the Opposition Leader's –
Whitlam's – staff came up with it. Not because we were brilliant. The
party was comatose. It couldn't come up with any ideas. So we had
to."[3] Without anything in the party platform and little evidence of any
deep thinking within the labour movement on the area of retirement
policy, Mathews explained "when we wanted to come up with policy,
we thought 'if we can't figure it out, we would investigate what are
they doing overseas'."[4] They looked at developments in the United
States and the United Kingdom, and settled on an idea of conducting, in
government, a wide-ranging inquiry on retirement and social-security
policy. What they did not know was what form superannuation would
take.

Noel Whitehead[5] notes that "[a] scheme developed by Professor
Richard Titmuss (London School of Economics) advocated the
introduction of inflation-proofed, universal, state-run, earnings-related
pensions based on funded principles. This was first adopted as official
[UK] Labour Party policy in 1957."[6] The pension system prepared by
Titmuss proposed a new form of "national superannuation", linked to
earnings and accumulated contributions, rather than on the payment at
a single flat rate.[7] This idea struggled to win support in political and
bureaucratic circles: "The only support for a comprehensive, universal,
state-run scheme of earnings-related superannuation along the lines
proposed by Titmuss was found in the Ministry of Social Security.
Here, the division of social security and the investment of a national

---

[3] *Ibid.*

[4] *Ibid.*

[5] Not to be confused with Donald Whitehead.

[6] Whitehead, Noel (2002), "Constructing the Public-Private Divide. Historical
Perspectives and the Politics of Pension Reform", Working Paper No. WP102,
Oxford Institute of Ageing Working Papers, August, www.ageing.ox.ac.uk/
files/workingpaper_102.pdf, p. 9.

[7] Burchell, Andrew (2012), "Crossman and Social Security", Warwick
University, August, http://www2.warwick.ac.uk/services/library/mrc/
explorefurther/digital/crossman/urss/socialsecurity.

superannuation fund in equities found its fullest endorsement."[8] It was not enough. There were strong countervailing pressures, such that there was the "re-conceptualisation of pension solidarity from the workplace to some abstract notion of shared (financial) citizenship."[9] Clark posits that at least some employers saw a national superannuation scheme as a rational process to de-risk defined-benefit scheme obligations by limiting, eliminating, or phasing out, such schemes. Clark summarises that as free market capitalism in the 1980s onwards progressed and defined-benefit schemes were phased out, "… workplace pensions became increasingly remote from the circumstances of companies and industries."[10] This was to become clearer as the 1980s progressed and pension-fund liabilities became an increasingly potent issue. This is why there was strong merit in evaluating the options, risks, and opportunities in recasting public policy in this field.

In 1973, the Whitlam government had established the National Superannuation Committee of Inquiry, chaired by labour-market economist and academic Professor Keith Hancock. His report was handed down in 1976, after Malcolm Fraser (Prime Minister, December 1975 to March 1983) took government. The Hancock Review came up with majority and minority positions. The majority report recommended superannuation as a government scheme paid from taxation, invested by government and organised along the lines of the public service funds as they then existed. They envisaged that this would be implemented through a universal, partially contributory pension system with an earnings-related supplement. A minority recommendation suggested a non-contributory, flat-rate universal pension, a means-tested supplement, and encouragement of voluntary savings through expanding occupational superannuation.

The minority report proposed improvements and extensions in the existing system of superannuation through a multiplicity of providers,

---

[8] Whitehead, Noel (2002), *Loc. Cit.*, p. 15.
[9] Clark, Gordon L. (2012) "From Corporatism to Public Utilities: Workplace Pensions in the 21st Century", *Geographical Research*, Vol. 50, No. 1, February, p. 32.
[10] *Ibid.*, p. 34.

but with new rules to universalise coverage and entitlements. Because of the divergence of views, the Fraser government initially prevaricated, but ultimately rejected the majority recommendations and ignored the minority, taking no steps to implement specific proposals. Other than referring some matters raised in the Reports to inter-departmental committees, that was it. For a long time, however, some of the union leaders continued to hope that the Hancock national superannuation reforms would be implemented. Greg Sword recalls, "Hancock was a speaker at some of those conferences I went to because he was talking about his report. In the early years, we did not give up hope that there would be a chance... for a national scheme, so most of the agreements we – in fact, all of the earlier agreements that we negotiated with the employers – all said: in the event of there being a national scheme, then this money will go into the national scheme."[11]

The second phase of considering legislative change came through the development of award-based superannuation in the 1980s and then, in 1992, legislative enactment for compulsory superannuation. Kelty claims that in the 1980s the unions were determined to think strategically and on a national scale. "We made up our mind to get national superannuation. We had to do it in steps. The 3 per cent [campaign in 1984-85] was always just a step."[12] The first 3 per cent was secured in strategic industries, the building and construction industry, transport, oil, and the metal industry. Now that industry funds were established industrially, the challenge was how to set them up on a secure basis. Kelty comments, "whatever I say about Garry [Weaven], he was wonderful in terms of establishing the industry funds. The funds then become vibrant and alive themselves. The funds exist, the fibre is alive, the money is growing, we are getting a reasonable rate of return, doing a steady job, organisations and the people involved are getting credibility, they are working with employers. They started from being strongly opposed to them, compelled to be in them, to

[11] Greg Sword interview, June 2012.
[12] Bill Kelty interview, March 2013.

strong supporters of them."[13] The interactions in getting there were far from sweetness and light. Some employers saw superannuation as just another cost impost. Bert Evans remembers, "I kept saying to Kelty, 'it's the greatest load of bullshit I have ever heard. You said, 'this was 3 per cent productivity.' I said if it was productivity it would have been distributed 10 times over. It was a load of crap. 'You were saying that there was 3 per cent. It is just bullshit. You and Keating have conned everybody!' And I still tell them that."[14] Evans came to be a great supporter of industry super, but he thought the impetus for the idea rested on a myth, and that such comments regarding the trade-off should be weighed against the facts – including the decline in real wages, even with increases in superannuation – at that time.[15] This is clearly a vital point. Were the unions playing games or was there really a wages-superannuation trade-off? This question is answered next.

The Wage-Superannuation Trade-Off

One of the features of the Accord experience was that real unit labour cost continued to decline while the Superannuation Guarantee was phased in. Keating notes that the prediction that the SGC legislation might prove prohibitively expensive to employers was not borne out by the evidence. He notes:

> It is worth reminding people that in every year the Superannuation Guarantee Charge (SGC) grew by a further one percentage point of employer contributions towards the 9 per cent target, unit labour costs fell markedly. This meant that the cost of superannuation was never borne by employers. It was absorbed into the overall wage cost. Indeed, in each year of the SGC growth between 1992 and 2002, the profit share in the economy rose. The growth in trend productivity over the period was so large it paid for generous wage settlements, including superannuation, while accommodating a higher and higher

---

[13] *Ibid.* Kelty saw Barry Watchorn as one of the first employer catalysts to propose that the employers join with the unions in creating joint, well-run schemes.

[14] Bert Evans interview, May 2013.

[15] Email exchange, Bill Kelty to Mary Easson, 28 November 2013.

share of national income going to profits. And those wages and profits were paid consistent with an inflation rate of 2.5 per cent, on average, across the period.[16]

In other words, had employers not paid nine percentage points of wages as superannuation contributions to employee superannuation accounts, they would have paid it in cash as wages. Otherwise, the profit share in GDP would have risen to unprecedented levels and would have shot beyond reasonable bounds.

Figure 28: Real Unit Labour Cost & the Superannuation Guarante

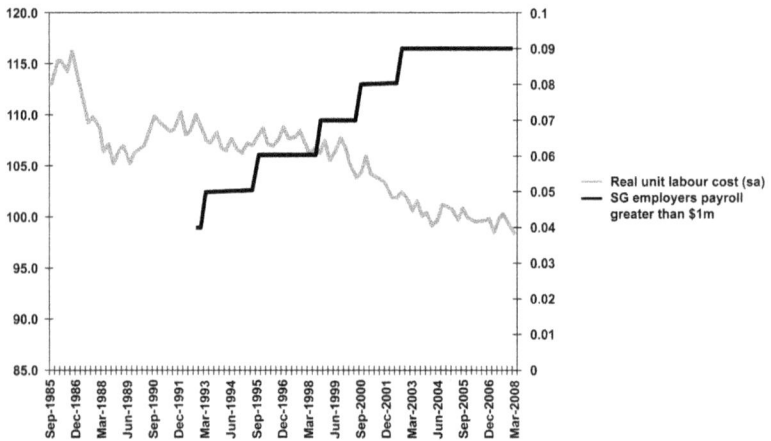

Source: Don Russell, 2008; ABS 5206.0 Australian National Accounts, Table 38. Unit Labour Costs, March 2008; Drew & Stanford (2003b)

In support of this contention that a direct swap of real labour cost for superannuation savings occurred, a former head of Keating's office, the economist and former Treasury official Dr Don Russell, developed charts on superannuation, wages, and real unit labour costs, which are shown above and below. The material, which the Charts highlight, make the point that at the time "employees pa[id] the SG,

---

[16] Keating, Paul (2007b) "The Story of Modern Superannuation", speech delivered to the Australian Pensions and Investment Summit, 31 October, http://www.keating.org.au/shop/item/the-story-of-modern-superannuation-31-october-2007, accessed 1 September 2016.

not employers."[17] Figure 28, above, shows that real unit labour cost continued to decline while the SG was phased in. The decline in real unit labour costs 1998 to 2003 was particularly pronounced; at the same time the SG rose from 6 per cent to 9 per cent. Here the contention is that, in effect, a drop in real wages for workers occurred and at that the overall impact of that was diminished or partly offset by superannuation contributions. The profit share was on the rise well before the surge in the terms of trade, as the following charts show. Figure 29, below, clearly shows the correlation.

Figure 29: Profit Share and the SG

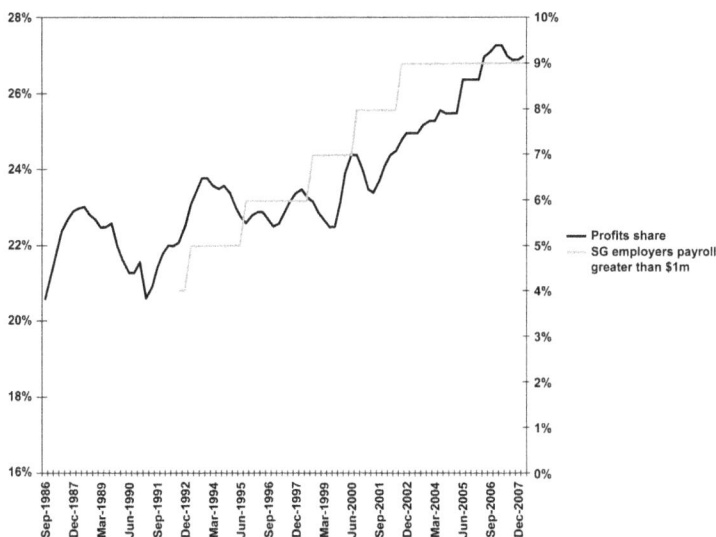

Source: Don Russell, 2008; ABS 5206.0 Australian National Accounts, Table 20, Selected Analytical Series March 08; Drew & Stanford (2003b).

The wage share of total compensation adjusts quite quickly to offset the initial impact of a higher social share:

- CORRELATION (change in wage share; change in social share lagged 1 quarter)   -0.6271

---

[17] Email exchange, Don Russell to Mary Easson, 2 December 2013. I am grateful to Dr Russell for providing these charts and allowing me to reproduce them here.

- CORRELATION (change in wage share; change in social share lagged 2 quarters) -0.5434

- CORRELATION (change in wage share, change in social share lagged 3 quarters) -0.3096

- CORRELATION (change in wage share, change in social share lagged 4 quarters) -0.2248[18]

What seems incontrovertible at this time is that "the trade-off of decline in real wages and increase in superannuation – [was] unprecedented and verified,"[19] as Figure 30 also highlights.

Figure 30: Social Contribution Share of Total Compensation

Source: Don Russell, 2008; ABS 5206.0 Australian National Accounts, Table 7, Income from GDP, current prices March 08.

It is contended in this book that an ALP/union-negotiated deal (the

---

[18] Estimates provided by Dr Don Russell.
[19] Email exchange, Bill Kelty to Mary Easson, 28 November 2013. Mr Kelty suggested that I contact Dr Russell for the above-mentioned information.

Accord and all that went with it) resulted in superannuation coverage across the board. It might seem odd to say that this was a triumph for the labour movement as the victory was associated with a drop in workers' *real* wages and that the drop was only *partly* compensated or offset by concomitant occupational superannuation arrangements; with company profit share on the rise. The argument here, however, is that this was the labour movement's singular commitment to getting the Australian economy on track, growing GDP and employment, and encouraging the repair of the damage done in the decade before Hawke's election as prime minister in 1983. A reason the founders of the modern Australian superannuation system are aghast at the efforts to weaken the industry funds is because they know that the system was built on the sacrifices and trade-offs so convincingly outlined by Russell.

The Superannuation Guarantee

For the unions, the challenge was how to convert the creation of a series of small savings funds into to a proper retirement system. With the early 3 per cent schemes, "… that is all it is – a small retirement fund – and it is aided and abetted by some better industrial schemes, but it is very vulnerable because if someone comes to the government and says, 'You can have your $3,000 back', people will take the money. You have got to then go to the next step. We know… we are always going to get there to 9 per cent, so every one of these things is a step."[20] A critical negotiation was the Accord Mark II to raise contributions from 3 per cent to 6 per cent. Hawke and Keating agreed with the ACTU, but the Commission rejected the proposition.

At the time, a well-sourced article stated:

Mr Keating pioneered the Accord-based approach to the introduction of privately funded national superannuation and sees it as the key to giving all workers income security in retirement and to lifting national savings. But the Federal government's strategy for using the Accord to spread superannuation to cover all workers – a 3 per cent award-based

---

[20] Bill Kelty interview, March 2013.

payment was part of the September 1985 Accord and a second phased 3 per cent was agreed last year – has fallen far short of its objectives.

Although the first 3 per cent is now included in 85 per cent of awards, it is estimated that only slightly more than half the workforce has superannuation cover.

This is because a significant part of the workforce is not covered by awards and because many employers have not complied with awards on superannuation ... The Commission's refusal to endorse the 3 per cent second phase of award-based superannuation is a major blow to what the government regards as arguably its most important single social and economic reform.[21]

Kelty recalls:

I had sensed it in advance, and sat down at the India House restaurant [in Melbourne] – Don Russell, Paul Keating, Iain Ross, and me. Paul said, 'what do you think the Commission is going to do?' And I said, 'the Commission will reject it, so we will defer, I think, superannuation. And they will reject the movement of enterprise bargaining, and they will give us some wage increase to keep us happy.' I said, 'that's what they'll do.' And he said, 'why would they do that?' I said, 'for a range of reasons but that's what I think they'll do.' So he said, 'what are we going to do?' I said, 'we will then legislate for super and we will increase it from 6 per cent to 9 per cent, but we will establish our legislative super framework when we have got this tiny window of opportunity.' Keating says, 'no, we won't legislate for 6 per cent. We will legislate for 9 per cent over a period of time'.[22]

And he changes it from 6 per cent to 9 per cent, and he says to Don Russell [his private secretary], 'that's right. That's what we are going to do.' Don Russell says, 'there's no reason we can't legislate,' and Iain Ross [says], 'there is nothing you can't legislate'; he [says], 'we'll put it under the corporations' power and not industrial relation's power.'[23]

Keating says to Don Russell, 'your job is to get it,' and to Iain Ross

---

[21] Kitney, Geoff (1991) "Government May Legislate to Implement Super", *The Australian Financial Review*, 26 April, p. 1. This article was both copied and underlined for me and this quote read into the transcript of my interview with Mr Keating. Paul Keating interview, March 2013.

[22] Bill Kelty interview, March 2013.

[23] *Ibid.*

'your job is to get it' – 'we are going to legislate super if they reject it. If they don't reject, then superannuation will go from 3 per cent to 4 per cent.' Now what did they do? They rejected it. They deferred the super and said we were immature in handling the industrial-relations system. We said, 'history is short, mate. We won't ever get this again. We are going to legislate for super or we are going to change the wages system right now.' So we accelerated the changes in the industrial system. We accelerated the legislation. Now, Iain Ross did all the hard work. Ross, from the time he came into the ACTU, was... the intellectual catalyst and he was working with us. He would say [that] the High Court would reverse their view. And they did. 'The High Court will reverse their view and allow superannuation to be legislated. They will'. He was the one who worked that out.[24]

The Government, however, was facing difficult economic times, complicated by growing tensions concerning the leadership.[25]

Kelty recalls that to his surprise, "Bob [Hawke] said 'I am not sure of any commitment about the 6 per cent'."[26] This was an explosive position to canvass, potentially testing the Accord. "Paul was on the backbench. I said, 'Paul, we've got a few problems here. They want to walk away from the 6 per cent. He said, 'there's no problem. I'll help you out.' So, he made a speech about superannuation going to 12 per cent.[27] He's out there putting public pressure, raising the ante all the time."[28] Keating recalls, "I go to [the] Graduate School of Management and I say, 'it has got to be 12 per cent because we can't get to a 70 per cent replacement rate in retirement off 6 per cent.' The Treasury resisted. Hawke was going to knock it over with [Treasurer

---

[24] *Ibid.*

[25] Keating challenged Hawke in June 1991, resigned as Treasurer, and then beat Hawke in a second ballot of the ALP Parliamentary Caucus in December 1991.

[26] Bill Kelty interview, March 2013.

[27] Keating, Paul (1991) "A Retirement Incomes Policy", address to the Australian Graduate School of Management, July 25, typescript, 17pp..

[28] Bill Kelty interview, March 2013. Cf. Oakes, Laurie (1991) "The Super Champ" 6 August column in *The Bulletin*, reproduced in Oakes, Laurie (2011) *Power Plays: The Real Stories of Australian Politics* [a collection of published articles], updated edition, Hachette, Sydney.

John] Kerin, and the compromise, under pressure from me and Bill [Kelty], was 9 per cent. That was where the 9 per cent came from. Otherwise it would have been 12 per cent."[29] This was aimed at cementing the alliance with Kelty,[30] who recalls, "Bob sees me, yells at me, he [says], 'I've knocked him off' [a reference to Keating's first leadership challenge in June 1991 where Hawke prevailed 66-44 in the ALP parliamentary caucus. Keating was eventually prevail, 56-51, on 19 December 1991]. I said, 'Bob, you made a commitment to us. You've delivered all you ever said. We are getting the damn 6 per cent, we are getting the 9 per cent now and we are not going backwards. I don't care whether you are the leader or not. If it means I walk away from you, it means that we are out there doing you over, then so be it.' So Bob wasn't happy. He said, 'all right. No, mate, it's no problem'. He was good like that."[31]

Weaven acknowledges "then the really big next step ... was getting that legislation to insert a scale from 3 per cent to 9 per cent over 10 years. That, because the 3 per cent on its own, in legislation, was basically going to get most people in Australia, who were already in agreements, ultimately ... covered by awards – state and Federal. A bit of a lag with some of the States, but ultimately [everyone] would have been covered. That was a big, big chunk of the workforce, but we would never have got to 9 per cent [without legislation]."[32]

At the May 1991 ACTU Executive meeting, a decision was taken:

That the Executive establish a small negotiation sub-committee to examine the option of legislating to provide for all employees to have a minimum superannuation entitlement equivalent to 6 per cent of ordinary time earnings. The sub-committee would enter into

[29] Paul Keating interview, March 2013. Bramston, Troy (2016) *Paul Keating. The Big-Picture Leader*, Scribe Publications, Brunswick [Australia], p. 381.

[30] Edwards, John (1996) *Keating. The Inside Story*, Viking, Ringwood [Victoria, Australia], p. 440.

[31] Bill Kelty interview, March 2013. This account corresponds with Keating's interpretation of events. See O'Brien, Kerry (2015) *Keating*, Allen & Unwin, Crows Nest, NSW, p. 429..

[32] Garry Weaven interview, March 2013.

preliminary discussions with the Treasurer and Minister for Industrial Relations. The negotiation sub-committee to comprise: Iain Ross (ACTU), Mike McKay (ACTU), Greg Sword (NUW), Jim Maher (SDA), Brian Daley (FMWU) and Anna Booth (CATU).[33]

This was a good mix of expertise and experience. Ross, the ACTU Legal Officer, labour law expert and strategist; McKay, ACTU Industrial Officer, who was increasingly involved in CBUS and other funds; Sword, who had founded

Figure 31: Then former Treasurer Paul Keating makes an appearance on the *Midday Show* hosted by Ray Martin, at the Channel Nine studios, 17 July 1991, *Sydney Morning Herald* photo by Robert Pearce. Source: Fairfax Archives.

LUCRF, was national secretary of the National Union of Workers; Maher, immensely respected on the Right of the labour movement, who had come around to supporting the big retail scheme, REST;

---

[33] ACTU records, www.actu.org.au/Images/Dynamic/oldsite/public/papers/1991may/1991may.rtf, accessed March 2014.

Daley, the actuary working at AMP turned union official who was a walking encyclopaedia on superannuation; and Booth, national secretary of the Clothing and Textile Union, on the Board of the Australian Retirement Fund superannuation scheme, who was then considered a potential ACTU President.

This committee negotiated the format of the SGC legislation. The Superannuation Guarantee was announced by the then Treasurer, John Kerin, as part of the 1991-92 Budget speech. He noted that:

> Over the past eight years, major progress has been made in extending the superannuation system in Australia. In 1986, 3 per cent superannuation was awarded by the then Conciliation and Arbitration Commission as part of a productivity and wage package. This award requirement has not been complied with in full.

> The Government will therefore introduce a superannuation guarantee levy, starting from July next year [1992] ...

> This new superannuation guarantee levy will underpin the Government's retirement incomes policy. Superannuation will be extended to many Australians for the first time. In addition, an efficient mechanism for the orderly increase in the level of superannuation support over time will be put in place.[34]

Hawke was replaced by Keating as prime minister at the end of 1991. The Superannuation Guarantee legislation was introduced by the new Treasurer, John Dawkins, into the Parliament in April 1992.[35] After considerable debate, the Bills passed both houses and were given Royal Assent in August 1992.[36] Before the Bill was passed there was some doubt it would get through. The Australian Democrats

---

[34] John Kerin (1991) Treasurer, "Second Reading Speech: Appropriation Bill (No. 1) 1991-92", House of Representatives, *Debates*, 20 August 1991, p. 13.

[35] Australia, House of Representatives, *Votes and proceedings*, no. 120, 2 April 1992, p. 1424, http://parlinfo.aph.gov.au/parlInfo/search/display/display.w3p;query=Id per cent3A per cent22chamber per cent2Fvotes per cent2F1992-04-02 per cent2F0028 per cent22, accessed 28 May 2013.

[36] Australia, Senate *Journals*, no. 183, 8 September 1992, pp. 1364-5, http://parlinfo.aph.gov.au/parlInfo/search/display/display.w3p;query=Id per cent3A per cent22chamber per cent2Fvotes per cent2F1992-08-18 per cent2F0013 per cent22, accessed 28 May 2013.

were uncertain, with elements of the party calling for national superannuation along the lines proposed in the Hancock Review. Former Senator Cheryl Kernot comments that in the end, "the staged thing was fine. The ACCI [Australian Chamber of Commerce and Industry[37]] convinced me at one level – it was Ian Spicer,[38] CEO then, not to go further."[39] But the ACTU's lobbying, particularly by Iain Ross, was effective.[40] In Keating's summary, "in 1991 the commission rejected the government's support for the second 3 per cent. In August 1991 then as a back-bencher, I do the Graduate School of Management speech. The speech forms the basis of the SGC, which I introduce as Prime Minister in ... 1992. And then the Superannuation Guarantee regime ensures virtually all workers would be subject to the scheme. Employer contributions would rise from 4 per cent of ordinary-time wages in 1992-93 to 9 per cent by 2002-03."[41] Between 1992 and 2002 the Superannuation Guarantee charge rate increased incrementally according to the timetable established in 1992, from 3 per cent in July 1992 to 9 per cent in July 2002.

Crucial to the legislation succeeding was Kernot, the then spokesperson on superannuation matters for the Australian Democrats, who later reminisced: "I knew nothing about the technicalities of superannuation. It was mind-boggling for the first few months but, you know what it's like on committees, bigger themes emerge. It's an immersion course."[42] Kelty says, "we've got another trade-off.

---

[37] Founded in 1992, the Chamber is the largest peak council of Australian business organisations and effectively replaced the Confederation of Australian Industry.

[38] Spicer was then the ACCI CEO. See the "Biographies" section at the end of this book for details.

[39] Cheryl Kernot interview, February 2013; supplemented by email correspondence, Cheryl Kernot to Mary Easson, 30 October 2013.

[40] *Ibid.*

[41] Paul Keating interview, March 2013.

[42] Cheryl Kernot interview, February 2013. On Kernot's contribution to the eventual passing of the legislation, see: Megalogenis, George (2012) *The Australian Moment. How We Were Made for These Times*, Viking, Camberwell, Victoria, p. 243.

Figure 32: Cheryl Kernot announces her resignation from the Democrats at a press conference with Gareth Evans and Kim Beazley at Parliament House, Canberra, 15 January 1997, photographer Andrew Campbell. Source: Fairfax Archives.

We've got another system. We've got the 9 per cent legislated. The Democrats were fantastic. Cheryl Kernot was actually fantastic.[43] Iain Ross was superb."[44] Kernot reflected, "the other thing that influenced my thinking was an innate ... I suppose, just my own experience with Australians. When I would talk to them about 'would you compulsorily save this over a lifetime or would you prefer to be made to save it?', 99 per cent would say, 'make me save it! Make me save it! I won't do it otherwise.' And I think we're like that about a lot of things."[45] In the lead up to the 1993 Federal election, Kernot's support – and that of her party – was firm: "While Labor supports the SGC, the Coalition is proposing to freeze the minimum contributions level at the current 3 or 5 percent. This ideological obsession with 'voluntarism' was rejected by the Democrats ..."[46]

---

[43] Her profile positioned her to take over the leadership of the Democrats, which she did in 1993. Dowling, Joseph (1992) "Super Makes Kernot a Rising Star", *Superfunds*, No. 152, September, pp. 34-5.

[44] Bill Kelty interview, March 2013.

[45] Cheryl Kernot interview, February 2013. See: Dowling, Joseph (1992) "Super Makes Kernot a Rising Star", *Loc. Cit.*

[46] Kernot, Cheryl (1993) Senator Cheryl Kernot, Australian Democrat Treasury Spokesperson, contribution to "Super Policies", *Superfunds*, No. 157, March, p. 6.

On the minds of all the participants debating superannuation reform in 1991-92 was the agenda staked out by Keating in his speech to the AGSM, in setting out the strategy for future reform. In that speech Keating stated, "today I wish to propose a creation of a comprehensive National Retirement Income Scheme. Such a scheme should be based on the age pension and be augmented by a privately funded and employment related national super fuelled by a fully mature level of contributions."[47] He explained, "such a scheme would maintain the Age and Service Pensions as the foundation of equity and adequacy in retirement income arrangements, but be complemented by the income of private superannuation with the dual systems integrated through to tax and social security systems.[48]

Keating continued, "for an adequate and mature level of contribution to be established I suggest that by the year 2000 that we reach a national benchmark where each and every employee has a contribution to superannuation equal to 12 per cent of wage and salary income paid into his or her superannuation account."[49] The proposal was "to fill out the half of the second 6 per cent with tax cuts paid by the commonwealth on behalf of the employees of the superannuation fund."[50] And he speculated that the move to 15 per cent would be the next set of reforms.

The funds did not grow to 15 per cent, still less creep up to 12 per cent. What was legislated for in 1992 was implemented over a decade – a phasing of superannuation through the Superannuation Guarantee (SG) to 9 per cent by 2002. There matters rested until a decade later, when another Labor government proposed a further phased increase of contributions to 12 per cent by 2020. Only the first two increments, 9.25 per cent in 2013/14 then 9.5 per cent in 2014/15, were implemented, when the Abbott government decided on a pause and a

---

[47] Keating, Paul (1991) "A Retirement Incomes Policy", address to the Australian Graduate School of Management, July 25, typescript, p. 7.

[48] *Ibid.*, p. 8.

[49] *Ibid.*

[50] Paul Keating interview, March 2013.

Figure 33: Iain Ross, undated, circa early 2000s, photographer Erin Jonasson, Fairfax Archives

new timetable for a delayed phase-in.[51] Kernot now regretfully muses, "… I know why it didn't get to 15 per cent. It was because I didn't let them, sadly."[52] While Accord Mark VIII was an agreement to go there, it was never implemented. Partly this was because the political judgement was made that it might be too big a leap, and partly because Keating thought that the electorate should make a decision between him and the Opposition on the issue. In Kelty's recollection, "we sat there and Paul says, 'I don't know whether we should legislate.' I said, 'you are going to lose, mate. Why don't you legislate?' He said, 'no, no. People have got to know what the loss has done.' So he doesn't legislate to the 15 per cent. He goes to the election campaign. We lose. The [Liberals] immediately walked away."[53]

Before the March 1996 Federal elections, the Opposition

---

[51] See towards the end of Appendix 4.
[52] Cheryl Kernot interview, February 2013.
[53] Bill Kelty, interview March 2013.

promised to let the superannuation phase-in to 9 per cent stand. It was an important concession. For a moment, there was bi-partisan consensus. In the twenty years since, superannuation has changed utterly. The industry has grown exponentially. The retail funds and, especially, the SMSF sector are considerable competition for the industry fund segment of the market. No one completely dominates. It might seem with the experience of over thirty years of the big industry funds, their leading role in debates on alignment, performance, and fees, their credibility in the market, the depth and strength of their relationships, place them in an extremely strong position, far removed from the parlous shape they were in at first dawn. Such a recapitulation, however, would be to under-estimate the political environment.[54] There are troubles ahead – as are described in the next Chapter.

---

[54] For completeness, the uniformly favourable comments in this Chapter about the credibility of the industry funds might be tempered given some of the scrutiny in the Justice Dyson Heydon AC QC Royal Commission on Trade Union Governance and Corruption (which reported on 28 December 2015) of alleged improper dealings with certain unions. This raises a subject too complicated for constructive commentary here, subject to this observation: There was no systematic failure of the industry fund model. There was a relatively small number of misdemeanours identified. The culpable individuals concerned were disowned by the particular funds. See also the commentary on governance in the next Chapter.

6. THE TROUBLES AHEAD

Consider this scene: a holiday in the Hawaiian Islands, an airport, you get off the plane to walk to the terminal, collect your bags, and ready to go to your hotel. Suddenly a sprightly, bright smiling lady in her mid-70s greets you and ushers you into the van to take you to your destination. She is employed by the resort company and works 5 – sometimes 6 – days a week. Maybe she hates to be bored at home and needs to be "doing something". Retirement, with nothing to do, is death. She has a winning charm and she dotes on the kids. But after a quick chat she explains "I could not possibly afford to retire." She needs to earn an income. And you think of a grandmother, an aunt, someone you know back home in Australia and you realise we have it very lucky. In Australia, retirees are not left destitute. The pension is around 25 per cent of average award earnings; people are covered by superannuation. Average balances achieved in 2013-14 for all persons 15 years of age and over were $98,535 for men and $54,916 for women. These averages are well up (by around 20 per cent) on the balances of $82,615 for men and $44,866 for women in 2011-2012.[1] These are not fortunes, but they might appear so by that lady I met in Hawaii.

This book tells part of the story of why we live the way we do in Australia, where the safety net, a helping hand, and the three pillars of retirement policy – public pension, savings garnisheed by employers,[2] and voluntary contributions – underpin the dignity and

---

[1] Clare, Ross (2015) *Superannuation Account Balances*, ASFA, Sydney, December, p. 3. These figures highlight the gap in men's and women's superannuation.

[2] Actually, as noted earlier, it is not *from* employers – superannuation was principally in lieu of immediate wage increases.

lifestyle of an Australian in old age. As outlined in earlier Chapters, a great deal of credit for this must go to the labour movement, political and industrial, the ALP governments of 1983 to 1996 and the ACTU, and in particular Bob Hawke, Paul Keating, Bill Kelty, Garry Weaven, and Iain Ross. Appendix 4 provides an overview of the array of changes in superannuation over 40 years. Australians can be proud of our achievements. We tend to knock ourselves for what goes wrong more than recognising the fundamental, breath-taking accomplishment of the modern system of Australian superannuation.

No one, however, should ever be merely satisfied. All good things can be improved.[3] So what are the criticisms of the system that emerged and is described in this book? This Chapter examines potential changes ahead, including threats to what has been created. Discussed herein, in the context of looking to improve a healthy system, rather than throwing the bathroom out with the bath water, are some critiques, including the Financial System Inquiry,[4] the Henry Tax Review,[5] the Grattan Institute critique of excessive charges by rent seekers, and the current policies of the Liberal-National Coalition.

As an aside, it might be thought that given the regularity of change, governments over 40 years have behaved as if permanently dissatisfied, constantly itching for "reforms" to retirement savings policies and practice. In the second Rudd ALP government in 2013, there was a promise that there would be a moratorium on changes to the superannuation system for five years. Many Australians breathed a sigh of relief, hoping for an end to the constant amendment and floating of new regulatory rules – which threaten to undermine confidence in the system. AustralianSuper's Ian Silk noted that the industry itself

---

[3] Some of my thinking is here influenced by Keating, Michael (2015) "The Financial System Inquiry. Part 2: Superannuation and Retirement Incomes", in *Pearls and Irritations*, blog compiled by John Menadue, 20 January.

[4] See Murray, David, Chair, *et. al.* (2014) Report of the Financial System Inquiry, http://fsi.gov.au/publications/final-report, accessed 7 July 2015.

[5] See Henry, Ken, Chair, *et. al.* (2010) Australia's Future Tax System Review, http://taxreview.treasury.gov.au/content/Content.aspx?doc=html/home. htm, accessed 3 February 2015.

frequently advocates alternatives to current regulation.[6] Sometimes it seems that the protagonists believe that only good revision is the one they have thought about and sponsored.

Compared to most developed countries Australia's system ranks well – with a lower level of unfunded promises by government, therefore less risk to future tax payers, and provides better assistance for those on very low incomes and/or who have had broken work histories. Since the introduction of compulsory superannuation in 1992 with the Superannuation Guarantee, the total assets of superannuation funds have increased steadily from $59.6 billion in September 1988 to over $2.0 trillion today – a compound growth of 13.4 per cent. Apart from the family home, superannuation is the most important asset for most people. The industry is a major source of financial strength and stability for Australia. Superannuation funds typically have low levels of debt. Based on an assessment of adequacy, sustainability, and integrity, the 2015 Melbourne Mercer Global pension index rates Australia's superannuation system third out of 25 countries.[7] Denmark and The Netherlands ranked higher, considered Grade A, a "first class and robust income system that delivers good benefits, [that] is sustainable with a high level of integrity". Australia is the only country in the next category, B+, a "system that has a sound structure, with many good features, but has some areas for improvement that differentiates it from an A system."[8]

Despite such positive judgements, a number of studies are critical of the efficiency of the superannuation industry, with administrative costs considered too high. The Financial System Inquiry (FSI) report (2014), also known as the Murray Report, found that although the size of the average fund increased from $260 million in assets in 2004 to $3.3 billion in 2013, average fees only fell by 0.2 per cent over the same period, with two thirds of the estimated benefits from scale

---

[6] See Silk's remarks in the next Chapter.
[7] Mercer (2015) *Melbourne Mercer Global Pension Index*, Australian Centre for Financial Studies, October, p. 7.
[8] *Ibid.*

and lower margins being offset by increases in fund costs. While the FSI acknowledged that reforms to MySuper[9] might result in lower administration costs in future, the evidence suggested that these reforms might not fully succeed. Instead, the FSI recommended more competition so that if costs had not fallen sufficiently by 2020, new default members of superannuation funds should be allocated to MySuper products by a formal competitive process.[10] At the time of writing, as discussed below, this issue is being assessed by the Productivity Commission.

The FSI found that "superannuation assets are not being efficiently converted into retirement incomes due to a lack of risk pooling and an over-reliance on account based pensions". The meaning of that statement needs to be unpacked. The implication is that individuals are exposed to considerable risk from longevity and inflation, potentially causing them to endure a lower standard of living in retirement than necessary. The FSI accordingly, in response to the lack of products to manage longevity risk – that is, the prospect of retirees exhausting savings before they die – recommended introducing a comprehensive income product for retirement (CIPR). The merit here is that by managing the longevity risk through effective pooling in a CIPR this could significantly increase private incomes for many Australians and provide retirees with greater peace of mind that their savings will endure through their retirement, while still allowing them some flexibility to meet unexpected expenses.

The tax concessions in the superannuation system are poorly targeted and inequitable, with most of the value of the concessions accruing to the top twenty per cent of income earners. As a result, the return on investment in superannuation is about four times as

---

[9] MySuper accounts, mandated from 1 July 2013, are meant to offer lower fees and apply restrictions on fees. See the definition in Appendix 9.

[10] In passing, it may be noted that s.194(h)(i) of the *Fair Work Act 2009* provides that a term of an enterprise agreement is an "unlawful term" if it is a term that has the effect of requiring or permitting contributions, for the benefit of an employee who is a default fund employee, to be made into a superannuation fund or scheme that is specified in the agreement but relevantly does not offer a MySuper product.

high for people on the top marginal tax rate as for people on a low to zero tax rate, after taking account of tax concessions and means-testing of the age pension entitlement. It seems that planned, excess superannuation savings of high income people are a way of sheltering future tax-enhanced bequests, which is inconsistent with the objective of providing an adequate income in retirement.

It is a truth universally acknowledged that differences in the taxation of forms of income and savings shape and distort resource allocation. Superannuation tax concessions are so inadequately targeted that they increase the cost of the system to taxpayers and undermine confidence in the system. Given the present and future Budget outlooks, there are concerns about the sustainability of present taxation rules for superannuation, begging the question of what improvements in cost-effectiveness and fairness are needed to compliment another objective – that of generating significant Budget savings.

Without going into those earlier reforms proposed in the May 2016 Budget,[11] on 15 September 2016, Federal Treasurer Scott Morrison announced new measures applying to superannuation which, among other matters, will:

- Replace the earlier proposed $500,000 lifetime non-concessional contributions cap with an annual $100,000 limit, down from the previous $180,000.

- Provide an annual cap on concessional (before tax) superannuation to $25,000 (previously $30,000 for under 50s and $35,000 for over 50s).

- Allow individuals aged under 65 to continue "bringing forward" three years' worth of non-concessional contributions.

- Bar individuals with a super balance exceeding $1.6 million from making any further non-concessional contributions from 1 July 2017.

---

[11] For a summary, see: http://www.superannuation.asn.au/media/media-releases/2016/asfa-statement-2-june-2016, accessed 3 July 2016.

- Delay the commencement date of proposed catch-up concessional super contributions deferred to 1 July 2018.[12]

The measures mean that individuals are able to contribute $125,000 each year and, up to $325,000 in any one year, until such time as they reach $1.6 million.[13]

The rules, constantly reset, are a Bermuda Triangle for the uninformed – and even for many who are well-informed. In September 2016 the *Australian Financial Review's* Jennifer Hewett said that the twists and turns on then recent changes had "massively damaged broader public trust in the system," a breach not easily or quickly fixed. She noted that under changes introduced by Mr Morrison when Social Services Minister, even a part-aged pension cuts out for a single homeowner with assets beyond the family home of more than $547,000 from January 2017, for example – down from around $800,000 previously. For a couple, eligibility for just a part pension falls from assets of $1.175 million to $823,000. She noted that:

> At a non-risky return rate of 3 per cent per annum, that's only around $16,500 for a single homeowner and $25,000 for a couple – much less than the aged pension. Super 'reforms' – whether the government's or Labor's – make those harsh sums even harder to add up for an awful lot of people.[14]

Although the Turnbull government went through political hell attempting superannuation change in its 2016-17 Budget, there is likely to be continued pressure to reduce the rorts and loopholes and to consider options, such as levies and additional earnings taxes on

---

[12] See: http://treasury.gov.au/SuperReforms#reforming, accessed 24 October 2016.

[13] There was controversy about the "retrospective" effect of changes such as the lifetime cap. Prior to the 2016 Federal Budget, the ASFA standard had proposed AUD 2.5 million as an appropriate ceiling on tax-preferred individual savings.

[14] Hewitt, Jennifer (2016) "The Government Comes from Behind on Superannuation", *Australian Financial Review*, 15 September.

superannuation account balances above a certain limit. Potentially, too, there is the idea of implementing the recommendation by the 2010 Henry Review of Australia's Future Tax System to tax superannuation contributions at marginal rates less a flat-rate rebate.

Of all of the options, an important consideration is to limit the complexity of administration, strengthening the equity objective for superannuation, and providing consistency and certainty.

The retirement income system faces increasing challenges as the 21st century unfolds, including the ageing of the population, longer life expectancies (for example, more people living to a hundred years of age), and the fact that many more people will interact with the system. Some are unclear, arising from the diverse range of risks and uncertainties about future economic, social, and environmental circumstances. Those complexities test the sustainability, adequacy, acceptability, and coherence of the system.

In its final 2010 Report, the Henry Review observed: "The key finding of the Panel is that the three-pillar architecture of Australia's retirement income system, consisting of the means-tested Age Pension, compulsory saving through the superannuation guarantee and voluntary saving for retirement, should be retained." The Panel noted that the three-pillar system enjoyed strong community support. All things being equal, this suggests caution and prudence in making any changes.

Henry suggested a range of improvements to – rather than wholesale redesign of – the system such that governments should provide for minimum and essential needs and facilitate self-provision. Such policy options should be pursued in an equitable and targeted way. Individuals should save and/or insure during their working lives to provide resources in their retirement. Inevitably under this approach, retirement outcomes will differ for different people, depending on the extent to which they can and do make self-provision. The tests – and aims – of the system are adequacy, acceptability, robustness, simplicity, and sustainability. In combination they inevitably involve trade-offs.

Key Recommendations of the Henry Tax Review in Relation to the Retirement Income System

Key recommendations were:

1. *The superannuation guarantee rate should remain at [the then level of] 9 per cent.* The Panel considered carefully submissions proposing an increase in the superannuation guarantee rate. Notably the unions and all the industry funds campaigned for this measure. The Panel noted that such an increase could be expected to lift the retirement incomes of most workers.

But, perhaps surprisingly, the Panel considered the rate of compulsory saving to be adequate. The Panel argued that the Age Pension and the 9 per cent superannuation guarantee (when mature) could be expected to provide the opportunity for people on low to average wages with an average working life of 35 years to have a substantial replacement of their income, well above that provided by the Age Pension. The Panel suggested that more could be done through preservation and other rules to ensure that the 9 per cent contribution rate produces an adequate retirement income for greater numbers of people. Though not fully spelt out, this alluded to the potential of tax changes to enhance the savings of future retirees.

If the tax on superannuation earnings was halved to 7.5 per cent, as recommended by the Henry Review, then the retirement income for a median income earner was projected to result in replacement rates of as much as 88 per cent and a replacement rate of 76 per cent for an average income earner. The Henry proposal was to reduce a contributor's disposable income, but retirement incomes would increase as the fund would no longer pay contributions tax, and so the effect would be similar to requiring employees to make an additional contribution to superannuation. As such, this option is an alternative to the proposed phase-in of the contribution rate from the present 9.5 per cent to 12 per cent. But a lot turns on the government of the day agreeing to such tax measures and consistently sticking to them. The better option, in the opinion of this author, is to actually increase the SG contributions rather than to effect tax changes of the type proposed.

What an individual contributes is theirs – and politically harder for government to take away.

2. *The superannuation guarantee broadly should continue to cover employees.* While those who derive business income should make provision for their retirement during their working lives, the diverse and varying risks and circumstances of business and entrepreneurship argue for allowing full flexibility in their saving and investment decisions. The voluntary superannuation system is available to small business people for contributing to meeting their retirement needs. The Panel said that the $450 per month threshold should continue to apply,[15] as the compliance costs to the employer of providing superannuation guarantee contributions to marginally attached workers are outweighed by the benefits to the employee.

3. *Australia's retirement income arrangements should be adjusted to respond to increasing life expectancies.* This was a vexed question and in a nutshell: "Increasing life expectancies mean that: people are spending more time in retirement relative to working life; savings during working life are less able to meet retirement needs; and aggregate budgetary costs of the Age Pension are increasing." Henry proposed that the general age for access to the Age Pension and for access to preserved superannuation benefits should be increased. The Panel recommended that eligibility age for the Age Pension should be increased to 67 years. More radically, the Panel advocated that the general access age for superannuation benefits should also increase to 67 years. This would arguably improve the coherence of the system by strengthening the integration between the Age Pension and superannuation.

4. *Means Test Reform.* The Panel found that: "There is a case for reforms to improve the fairness and coherence of Age Pension means tests through a single means test that removes the assets test and extends the income test by deeming returns on a greater range of assets." This was a Godzilla step too far for the government. The

---

[15] That being a reference to the minimum weekly income a person receives before the SG is deducted. Lower weekly earnings do not attract the SG.

policy point here being that a single means test has the potential to improve the fairness and coherence of the retirement income system, but would be incredibly controversial.

The Panel also found that the broad intention is to find ways to simplify substantially the experience of part-rate pensioners in complying with the two systems, while also striking an appropriate balance between the targeting of pensions and maintaining incentives for work and saving.

5. *Aged Care System Review*. The Panel contended that: "The interaction of the tax-transfer system and the aged care system, particularly the means testing arrangements, needs to be explored further." The quality of life of older Australians is affected significantly by their access to and experience of age-related services, such as aged care and health. As future government spending on these services is projected to increase substantially, the Panel argued for giving consideration to a range of interactions between the tax-transfer system and other systems (such as the funding of housing assistance and health care). This is one of the greatest challenges of the Australian superannuation system and its integration with health and aged care – a subject that is considerably under-explored in the industry and by policy makers.

6. *Superannuation Tax Review*. The Panel noted that "[t]he tax advantages provided for superannuation serve the dual purpose of providing incentives for contributions and delivering more neutral overall tax treatment of deferred consumption relative to current consumption." True, up to a point, that point being that current arrangements do not provide fair or adequate incentives to all.

7. *Retaining Assets for Retirement Purposes*. The Panel warned that "[w]hile superannuation generates assets for retirement, current arrangements do little to ensure that those assets can be used for income purposes throughout the years of retirement. As people live longer, there is a growing risk that individuals will exhaust their assets before they die." There are policy and practical issues at stake here. Among the latter is the problem of the lack of products that retirees

can purchase to insure against longevity risk – a structural weakness in the system. Better retirement income products should be available for purchase so a person can ensure an income higher than the Age Pension throughout their retirement. The Panel noted that "[a] range of complex issues need to be addressed to deliver this outcome, including the scope for public and private provision, regulation and incentives to address market failures, and interactions with means tests and the tax system." This is relevant to the earlier discussion on the CIPR.

8. *Awareness*. The Panel noted that education and knowledge are important for making informed decisions. Otherwise, in my words, it is just gambling: "There is evidence that a lack of awareness and engagement affects the coherence of the system and, potentially, its adequacy. Simpler arrangements, such as a single means test, can contribute to this task, but more needs to be done, particularly in building understanding of issues such as longevity risk. Government and the superannuation industry should share in the responsibility of assisting individuals to better understand and engage in the system." Providing access to information so as to allow informed decision-making is another on-going challenge, as earlier noted.[16]

In the light of the above, it seems reasonable that the objectives of each of the three pillars should be:

(a) The means-tested Age Pension should ensure that all Australians receive a safety net level of income throughout their retirement that is adequate to provide a reasonable minimum standard of living.

(b) Compulsory superannuation should ensure that a reasonable minimum share of employee income is saved to contribute additional resources to retirement. Because it is a defined contributions system, rather than defined benefits system, it

---

[16] At the time of writing, ASIC is requiring superannuation and investment products to disclose fees and charges with a deadline date of September 2017 to implement. See: http://asic.gov.au/regulatory-resources/find-a-document/regulatory-guides/rg-97-disclosing-fees-and-costs-in-pdss-and-periodic-statements, accessed 8 December 2016.

is not appropriate or practicable to set a target replacement income rate for the superannuation guarantee. The rate of the superannuation guarantee, however, can be benchmarked by reference to moderate potential replacement rates for retirees with a full history of contribution at median to average earnings.

(c) Voluntary, additional superannuation contributions should provide a tax-assisted means for all to make self-provision for retirement in accordance with their circumstances and preferences. For reasons of both acceptability and sustainability, the extent of tax concessions should be the subject of reasonable caps because superannuation has as its principal purpose reasonable retirement incomes, rather than being a mechanism for socially inequitable tax minimisation for high income earners.

In sum, the Henry Review insisted that with such important reforms, the three-pillar architecture would be strengthened, in continuing to provide a balanced and flexible response to the challenges of a changing dynamic environment that retirement savings policy needs to attend to. Overall the principles underlying such proposed reforms still merit consideration. They would make a very substantial contribution to a less expensive and fairer retirement incomes system.

It is also noteworthy that, for the average male wage earner, the FSI has calculated that its reforms would have the potential to increase his retirement income by around 25 to 40 per cent (excluding the age pension) – no mean achievement, and at less cost after reform of the tax concessions than the present system.

Some industry leaders continue to argue that funds compete vigorously, so the outcome must be close to efficient, with little more than a few loose ends to be tied up. Against such a relaxed perspective is the alternate view that there are too many funds and too many accounts – adding to costs. Barely distinguishable products sell over a broad range of fees. Even identical products attract varying fees – for example, across the 'platforms' used by financial advisers. Is MySuper any better? One concern is that a few years ago APRA did not reject any application of the 127 products currently registered. They were not quality assessed or ranked. Apparently all applications were approved. The bulk of the MySuper market is served by industry funds. For the most part, their fees are lower than elsewhere in the market. But even here, smaller funds are usually materially *more expensive* and even the larger funds are not as lean as they should be. Price-insensitive customers are profitable; and as scale is so important to viability, funds incur excess costs in seeking to win and retain customers. Competition can therefore add to costs.

Average costs have fallen only slowly even as the system has grown, and they remain in excess of what could be feasible. Default fees could and should be arguably below 0.7 per cent per year with no change to service or investment performance, not today's 1 per cent and much higher – with some fees poorly disclosed or hidden. What does this mean for policymakers? The FSI was rightly concerned about efficiency in the sector. Consistency in disclosure is essential for comparisons. But presumably the most important figure is the return to investors over time, given particular risk parameters.

On another topic, a significant threat to the industry funds, is any potential move to cut the link between industrial awards and defaults, as is Coalition policy. But this appears unlikely to be a game-changer for efficiency: It will put pressure on some inefficient industry funds, but it will also potentially result in funds incurring higher selling and marketing costs as well as increasing member and employer engagement costs. The net result could even be an increase, not a decrease, in average fees.

The FSI recommended that the government design and run a tender to select default funds, unless the industry is shown to be much more efficient by 2020. The criterion against which efficiency might be measured was never spelt out comprehensively. The current review by the Productivity Commission of the efficiency in the industry is addressing this challenge. Clearly, inducing small funds to merge with industry-akin larger funds, helping account holders consolidate their super into a single account, and improving transparency and consistency – thereby facilitating the comparability of superannuation products – would help.

Australians are paying far too much for their superannuation. On one summation, "[w]e pay about $20 billion in fees, including the expenses of self-managed funds."[17] Customers of superannuation funds pay an average of $1300 per account-holder every year. On one estimate, those payments to the superannuation industry can and should be reduced by at least half, potentially saving Australians at least $10 billion a year, according to the Grattan Institute's report, *Super Sting*. That report argues that superannuation fee reform is the largest single opportunity for micro-economic reform in the economy.[18]

High fees hurt account holders. Even the average Australian fee of 1.2 per cent reduces the amount of superannuation at retirement more than 15 per cent. On conservative assumptions, a 50-year-old Australian will have his or her superannuation balance reduced by almost $80,000 in fees at retirement. A 30-year old will lose more than $250,000 or about a quarter of his or her total balance. Under a fairer and more transparent fee structure, at least half that money could be saved.

High fees also hurt taxpayers, who pay more for pensions when superannuation runs short. On the evidence, usually high fees cannot even be justified by the promise of higher returns: Many of the Australian funds that charge the highest fees consistently deliver lower returns than others once their fees are taken out. Since 2004, some of the most expensive retail superannuation funds have delivered a negative return after fees and inflation.

Superannuation is inherently opaque, and few people can make — or care to make — a fully informed choice. About 70 per cent of Australians pay automatically into default funds chosen by their

---

[17] Minifie, Jim (2014) "How to Halve our Super Fees", *The Australian*, 28 April.

[18] Minifie, Jim (2014) *Super Sting: How to Stop Australians Paying Too Much for Superannuation*, The Grattan Institute, Melbourne, April, *passim*. This and the next few paragraphs have been influenced by this research.

employer or specified in an award.[19] The result is that funds do not compete primarily on fees. Instead, they are trapped in a costly game of competing on service levels, marketing, and product features. All these push up fees and drive down net returns.

One of the great achievements of the modern Australian superannuation system is that the provision of group insurance in industry and other fund products mean that Australia's superannuation system has produced the most efficient, extensive coverage of life and disability insurance arrangements than anywhere in the world. Workers and their dependents who would be otherwise uncovered are embraced by present arrangements and the bargaining position of the industry is strong to ensure a high payout by the insurers. More can be done to improve the system, especially where there are multiple

---

[19] Worth noting is the practical effect of various Federal industrial agreements. They limited choice. There was just no alternative for employers or employees – i.e., the superannuation payments could lawfully be made only to one of the industry funds specified in the award (that was the situation until about 2005) or enterprise agreement (to date) – for example to HESTA, NGS Super, Catholic Super, CBUS, Australian Super, and the rest. In many enterprise agreements, only one industry superannuation fund (e.g., in the private haulage industry, TWU Superannuation Fund) is actually named – with the result that occupational superannuation contributions can lawfully go only into that particular fund. Dyson Heydon made recommendations about this in his final report into trade unions, and used the example of a particular employee and his lack of choice under a Federal enterprise agreement. But this seemed an odd focus given the remit of his Royal Commission mandate, earlier referenced. In contrast with the Federal arena, the Greiner government's Industrial Relations Act 1991 (NSW) s.180 provided for the right of an employee to nominate in writing any (complying) superannuation fund other than a fund or funds which may have been specified in a relevant State award or enterprise agreement. The Carr government's Industrial Relations Act 1996 (NSW) carried-over that provision as s.124 in relevantly identical terms. At the time, there was absolutely no issue raised by anyone (the Labor Council of NSW – now called Unions NSW – included) suggesting that the Greiner government's s.180 of the 1991 Act should not be carried-over into the Carr government's new legislation. In this sense, freedom of choice for employees concerning their own superannuation was an entirely uncontroversial feature of the NSW system of occupational superannuation. This could be a precedent for any new national arrangements.

accounts and therefore excess coverage for certain individuals. But the associations, across retail to industry funds, are looking to remedy particular deficiencies.[20]

The average Australian superannuation fund today is six times larger than it was in 2004, yet the savings that such growth should deliver have been almost wholly absorbed by rising costs – part of which is due to the cost of new government regulation. Successive government reforms that have sought to expose funds to greater competition have also had little impact on fees (sometimes, perversely, with increased regulation increasing them). The latest round of reforms, Stronger Super, including MySuper, provides for a more uniform set of products for people who do not actively choose their funds. It makes funds somewhat easier to compare, but does little to put downward pressure on fees.

The other main Stronger Super reform, SuperStream,[21] will reduce some costs, but does nothing to address the costs of marketing, sales or excessive active asset management.

Historically, the main reforms have turned on particular perspectives or ideology concerning the world. There is a clear difference between what the associations champion in the retail funds sector versus their equivalents in the industry fund sector. Though one would hope that fundamentally all should have their eye on a single objective – what works best for the member. Industry fund pioneer, Ian Silk, exasperated with petty rivalries, in 2015 called for a compact between the superannuation sector and the parliament, saying:

> We should be looking to build a self-reinforcing compact between the parliament on the one hand that established the system, the industry that's operating that system, and the beneficiaries of the system.

---

[20] See the speech by former TAL Insurance CEO and former ASFA President and Interim CEO, Jim Minto, at the 2016 ASFA conference. Minto, Jim (2016) "ASFA Oration", 9 November 2016.

[21] SuperStream is the name given by the Super System Review to its package of measures designed to enhance the 'back office' of superannuation. See the definition in Appendix 9.

Trust needs to be at the heart of this system, and we should have at the epi-centre of the system the guiding principle of acting in the best interests of members and not diluting a singular focus on that objective.[22]

But rivalries and a 'divide and conquer' approach of the government of the day have not allowed that objective to be achieved.

It is a curious thing, what stakeholders and actors in superannuation are thinking now needs to be done. Given the Melbourne Mercer report ranking the Australian system in the top three in the world, a reasonable hypothesis might be to seek to improve from B+ to a clearly A-grade system.

As noted early in Chapter 2, consumers and participants in a process, system, or in purchasing goods and services, have choices when it comes to an unsatisfactory experience. To appropriate Hirschman's schema, where a service or system, say, meets objectives or is steadily improving, then "loyalty" is a natural disposition. Where, however, this is not the case, the ways of reacting to deterioration in performance and/or, generally, to dissatisfaction is to "exit" – to quit the system and/or to switch to or to create a competing product. Alternatively, if disaffection is not so drastic, to "voice" ideas for change, by agitating and seeking to influence change "from within". Unresponsive reaction to voicing is a precursor to exit. If you are not listened to, then why belong?

Are the rumblings of dissatisfaction with the Australian system likely to lead to super-exit – a move by some leading parties to create a new system?[23] In that respect, it is interesting to contrast today's scenarios with those of the mid-1980s. Back then the unions, after voicing complaints about the efficacy of the existing system, admittedly the bulk of them haphazardly and

---

[22] Silk, Ian (2015) 'ASFA Oration', 25 November, p. 2.
[23] Clearly, I am adapting a contemporary phrase, Brexit (the decision in 2016 by Britain to exit the European Union), to superannuation. Here in the sense of exiting the current Australian superannuation model.

with various degrees of application, then decided to exit and create something new.[24] Today, the union-related industry funds want to retain most features of the existing system, voicing suggestions for improvement. In the mid-1980s they saw fundamental and multifarious flaws, inequities, and injustices: Blue collar workers and women in many enterprises missed out, the system was incapable of self-correction, so radical change was needed. Today, sections of the retail sector see their profitability cut back by recent regulations (MySuper, restrictions on cross-selling, and tight regulations covering the giving of financial advice and conflicts of interest) and envy some of the advantages of the industry funds – with default positions in many awards and enterprise agreements. A few retail representatives are tempted to go for radical change, desiring to exit the current system if they could – by gaming on winning in an auction system.[25] Most, however, are not so bold, preferring greater contestability to full-scale competition or an auction system.[26] One recent study of the sector noted that "[t]he major banks' wealth management activities have not lived up to initial expectations for income growth and cross-selling opportunities, and are generating lower returns than core banking activities".[27] But this is not to say the sector is unprofitable; but the wealth management side of the listed banking sector in Australia drags down the top 4 Australian retail banks' overall return on capital (ROC).

---

[24] With the superannuation system of the 1970s, it might be argued that the unions were in one sense exiting nothing. To the extent that occupational superannuation actually existed, it was then mostly only in small pockets of employment – until matters gained industrial and legislative momentum. The latter created something new, rather than tinkering with an impossibly flawed system.

[25] This point is based on several conversations with the author. I do not, however, claim that in this instant the "exit" view is representative or widespread.

[26] Notably, however, when he was CEO of the Financial Services Council from 2009 to 2015, John Brogden, for example, often wrote and spoke about the contestability of the industry v. retail funds.

[27] Golat, Theodore (2016) "Banks' Wealth Management Activities in Australia", *Bulletin of the Reserve Bank of Australia*, September Quarter, p. 59.

As a solution to current challenges, exit is questioned for certain important situations. As exit often undercuts voice while being unable to counteract decline, loyalty is seen in the function of retarding exit and of permitting voice to play its proper role. The interplay of the three concepts – loyalty, voice, and exit – illuminates a wide range of economic, social, and political phenomena. Exiting from the existing superannuation system, however, is an unlikely response from any future Australian government. But anything is possible – especially with so much pent up opposition within the present Turnbull government to the industry funds, together with the retail funds wishing to be part of the market which is presently, by the operation of the naming of industry funds in modern Federal awards is primarily the domain of the industry funds. One potential threat to the current industry fund model is to change governance arrangements in a way that could corrode the character of representation on boards. This is a matter currently under close examination by the government and the industry associations.[28] At the time of writing the government has commissioned the Productivity Commission (PrC) to review the efficiency of the system. In discussion papers, the PrC has contemplated recommending consideration of the New

---

[28] The government in mid-2015 introduced a Bill proposing that all non-SMSF superannuation boards should have an independent Chair with a third of directors on such boards independent. But the proposed definition of the latter was overly restrictive and led to various Senators holding the balance of power in late 2015 opposing the proposal. The government then withdrew its Bill. In December 2015 Bernie Fraser was commissioned by Industry Super Australia and the Australian Institute of Superannuation Trustees to write up a report on governance, which is intended for sharing with independent Senators. It is possible, even likely, that more independent directors, depending on skills gaps on particular boards, will be appointed in the future by the industry partners. This is surely no bad thing and will strengthen governance. Such minimum representation was recommended by the Cooper and Murray reviews. As at early 2017, this matter is likely to be debated with much turning on politics and the context and content of any proposed reforms, including the question of what "independence" should entail. Weakening the viability and character of the industry funds would be poor policy. But *animus* seems to be part of the Turnbull government's positioning.

Zealand "KiwiSaver"[29] or the Chilean system[30] of auctioning the equivalent of MySuper default schemes. This could mean that 9-20 default schemes are registered by the government, resulting in the Australian Tax Office randomly allocating individuals to one of them.

There are several objections to default proposals. One is whether the existing system is *so* bad that such a drastic measure is merited. Second, a Spanish proverb comes to mind: "If you have to boil the ocean to make a cup of tea, you have made the solution too complicated". And cumbersome would be the "reforms". Third, the significant transition costs are not to be underestimated. Fourth, unintended consequences cannot be ignored – including confusion, increased marketing costs, and divorcing people from identifying with their particular industry. The de-personalising approach, what Clark calls "the process of discounting workers' company and industry identities..."[31] would accelerate at a faster pace. Nothing can be taken for granted. There is much that is unpredictable with current policy settings in Canberra. Relentless threats there are aplenty.

---

[29] KiwiSaver is a voluntary, work-based savings initiative of the New Zealand government to assist employees and employers with long-term saving for retirement. Default products are chosen by the tax office and member accounts routinely allocated to default managers from new member accounts. See: http://www.kiwisaver.govt.nz, accessed 4 May 2016.

[30] See ASFA (2016) "Alternative Default Models", Submission to the Productivity Commission, October.

[31] Clark, Gordon L. (2012) "From Corporatism to Public Utilities: Workplace Pensions in the 21st Century", *Geographical Research*, Vol. 50, No. 1, February, p. 42.

7. IMPLICATIONS AND AREAS FOR FUTURE RESEARCH

This chapter explores some of the main challenges facing the superannuation industry funds. Many of the insights are either prompted by or drawn from an extensive interview with Ian Silk, industry-fund veteran and current CEO of AustralianSuper. One of the key issues is the place of industry funds in the Australian network of superannuation providers. Competition between models of superannuation provision, and between funds, is likely to grow in intensity. Consolidation (amalgamation) of funds is an existing trend also likely to continue.

Performance and fees are likely to be key differentiators and provide comparative advantage (or otherwise) between funds and competing investment models. The industry funds stole a march on their retail and corporate competitors by their asset-allocation bias towards infrastructure, property, and private equity – compared to the retail and corporate funds. This advantage for the industry funds could diminish as others mimic these asset-allocation preferences. Arguably, the industry funds could still retain an advantage, however, due to their structure and the relatively benign intent of members to "let the experts run the thing". This is in comparison to the more liquid, member-demanding, financial-adviser chopping and changing asset-mix approach of the retail funds in particular, which tend not to encourage long-term investing as much as industry funds do.

It is interesting to note that in recent decades one of the biggest changes to the composition of the industry has been the disappearance of corporate funds, down from 1,224 in 2005 to just 32 in 2016, as companies have decided that superannuation is not their core business.[1]

Fees and fee models are an ongoing issue as the industry funds distribute their profits to their members, rather than to external shareholders. This means that, over time, with two equally performing fund managers, a member ends up with less in a retail fund compared to an industry fund. As true performance is the lifetime return to the member, the industry funds have a compounding comparative advantage over their competitors.

The ability to secure the phase-in from 9 per cent to 12 per cent is affected by the political risk that, until the phasing is implemented, the government might renege. Already, the phase-in has been "paused" – frozen at 9.5 per cent until 2021-22 with 0.5 per cent increments thereafter till 2025-26 when the 12 per cent target is due to be reached. Perhaps the risk is greatest to the member rather than the funds. Having more funds under management is a priority for fund managers, but for the member, extra funds flowing into their personal superannuation account is crucial to a decent retirement. Indeed, it is worth noting the arguments against the "pause" – including that unions contend they had moderated wages claims during rounds of negotiations on the basis that it was expected that certain superannuation increases would occur, but then they did not eventuate. In consequence, it is apparent that many workers have been disadvantaged in that claims for higher wages were not pressed because it was expected that, instead, superannuation targets would be met.

Moving to 15 per cent is the long-term aim of all the funds. As Garry Weaven says, "people would say, 'how much is enough?' And I would say, 'more'. What should it be? More. It should be more. How much should it be? More!"[2] To the extent that the industry funds are campaigners for the next shift to 15 per cent as well as defending the

---

[1] Smith, Matthew (2016) "What's Eating Asset Consultants", 2 June, http://finsia.com/news/news-article/2016/06/02/what-s-eating-asset-consultants, accessed 20 September 2016.

[2] Garry Weaven interview, March 2013.

current roll-out to 12 per cent, their credibility and favourable market presence are enhanced.

A significant dilemma is the question of retaining the character of the industry-fund model. All organisations are at first inspired by the ideals and ethics of their founders. But in time, as they necessarily become more bureaucratic, those defining principles are diluted. Ensuring that the mutual-like character of the funds is maintained is an enduring challenge. As Tom McDonald remarks, "in the big-picture sense, from a left-wing point of view, what we have done with industry funds is to create the biggest workers' cooperative in Australia's history."[3] Expanding on the point, he argues: "What is a cooperative? A cooperative is a body, an organisation where the total benefits and assets belong to the members on an equitable basis and they, the cooperative, are their own managers. So, in the area of management, you've got the greatest cooperative movement in history."[4] In the long term, however, history suggests that one day there will be pressure by management to demutualise.

It is useful to look at the character of the superannuation industry today in more detail. It is structured into five sectors: the self-managed sector, the corporate superannuation fund sector (with funds open to the employees of the particular corporation), public-sector funds (only available to public servants), retail funds (mostly owned and run by big banks, big fund managers, and big insurance companies), and the industry funds. The largest, as measured by asset-wealth is the self-managed fund sector, which has experienced explosive growth in the past decade. The toughest competition is between retail funds and industry funds, but the industry-funds sector is very fragmented. In banking, the big four banks dominate the sector. By contrast, the four biggest superannuation funds have less than 20% market share of superannuation. Silk says "it is an incredible number, a huge number of small funds. People look at AustralianSuper and see this behemoth of a fund. Well, we have got about 4 per cent of market

---

[3] Tom McDonald interview, August 2012.
[4] *Ibid.*

share, so [we are] actually a minnow in the context of the industry."[5] But it is growing. While AustralianSuper is small within the industry as a whole, it is a giant when measured against any one of the tens of thousands of small players. If scale is an important element in superannuation, then there is likely to be greater consolidation in the future. Gordon Clark makes a counter argument, however, writing "[i] t would seem that management entrenchment combined with board member entrenchment has dampened the rate of consolidation among industry funds ..."[6] Ian Silk, on the contrary, contends that, in fact, "[i] ndustry funds, retail funds, and public sector funds have all halved in number in the last 12 years. The number of corporate funds has fallen by about 95 per cent as [corporations] say, 'we will stick to our knitting and make our widgets, and we will outsource our superannuation to the so-called experts.' There has been a doubling in the number of self-managed funds."[7]

The Australian Taxation Office has the job of consolidating accounts on request for people who have multiple accounts. In 2012, there were about 11 million people in the Australian workforce and about 33 million superannuation accounts. Therefore, the average person has 3 accounts. Since then, with government regulation reducing the number of accounts, closing dead accounts, and so forth, this number has reduced – with the average member in late 2016 holding 2.5 accounts. Testily, in 2015 addressing a superannuation conference, Ian Silk commented that:

> This industry has around two-and-a-half accounts on average for every member in the system. Is that a good outcome for consumers? Manifestly not. Is it a good outcome for the industry? Well, many of us seem to think so. If regulators and governments don't impose a system

---

[5] Ian Silk interview, March 2013; supplemented by email correspondence, Ian Silk to Mary Easson, 4 November 2013. See Appendix 5 for a list of the major funds.

[6] Clark, Gordon L. (2012) "From Corporatism to Public Utilities: Workplace Pensions in the 21st Century", *Geographical Research*, Vol. 50, No. 1, February, p. 38.

[7] Ian Silk interview, March 2013.

on the industry that encourages much greater automaticity of account consolidation, what is to stop us coming together as an industry to provide a better system for members? There's only one thing stopping us: self-interest; the interest of the agents of the industry, not the interest of the beneficiaries of the industry.[8]

Ideally, holders of multiple accounts will consolidate them – as they are paying fees in each one. But the evidence shows that most people adopt a "forget and regret" approach, not bothering to consolidate and belatedly discovering how their balances, over time, are eroded by fees and charges.

Opinion is divided about the future trajectory of self-managed funds. Will they continue to grow at the current rate, or will the number of regulatory changes, including the capping of amounts of money people can voluntarily put into super, constrain their growth? Some of the worse behaviour in financial and conflicted advice occurs in the SMSF sector. There is a good deal of ill-informed decision-making. It is peculiar that this sector is discretely regulated compared to the rest of the industry.

Certainly, consolidation is likely to occur in the other three sectors. Corporate funds seem set to fall even further as a portion of the total, as fewer companies maintain individual funds. IBM's decision in 2012 to merge its superannuation fund into AustralianSuper illustrates this trend to outsource, and is particularly noteworthy given the negligible unionisation of employees at IBM. The decision, arrived at after a tender, was based on what management considered to be in their employees' best interest.[9] Thus, consolidation is most likely to occur in the public sector, retail, and industry funds. The merger of Health Super and First State Super is another case in point.[10] But there is a

---

[8] Silk, Ian (2015) 'ASFA Oration', 25 November, p. 4.

[9] See http:/ http://forms.australiansuper.com/WelcomeIBM, accessed 22 June 2013. AustralianSuper won this mandate after a competitive tender initiated and managed by IBM.

[10] First State Super merged with Health Super on June 30, 2011 with the full integration of the Funds completed in mid-2012. It is an interesting hybrid: a public-sector scheme merging with a significant private-sector presence in health. See www.firststatesuper.com.au/healthsuper, accessed 9 July 2013.

good deal of stubbornness by some of the smaller funds and the minor fiefdoms around them.[11] Change will not be easy.

Turning to investment performance, Silk says "what distinguished industry funds from the other sectors was that back 15 to 20 years ago, Bill [Kelty], but also Garry [Weaven], pushed industry funds to invest in infrastructure. [That was] just part of the visionary thinking of Bill in particular, but also Garry."[12] In part, this was a responsible response to the clamour, in *Australia Reconstructed* and elsewhere, for the industry funds to help "develop Australia". In fairness to the retail funds, they have a more volatile membership, with competition and potential movement of funds requiring greater liquidity compared to the industry funds. The latter, buttressed by award superannuation clauses and sponsorship by unions and employers, have an advantage. A more stable investment base makes for easier asset allocation to long-term investment in alternatives, including infrastructure and private equity. Silk argues that it was a logical investment for the industry funds, because if a fund manager is investing in a big infrastructure asset, a toll road or a public-private partnership with a hospital for example, the ability to do that is enhanced if liquidity is not an issue and there is little to no pressure to sell the toll road tomorrow, having bought it yesterday. In contrast, shares are much more easily converted into liquid capital.

Silk comments that "for a fund like this [i.e., AustralianSuper] to have a third of its assets outside the share market, outside government bonds and outside cash but in infrastructure, private equity and unlisted property – now, that is not unexceptional. But 20 to 25 years ago, that was an allocation that nobody had heard of. Bill [Kelty] dreamed it up, basically."[13] This was not a conservative allocation for its time. But the rest of the portfolio usually followed cautious instincts. Part of the background was the fevered atmosphere in which compulsory

---

[11] Not that bigger is better in every case – to allude to a point by Gordon Clark mentioned at the end of the last Chapter.

[12] Ian Silk interview, March 2013.

[13] *Ibid.*

super was introduced. Some schemes were hurriedly set up in the mid-1980s: "… if it had not been a conservative approach and things had gone wrong … heaven help us," mused Silk. "We were incredibly lucky."[14]

The most extreme example of conservatism is to invest in capital-guaranteed products. When the industry funds were established, there was no appetite for loss, so many of the trustees insisted on money going into capital-guaranteed products. During and just after the 1987 crash, most of the industry funds produced double-digit positive returns because they were overweight in those capital-guaranteed products. Silk says, "I don't think they have been excessively conservative, but if I was one of the warriors who had fought for it, and I had grand visions, I might have thought the funds might be more prepared to be more aggressive or ambitious in their investment arrangements."[15]

In debates on asset allocation and member choice, it is interesting that according to Silk "industry-fund members, almost universally, were not engaged with super …"[16] This, ironically, created an opportunity to differentiate them from retail funds. He says that the industry funds had the great luxury of very strong cash flow and members who were not engaged "so that the trustee could do, frankly, whatever they liked with the money knowing they weren't going to be put under pressure by members saying, 'I want my money out'; whereas, generally, the retail funds did not have unlisted assets, like infrastructure, on their radar screens. It wasn't even a conscious thing, but as they have over the time realised that the industry funds stole a march over them, they've tried to get it back and they have moved more into unlisted assets."[17]

The retail funds have not been able to do so to the same extent because most of their members are either themselves more engaged

---

[14] *Ibid.*
[15] *Ibid.*
[16] *Ibid.*
[17] *Ibid.*

and more likely to move their money around, so liquidity becomes an issue, or they are advised by a financial advisor. Generally, advisors are keen to demonstrate their value to clients by saying "we should move from here to there." "Set and forget" is not typically the business model of financial advisors. Consequently, the liquidity requirements for retail funds are much higher than those for industry funds. In Silk's assessment, "this has been the single most important investment-performance differentiator between the industry and commercial funds. So, those 'compare the pair' advertisements go to fees,[18] but if you add in investment performance it is mainly because we have had a big exposure to infrastructure and unlisted assets and they have had a much smaller exposure."[19] Silk further notes, "we have an investment committee that meets at least once a month, and its most important decision is to decide the asset allocation of the fund: how much we will be investing in Australia, in shares, international shares, property, infrastructure, bonds, cash and so on."[20] In AustralianSuper's case, the fund has about 13 to 14 per cent allocated to infrastructure and unlisted property, and around 4 per cent to private equity (for a total of about 32 per cent).

Like investment performance, fees are also a differentiator. The key difference between industry and retail funds, in terms of their organisational model, is that the latter are owned by shareholders. They exist to serve those shareholders by acquiring customers and putting a profit-margin on their interactions. The industry funds, however, do not have shareholders. There is only one stakeholder: the

---

[18] Through advertisements and general marketing, the industry funds encourage direct fund-to-fund comparisons and purport to show that fees charged in the retail sector compared to the industry funds are higher and significantly dilutive to long-term members' returns. See http://industrysuper.com/tools-forms_superfund-comparator.aspx, accessed July 9, 2013. Such advertising seeks to establish on a like-for-like basis that there are significant differences between member, not-for-profit funds, the industry and government sector ones, and the retail for-profit funds. Anecdotally, it is apparent that the advertisements are highly effective.

[19] Ian Silk interview, March 2013.

[20] *Ibid.*

members themselves. A retail fund has two stakeholders: the clients and the shareholders.

Industry funds are often referred to as "not-for-profit" funds. Silk, however, says "I hate that term because who wants to be in a super fund that is not really interested in profit? Well, I don't."[21] The point is that the legal structure – the trustee – is not for profit, but the fund itself is unashamedly profit-oriented. Although many of the industry funds were not the sharpest and most commercially-oriented organisations in their early days, the larger funds have become very commercial. Their approach is to balance a member's orientation with commercial rigour. Ian Silk asserts "every time we do something because it is a nice thing to do, if that is at the expense of the commercial orientation of the fund, and what we are going to put into your account, then that is actually not a 'members-first' position at all."[22] Bert Evans recalls putting matters more bluntly. "Very early in the piece there was suggestion to buy an apple-packing factory at Batlow to save 40 jobs ... and I said, 'pig's arse!'"[23] He could not see how such a decision could be in the interest of STA members.[24] "Could you imagine it, if we owned every darn factory in Australia? This is my monument to super. One of my mates in the metal unions said to me, 'listen, Bert, we owe it to you to tell you, we are going to use this money for social purposes.' I said, 'no you are not.' He was on the board and he took me aside in North Sydney in the office and I said, 'no, you're not. Just write on the back of your hand 'my house' because it is my house. There is not going to be one decision taken that puts my house at risk'."[25] This story highlights how invaluable were the employer representatives' contribution to the development of the industry fund model. They were not in any sense after 1986 "union funds". They were bi-partite in their board composition and nearly as one on most issues.

---

[21] *Ibid.*

[22] *Ibid.*

[23] Bert Evans interview, May 2013.

[24] That is, the then Superannuation Trust of Australia, later to merge with the Australian Retirement Fund to form AustralianSuper in 2006.

[25] Bert Evans interview, May 2013.

The industry funds in the early days were determined to pick prov-en managers they could work with and to choose the best indiv-iduals they could find for each role. "From the start it was very much this 'best-of-breed' approach," recalls Ian Silk.[26] In other words, the indus-try funds each decided to piece together their structure "… to construct our own organisation, rather than just going to a one-stop shop."[27]

Weaven comments that in conceiving the building-industry fund, "the standard trustee deed I was presented with by Colonial – which won the tender to do the administration – the deed was unbelievable. Things like, you had to have a member of the Institute of Actuaries and they had to approve everything you did."[28] The picking of established, brand-name advisors and service providers followed the pattern begun in the formation of the LUCRF scheme: choosing accomplished professional firms to work with in developing a credible, robust fund structure. Sword recalls going to the Ryan Carlisle Needham and Thomas law firm[29] and speaking to managing partner John Ryan to work on developing a set of rules for what was needed. He sought potential models: "I went around and talked to the Pulp and Paper Workers' Union, who had a similar scheme, but theirs was not fully vested and it was only for a couple of plants in their industry …"[30] Even so, the rudimentary structure of their scheme was something to go by. "I got one of their application forms and, you know, you'll remember the thing called Letraset; this sort of sheet of plastic letters. Yes, so it was a plastic sheet and if that was a 'P', you sort of go like that and peeled. So I got their application form, I whited out Pulp and Paper Workers and I put in 'LUCRF' because I didn't have a name to put in [for the] Storeman and Packers Super Fund and then printed those all up. So, I went out and I had to go shed by shed, and 87 per cent of them signed up for the super."[31] He mused, "… it was the

---

[26] Ian Silk interview, March 2013.

[27] *Ibid.*

[28] Garry Weaven interview, March 2013.

[29] Since 1983 known as Ryan Carlisle Thomas, lawyers.

[30] Greg Sword interview, June 2012.

[31] *Ibid.* Sword is referring to workers in the skin and hide industry in 1978.

error that the employers made because they misjudged the capacity to get those working people to understand what would be beneficial to them."[32]

Ryan took Sword to then top five global accounting firm Arthur Andersen to prepare a trustee and a trustee-company structure: "We wanted Arthur Andersen to be really good. Mind you, once we started, the union was going to run this, so we had to have pretty solid protection, [a] gold-plated sort of [auditing]; not Acme Auditing, but Arthur Andersen."[33]

For Silk, there is a clear, appropriate rationale for investment decisions: Leave it to the professionals. "I liken it a bit to a motor vehicle. Speaking for myself, if my car breaks down there is no point in me lifting up the bonnet, because I will be confronted with a problem not for me. I know my limitations. Clint Eastwood said, 'a man has got to know his limitations.' And that is one of my many limitations. I reckon super is a bit like that. At its most fundamental level, my employer puts money into super. I can put some money in if I like. As long as I am in a decent fund it will look after me. I might want to choose this or that investment option and I might want to increase my insurance. I could do either of those, certainly the latter, pretty straightforwardly, but do I need to know all the rules? Actually, I don't."[34]

Silk adds, "the industry beats itself up a bit about being so complex. We are complex for those who want to know the innards of it ..."[35] The issue is more about the constancy and the frequency of changes and the extent to which they are negative changes. "I am not saying that [the] super system has served everybody very well, but people speak about its complexity, which is a different issue. It is complex, but does it matter to most people? I would say it doesn't."[36]

---

[32] Greg Sword interview, June 2012.

[33] *Ibid.* Ironically, Arthur Andersen was to collapse as a global accounting firm in the period 2001/4 in the aftermath of the Enron oil company scandal in the United States.

[34] Ian Silk interview, March 2013.

[35] *Ibid.*

[36] *Ibid.*

Ironically, the industry is constantly saying to government "stop making changes!", but it also frequently proposes changes to make the system better. Many of the changes clearly have been seeking to tap savings for tax revenue. For example, before the 1996 election the Liberal Party opposed industry super right up until December 1995. The then Opposition from 1992 to late 1995 opposed compulsory superannuation.[37] They knew that policy had become a losing position, and the then-Shadow Treasurer Peter Costello abandoned the Liberal party's opposition at the end of 1995. But equally they went into that election promising no increase in taxes. Gary Weaven remembers, "once they were in, he [Costello] introduced a surcharge on super so he could say it wasn't tax. It was clearly a tax."[38]

The changes that have aroused the greatest controversy in the broader Australian community are those that negatively affect particular entitlements. As discussed in Chapter 6, the most vexing are typically about taxation, and sometimes access to the money itself. The more changes that occur – and the more negative changes that occur, obviously, the less public confidence there is in superannuation. There is a sovereign risk element – meaning the risk of government unilaterally changing the rules and upsetting the retirement strategies. This is manifest in two ways: a reduction in discretionary payments into the system; and diminishing public support for the whole system, as expressed in the lament, "I have been saving for 35 years and now you are going to whack a tax on me! That is not what I signed up for!"

Silk sees tax as an issue that will never dissipate. It will always be a threat – the government temptation to increase taxes and/or to change

---

[37] This had been the position with the Superannuation Guarantee legislation. In a radio interview on 10 July 1992, the then Opposition industrial relations spokesperson, John Howard, urged that "putting off this stupid superannuation guarantee levy that costs tens of thousands ... [of jobs]" was needed for economic recovery. Howard is quoted in Megalogenis, George (2012) *The Australian Moment. How We Were Made for These Times*, Viking, Camberwell, Victoria, p. 243.

[38] Garry Weaven interview, March 2013. See Appendix 4.

Figure 34: Ian Silk from the then Australian Retirement Fund, prior to 2006, *Australian Financial Review* photo by Eamon Gallagher. Source: Fairfax Archives.

policy. He comments on the desirable level of savings, the SGC, "this is sort of a heresy in some circles, but I don't think there is a particular magical figure. 12 per cent might be quite okay for you depending on what your income has been and what you have built up over time and what you expect your standard of living expectations are in retirement; whereas I might need 15 per cent, I have had broken work patterns, I've raised my kids and all those sorts of things."[39]

---

[39] Ian Silk interview, March 2013.

Minimum contributions to a maximum limit of 12 per cent are likely for quite some time because there is no indication from the Coalition that they will seek increases anytime in the foreseeable future, beyond 2025-26 when the final 12 per cent instalment applies. On the shift from 9 to 12 per cent, there was little controversy at the time outside of the mining tax imbroglio, further discussed below. There was a phase in of 9.25 and 9.5 per cent of the SG. Under Prime Minister Rudd, a decision was taken to increase the SG from 9 to 12 per cent. Rudd says, "as Prime Minister I remember a conversation with Paul Keating on the importance of climbing to 15 per cent with the SG, from 9 per cent to 12 per cent in order to provide long-term superannuation adequacy for working people."[40] On the Henry Review, the then-relevant Minister, Chris Bowen, said, "I couldn't see why he wouldn't just do the simpler thing and go from 9 per cent to 12 per cent and, as I say, finish the legacy. I put that argument to both Wayne Swan and Kevin Rudd, and I thought it was a big call, but we should reject the Henry recommendation and go from 9 per cent to 12 per cent."[41] Rudd further states:

> When I discussed with colleagues Treasurer Swan's proposal for the mining tax, the position I took was [that] there had to be a return to the Australian people in two respects: one, in terms of a national investment in infrastructure where people could see the physical dividend from the actual tax which [would] then [have been] collected – a long-term mechanism for funding the needs of the Building Australia Fund and Infrastructure Australia. Two, we needed to deliver something back to working people across the country as well. I said to the Treasury at the time that it was important that they now framed a proposal on how we could implement the 9 per cent to 12 per cent. I then said that there were no circumstances under which, as Prime Minister, I would support proceeding with the mining tax unless that was contained within the same proposal.[42]

---

[40] Kevin Rudd interview, May 2013.

[41] Chris Bowen, interview, May 2013. Cf. Bateman, H., & Kingston, G. (2010) "The Henry Review and Super and Saving", *The Australian Economic Review*, Vol. 43, pp. 437-48.

[42] Kevin Rudd interview, May 2013.

The economic circumstances were difficult, however. Hence Senator Nick Sherry's reservations about the timing of any major changes in benefits and cost to employers.[43] Bowen recalls "there were all the arguments about impact on small business and wage costs and all that sort of stuff, and I made the point that the same arguments were put against the 9 per cent to start with, but jobs grew, real wages absorbed the increase, etc … I had the view that if we didn't do it now – I think this was the clincher for Kevin – if we didn't do it now it was never going to happen."[44] In Rudd's words, "I wanted to complete the task – based on long conversations with Keating about it over a long period of time."[45] Although Treasury were opposed,[46] the government's proposals were relatively uncontroversial for two reasons. First, they were part of the package of tax changes associated with the mining "excess profits" tax which, however, proved hugely contentious. Second, the government's moderate claim of implementing a long overdue reform (the last Superannuation Guarantee improvements had been legislated for a decade before), simply passed without much attention, given the first point. Chris Bowen recalls, "the other thing we tied it to – my argument – was 'let's not just make it from 9 per cent to 12 per cent, but let's rejuvenate the whole thing'. If the sector is getting 9 per cent to 12 per cent, which they really want, then they have also got to lift their game. We did FOFA – Future of Financial Advice – and abolished and banned commissions for financial advisors, which [were] distorting where superannuation investments were going. We did Cooper – the response to the Cooper Review. I said, 'If they are going to get from 9 per cent to 12 per cent, they need to improve their efficiency.' … We announced FOFA the weekend before we announced the 9 per cent to 12 per cent"[47]

Keating notes, "you may know I encouraged Kevin Rudd and Chris Bowen and Wayne Swan to go from 9 per cent to 12 per cent

[43] Nick Sherry interview, March 2013.
[44] Chris Bowen interview, May 2013.
[45] Kevin Rudd interview, May 2013.
[46] *Ibid.*
[47] Chris Bowen interview, May 2013.

in the period of [their] government. So, when we get to 12 per cent in 2019, this would assume both parties supported it, we will be at the 12 per cent that I spoke of in 1991 – many years too late, but better late than never."[48] Bowen argues that the context was all-important to promoting the change. "When I announced [the] FOFA [reforms], I said, 'this is the biggest change to superannuation in 20 years,' and then the next week I said, 'last week I said, "that was the biggest change but now we have got a bigger one', but it was a package. I said to the sector, 'this is a package. Nine per cent to 12 per cent doesn't come for free. You are going to have to work with us on these things.'"[49]

Although incredibly influential, the Cooper reforms[50] have not been met without dissent. For example, Clark writes that at one level one might say "… the Federal government's introduction of a generic pension product represents a profound critique of the costs and consequences of the super industry."[51] This is to allude to the justification for the MySuper generic product, that costs would be kept low for members who simply wanted a 'no frills', conservative investment strategy. de Bruyn, however, makes a different point highlighting the administrative and associated costs in doing so – arguing that the industry funds, such as REST, were offering exactly that, a low cost service to members. Additionally, because the industry superannuation funds do not make profits, the only way to cover expenses is out of the fees that members pay. The compulsory reforms that the government introduced, for example, required that funds over

[48] Paul Keating interview, March 2013. Keating is alluding to the speech he gave in 1991. See Keating, Paul (1991) "A Retirement Incomes Policy", address to the Australian Graduate School of Management, July 25, typescript, 17pp.

[49] Chris Bowen interview, May 2013; supplemented by email correspondence, Chris Bowen to Mary Easson, 29 October 2013.

[50] Cooper, J. (2010a) "Super System Review, Final Report Part One: Overview and Recommendations", www.supersystemreview.gov.au, accessed June 1, 2013; and Cooper, J. (2010b) "Super System Review, Final Report Part Two: Recommendation Packages", www.supersystemreview.gov.au, accessed 1 June, 2013.

[51] Clark, Gordon L. (2012) "From Corporatism to Public Utilities: Workplace Pensions in the 21st Century", *Geographical Research*, Vol. 50, No. 1, February, p. 32.

about five or six years would have to pay compliance costs to the Federal Government. For example, the cost for the upgrade of the Australian Taxation Office computer systems was around $335 million, paid for by a levy imposed upon the industry. de Bruyn says, "one of the administrators – who do the administration for REST – [says] to us that collectively around Australia, superannuation funds are spending around $800 million in getting their administration systems upgraded to comply with the new requirements. If you add $800 million with the $335 million levy from the government over several years for ATO computer upgrades, there is well over $1 billion in costs to set up a system which is largely no different to what the industry funds today are already providing, which is a simple, low-cost, vanilla superannuation product."[52] Perhaps, also, an unintended consequence of attempting to stamp out rorts in the wider industry is to weaken identity with the very schemes that have excelled in member-aligned performance. Clark queries if this has been thought through: "It would seem that with the advent of MySuper and the development of so-called generic default products, the process of discounting workers' company and industry identities will be complete."[53]

In some industrially weak industries, where the unions are poorly organised, the superannuation surcharge has been entirely traded off, but in others employers have just added it to the total salary/wages package. A similar outcome in pockets of the economy is likely with the ratcheting from 9.5 per cent to 12 per cent. Some employers will want to ensure a discount to what would otherwise be wage increases. From 1 July 2013, the SG went from 9 to 9.25 per cent and a year later to 9.5 per cent. But in some corners of industry employers who had been intending to give a 3 per cent wage increase then proposed "on economic grounds'" 2.75 per cent, with the remaining 0.25 per

---

[52] Joe de Bruyn interview, March 2013. Cf. SDA (2012), "Submission to the Productivity Commission concerning Default Superannuation Funds in Modern Awards", http://www.pc.gov.au/__data/assets/pdf_file/0013/116302/sub024-default-super.pdf, accessed 28 May 2013.
[53] Clark, Gordon L. (2012) "From Corporatism to Public Utilities: Workplace Pensions in the 21st Century", *Loc. Cit.*, p. 42.

cent going to superannuation. Not for the first time, then, workers are paying for their superannuation.

According to industry fund pioneer Greg Sword:

> The competition in the market place currently is between industry funds, where there is a democratic management system, and it's not for profit, and then there are the banks. There is an AMP Group on the sidelines, but it's not a player. Every other product is owned by the banks. So, all the noise that you hear about super funds that are not performing, or they have bad performances or whatever, it may be it's all about that competition between the banks. The really important governance model governs the foundation for the industry fund; that is, it remains that social partnership. Independent directors can play a role here and there but they are not the solution and they are not the most important element of effective governance. It's the competition that matters most; banks are losing the competition.[54]

Yet it is not the case that industry funds are triumphant and remorselessly eclipsing all competition. As noted in Chapter 1, the industry funds currently represent less than a quarter of all Australian savings in superannuation.[55]

As this book and this Chapter in particular documents, however, the industry funds have had profound impacts on the Australian superannuation model over the past 30 years. This is so in five main respects.

First, the extension of superannuation as a near universal employment right was won for the industry funds – principally in most cases by their initial union leadership, by the employers who came on board who in many cases were decisive in creating and shaping particular schemes, in combination with their political allies – and by no-one else. Superannuation did not come about from Treasury modelling. It did not really come out of Labor Party policy either, as important as policy was to become with the SGC. It came from the unions. They fought for it as a major right and entrenched it in

---

[54] Greg Sword interview, June 2012.
[55] Note Appendices 5 and 6 for details of the major funds.

different industries, and its growth started from there. This provides a legacy of huge credibility in the on-going competition between superannuation fund models, and in the context of some of the drastic changes now being contemplated by the Turnbull government, as discussed in Chapter 6.

Second, the industry funds broke the dominance of the virtual-integrated financial services model of the AMP,[56] National Mutual,[57] Colonial Mutual,[58] MLC,[59] and the rest. In the selection of "best of breed" fund administrators, investment-fund managers, and other service providers, the industry funds created their own, distinctive management model. This is not to say that the previously significant players disappeared. They have all restructured, adapted, and are significantly larger due to the superannuation savings revolution described in this book.

Third, the industry funds inspired greater transparency on fees and performance and then drove fees down, thereby contributing to a more performance-driven, accountable system across the whole industry. The system, however, requires still greater transparency, clarity, and agreement on the definition of costs and fees. "Look through" transparency is needed. What are all the management expenses, the aggregation of fees, costs, and charges that affect overall returns? If the answer to that question becomes too complicated, then overall

---

[56] Formed in 1849 as the Australian Mutual Provident Society, demutualised in 1998, AMP is Australia's largest retail and corporate superannuation provider.

[57] The National Mutual Life Association of Australasia, National Mutual, was a mutual insurance company formed in 1869 in Melbourne and demutualised in 1996, with French firm AXA purchasing 51 percent of the shares, and renaming the company to AXA Asia Pacific in 1999.

[58] The Colonial Mutual Life Assurance Society Limited, later Colonial Limited, demutualised in 1997 having in 1994 acquired the State Bank of New South Wales. In 2000 the Commonwealth Bank acquired Colonial. Colonial First State Investments is now a major financial services business of the bank.

[59] MLC Limited, a mutual tracing its history back to formation in 1886, was half acquired by Lend Lease in 1982, and fully acquired in 1985 and sold to the National Australia Bank (NAB) in 2000. It is now a key part of the wealth management arm of the NAB.

returns to members depending on risk guidelines need to be considered – with the industry devising its own guidelines and publicising results, on a like-for-like basis. Or perhaps a new Superannuation Standards Commission,[60] regulating the entire industry, would be suited for this task, if the industry is incapable of meeting it.

Fourth, the retail funds were shaped by the impact of the industry funds, the discipline of competition and the plethora of regulation to stamp out third-line enforcing and to call to account the financial advisory industry. They are stronger for this.

Fifth, the lively competition between the industry funds and their competitors changed the mix of offerings in the market. The gradually diminishing presence of corporate funds is one manifestation.

The history of superannuation in Australia raises interesting questions. To what extent has the asset allocation strategy and resulting performance of the industry funds been superior to their competition (or otherwise)? Does this provide scope for exploitable, sustainable advantages to the industry funds? How is this changing? Is asset allocation and related performance a consistent advantage that persists in changing markets over time? How has the asset-allocation model – or at least the theme of greater weighting to indirect investments, including infrastructure, property, and private equity – across the industry funds affected the rest of the industry, such as influencing competitors and inspiring alternate models? Why did the industry-fund model survive despite the change of government in 1996 and various steps taken to weaken the industry funds' position (including legislation for "freedom of choice" and removing the link between industrial awards and particular superannuation schemes in the Federal industrial relations system)? Is the NSW experience, earlier referenced, in promoting freedom of choice in the context of occupational arrangements in industrial instruments a useful precedent and model nationally? How does the development of the

---

[60] This body, which presently does not exist, might bring under one roof the entirety of superannuation regulation. Currently APRA, ASIC, and the ATO manage parts of the task.

Australian system of superannuation fit in the context of financial innovation in the 1980s in Australia? Is the case for a national superannuation scheme forever off the national agenda? Because "[u]ltimately, the 'final' value of such schemes is not the responsibility of the employer,"[61] is this burden ever likely to be government's responsibility or will what Clark calls 'public utilities', regulated entities, superannuation funds, be all compelled to provide low-fee benefits to fund members?

The overall impact of the industry funds on the fees payable in the industry, in absolute quantum, the scope of coverage for such fees and the impact on service providers, is another interesting issue. Silk once noted that "my job" is to improve "the quality of service to members (low costs are an integral part of this), as well as broadening the range of services."[62] Mapping the changes over time from the 1980s, including the impact of technology, is a task worth doing. To cite just one instance, in the development of their own administration-delivery vehicles, the industry funds have utterly transformed themselves, with industry-funds management, Australian Administrative Services (AAS) – founded in 1987 – at one point dominating the sector as they ousted traditionally significant players and caused competitors to adapt to survive. In the end, AAS was sold to Link Group in 2006, as its services were seen as non-core and commoditised. And it has to be said that the under-investment in technology, processes, and management meant that this service was a "loss leader". "You do not need to do everything yourself to have a positive impact for members" seems to be the appropriate lesson drawn by the industry fund movement.

Some of the collective, or mutual, activities by funds have been extremely important, as Garry Weaven notes: "… a lot of that collective action between the funds … probably won't be a force so much in the

---

61 Clark, Gordon L. (2012) "From Corporatism to Public Utilities: Workplace Pensions in the 21st Century", *Loc. Cit.*, p. 34.
62 Way, Nicholas (1994a) "Under Fire, But Smooth as Silk", *Superfunds*, No. 176, November, p. 69.

future as they all get very big in their own right, but it has been very, very important, for example, in setting up industry super property trust as a collective."[63]

Weaven argues: "doing it our own way and saying this is for our members' benefit and not for the benefits of the fund manager but the way we need it – setting up IFM and IFS, setting up the Australian Council of Super Investors for the corporate governance and voting and the proxy voting role, setting up the Australian Institute of Super Trustees for advocacy for the representative trustee system and industry super network for the same reason, the collective advertising of Industry Super campaign to really pull the rug out of the nay-sayers and make it hard for politicians to develop an anti-industry fund position – they still can but it is much harder for them when the numbers are up there."[64]

He goes on to observe "all of those things were tremendously important parts of developing the actual representative trustee system sector and measurement. We really pioneered measurement. There was no proper measurement of super – of group performance. There was no proper measurement. The fund managers who ran super used to publish any numbers they liked and no-one could gainsay them."[65] This is, however, an ongoing area of reform as the total industry is a long way away from true, full look-through disclosure of fees and charges – and management expense ratios (MERs).

The success of the industry funds and the exponential overall growth of funds under management pose challenges to success. Various organisations – Rice Warner and Deloitte, for example –

---

[63] Garry Weaven interview, March 2013. Weaven is alluding to Industry Super Property Trust (ISPT). Originally founded in June 1994 as an unlisted property trust by four leading industry superannuation funds, ISPT has grown to be co-owned by 21 prominent industry super funds and other "like-minded" organisations. See: www.ispt.net.au, which describes over $11.0 billion in investments as at June 2016.

[64] Garry Weaven interview, March 2013.

[65] *Ibid.*

see it as exponential growth.[66] One consequent issue is the taxation policy that should apply and the impacts of current and future policy. The Henry Tax Review's analysis and prescriptions, notwithstanding the Review's limited terms of reference, still provide guidance on alternative approaches.

Figure 35: Susan Ryan, campaigner for gender equity in superannuation, then President of the Australian Institute of Superannuation Trustees, 16 December 2004, Australian Financial Review photo by Louise Kennerley. Source: Fairfax Archives.

Emerging issues include whether the available evidence suggesting that the current taxation "gaming" associated with private occupational superannuation represent a substantial and regressive distribution of resources. The Henry Tax Review identified the need to encourage private savings as part of the policies required to manage Australia's ageing demographic profile. Private savings, however,

---

[66] See for example, Deloitte (2015) "The Dynamics of the Australian Superannuation System. The Next Twenty Years, 2015-2035", https://www2. deloitte.com/au/en/pages/financial-services/articles/dynamics-australian-superannuation-system-2015.html, accessed 2 June 2016.

can be made through a range of devices. People with higher incomes are presumptively well-placed to undertake their own savings, without unduly concessional taxation arrangements. Moreover, few arguments suggest that there should be further reliance on regressive, superannuation-taxation concessions. The other elephant in the room is the long-term viability of Australia's three-pronged retirement-incomes policy. What are the implications for the Aged Pension as either a default safety net or a continuing right?

Compulsory superannuation combined with buoyant economic growth has turned Australia into a "shareholder society", where most workers are now indirect investors in the listed and unlisted markets. One consequence is a lively personal-investment marketplace, and many Australians take an interest in investment topics. Occupational superannuation is based on individual ownership of contributions made into private funds, with entitlements directly related to savings over a lifetime.

There is a danger that the aged pension might only become a safety net for those who have not done so successfully in the market, not a right of citizenship.[67] This would be a deleterious outcome. Low-income earners, people with disabilities, those who have devoted themselves to carer's responsibilities, employees with broken service, particularly women, deserve to do better than to struggle in retirement. Mandated superannuation helps, but high-income earners benefit the most. Making sure those who can afford to save are encouraged – and mandated – to do so assists in ensuring equity all round. The optimum level of savings required – 12 per cent, 15 per cent or more – is obviously an important on-going issue, especially as life longevity increases. Modelling for the future is always going to be a dynamic area for research, and very much related to economic performance.

---

[67] This is not to express an affirmative view. Entitlements are affected by the market in adverse ways. The author, for example, has had conversations with individuals in superannuation funds which had invested their money so badly that they had to defer planned retirement for a couple of years. This being a telling reflection on poor investment by the fund in which his or her money was entrusted.

Whether increases to the eligibility age for retirement, including eligibility for the old age pension, is equitable is an important question. On the issue of whether, in those early days of the creation of a new system, superannuation would supersede a national old-age pension, Keating is explicit: "Everything the Labor Party ever spoke of, retirement income always had the [Aged] Pension as the building block... That was the anti-destitution payment, and as you grew your pension sums, your lump sums and [what] you're earning in retirement, there would be a withdrawal rate from the full pension."[68] One question is the gender impact of changes up until now and likely future consequences.[69] Women have on average around 57 per cent of the superannuation savings of men.[70]

Figure 36: Portrait of former Prime Minister Paul Keating in his offices in Potts Point, *Sydney Morning Herald* photo by Nic Walker, 7 October 2015. Source: Fairfax Archives.

---

[68] Paul Keating interview, March 2013.

[69] This point was particularly emphasised in interviews with Anna Booth, August 2012, and Susan Ryan, March 2013.

[70] Kaine, Sarah (2015) "Women, Work and Industrial Relations in Australia in 2015", *Journal of Industrial Relations*, Vol. 58, No. 3, pp. 328-9.

Determining who falls between the cracks of opportunity, and the role of government in the overall design of the system to assist low-paid workers is another important issue, as is whether certain types of jobs need retirement tailored to the needs of that industry's employees, rather than rules rigidly applied to all. In building, for example, someone approaching sixty years of age is typically in a tougher position than a desk worker. They physically may be unable to keep going. Do increasing age limits on pension eligibility hurt them disproportionately? How should public policy adapt? Weaven suggests, "…for many people, you can't work. If you are a bricklayer, you can't. Even if you are a production-line worker you are very unlikely to be able to go on until your 70s because your body won't do it. As long as the system is sufficiently accommodating for that, there is nothing wrong with edging the preservation age up as life expectancy increases."[71]

Maintaining the cultural traditions and ethic of the industry funds is a challenge for the longer term. Silk states, "people say, 'what is the biggest challenge for Australian superannuation? Is it change of government, is it the investment market?' For me, it is none of those things, because they are just issues that you have to manage. Some hurdles are put in front of you – you had better deal with it some way… AMP started life 150 years ago as a mutual organisation established for, and working diligently on behalf of, its policy holders. It legally demutualised in the late 1990s, but it ceased to be a genuine mutual before that. It was captured by other stakeholders, in particular management. Then, when they were demutualised, there was this huge transfer of wealth to management. Now whilst we don't have that model yet, I reckon at some point there will be pressure on these funds to demutualise in some way. Even if that legal change isn't proposed, it is not hard to see a fund saying, 'we have got two million members. In four years' time we are going to have $100 billion. King of the universe …' Just the way we treat our members, the way we treat service providers and the relationship with unions.

---

[71] Garry Weaven interview, March 2013.

We must never forget that we wouldn't be here were it not for the unions."[72]

Silk personally invests time conveying and retaining the culture built up over many years. "Here we are on the top floor of a building in the CBD [in Melbourne]. I meet with every new staff member that starts here and I take them through the history of the fund, and so I say, 'never forget the real stakeholders here. It is a welder out in Footscray or a cleaner out in Narre Warren' – and it is an issue, because these funds are employing more and more professionals that come from the professional services industry."[73]

All organisations evolve: "… It is a function of time, I think, because Bill [Kelty] is entirely out of the industry. He was on our board for 20 years, and it was a really sad day when he left because he was such a remarkable contributor, not just to our fund, much less his broader views. But Garry [Weaven] would [also] be gone in a few years' time... It is a great institutional challenge to maintain the faith and the passion."[74] To adapt Edmund Burke's line, the industry fund movement represents a *contract* between the past, the present, and those yet born.[75] How the industry retains its traditions, renews, and excels into the future is the challenging part of that possibility.

---

[72] Ian Silk interview, March 2013.

[73] *Ibid.*

[74] *Ibid.*

[75] Cf. Burke's observation was that "[s]ociety is indeed a contract... a partnership not only between those who are living, but between those who are living, those who are dead, and those who are to be born." Burke, Edmund (1790; 2003) *Reflections on the Revolution in France*, Turner, Frank M., editor, Yale University Press, New Haven and London, p. 82.

8. Concluding Observations

Economic historian Max Corden once said, "Australian economists have probably made their most original contributions in writing on wages policy and the arbitration system."[1] Professor Donald Whitehead was one such economist: his greatest and most lasting influence was on the intellectual development and strategic thinking of his former student, Bill Kelty, himself trained as an economist.

Whitehead speculated in the early 1970s that the rigidity of the Australian industrial-relations system meant that "the most likely outcome for Australia seems to be a rate of inflation that is high by international standards and which is likely to continuously accelerate".[2] This was before the oil shocks of 1973/74, which made his projections gain even greater acuity. He recommended stronger central union organisation, which he deemed "necessary to implement a wages policy"[3] and recommended the involvement of unions in economic planning. He saw progress as possible only through a "package deal" of reforms – including wages policy, tax cuts, superannuation savings, and social wage improvements. This would require a "bargain" between organised labour, the government, and employers that would

---

[1] Corden, M.W. (1968) *Australian Economic Policy Discussion: A Survey*, Melbourne University Press, Parkville, p. 2.

[2] Whitehead, Donald Henry (1973) *Stagflation and Wages Policy in Australia*, Longman, Camberwell [Melbourne, Victoria], p. 123.

[3] Blue- and white- collar workers were united under the aegis of the ACTU with the merger of the Australian Council of Salaried and Professional Associations (ACSPA) in 1979 and the Council of Australian Government Employees (CAGEO) in 1981. See Griffin, G., & Giuca, V. (1986) "One Peak Council: The Merger of ACSPA and CAGEO with the ACTU", *Journal of Industrial Relations*, Vol. 28, No. 4, pp. 483-503.

Figure 37: Professor Donald Whitehead. Source: Archives of La Trobe University.

strike a fair balance for economic reform. Ultimately, the Hawke and Keating governments working in tandem with the ACTU were the architects of the kind of changes sketched by Whitehead.

Whitehead's politics were conservative leaning, but he was not anti-union. He suggested an attractive array of programmes for training and re-equipping workers to better participate in the workforce. He also urged for something that "would involve comprehensive superannuation arrangements geared to the earnings of the employee during his working life. Unions should be involved in the operation of the superannuation scheme."[4] He saw merit in the unions becoming more actively engaged in solving Australia' economic problems – by participating in the task of growing the pie, not just its cutting. He wanted unions to consider themselves as more than just "wage-bargaining institutions". He thought some control of profits would be necessary as part of the package. He paused to note at the end of his book on stagflation that what he was recommending "underlies the complexity of a viable wages policy."[5] He thought nothing less ambitious could meet the task.

In large measure, as we have seen, much of this agenda informed Kelty's approach to the challenge of wage policy, economic adjustment associated with the opening of the Australian economy with the floating of the Australian dollar in late 1983, and financial deregulation thereafter. Between 1983 and 1985 wages were adjusted quarterly according to movements in the Consumer Price Index (CPI) except in 1984 when indexation was discounted to leave out the inflationary effect of the government's introduction of a levy on personal incomes to help pay for the national health insurance scheme, Medicare. Colloquially known as the "Medicare fiddle" this traded off a real wage increase for medical insurance, an improvement in the social wage, implemented under the Accord. The Accord was vital to shaping not only industrial relations and economic policy for the life of the Labor governments, 1983 to 1996, but also to the development of superannuation policy. Real wages declined, with "catch up" partly taking the form of superannuation. But the economy prospered and there was a spurt of employment growth. Eventually the back of inflation was broken and, as a result of the reforms under the Hawke and Keating governments, the foundation for a robust economic investment was laid.

Prior to the 1970s, occupational superannuation existed as a fringe benefit among relatively well paid white-collar and public-sector

---

[4] See Whitehead, Donald Henry (1973) *Stagflation and Wages Policy in Australia*, *Loc. Cit.*, p. 124.
[5] *Ibid.*, p. 128.

workers. As noted in Chapter 2, the viability of the mostly defined benefit plans in the private sector relied on poor vesting and inadequate portability terms. During the 1970s, the private, occupationally-based system of superannuation was significantly expanded to cover a broader range of employees in response to the trade unions' growing campaigns to increase access to this form of employment-related benefit. The Hancock Review under Whitlam outlined the problem that needed to be addressed: How to extend superannuation coverage to all employees as a right. In reaction to campaigns by stevedores, sections of the pulp and paper industry, the storemen and packers, and other pockets of unionised industry, superannuation was on the national agenda. In 1979 the ACTU Congress voted to make superannuation a major policy issue.[6] Tom McDonald notes that "Bill Kelty attributes much of the vision of creating an industry-based superannuation scheme to Charlie Fitzgibbon, where the wharfies were one of the first to 'go off'. They had to engage in a significant industrial action to achieve superannuation. The price the employers wanted them to pay was to agree to the workers being permanent, and initially the union was opposed to this."[7]

The late 1970s in Australia were characterised by policies aimed at achieving wage restraint through a process of wage indexation: wage increases were tied to measured changes in prices. Campaigning for occupational superannuation, as a form of deferred wages, provided one way of circumventing the wage-indexation processes sanctioned by the Australian industrial relations tribunals at the time.

---

[6] Plowman, David & Weavan, Garry (1989) "Unions and Superannuation", in Ford, Bill & Plowman, David (1989), editors, *Australian Unions. An Industrial Relations Perspective*, Second Edition, Macmillan Company of Australia, Crows Nest [Sydney], p. 251.

[7] Tom McDonald interview, August 2012. Wharf-side employees – "wharfies" – resisted becoming permanent employees of a particular company because under the guild-like, union organised roster scheme, they regarded themselves as being "free". See: Sheridan, Tom (1998) "Regulating the Waterfront Industry 1950-1968", *Journal of Industrial Relations*, Vol. 40, No. 3, pp. 441-60.

Figure 38: Gary Weaven, executive chairman of Industry Funds Services in his Melbourne office, 31 January 2006, *Australian Financial Review* photo by Jessica Shapiro. Source: Fairfax Archives.

The political environment played a crucial role. As Simon Crean says, "my recollection [was] that [the Hancock reforms] were blocked, and [we thought], 'if we can't do it politically, then let's do it industrially.'"[8] The expansion of occupational superannuation arrangements continued throughout the 1980s and 1990s, and may be attributed to wage-fixing arrangements, legislative provisions, and a range of political imperatives. The building unions created the first major, mass-membership industry fund. As shown in Chapter 3, it was a model of drift and stab and creative opportunism, where several players, Bill Kelty and Paul Keating in particular, changed the agenda for everyone else. In 1985, the ACTU agreed to limit a national productivity claim in return for an extension of occupational

---

[8] Simon Crean interview, May 2013. The proposed reforms were discarded under the Fraser government. Under the Whitlam government certain public-sector superannuation reforms were blocked in the Senate, but not the Hancock Report's recommendations themselves.

superannuation entitlements from the Federal Government. From the government's perspective, the agreement provided a mechanism to grant wage increases (albeit deferred), while not deeply adding to rising inflationary pressures. Employer groups, however, were opposed. In 1986 they appealed to the High Court of Australia, challenging the definition of superannuation as an industrial issue. In May of that year, the High Court handed down a landmark decision finding that superannuation was a workplace matter and could be included in the pay and conditions specified under particular awards. This decision facilitated the incorporation of superannuation provisions into awards and led to further rapid growth in superannuation coverage. At the same time, occupational superannuation fed into policy concerns about the consequences of relatively low savings levels in Australia and the ageing of Australia's population.

The expansion of occupational superannuation culminated in the introduction of the *Superannuation Guarantee Act* in 1992, which made occupational superannuation a form of mandated savings that received favourable taxation treatment. By dealing with the retirement needs of employees in the context of macro-economic policy, the expansion of occupational superannuation was envisaged as a good for all. The legal powers of the Commonwealth, including the role of the industrial tribunals in conciliating and arbitrating disputes on superannuation, was constitutionally expanded in the 1980s and 1990s. The use of industrial relations law – extended and amplified through the use of the corporations' power – expanded occupational superannuation as the effective creation of property rights to superannuation.[9] This reference to "property rights" emphasises that access to mandatory employer contributions and employment-related, above-minimum provisions was associated with a person's relative status in the labour market. Employment was the means to attain that right. Those in favourable labour-market positions, with higher wages and greater employment

---

[9] Cf. Kelly, Paul (2011) *The March of Patriots, The Struggle for Modern Australia*, Melbourne University Press, Carlton (first published in 2009, updated in 2011), p. 59.

stability, had relatively high levels of superannuation coverage, which in turn was more likely to be at above-minimum SG rates.

Despite the considerable rhetoric about superannuation being one of the "three pillars" of Australia's retirement-income system, it is not an entirely settled position. There is still a good deal of uncertainty about the "objectives" of superannuation. Is it intended to supplement or to entirely replace reliance on the aged pension? The taxation arrangements surrounding superannuation have important implications for the Commonwealth budget and for retirement-income equity. It is here where the uncertainty on Australia's current Budgetary settings clouds what might otherwise be a more settled position on reasonable benefit limits and taxation of superannuation.

Figure 39: Two former ACTU Presidents who made a difference in superannuation changes: Then Minister for Trade, Simon Crean, and Minister for Resources, Energy and Tourism, Martin Ferguson, chat in the House of Representatives 27 May 2008, *Sydney Morning Herald* photo by Glenn McCurtayne. Source: Fairfax Archives.

The development of the modern system of superannuation in Australia can be summed up simply. As Bob Hawke put it, "... to use the language of our Chinese friends, it was win-win."[10] Even so, there was no magical, logical or easy progression to that outcome. Kelty and Keating were the main authors of this creation story. As Sword said, "… you have to give credit to Keating to make the right decision at the right time, when he was confronted with it."[11] In Keating's words, "oh, it is a piece of social science, the whole thing."[12] With Federal Treasury sceptical about the system, however, there has to be doubt about whether the current 9.5 per cent Superannuation Guarantee will reach 12 per cent, still less beyond.

Keating argues that from the start of the Hawke government, superannuation was on his agenda: "I wanted to see superannuation be equitably and generally available to the public. How precisely we would do that, we were not sure. But one thing we had to do was change the preferential tax treatment of lump sums. I did that two months after getting the job. The marginal rate on 5 per cent of the sum – effectively 3 per cent – then became a rate of tax of 15 per cent up to $50,000, and then 30 per cent over $50,000 when you took the lump sum out, but we were not taxing the funds themselves."[13] He wanted to encourage savings, true retirement savings, with regular payments drawn down over an individual's retirement period. Superannuation should not be like a one off lottery win, paid as a lump sum and quickly spent prior to retirees going on the aged pension. The reforms were aimed at increasing savings for annuities in old age. Keating explains, "[w]e had to stop people taking the money out and getting paid and leaving. Even [people] who changed jobs got their lump sum and they thought 'what will we do? We will have a cruise or pay the loan off?' None of it was about retirement income. I wanted a vested [retirement age of] 55 and have portability. These reforms were all done in 1983 to 1984."[14] Actually, 1983-84 merely marked the beginning of reforms that would eventually be applied to the whole industry.[15]

---

[10] Bob Hawke interview, December 2012.

[11] Greg Sword interview, June 2012.

[12] Paul Keating interview, March 2013.

[13] *Ibid.*

[14] *Ibid.*

[15] See Appendix 4 for details.

Then the government and the ACTU supported the attainment of the first 3 per cent industrially. Keating became instrumental to implementing the unions' superannuation aims. In the words of an informed observer at the time, "Mr Kelty acknowledged as much ... saying privately that it was Mr Keating who first articulated national superannuation as a politically achievable end – and a desirable priority – when Labor first came to power."[16] In fact, it was both of them, Kelty and Keating, from different perspectives, who united to smithy-forge a new system into shape. In 1989 the second 3 per cent in superannuation was pursued industrially, but the Australian Conciliation and Arbitration Commission[17] knocked it back. This was the genesis of the SGC legislation.

Gradually, superannuation funds were growing, and portability and vesting reforms were being achieved. In 1987, the Occupational Standards Act was introduced into Parliament. It set out prudential standards for the management of superannuation benefits. Keating's recollection is that "in 1988 [by] changing the tax treatment on the way into the fund [fund contributions] and in the fund [taxing earnings], streaming imputed credits of the fund [- these were the first reforms] – and now I have got the system up and ready to rumble."[18] This is to refer to the 15 per cent tax on contributions going in, the 15 per cent tax on earnings, the introduction of favourable, discounted capital gains tax policy to superannuation, and the rest. See Appendix 4 for a summary of those and other reforms. But the stumbling block was how to get the second 3 per cent through. "The [Industrial Relations] Commission knocks us back so I said to Bill, 'not only will I legislate for the two lots of 3 per cent, I will pick up all the ones that didn't get it',"[19] was Keating's promise.

---

[16] Noonan, Gerard (1985) "The Significance of the Super Deal", *The Australian Financial Review*, 13 September, p. 1. This section is highlighted in the copy of this clipping I received from Mr. Keating.

[17] See footnote 2 of Chapter 1 for changes in name over time of the main Commonwealth industrial relations tribunal.

[18] Paul Keating interview, March 2013.

[19] *Ibid.*

Keating believed that the government should legislate: "They all thought I would legislate this going to 6 per cent, but I had other thoughts. First of all, 50 per cent of the workforce hadn't got the first 3 per cent. They certainly wouldn't have got the second 3 per cent. We wanted a national scheme, because somehow if you give people no bargaining power and no awards, you can pick them up under the corporations' power by legislating for them. Then I wanted to go to 12.5 per cent, because you can't have a retirement-income policy stuck at 6 per cent. So I made this speech[20] because Kerin – the new Treasurer – and Hawke were backsliding on this."[21]

Keating acknowledges that both wings of the labour movement combined for a common purpose: "I don't claim sole credit by any means. The building and transport industries led the way, the ACTU pushed for it, many employers saw the wisdom of it, my cabinet colleagues supported it and of course, the I[ndustrial] R[elations] C[ommission] – a braver show then – implemented it."[22] The Australian superannuation story is part of the labour movement's historic mission to "civilise capitalism", to borrow Bede Nairn's terminology.

In Keating's summation, "these reforms have changed super-annuation from an income tax avoidance scheme for the affluent to an equitable and attractive retirement-income arrangement for ordinary Australians."[23] In Keating's view, he did not need to be prodded by the unions to enact superannuation reform. He had a coherent perspective and had been active from the start of the government in enacting reforms. Ultimately, however, the unions and the government were driven to pursue a common agenda. They influenced each other. In

---

[20] Keating, Paul (1991) "A Retirement Incomes Policy", address to the Australian Graduate School of Management, July 25, typescript, 17pp.

[21] Paul Keating interview, March 2013. From the public record, it is not clear that Hawke and Kerin were actually "backsliding", but there was concern in the ACTU and elsewhere that they might be, hence Keating's intervention. Unfortunately Hawke's memoirs are unrevealing on this point. Hawke, Bob (1994) *The Hawke Memoirs*, William Heinemann Australia, Port Melbourne.

[22] Keating, Paul (1991) "A Retirement Incomes Policy", *Loc. Cit.*, p. 3.

[23] *Ibid.*, p. 3.

Kelty's words, "the philosophical framework [of the Hawke and Keating governments might seem] a bit oblique, but in reality it was clear: Open up [the economy] to the rest of the world, increase productivity, promote competition – but part of the distribution would be powerful safety nets in national health care, superannuation, and wages. In turn these super safety nets would promote adaption and change, thus increasing productivity."[24] This was the Australian social democratic agenda of the 1980s and 1990s. Weaven observed in 2016 that this "foresight has ensured that the system has become an indispensable part of Australia's economic and social policy, notwithstanding waning union power and often hostile opposition by the Liberal Party."[25]

Compulsory superannuation savings (along with other factors such as China's growth and its demand for Australian raw materials and services) helped Australia weather the storms of the global financial crisis toward the end of the first decade of the twenty first century. In 2015 the superannuation industry paid out, in the form of superannuation benefits to Australians, more than $61 billion. That is more than the government pays out by way of aged pension payments.[26] Whatever some of the short-term Federal Budget impacts of favourable tax change concessions for low and middle class savers, the overall long term benefit for the Budget is substantial – and critical for individuals and couples living in dignity in their retirement years.

The past is never a certain guide to the future. As Weaven says, "if we can get decent long-term returns with the effective compounding interest, then it will continue to be popular, and [the Australian system of superannuation] won't be that easy for future governments to adversely meddle. But I think there is a real, genuine danger to the system."[27] Future success depends on the continuing performance

---

[24] Email exchange, Bill Kelty to Mary Easson, 28 November 2013.

[25] Weaven, Garry (2016) 'Workers' Capital: The story of Industry Funds and Australia's Superannuation Revolution', Foenander Lecture at the University of Melbourne, 15 November 2016, p. 13.

[26] Silk, Ian (2015) 'ASFA Oration', 25 November, p. 1.

[27] Garry Weaven interview, March 2013.

of investment returns to members, structure and governance, and the alignment of interest between beneficiaries and the providers of services. The question, always, is whether the industry as a whole is performing optimally or just "well". There must be a never ending focus on doing better, in harmony with the best interests of the fund member. There is a great deal of diversity in the Australian superannuation industry. Although this book has concentrated on the industry funds, who make up less than 25 per cent of the total, their impact has been substantial – across the whole of industry. Keating and Kelty's superannuation legacy applies to all sectors – including government, retail, corporate and self-managed funds.

Knowing where the journey started is a useful platform for looking ahead. This book, in uncovering the creative innovation associated with the invention of mass superannuation in this country, provides a firm vantage point from which to view the story's beginnings – and to look ahead, mindful of the battles, scars, and dynamics that forged the modern system of superannuation in Australia. With so much at stake, the threats loom large, unrelentingly so. There will be more to come in this narrative.

APPENDIX 1: INTERVIEWS

Anna Booth, 29 August 2012

Chris Bowen, 26 May 2013

Simon Crean, 14 May 2013

Joe de Bruyn, 8 March 2013

Bert Evans, 22 May 2013

Bob Hawke, 13 December 2012

Paul Keating, 11 March 2013

Bill Kelty, 6 March 2013

Cheryl Kernot, 14 February 2013

Race Mathews, 20 June 2012

Tom McDonald, 30 August 2012

Kevin Rudd, 15 May 2013

Susan Ryan, 11 March 2013

Nick Sherry, 21 March 2012

Ian Silk, 6 March 2013

Greg Sword, 6 June 2012

Garry Weaven, 5 March 2013

General

Potential prompting questions:

By asking an indirect question which places people in a context they can understand and which allows them to tell a story about themselves or someone they knew.

Eliciting Anecdotes:

A real account of someone's experience, told from a particular perspective of the teller, refers to an historical event fixed in time.

Prompting sentences, such as:

Tell me about a time when someone had a major influence on the proposal?

If you were asked to give an address about the development of superannuation to a public meeting what would you tell your audience?

Imagine you are chatting to a friend about your experience, what would you talk about?

Pressing for Answers

Although the intention of the interview technique is for the interviewee to state their case as they see it, some questions were asked to prompt answers as to how decisions were taken. The intention was to enable informed consideration of the hypothesis that the ultimate determining factor of the decision-making process in superannuation policy delivery was political power – not the power (or the rationality) of technocrats.

Specific Questions

1. What were the problems that needed changing that caused you to consider campaigning for superannuation reform?

   Question Prompter: portability of superannuation benefits;

different benefit levels to blue and white collar workers; transferability on termination; adequacy of benefit levels; defined contribution versus defined benefit; whether offered at all to some workers, etc.

2. How were these issues manifested in your industry or other industries you were involved in?

   Question Prompter: Were there good examples of super benefits with certain employers? What were the examples of atrocious discrimination?

3. In your view, what were the origins of superannuation in Australia's unique industrial relations system in the mid-1980s?

   Question Prompter: ability to bargain, right to take industrial action in campaigning for superannuation benefits, or legal issues such as secondary boycotts.

4. How did your fund come into being? Were employers opposed? How were some won over?

   Question Prompter: There must be a story about how this happened? (Not a Question for all interviewees).

5. How significant was the 'Australia Reconstructed' visit?

   Question Prompter: Were you there? Would the reforms have happened anyway? Who associated with that visit was influential? (Not a Question for all interviewees).

6. Can you describe the phases of change?

   Question Prompter: 3 per cent becoming universal, then the campaign in your industry, the role of the Accord?

7. How did the Accord signify and come into prominence?

   Question Prompter: How did that happen?

8. What was your personal role?

   Question Prompter: And who do you think deserves to be singled out (i) overall; and (ii) in your industry?

9. What was the impact on Australian markets, including the stock markets?

Question Prompter: Do you have a view on this, or was this a question for the experts?

10. Would you like to make any international comparisons with regard to Australia's superannuation system?

Question Prompter: How do you think we compare with other retirement income systems?

11. Do you think that the Australian system is transferable to other jurisdictions?

Question Prompter: Have you been asked this? Is there anyone you would recommend making further contact with? In Australia or elsewhere?

12. What do you see as the identifying characteristics of the Australian model, including so-called industry funds?

Question Prompter: How would you summarise this? How does your industry's experience differ from others?

13. What do you perceive to be the unintended consequences of compulsory superannuation?

Question Prompter: For example, an interesting topic is whether, as Vince Fitzgerald and others asserted in the late 1980s to mid-1990s that a consequence of compulsory superannuation would be a reduction in personal savings and not much of an increase, if increase at all, of net savings. What about for low wage people having an opportunity to save for family home? What about the increased impost on ordinary people now required to make extraordinary financial decisions?

14. What are the potential future implications of the Australian model?

Question Prompter: What are challenges ahead? Could you imagine circumstances that could significantly affect the system as it currently exists?

15. What other reforms should be on the agenda and why?

Question Prompter: Should the compulsory contribution rate be 9 per cent to 12 per cent, or 15 per cent or something else? Any other priorities? What about loans for housing deposits, etc.?

16. Do you have any disappointments with the outcome?

    Question Prompter: For example, with the changes to banking and the role of Members' Equity?

17. In retrospect, what did you think you and others were doing at the time the Australian system was created? Did you foresee the superannuation industry as it exists today?

    Question Prompter: Was it improvised? What was the role of the ACTU, unions, employers, Government?

18. What was the role of experts?

    Question Prompter: For example, actuaries and professional firms, including asset consultants, lobby and interest groups, policymakers, consultants, and academics?

19. How significant was the Business Council of Australia (BCA) and other employer bodies?

    Question Prompter: The BCA was formed in 1983 and played a major role in the Hawke-Keating years in putting the voice of 'Big Business' to government.

20. How important was the 1977 decision by the Fraser government not to introduce a national superannuation system?

21. Who were the 'decision-makers' on superannuation between 1977 and the release of Accord Mark 2 (1985)?

22. Did the early supporters of broad based superannuation foresee the impact on the financial sector?

    Question Prompter: For example, layers of jobs for consultants, investment managers, financial advice, financial planners etc.?

23. Were the early discussions just about coverage and accumulations – or was the decummulation phase also considered?

Question Prompter: Did anyone foresee or discuss that moving to DC (Accumulation) schemes would leave members vulnerable to market and other risks?

24. Who else do you think should be interviewed?

Question Prompter: Especially in employer, arbitration, government and expert ranks.

Appendix 3: Australia's Economic Performance Based on Select Indicators

Figure 40: Inflation, 1956-2016

Since the mid-1970s there has been a steady reduction in inflation; the Accord assisted in breaking the wages-inflation spiral. Source: www.tradingeconomics; Australian Bureau of Statistics

Source: www.tradingeconomics; Australian Bureau of Statistics

Figure 41: Unemployment Rate, 1976-2016

Unemployment fell in the period of the Accord, but shot up fast in the early 1990s recession, then slowly dropped co-inciding at the start of the 1990s with wage-tax cuts and the SGC legislation. Source: www.tradingeconomics; Australian Bureau of Statistics

Source: www.tradingeconomics; Australian Bureau of Statistics

Figure 42: Growth in GDP Rate, 1960-2016

The volatility of GDP growth in the Hawke-Keating period is starkly illustrated here - a sharp economic recovery, then the impact of the recession in the early 1990s, followed by a long, continuous boom. Source: www.tradingeconomics; Australian Bureau of Statistics

Source: www.tradingeconomics; Australian Bureau of Statistics

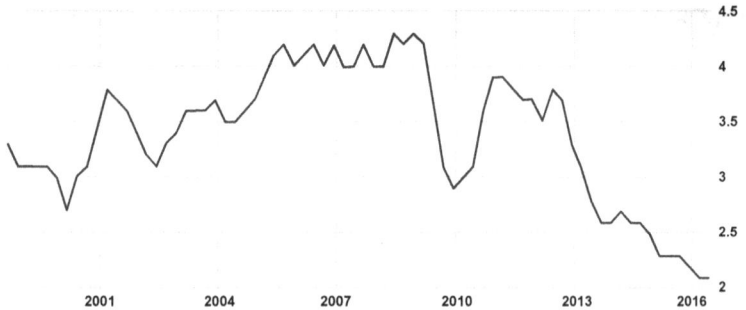

Figure 43: Annual Change in Hourly Rates of Pay, 1998-2016

Annual wage growth is now amongst the lowest since data has been collected. Source: www.tradingeconomics; Australian Bureau of Statistics

Source: www.tradingeconomics; Australian Bureau of Statistics

234

Figure 44: Australian Population Growth, 1960-2016

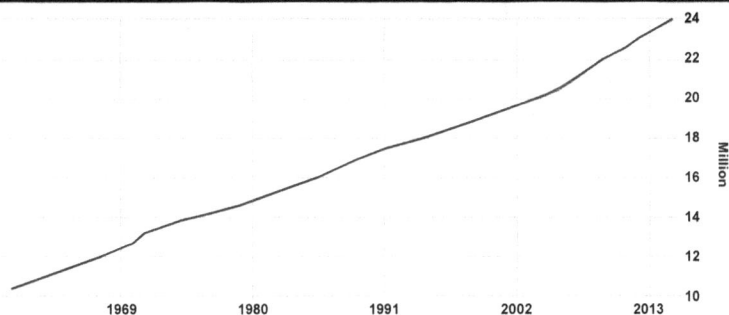

Steady population growth has been a feature of Australia's economic story in the past 50 years. Source: www.tradingeconomics; Australian Bureau of Statistics

Source: www.tradingeconomics; Australian Bureau of Statistics

Appendix 4: Major Superannuation, Industrial Relations, and Related Changes in Australia

Details showing industrial, political and economic events relevant to superannuation. See Appendix 3 for certain over-lapping lead economic indicators.

Period	Change	Implications
2 December 1972	Labor elected to government after 23 years in Opposition.	Gough Whitlam becomes Prime Minister, Frank Crean Treasurer, Clyde Cameron Minister for Industrial Relations.
March 1973	Whitlam government establishes the *National Superannuation Committee of Inquiry*.	Chaired by Professor Keith Hancock, Australia's retirement policies are reviewed together with consideration of a national superannuation system.
1973-74	Oil shocks.	Australia's industrial relations system copes poorly, with inflation and wages spiralling upwards.
September 1973	Partial abolition of the means test for the Age Pension	For those aged 75 years
1974	Australian Bureau of Statistics conducts the first national survey of superannuation coverage.	Survey shows 32 per cent of the workforce is covered by superannuation – 36 per cent male; 15 per cent female. 24 per cent of people in the private sector have super cover compared with 58 per cent in the public sector.
31 January 1975	Final report of Taxation Review Committee (Asprey Committee) completed.	Review commissioned in 1972 by the previous government headed by Mr Justice K. W. Asprey, of the NSW Supreme Court, includes in its final report consideration of the tax treatment of superannuation contributions, income, and benefits. Review puts forward two alternate 'views' on taxation arrangements supporting the status quo or fundamental changes applying to new schemes only. The Review is critical of the relatively low tax rate of 5 per cent applied to lump sum superannuation benefits that had been in place since 1915.
May 1975	Further partial abolition of the means test for the Age Pension.	For those aged between 70-74 years.

236

Appendix 4: Major Superannuation, Industrial Relations and Related Changes in Australia

June 1975	Old Age Pensions linked to 25 per cent of average weekly earnings.	Government policy that pensions will be indexed annually.
November-December 1975	Whitlam government dismissed by Governor General Sir John Kerr, Malcolm Fraser appointed Prime Minister and wins election.	Labor is swept from office in a landslide defeat.
1975-1981	A centralised wage indexation system operates between 1975 and 1981.	Partial indexation to limit the wage-inflation cycle. After a wave of strikes, the metal industry agreement (December 1981) for a $39 wage increase and 38-hour week flows through the Australian labour market.
1976	Pensions become subject to automatic increases twice yearly.	Also, the Age Pension assets test is abolished.
20 June 1977	Fraser government declines to establish a contributory national superannuation scheme.	Key Hancock Report recommendation rejected. Other recommendations under consideration.
1978	LUCRF Super formed.	Building on earlier attempts by other unions, the Storemen and Packers' Union popularises the case for superannuation among Australian trade unions.
12 July 1979	Fraser government formally rejects Hancock Inquiry recommendations.	Government announces the establishment of a Task Force to consider the role of occupational superannuation in providing for retirement and whether there is a need to revise or impose new standards for schemes.

November 1981	Report of the Committee of Inquiry into the Australian Financial System (Campbell Inquiry) released.	The Committee, which started its work in 1979, recommends sweeping changes across financial regulation including banking deregulation which the Fraser government refrained from. On superannuation, it concludes that existing taxation advantages for superannuation are inequitable when compared with other savings vehicles and suggested means of removing those inequities. Recommendations include: • income (investment income and employer contributions) should be taxed in the superannuation plan at an average marginal rate applicable to contributors; • that the 30/20 rule regarding investment in public sector entities should be abolished; • all contributions, both member and employer, should be tax deductible; and • all benefits, whether in pension or lump sum form, should be free of income tax.
1981-1982	Wages explosion.	Unemployment hits 10 per cent.
30 July 1982	Fraser Government rejects Campbell recommendations applying to superannuation.	Government says it has no intention to change the taxation treatment of lump sum superannuation benefits or to set a limit on the level of superannuation benefit that may be paid in the form of a lump sum.
1982	Reintroduction of wage indexation.	Centralised wage system re-instated after the 1981-82 wages explosion.
August 1982	The ALP and the ACTU reach agreement in principle on wages and related policy.	This is the first draft of what will be the first Accord, adopted in February 1983, which will see unions trade off wage rises if prices and other incomes are controlled under a Labor government.
November 1982	Temporary wage freeze.	Prime Minister Malcolm Fraser announces six month wages freeze.
January 1983	Peter Nolan suddenly resigns as ACTU Secretary.	Replaced by Bill Kelty as ACTU Secretary.
3 February 1983	Bob Hawke replaces Bill Hayden as leader of the Australian Labor Party (ALP)	Hawke widely seen as a credible leader; he campaigns under the mantra of "national reconciliation, national recovery, national reconstruction."
3 February 1983	Malcolm Fraser calls election for the House of Representatives and half the Senate.	Fraser had hoped a snap election would surprise Labor with "their pants down" as he put matters, and cause Labor to rally behind its existing leader Bill Hayden. But earlier on the same day, Labor switched leaders.

Appendix 4: Major Superannuation, Industrial Relations and Related Changes in Australia

21 February 1983	Prices and Incomes Accord signed between the ACTU and the ALP.	Under the Accord between the ALP and the ACTU, trade unions agreed to make "no extra claims" in exchange for real wage maintenance "over time", with social wage improvements, and union involvement in policy-making as part of the package. The Accord agreement signed during the election campaign, with inflation and unemployment hovering around 10 per cent.
5 March 1983	The ALP elected to government.	Bob Hawke as Prime Minister and Paul Keating as Treasurer.
11-14 April 1983	National Economic Summit held in Canberra.	The summit involved all political parties, unions and employer organisations and aimed to form a national consensus on economic policy. The Confederation of Australian Industry "expressly disagrees" with certain features of the Accord.
19 May 1983	Statement by Treasurer Keating announcing changes to the tax treatment of superannuation.	Policy initiatives in May 1983 include: higher levels of taxation on lump-sum superannuation and related payments; a non-retrospective tax increase on lump sums, excluding non-deductible contributions by individuals from a maximum effective rate of 3 per cent (i.e., 60 per cent on 5 per cent tax) to a maximum rate of 15 per cent for lump sums below $50,000 for recipients aged 55 or over, and 30 per cent for any excess over $50,000. For lump sums received by people under 55, a maximum rate of 30 per cent applies. Lump sums, however, are exempt from this tax if rolled over into another superannuation fund, an annuity or superannuation pension or an approved deposit fund – therefore "assisting portability" and encouraging savings.
26 May 1983	Final report of the Commonwealth Task Force on Occupational Superannuation, commissioned by the former government.	Proposals in the report include: • Eligibility for tax concessions for superannuation funds to depend on the vesting and preservation of retirement benefits in accordance with minimum prescribed standards. • A requirement for the regular disclosure of certain information to members of superannuation funds. • The removal of certain constraints to facilitate the achievement of a limited market for annuities among certain groups such as those using annuities for pre-retirement purposes and some age pensioners aged 70 years or over.
15 August 1983	A joint media release by the Treasurer, the Confederation of Australian Industry (CAI) and the ACTU on reform.	Government commissions an Inter-Departmental Committee on Issues and Broad Options Concerning National Superannuation. Committee reports in October 1984.

23 September 1983	In the National Wage Case, the Commission reintroduces six monthly wage indexation.	The Commission observes that lack of commitment had ended the previous indexation system. The Commission will now require a 'no extra claims' commitment to be made when each award is varied. This commitment is included as a requirement for National Wage increases up to September 1994. A package of principles adopted by the Commission provides for a 38 hour week to be introduced by consent, if there are "cost offsets", and provides tests for other award increases.
12 December 1983	Float of Australian dollar	The exchange rate reform was recommended by the Campbell Inquiry.
4 April 1984	Commission's National Wage Case decision	Awards are generally varied to give effect to the 4.1 per cent CPI increase, effective first pay period on or after 6 April 1984.
1984	BUSS – superannuation for the building industry – created.	Model for subsequent industry funds is supported by the ACTU, with a Board comprising equal numbers of employer and employee/union representatives.
June 1984	40 new foreign exchange licenses granted	Treasurer Keating continues financial deregulation and opening of the Australian financial system.
1984	Age pension assets test reintroduced.	Family home excluded.
11 September 1984	Abolition of the '30/20' Rule.	This Rule had applied from 1961 when the Government introduced a requirement that life insurance and superannuation funds hold 30 per cent of their assets in the form of government securities, at least two thirds of which had to be Commonwealth Government securities. It was originally driven by a perceived need to ensure a market for government debt.
1 December 1984	Labor returned to government.	Prime Minister Bob Hawke defeats Andrew Peacock, Opposition Leader & Leader of the Liberal Party.
February 1985	16 banking licenses granted to 16 foreign banks	Treasurer Keating continues financial deregulation and opening of the Australian financial system.
3 April 1985	Commission's National Wage Case decision	Increase of 2.6 per cent operative 6 April 1985 made by the Commission.

Appendix 4: Major Superannuation, Industrial Relations and Related Changes in Australia

September 1985	Accord Mark II	Support for superannuation in awards. Key areas of agreement include: • Superannuation should be extended and improved on an industry by industry, occupation by occupation or, in limited circumstances, company by company, basis. • The improvement should be offset against national productivity and be based on a three per cent wage equivalent. • Negotiations can proceed on superannuation on the above basis provided that the cost impact of new or improved arrangements except in very isolated circumstances will not occur before 1 July 1986. • Before the expiration of the current parliament the Government will legislate to establish a national safety net superannuation scheme to which employers will be required to contribute where they have failed to provide cover for their employees under an appropriate scheme.
September 1985	The ACTU presents claims to the Conciliation and Arbitration Commission in the National Wage Case.	The government supports the ACTU's claim that three percentage points of wages should be contributed by employers to an individual superannuation account. In supporting the unions, the government argues before the Commission that employees should enjoy a structural or ongoing benefit in recognition of their years' of wage responsibility – adding the layer of superannuation to the agenda as part of an expanded social wage.
4 November 1985	Commission's National Wage Case decision.	Decision to increase awards by 2.6 per cent operative on 6 April.
February 1986	Commission decides in the ACTU's and the government's favour, agreeing that up to 3 percentage points of wages can be vested in each employee's name in a superannuation fund through a process of award negotiation between individual trade unions, employer groups, and enterprises.	Negotiations involved the splitting of productivity "gains" with employers and went to deciding what part of the wages growth would be paid as take-home pay and what part would be withheld as employee savings – to go to superannuation.

241

1986	Employer groups, including the Confederation of Australian Industry, challenge the Commission's decision in the High Court.	The employers' argument is that superannuation is not an industrial matter within section 51 (xxxv) of the Constitution.
14 May 1986	Keating's "banana republic" statement.	On a radio programme with Sydney radio's John Laws, Keating says: "If this government cannot get the adjustment, get manufacturing going again, and keep moderate wage outcomes and a sensible economic policy, then Australia is basically done for. We will just end up being a third-rate economy, a banana republic."
15 May 1986	High Court rules in favour of the Conciliation and Arbitration Commission on superannuation as a valid matter capable of being considered by the tribunal.	The matter is known as the "Manufacturing Grocers' Case" (after the union that brought the matter to Court) or the "Superannuation Case" (1986) 160 CLR 341.
26 June 1986	National Wage Case – Commission issues new guidelines.	Commission agrees to six monthly wage indexation with some changes to the wage guideline principles. In particular a new superannuation principle provides for agreements to be approved for superannuation contributions of up to 3 per cent, but the Commission rejects a claim for such payments to be arbitrated. The package operates for two years from 1 July 1986. It also provides for a national wage increase of 2.3 per cent from 1 July 1986.
23 December 1986	Commission adjourns the National Wage Case.	
June 1986 to March 1987	Worsening economic conditions in Australia.	Evidence to the Commission cites CPI increases of 10 per cent per annum compared to the OECD average of 2.5 per cent, increases in the national debt and the costs of servicing it, pressure on interest rates, no growth in non-farm Gross Domestic Product, negative growth in terms of trade, and a rise in unemployment from 7.6 per cent in June 1986 to 8.2 per cent nine months later.
March 1987	Commission issues New Wage Guidelines – Two Tier Adjustments.	The new principles do not provide for wage indexation. They provide for 'two tier' increases, with the first tier a $10 per week increase to award rates. A second tier adjustment not exceeding 4 per cent is available in return for "measures implemented to improve efficiency" under the "restructuring and efficiency principle", including changes to "work practices and management practices". It provides for arbitration of superannuation claims.

May 1987	The *Occupational Superannuation Standards* Bill is introduced into Federal parliament, which sets for the first time separate prudential standards for the management of superannuation accumulations and their benefits.	The Bill seeks to universalise minimum superannuation standards. The Bill includes provisions for: (i) the vesting of benefits in the employee, not the employer, prior to retirement; (ii) preservation of all benefits to age 55; (iii) greater member involvement in the control of superannuation funds; and (iv) a requirement that funds submit returns to the regulatory authority to certify compliance with the required standards. The proposed legislation provides for regulation in insurance, superannuation, and actuarial areas to be brought under the responsibility of a single statutory body, the Insurance and Superannuation Commissioner.
1987	Insurance and Superannuation Commission (ISC) is established.	Commissioner appointed.
June 1987	Accord Mark III	End of formal indexation of wages with formation of a two-tier wages system based on requiring efficiency offsets for wage increases.
11 July 1987	Labor returned to government.	Prime Minister Bob Hawke defeats John Howard, Opposition Leader & Leader of the Liberal Party.
20 October 1987	"Black Tuesday" stock market crash	Known as "Black Monday" in the United States (due to time differences), this marks the crash in global stock markets and the beginning of tough economic times. There is a 41.8 per cent fall in the Australian stock market by end of the month.
17 December 1987	Commission adjourns the National Wage Case.	
21 December 1987	Hawke Government introduces the *Occupational Superannuation Standards Act 1987* (OSSA).	Operating standards are prescribed for the vesting of benefits from employer and employee contribution; preservation of benefits until age 55; more member involvement in the control of superannuation funds; and security of members' benefits.
5 February 1988	Commission issues new Wage Adjustments.	A flat increase of $6.00 is operative from 5 February.

May 1988	Policy statement issued by the Treasurer on the *Reform of the Taxation of Superannuation*	Contained measures to bring forward payment of superannuation taxation liabilities by introducing a tax on contributions and reducing tax on benefits. Included proposal for reasonable benefits limit (RBL) arrangements.
May 1988	Keating's "bringing home the bacon" 1988/89 Budget speech.	Keating exuberantly says that the Budget and all the economic reforms of the government will soon pay big economic dividends.
June 1988	Kirribilli Agreement	Agreement between Prime Minister Bob Hawke and Treasurer Paul Keating, witnessed by businessman Sir Peter Abeles and ACTU Secretary Bill Kelty, on an orderly transition from the former to the latter in heading the government.
1 July 1988	Reasonable Benefits Limit changes.	The 25 May 1988 announcement takes effect.
Accord Mark IV	Structural Efficiency Principle.	Introduces the Structural efficiency Principle and commencement of award restructuring aimed at minimising demarcation disputes between unions and introducing more flexible job descriptions in awards.
12 August 1988	Commission issues New Wage Guidelines – "Structural Efficiency Guidelines".	Two increases at least six months apart are made available, the first one of 3 per cent (after 1 September 1988) and the second a flat rate of $10 (at least six months later). The 'restructuring and efficiency principle' is replaced with the 'structural efficiency principle'. Under this principle increases are available if the parties to the award formally agree to cooperate positively in a fundamental review of the award with a view to implementing measures to improve the efficiency of industry and provide workers with access to more varied, fulfilling and better paid jobs. All aspects of award provisions are mentioned as being appropriate for review, including classification structures, and provisions regulating working hours.

1988	The *Taxation of Superannuation* statement is made by the Treasurer.	New policy is announced that the tax treatment of superannuation will be brought into line with the tax treatment of other forms of savings such as bank deposits. That is, income will be taxed on the way into the superannuation account, as with the after-tax income of deposits in a bank account; earnings in the super account will be taxed as they accumulate, as interest in a bank account accumulates and is taxed; and that funds will be free to be taken out, as savings can be freely taken from a bank account. New tax rates nominated: Tax at 15 per cent to be applied to all employer contributions and to tax-deductible contributions made by the self-employed. A further tax, at 15 per cent, to be applied to the earnings within a fund. The extension of dividend imputation system to superannuation announced. The Reasonable Benefits Limit or RBL regime is introduced to limit the total amount of concessionally taxed superannuation a person can receive over their lifetime. This is designed to stop chief executive officers and people at the top of industry on the cusp of retirement protecting income by being awarded large sums by way of employer superannuation contributions.
February 1989	Commission adjourns consideration of a review of the Wage Principle Guidelines.	
1989	Treasurer Paul Keating, and the Minister for Social Security Brian Howe, outline the government's retirement income policy: *Better Incomes: Retirement Income Policy into the Next Century.*	The document formulated the argument of the "three pillars": • a taxpayer-provided age pension, the basic anti-destitution payment; • a mandated fully funded, privately managed occupational contribution scheme, superannuation; and • a voluntary retirement savings system of discretionary superannuation contributions encouraged and supported by concessionality of the tax system.

7 August 1989	In the National Wage Case, Commission issues refinement Guidelines – introducing tests for what is expected to be achieved under the structural efficiency principle.	Adjustment of pay will be allowable for completion of successful exercises under the structural efficiency principle. It provides for all award rates to be "broad-banded" into generic classification levels, to replace the hundreds of award rates set by reference to a narrow function. Award rates are to be set by reference to the metals and building tradesperson rate of $356.30 and $50.70 per week supplementary payment. They are to be set on the basis of relative skill, responsibility and the conditions under which the particular work is normally performed. The decision provides a first increase of $10 per week for workers at the basic skill/trainee level; $12.50 per week at the semi-skilled worker level; and $15.00 per week or 3 per cent, whichever is the higher, at the tradesman or equivalent level and above; and a second increase of the same order as the first increase, to be paid not less than six months after the first increase. The second instalment of the structural efficiency adjustment should only be available if the Commission is satisfied that the principle has been properly implemented and will continue to be implemented effectively.
February 1990	Under Accord Mark VI, the ACTU approached the Conciliation and Arbitration Commission to approve the industrial negotiation of a further three percentage points of superannuation contributions under the Award system – to bring the quantum under award superannuation to 6 per cent of wages. The government committed to extend the 3 per cent contribution in awards and agreements to 6 per cent. The claim is rejected.	After the Commission rejects the ACTU's claim for the further Award contribution to superannuation, its decision triggers a commitment to the ACTU by the government that, under the Corporations power of the Constitution, the government would legislate for at least a further three percentage points of wage-equivalent superannuation contributions to be paid on behalf of all employees. The Treasurer pledges that this will include bringing the first three percentage points to those employees who lacked the bargaining power industrially to secure it in the first instance – in the main, part-time workers and the low-paid, a high proportion of whom were women.

Appendix 4: Major Superannuation, Industrial Relations and Related Changes in Australia

24 March 1990	Labor returned to government.	Albeit narrowly, Bob Hawke again defeats Liberal and Opposition Leader Andrew Peacock.
29 November 1990	Treasurer Keating declares "this is the recession that Australia had to have".	September quarter of 1990 shows a 1.8 per cent fall in Gross Domestic Product.
16 April 1991	In the National Wage Case, Commission issues refinement Guidelines – declining to approve enterprise bargaining guidelines.	The structural efficiency principle continues with changes. It provides for a 2.5 per cent general increase in award rates, subject to the requirements of the structural efficiency principle. The Commission decides not to move to a system of enterprise bargaining supported by the ACTU and government, and opposed by employers, because the parties lacked the "maturity" to undertake such bargaining, and because the Commission has "major concerns" about: • The incompleteness of the award reform process and its application at the enterprise level; • The inadequate development of the 'receptive environment' necessary for the success of enterprise bargaining beyond the scope of the present system; • The fundamental disagreements between the parties and interveners about the nature of the proposed form of enterprise bargaining and their failure to deal with various significant issues; and • The potential for excessive wage outcomes. • It states that the unresolved issues require further attention and debate, if "industrial disputation and excessive wage outcomes" are to be avoided.
3 June 1991	Keating resigns as Treasurer after unsuccessfully challenging Bob Hawke for the leadership of the Parliamentary Labor Party and *ipso facto* the Prime Ministership.	Keating quits ministerial office and goes to the backbench. John Kerin becomes Treasurer.
July 1991	With the 1991 Budget process the new Treasurer is advised by Treasury not to proceed with a compulsory charge for superannuation.	In discussions and media "leaks", the ACTU makes clear to the Prime Minister and Treasurer that if the government walks away from compulsory superannuation, to at least 6 per cent of wages, the ACTU will no longer operate general wages policy within the Accord framework.

25 July 1991	Keating's delivers a landmark speech on superannuation to an audience at the Australian Graduate School of Management at the University of NSW.	Keating argues the government should legislate a mandatory twelve percentage point charge to be paid by employers as part of productivity sharing under the Accord wage restraint model. The speech helps shape the debate within the government on superannuation policy, reaffirms Keating's leadership credentials, and sketches out a future for the superannuation system under a compulsory model.
20 August 1991	The Budget Speech sets out a 9 per cent target for the guarantee charge but said a further 3 per cent, that is, the full 12 per cent, will be considered, including reaching it by way of tax cuts.	In the Budget, Treasurer John Kerin announces that from 1 July 1992, under a new system to be known as the Superannuation Guarantee (SG), employers will be required to make superannuation contributions on behalf of their employees.
30 October 1991	Commission issues National Wage Case guidelines.	Commission continues the availability of the April 1991 increase. It also provides for a new Enterprise Bargaining Principle, under which an enterprise agreement might be approved if certain tests were met, including that wage increases were 'based on the actual implementation of efficiency measures designed to effect real gains in productivity'. The Commission says that the submissions of the parties supported the introduction of enterprise bargaining but also 'revealed a diversity of opinions and a failure to confront practical problems'. It says that there is "little prospect … that further postponement will lead to more fully developed proposals or to the resolution of the points of disagreement."
December 1991	John Kerin resigns as Treasurer.	On 9 December Ralph Willis is appointed Treasurer.
21 December 1991	Having defeated Bob Hawke in a leadership ballot, Paul Keating is sworn in as Prime Minister. '	John Dawkins becomes Treasurer.
February 1992	Prime Minister's "One Nation" Statement	Prime Minister Keating promises a number of transport and other infrastructure development to stimulate the economy.
1992	"L-A-W law" tax cuts promise is made by the Prime Minister.	In responding to the Opposition's "Fightback!" policies, the Keating Government responds by promising to match the income tax proposals without a Goods and Services Tax (GST). To demonstrate strength of intent, Keating promised two rounds of income tax cuts, legislating them and describing them as final. But four months later Keating announces that only half the promised tax cuts will be paid.

Appendix 4: Major Superannuation, Industrial Relations and Related Changes in Australia

1992	*Security in Retirement* Statement.	Treasurer Dawkins announces an increase the preservation age from 55 to 60, phasing in from July 2015 for people born after 30 June 1960.

2 April 1992	Treasurer John Dawkins introduces into Parliament the *Superannuation Guarantee Charge* Bill.	Employer superannuation contributions rise from four percentage points of ordinary-time earnings from 1 July 1992 to nine percentage points of ordinary-time earnings by July 2002.
		
		Financial Year
		Employer Annual Payroll < 1,000,000
		Employer Annual Payroll > 1,000,000
		
		           1995/96 5 6
		           1996/97 6 6
		           1997/98 6 6
		           1998/99 7 7
		           1999/00 7 7
		           2000/01 8 8
		           2001/02 8 8
		           2002/03 9 9
		
		From 1 July 1992, the government imposed a levy on those employers (the Superannuation Guarantee Levy/ Charge or SGC) who did not contribute the required amount to an employee's super fund

13 March 1993	Labor re-elected to government.	Widely expected to be defeated prior to polling day, Prime Minister Keating refers to the victory over Opposition and Liberal leader John Hewson as a "victory for the true believers".
1993	*Superannuation Industry (Supervision) Act, 1993.*	Legislation sets out minimum prudential and other standards that all funds need to comply with. The OSSA continues in force but many of its provisions were repealed and transferred to the SIS Act.
1993	World Bank endorses Australia's three pillars system.	In its *Averting the Old Age Crisis* Report, the World Bank regards the Australian system for the provision of retirement income as best practice.
June 1993	*National Saving: A Report to the Treasurer* (Vince Fitzgerald Report) is released.	The Report advocates increasing household savings via superannuation but recommends that national savings also be increased by increasing public sector savings. Superannuation's role in increasing national savings is no longer seen as paramount, partly because Fitzgerald had doubts on the ultimate significance of superannuation to total national savings.
July 1993	*Second round* "L-A-W law" tax cuts deferred	Second round delayed because of Budget difficulties. The Prime Minister then states he will divert them to superannuation but his government doesn't last long enough to implement this plan.

1993	*Industrial Relations Reform Act*	Government extends powers and jurisdiction of the industrial relations tribunals by using "corporations powers" under international treaties to which the Commonwealth is signatory. Effectively, this extends the jurisdiction of Commonwealth law including more clearly in determining powers to determine superannuation matters.
October 1993	Commission's *Wage Fixing Principles* Decision	The Commission continues to make available structural efficiency increases, and provides for an additional $8 increase to be generally available award by award.
December 1993	John Dawkins resigns as Treasurer.	Ralph Willis appointed Treasurer.
1994	Decision that the pension age for eligible women to be raised to 65, in a phased process.	Phased process between 1994 and 2014.
1 July 1994	Superannuation Complaints Tribunal was established.	The Tribunal deals with complaints about superannuation, specifically in the areas of regulated superannuation funds, annuities and deferred annuities.
August 1994	Commission in new National Wage Case sets out principles for enterprise bargaining.	Commission hands down a new package of principles. The principles make earlier increases available, without establishing new increases. The principles do not include the 'no extra claims' commitment, and describe the role of awards as a 'safety net' for enterprise bargaining.
May 1995	In the Budget of 1995, Treasurer Ralph Willis announces the government's intention of lifting superannuation contributions for all employees from nine percentage points of wages to fifteen percentage points by the 2002 income year.	The Treasurer foreshadows that the next three rounds of personal income tax cuts will be paid as savings rather than as cash – designed to bring the superannuation contributions of each employee to the equivalent of twelve percentage points of wages.

There is a condition, however, as under Accord Mark VIII it was agreed that a new principle would be established within the wages system, whereby a co-payment would be made by each employee, matching that provided by the government by way of the tax cuts. This would amount to one percentage point of wages to be paid by the employer on behalf of each employee to their superannuation fund in lieu of one percentage point of cash which would have otherwise gone to their wage packet. This one percentage point was to have been withheld and paid over each of the three years, 1997-98, 1998-99 and 1999-2000. Three percentage points in all.

Those three percentage points of personal saving, matching the government's three percentage point tax cuts, total six percentage points, meaning that the overall level of superannuation contributions would be to fifteen percentage points. |

Appendix 4: Major Superannuation, Industrial Relations and Related Changes in Australia

1995	Superannuation coverage for women reaches 85 per cent.	This is up from 25 per cent in 1983.
October 1995	Commission issues decision on Safety Net Adjustment.	The Commission provides for earlier increases including the October 1993 first $8, and a second adjustment of $8 from September 1994 at enterprise level, subject to certain tests, and a second $8 at award level from March 1995, subject to tests including a six month gap with the last award increase. It provides for a third $8 at enterprise level from September 1995, and at award level from March 1996, subject to various tests such as a 12 month gap between the second and third safety net increases. A new "minimum wage" clause is established to be included in awards, linked not to needs but to the minimum classification rate in most Federal awards. This is the rate of a classification in the Metal Industry Award. All awards are linked to the rates in that award as a result of the August 1989 structural efficiency reviews, an extraordinary feature of that era's wage fixation.
2 November 1995	Shadow Treasurer Peter Costello announces Opposition policy.	Costello supports SGC to 9 per cent – reversing previous opposition – and calls for employee choice and for funds to "compete for business" in an address to the Association of Superannuation Funds of Australia.
1996	In the 1996 election campaign John Howard promises to maintain the value of the Keating government's 1995 Budget superannuation measures.	On election, Howard walks away from Labor's SGC commitment as a 'non-core' promise and legislates to remove the 1995 Labor tax cuts payable to superannuation.
2 March 1996	Labor defeated, Liberal National Coalition elected to government.	With John Howard as Prime Minister and Peter Costello as Treasurer.
1996	Government reviews policy to allow employees be able to 'opt out' by having the opportunity to receive wages or salary instead of superannuation guarantee contributions.	Policy is deferred and then dropped.

1996 Budget	Introduction of the superannuation surcharge for higher income earners and other changes.	Other measures include: • Increasing the general age limit for superannuation contributions from 65 to 70 years; • Allowing banks, building societies, credit unions and life insurance companies to provide superannuation in the form of Retirement Savings Accounts (RSAs); • Offering an income tax rebate for people who contributed to the superannuation fund or RSA of a non-working or low income spouse; and • Allowing employees who earn between $450 and $900 per month to have the option of choosing between Superannuation Guarantee Contributions or the equivalent in wages and salary; • Abandoning increasing superannuation beyond the 9.0 per cent phase-in.
1 July 1996	Superannuation guarantee charge rises to 6 per cent of an employer's base year payroll for all employees.	Phasing in of the 9 per cent continues.
May 1996–March 1997	*Financial System Inquiry* commences chaired by businessman Stan Wallis.	Report is influential in informing the subsequent changes to superannuation industry regulation by the Australian Prudential Regulation Authority (APRA) and for measures to promote competition between funds, including the establishment of the SMSF arrangements and choice of superannuation fund by employees.
September 1996	High Court rules in favour of the constitutional validity of the *Industrial Relations Reform Act 1993*.	Confirms wider powers of the Commonwealth in the field of labour law, based on ILO and other international treaty obligations.
October 1996	*Workplace Relations and Other Legislation Amendment Act 1996*	Howard government passes new industrial legislation. The government's intention is to exclude superannuation as an "allowable award matter", but this is thwarted in discussions with the Australian Democrats, whose support is required for passage of the legislation through the Senate.
March 1997	Final report of the Financial System Inquiry (the "Wallis Report") is issued.	Report advocates superannuation choice and other changes to the superannuation system.
13 May 1997	1997-98 Budget announcements.	These include the establishment of a broad-based savings tax rebate, preservation of all benefits from 1 July 1999, increasing the superannuation preservation from 55 to 60 years on a phased-in basis and a 'Deferred Pension Bonus Plan' which offers a financial incentive to defer retirement.

Appendix 4: Major Superannuation, Industrial Relations and Related Changes in Australia

1 July 1997	Retirement Savings Accounts (RSAs) introduced.	RSAs are intended to provide a simple, low-cost and low-risk savings product which employers can use as an alternative to making contributions to superannuation funds for their superannuation contributions for employees. Individuals can also use RSAs for their personal superannuation contributions.
20 September 1997	The Old Age Pension is maintained at minimum of 25 per cent of Average Weekly Ordinary Time Earnings.	This is legislated for.
1 July 1998	The Australian Prudential Regulation Authority (APRA) is formed – a statutory authority of the Australian Government and the prudential regulator of the Australian financial services industry.	The Australian Taxation Office (ATO) continues to carry out some regulatory functions and administer the superannuation taxation legislation. The Insurance and Superannuation Commission ceased to operate on the same date. These changes were in response to the recommendations of the Wallis Inquiry.
1 July 1998	Superannuation guarantee charge 7 per cent of employer's base year payroll for all employers.	Phasing in of the 9 per cent continues.
30 October 1998	Prime Minister John Howard and Liberal-National coalition is re-elected.	Howard defeats Labor Opposition Leader Kim Beazley; the Prime Minister prior to the election promised to introduce a goods and services tax (GST).
8 July 1999	*A New Tax System (Goods and Services Tax) Act 1999* comes into law.	GST in operation from 1 July 2000.
21 September 1999	Capital Gains Tax changes	A complying superannuation entity that acquires a CGT asset and makes a capital gain from a CGT event happening to that CGT asset is able to receive a 33⅓ per cent discount on the capital gain, providing that the CGT asset was owned by the taxpayer for at least 12 months.

8 October 1999	ATO takes over regulation of the SMSFs sector	Associated changes include: • Excluded funds become SMSFs/SAFs. • Borrowing via unit trusts is closed with a 10 year transition period. • The SIS Act is amended to establish a new category of small superannuation fund, the Self-Managed Superannuation Fund. • All contributions made by or on behalf of a member, and all earnings since 30 June 1999, are preserved benefits.
1 July 2000	Superannuation guarantee charge 8 per cent of employer's base year payroll for all employees.	Phasing in of the 9 per cent continues.
January 2001	Financial Sector Legislation Amendment Act is passed.	• Allows the ATO to disqualify persons considered not to be 'fit and proper' to manage a fund.
10 November 2001	Prime Minister John Howard and Liberal National coalition re-elected.	The so-called "Tampa" and post "9/11" election defeats Labor Opposition Leader Kim Beazley.
10 December 2001	Productivity Commission delivers its final report to the government for its inquiry into the *Superannuation Industry (Supervision) Act 1993* and certain other superannuation legislation.	Major recommendations include: • The need for funds regulated by the Australian Prudential Regulation Authority to prepare a risk management strategy; • Protection of lost member accounts with balances in excess of $1,000 should be removed; and, • Part 23 of the *Superannuation Industry (Supervision) Act 1993* should be amended to require the Minister to table in Parliament, as soon as practicable, the Australian Prudential Regulation Authority's advice and the reasons for the Minister's decision on whether to provide financial assistance to funds which suffer substantial loss from theft or fraud.
1 July 2002	Compulsory employer contributions under the Superannuation Guarantee rise to 9 per cent of income.	Consequence of the ten year phase-in.
1 July 2003	Introduction of the Government co-contribution of up to $1,500 for lower income employees.	This is made available to employees who make personal contributions such that the government co-contribution provides for a matching contribution for eligible personal contributions for low income earners (those earning less than $27,500 with a reduction of $0.08 per dollar earned up to $40,000), with a maximum government contribution of $1,000.

Appendix 4: Major Superannuation, Industrial Relations and Related Changes in Australia

1 July 2003	Requirement for employers to make quarterly superannuation guarantee payments.	This means less risk for employees where an employer seeks to avoid a once-a-year payment.
25 February 2004	Treasurer Costello releases *A more flexible and adaptable retirement income system* as part of 'Australia's Demographic Challenges' announcement.	Amongst other things this report proposes to allow access to a person's superannuation, in the form of an income stream, before they leave the work force (that is, transition to retirement pensions) and to scrap the work test for those under age 65.
3 June 2004	Superannuation regulations are improved on portability.	Easier rules allow portability of money between different superannuation accounts.
2004	The *Superannuation Safety Amendment Act 2004*	*Inter alia*, this provided for: • Fund auditors and actuaries to lodge auditor contravention reports with fund regulators; • Super trustee licensing to begin 1 July 2004; and, • Work test governing contributions made under age 65 ceased to operate. Work test remains for contributions made above age 65.
1 July 2004	Superannuation government co-contribution matching rate is increased.	This rises from 100 per cent to 150 per cent up to a maximum contribution of $1,500. Eligibility income thresholds increase to $28,000 for full contribution with a reduction of $0.05 per dollar earned up to $58,000.
9 October 2004	Prime Minister John Howard and Liberal National coalition re-elected.	Defeats Labor Opposition Leader Mark Latham
June 2005	Superannuation Choice legislation is passed.	This requires employers to provide employees with a choice of fund into which superannuation guarantee payments can be paid. The choice of fund proposals were first announced in the 1997-98 Budget. In 1998, the Superannuation Legislation Amendment (Choice of Superannuation Funds) Bill 1998 was the first Bill introduced to implement the measure, however, the Bill lapsed with the election in 2001. The Superannuation Legislation Amendment (Choice of Superannuation Funds) Bill 2002 was then introduced in 2002 and this was subsequently renamed as a 2003 Bill. The 2003 Bill was amended in 2003 and 2004 before finally passing the Parliament.

1 July 2005	Transition to Retirement (Superannuation) pensions becomes available.	A member can commence to receive a transition to retirement pension without having to leave the workforce or retire.
9 May 2006	In the Budget Speech, Treasurer Costello announces 'Simpler Super' and pledges to simplify superannuation.	Included in the package are: • Exemption from tax on end benefits for Australians aged 60 years or over from 1 July 2007; • No tax on a lump sum; • No tax on a superannuation pension; • Reasonable benefit limits to be abolished; • Transferring super between funds made easier; and, • Implementation 1 July 2007.
24 November 2007	Howard government defeated by Labor at national elections	Kevin Rudd becomes Prime Minister; Wayne Swan as Treasurer; both sworn in on 3 December 2007.
13 May 2008	The Henry Panel taxation review is commissioned by Treasurer Swan.	Review of Australia's tax system chaired by the Secretary to the Treasury, Dr Ken Henry AC, together with panel members Mr Greg Smith (Australian Catholic University), Dr Jeff Harmer (Secretary Australian Department of Families, Housing, Community Services and Indigenous Affairs), Heather Ridout (Australian Industry Group), and Professor John Piggott (University of New South Wales). The Panel also responds to a specific request from the Treasurer to review and propose recommendations on the adequacy of the retirement income system and the appropriateness of the relevant taxation arrangements.
15 September 2008	Start of Global Financial Crisis (GFC)	Collapse of US investment bank Lehman Brothers sets off the global recession.
2009	Superannuation funds now able to offer limited financial advice to their members.	This accelerates the formation of and relationships with financial planners and superannuation funds.
29 May 2009	Super System Review (SSR) is commissioned.	Report commissioned by the Minister for Superannuation and Corporate Law with the review into the governance, efficiency, structure and operation of Australia's superannuation system.
23 November 2009	Report of the Inquiry into Financial Products and Services in Australia.	Report by the Parliamentary Joint Committee on Corporations and Financial Services, chaired by Bernie Ripoll, MP. Report known as the "Ripoll Report".

Appendix 4: Major Superannuation, Industrial Relations and Related Changes in Australia

26 April 2010	Future of Financial Advice (FOFA) reforms are announced.	Minister Bowen, in response to the Ripoll Report, announces a series of reforms, including: • A prospective ban on conflicted remuneration structures including commissions and volume based payments, in relation to the distribution and advice of retail investment products including managed investments, superannuation and margin loans. • The introduction of a statutory fiduciary duty so that financial advisers must act in the best interests of their clients, subject to a "reasonable steps" qualification, and to place the best interests of their clients ahead of their own when providing personal advice to retail clients. • Increasing transparency and flexibility of payments for financial advice by introducing "adviser charging" that will help align the interests of the financial adviser and the client; is clear and product neutral; and where the investor will be able to opt in to the advice in response to a compulsory, annual renewal notice. • Percentage-based fees (known as assets under management fees) will only be charged on ungeared products or investment amounts and only if this is agreed with the retail investor. • Expanding the availability of low-cost "simple advice" to provide access to and affordability of financial advice. • Strengthening the powers of the Australian Securities and Investments Commission (ASIC) to act against unscrupulous operators.
2 May 2010	Henry Tax Report released.	Australia's Future Tax System Review (AFTSR).
2 May 2010	Government proposes staged increase in the SG to 12 per cent.	Government rejects certain parts of Henry Report and favours SG increase.
24 June 2010	Rudd is replaced by Julia Gillard as Prime Minister.	Rudd loses office in an uncontested ballot of the Parliamentary Labor Party. Wayne Swan remains Treasurer and replaces Gillard as Deputy Prime Minister.
30 June 2010	Release of Cooper Review reports.	Super System Review (SSR) concludes
21 August 2010	Federal election sees Julia Gillard hang on as Prime Minister in a minority government.	Labor narrowly retains office with support of several independent MPs.

2012	Government co-contribution reduced to $500 for lower income employees.	Available to those employees who make personal contributions.
2012	Legislation is passed to lift SG contributions from 9.0 per cent to 12 per cent by 2019.	Renewal of phasing in of higher SG.
26 June 2013	Julia Gillard is replaced by Kevin Rudd as Prime Minister.	Gillard loses office in a contested ballot of the Parliamentary Labor Party. Wayne Swan resigns as Treasurer, replaced by Chris Bowen. Anthony Albanese becomes Deputy Prime Minister.
1 July 2013	Compulsory employer contributions under the SG rise to 9.25 per cent of income.	First phasing-in of 12 per cent superannuation guarantee.
1 July 2013	MySuper products introduced.	Funds must notify members with multiple accounts.
7 September 2013	Rudd government defeated by Liberal/National Parties.	Tony Abbott becomes Prime Minister, Joe Hockey, Treasurer, and Wal Truss, Leader of the National Party, Deputy Prime Minister.
January 2014	Contributions for employees who do not nominate a super fund must be made to MySuper products.	Considerably entrenches MySuper as the foundation of non-SMSF superannuation.
2013	Abbott government delays SGC increases.	Superannuation Guarantee (SG) rate to remain at 9.5 per cent for another 5 years, increasing to 10 per cent from July 2021, and eventually increasing to 12 per cent from July 2025 (see table below).

Financial Year	SGC Rate per cent
2012/13	9.0
2013/14	9.25
2014/15	9.5
2015/16	9.5
2016/17	9.5
2017/18	9.5
2018/19	9.5
2019/20	9.5
2020/21	9.5
2021/22	10.0
2022/23	10.5
2023/24	11.0
2024/25	11.5
2025/26	12.0

Appendix 4: Major Superannuation, Industrial Relations and Related Changes in Australia

20 November 2013	Financial System Inquiry process underway.	Draft terms of reference are issued by Treasurer Joe Hockey, and finalised in December; the inquiry was chaired by David Murray A0.
1 July 2014	Compulsory employer contributions under the SG rise to 9. 5 per cent of income.	Continued phasing-in of 12 per cent, but now paused to 2021/22
From July 2014	Use of electronic data standards becomes mandatory.	This becomes so for for employers with more than 20 employees.
7 December 2014	The Financial System Inquiry (Murray) Report is delivered.	Inter alia recommends narrow definition of the purpose of superannuation; urges government to take steps to reduce fees; and advocates consideration of an auction for default superannuation products.
14 September 2015	Tony Abbott is replaced by Malcolm Turnbull as Prime Minister.	Abbott is defeated in a ballot of the Parliamentary Liberal Party; Joe Hockey resigns as Treasurer, replaced by Scott Morrison.
2 July 2016	Turnbull government re-elected.	Narrow return of government, with a one seat majority in the House of Representatives, but generally reliable support from conservative independents.
From July 2017	Further entrenching of MySuper.	Existing default investments must be transferred to a MySuper account.

Sources: All information above has been independently gathered by the author from various sources.

APPENDIX 5: MAJOR INDUSTRY AND OTHER SUPERANNUATION BODIES

This information, current as at the time of writing, is drawn from published information, including APRA's "Superannuation Statistics 2016" funds' websites, and personal knowledge.

The information is divided into two sections, first, a list of the current top 20 funds; and second, a list of most of the industry and other funds with more than $1 billion in funds under management.

Top Funds in Australia

The 20 largest super funds in Australia control nearly two-thirds (62.8%) of all super money held by the 240 or so larger super funds, and their share of the total is accelerating. The table below highlights the majors.

Figure 45: Largest Superannuation Funds in Australia

Fund	Fund Type; Whether Public Offer	Total Assets in Billions, Approx.
1. AustralianSuper.	Industry & Public Offer.	$95.0
2. First State Superannuation Scheme.	Hybrid & Public Offer.	$76.0.
3. Colonial State.	Retail & Public Offer.	$65.0.
4. State Public Sector Superannuation Scheme (QSuper).	Public Sector & Not Public Offer (but may be likely to become so).	$60.0
5. Retirement Wrap (BT).	Retail & Public Offer.	$55.0.
6. UniSuper.	Industry & Not Public Offer.	$55.0.
7. AMP Superannuation Savings Trust.	Retail & Public Offer.	$54.0.

8. The Universal Super Scheme (MLC).	Retail & Public Offer.	$46.0.
9. Retail Employees Superannuation Trust (REST).	Industry & Public Offer.	$40.0
10. SunSuper Superannuation Fund.	Industry & Public Offer.	$36.0.
11. OnePath Masterfund (ANZ).	Retail & Public Offer.	$35.0.
12. HESTA.	Industry & Public Offer.	$34.0.
13. Construction & Building Unions Superannuation (CBUS).	Industry & Public Offer.	$34.0.
14. Wealth Personal Superannuation & Pension Fund (AMP, formerly AXA).	Retail & Public Offer.	$27.0.
15. ASGARD Independence Plan Division Two (BT).	Retail & Public Offer.	$21.0.
16. Mercer Super Trust.	Retail & Public Offer.	$21.0.
17. HOSTPLUS.	Industry & Public Offer.	$18.5.
18. IOOF Portfolio Service Superannuation Fund.	Retail & Public Offer.	$18.0.
19. Telstra Superannuation Scheme.	Corporate & Public Offer.	$18.0.
20. Public Sector Superannuation Scheme.	Public Sector & Not Public Offer.	$18.0
Total		$793.0

Source: Total assets data sourced from Superannuation Fund-level Rates of Return June 2015 (issued 10 February 2016), APRA, supplemented by personally checking individual funds' websites.

Appendix 6: Major Industry and Some Other Funds

AGEST was a default scheme for the Federal public sector which merged with AustralianSuper.

AMP Superannuation Savings Trust is a retail and public offer fund offered to employees and employers across Australia. With approximately $54 billion in funds under management, the fund has over 2,150,000 members. AMP is Australia's largest retail and corporate superannuation provider, as well as the largest life risk business with over $110 billion in total funds. Formed as a mutual in 1849, AMP demutualised in 1998 and listed on the Australian Stock Exchange. See: https://www.amp.com.au/amp/performance-and-unit-prices/superannuation-funds/retirement-savings-account.

ASGARD Independence Plan Division Two (BT) is a retail and public offer fund offered to employees and employers across Australia. With approximately $21 billion in funds under management, the fund has over 312,000 members. Formed in 1985 by the investment banking group Bankers Trust, BT Financial Group (BTFG) is now the wealth management arm of the Westpac Group, which following the Westpac and St. George merger in late 2008, also includes the wealth division of St. George bank. Westpac is one of the big four Australian domestic banks. See: http://www.asgard.com.au.

ASSET Super – see CARE.

AUST, the Allied Unions' Superannuation Trust merged with BUSS to form CBUS.

AvSuper Fund is a public sector and public offer fund dedicated to employees in the aviation and aviation safety industries. With approximately $2 billion in funds under management, the fund has over 6,500 members. See: www.avsuper.com.au.

Australia Post Superannuation Scheme (APSS) has around 46,000 members and over $6 billion in funds under management. See: https://www.apss.com.au.

AUSCOAL Superannuation Fund – see Mine Wealth and Wellbeing.

Australian Catholic Superannuation and Retirement Fund, headquartered in Burwood in Sydney, is an industry and public offer fund with around 93,000 members and over $7.1 billion in funds under management. See: www.catholicsuper.com.au. See also the Catholic Superannuation Fund.

Australian Government Employees Superannuation Trust (AGEST), founded in 1991, was the default Federal public-sector scheme; it merged with AustralianSuper in 2013.

Australian Meat Industry Superannuation Trust (AMIST) – not to be confused with MIESF (qv.) – has around $1.8 billion in funds under management with approximately 67,000 members. See www. amist.com.au.

Australian Retirement Fund merged in 2006 with the Super-annuation Trust of Australia to form AustralianSuper.

AustralianSuper is an industry and public offer fund. With around $95 billion in funds under management and over 2,100,000 member accounts, it is Australia's largest industry fund, having been formed in 2006 from the merger of STA and RTA and absorbed AGEST (2013), IBM Super (2012) and WestScheme (2011). See http://www. australiansuper.com.

AustSafe Super Fund is an industry and public offer fund focused on rural and regional Australia, with approximately $2.1 billion in funds under management with over 145,000 members. See: www.austsafe. com.au.

Retirement Wrap (BT) is a retail and public offer fund offered to employees and employers across Australia. With approximately $55 billion in funds under management, the fund has over 870,000 members. This is managed by BT Financial Group (BTFG) the wealth management arm of the Westpac Group, one of the big four Australian domestic banks. See: http://www.bt.com.au/personal/superannuation/ solutions.html.

Building Unions Superannuation Scheme, Queensland (BUSS(Q)), is an industry and public offer fund with approximately 87,000 members from over 8,400 employers, with around $3.5 billion in funds under management. See: www.bussq.com.au.

BUSS – see **CBUS**

CARE or **CareSuper**, originally named the Clerical and Retail Employees' Super fund, founded in 1986, is an industry and public offer fund which manages approximately $12.5 billion in funds under management, with nearly 260,000 members from over 70,000 employers. It describes itself as the largest industry fund specialising in super for people engaged in professional, managerial, administrative and service occupations. In late 2012, CareSuper merged with AssetSuper, which was established in NSW 1987 by the Employers Federation of NSW, the NSW Chamber of Manufacturers, and the Labor Council of NSW. That fund, as at November 2011 (prior to merger), had more than $1.6 billion for almost 85,000 members throughout Australia with more than 12,000 employers. See www.caresuper.com.au.

Catholic Superannuation Fund (CSF), headquartered in Melbourne, an industry fund, is the largest Catholic superannuation fund in Australia, with over 73,000 members and 14,000 participating employers, with around $7.3 billion in funds under management, covering Church institutions, including schools. See http://csf.com.au/about-us. See also the Australian Catholic Superannuation and Retirement Fund.

Club Plus Superannuation Scheme, formed in 1987, covers the Club industry, initially mainly in NSW but now Australia-wide. It has around $7.3 billion under management, with over 110,000 members and over 11,000 employers. See: www.clubplussuper.com.au.

Colonial First State First Choice Superannuation Trust is a retail and public offer fund offered to employees and employers across Australia. With approximately $65 billion in funds under management, the fund has over 774,000 members. Formed in 1988, Colonial First

State is a wealth management group owned by the Commonwealth Bank, one of the big four Australian domestic banks, and offers investment, superannuation, retirement, and related products to customers. See: www.colonialfirststate.com.au.

Construction & Building Unions Superannuation Scheme (CBUSS), also known as Cbus in its early days, was formed from the 1989 amalgamation of the first major funds, BUSS and AUST, becoming known as C+BUS (Construction and Building Unions Superannuation), with initial membership from the building and construction unions. It now has around $34 billion in funds under management, with nearly 750,000 members. See www.cbussuper.com.au.

Energy Industries Superannuation Scheme (EISS) manages two large superannuation funds. Pool A is a public sector and public offer fund with over $2.6 billion in funds under management and around 18,000 members. Pool B is a public sector and non-public offer fund with over $2.4 billion in funds under management and just under 4,000 members. EISS was established on 30 June 1997 by a Trust Deed made under an Act of the NSW Parliament for the purpose of providing retirement benefits for employees of certain Energy Industries entities in NSW. See: https://www.eisuper.com.au, accessed 20 September 2016.

Energy Super is a not-for-profit, public offer, superannuation fund, drawing members mostly from Queensland and Victoria. Presently it has nearly 49,000 members with more than $6.7 billion in funds under management. See: https://www.energysuper.com.au.

Equip Super was formed from energy-sector funds in the Victorian public sector, mainly centred on employees from the State Electricity Commission of Victoria. The Victorian Energy Industry Superannuation Fund changed its name to EquipSuper in 1998. Presently the fund has $7 billion under management. See www.equipsuper.com.au.

FIRST Super was formed in July 2008 when three industry funds merged – the Furniture Industry Retirement Superannuation Trust, the Pulp & Paper Workers' Superannuation Fund, and the Timber Industry

Super Scheme. The Pulp & Paper Workers' Superannuation Fund had been formed in August 1974 and was one of the pioneer industry funds that significantly influenced the formation of LUCRF scheme (q.v.). Presently it has over 60,000 members with more than $2.3 billion in funds under management. See: www.firstsuper.com.au

First State Super is a not-for-profit, public offer, superannuation fund. Presently it has nearly 760,000 members with more than $56.0 billion in funds under management. Established in 1992 to provide for the superannuation and retirement needs of NSW public sector employees, in 2006 the fund became open to all. In 2011, First State Super merged with Health Super to create one of Australia's largest super funds. Additionally, on 23 May 2016, it acquired State Plus (qv.), with $21 billion in funds under management. See www.firststatesuper. com.au.

Funds SA is the South Australian public sector scheme, a government, non-public offer superannuation fund available to public sector workers in the State with just over $25.0 billion in funds under management. See: https://www.funds.sa.gov.au.

Government Employees Superannuation Board (GESB), the Western Australian public sector scheme is a government, non-public offer superannuation fund available to public sector workers in the State with just over $22.0 billion in funds under management. See: www.gesb.com.au.

Harwood Superannuation Fund is a corporate fund that manages the retirement savings for 13,500 employees of building products suppliers CSR, Holcim Australia and Wilmar Sugar. In 2013 the fund outsourced nearly all of its functions including $1.4 billion in funds under management.

HESTA, the Health Employees Superannuation Trust Australia, is an industry and public offer fund established by the Australian Council of Trade Unions (ACTU) and the employer groups in 1987 to cover the health and community services industries. The scheme presently has approximately $34.0 billion in funds under management, with approximately 823,000 members. See: https://www.hesta.com.au

HOSTPLUS is an industry and public offer fund established by the Australian Hotels' Association (AHA) and the LHMU (now United Voice) union in 1987, which presently has approximately $18.5 billion in funds under management, with approximately 993,000 members and more than 75,000 employers. See http://hostplusexecutive.com. au/about-us/our-history, accessed 26 May 2013 and https://hostplus. com.au/super.

IOOF Superannuation, sponsored by IOOF is a retail and public offer fund, which presently has approximately $18.5 billion in funds under management, with approximately 432,000 members. IOOF originated in Melbourne in 1846 as a friendly society called the Independent Order of Odd Fellows. By the late 1980s, IOOF was the largest friendly society in Australia, with approximately 200,000 members, but demutualised in 2002 and acquired various businesses in subsequent years to become one of the largest providers of retail fund investments in Australia. See: https://www.ioof.com.au.

Legal Super is an industry and public offer fund in the legal and support staff profession with just over $2.7 billion in funds under management, with approximately 42,000 members. See: www. legalsuper.com.au.

Local Government Super is a NSW public sector and non-public offer fund for local government employees and public utilities in NSW and manages approximately $9.5 billion of funds under management with around 85,000 members. The fund is prominent in debates calling for greater sustainable developments or "green" investments. Its website describes itself as the industry fund for the sector. See: https://www. lgsuper.com.au.

LUCRF Super was formed by the Federated Storemen and Packers' Union (now the National Union of Workers, after a series of union mergers) in the late 1970s and by the mid-1980s adopted the 'industry fund model' of equal union and employer representation. The public offer industry fund has just over $5.0 billion in funds under management, with nearly 175,000 members. See: https://www.lucrf. com.au.

Maritime Super, an industry and public offer fund, was formed on 1 March 2009 as a result of the merger between two maritime industry super funds – the Stevedoring Employees Retirement Fund (SERF) and the Seafarers Retirement Fund (SRF). The fund has just over $5.0 billion in funds under management, with around 30,000 members. See: www.maritimesuper.com.au.

Meat Industry Employees' Superannuation Fund (MIESF) – not to be confused with AMIST (qv.) – has around $725 million in funds under management with approximately 26,000 members. See: http://miesf.com.au.

Mercer Super Trust is a retail and public offer fund with approximately $21 billion in funds under management and approximately 217,000 members. See: www.mercerfinancialservices.com.

Military Superannuation & Benefits Fund – see PSS.

Mine Wealth and Wellbeing, the old AUSCOAL fund, a hybrid government supported, industry and public offer fund, was renamed from July 2015 with $9.5 billion in funds under management, following merger between the Coalsuper Retirement Income Fund (COALSUPER), the Queensland Coal and Oil Shale Mining Industry Superannuation Fund (QCOS), and the Coal Industry Superannuation Fund of Western Australia. COALSUPER had been formed in 1941 under the NSW McKell Labor Government. See https://www.mine.com.au.

MTAA Super, formed by the Motor Traders Association of Australia, (MTAA), is an industry and public offer fund and presently has $9.2 billion in funds under management, with approximately 255,000 members. See: http://mtaasuper.com.au.

MUST in 1988 became the Superannuation Trust of Australia.

Non-Government Schools Super (NGS) is an industry and public offer fund in the non-government schools sector with just over $7.0 billion in funds under management, with over 100,000 members. See: https://www.ngssuper.com.au.

OnePath Masterfund is a retail and public offer fund offered to employees and employers across Australia. With approximately $35 billion in funds under management, the fund has over 1,125,000 members. Predecessor funds were managed by Mercantile Mutual and more recently by ING Australia. In 2009, the ING wealth business was acquired by the Australia and New Zealand Banking Group Limited (ANZ), one of the big four Australian domestic banks. See: www.onepath.com.au.

Prime Super Fund is an industry and public offer fund established in 1996 through the amalgamation of a number of smaller super funds, focused on servicing regional and rural Australia and, more recently, the health and aged care services sectors. With approximately $3.8 billion in funds under management, Prime has over 126,000 members. See: https://www.primesuper.com.au.

LGS Super, Queensland Local Government Super Board is a government, non-public offer superannuation fund available to Local Councils and utility workers in Queensland with approximately $6.0 billion in funds under management and 85,000 members. See: https://www.lgsuper.com.au.

PSS Scheme, the Public Sector Superannuation Scheme, is a government, non-public offer superannuation fund available to Commonwealth government employees with approximately $18.0 billion in funds under management and 231,500 members. See: https://www.pss.gov.au.

QSuper, the Queensland State Public Sector Superannuation Scheme is a government, non-public offer superannuation fund available to public sector workers in Queensland with just over $60.0 billion in funds under management and over 552,000 members. See: https://qsuper.qld.gov.au.

Qantas Super was established in 1939 and has grown to become one of Australia's largest corporate superannuation funds. Originally set up for employees of Qantas and related aeronautical businesses, the fund is a non-public offer fund with approximately $7.4 billion in funds under management and 33,000 members. See: https://www.qantassuper.com.au.

Queensland Independent Education & Care Superannuation Trust (QIEC Super) is an industry and non-public offer fund with over $1.2 billion in funds under management and around 26,000 members. The fund was set up in 1990 specifically for the benefit of all employees in the non-government education industry, child and other care, and community services in Queensland. See: www.qiec.com.au.

REI Super Fund, formed in 1975, is an industry and non-public offer fund focused on professionals and employees in the real estate industry, with approximately $1.3 billion in funds under management and over 31,000 members. See: https://www.reisuper.com.au.

Retail Employees Superannuation Trust (REST), established by the Retail Traders Association, then with the support of the relevant union, the SDA, is an industry and public offer fund with just over $40.0 billion in funds under management and over 2,150,000 members. See: www.rest.com.au.

State Plus, formerly known as State Super Financial Services (SSFS) provides financial advice to public sector workers and retirees. It was acquired by First State Super on 23 May 2016 with $21 billion in retirement funds and over 200 financial planners located in metropolitan and regional centres throughout Australia. Overriding a direction by the then NSW government not to compete with other financial advisory firms, SSFS was formed in the late 1980s by the NSW State Super fund and set up as an independent investment and financial advisory business at first limited to advice to former government employees and their families. See: https://www.stateplus.com.au.

Statewide Superannuation Trust (Statewide Super) is an industry and public offer fund which in 2012 merged with South Australian Local Government Superannuation to become the leading industry fund based in South Australia and the Northern Territory with in excess of $6.5 billion in funds under management and 140,000 members. See: https://www.statewide.com.au.

SunSuper Superannuation Fund is an industry and public offer fund established in 1987, based in Brisbane, Queensland, as a multi-industry superannuation fund to cater for virtually all workers across Australia. SunSuper presently has approximately $36.0 billion in funds under management, with approximately 1,150,000 members. See: www.sunsuper.com.au.

Superannuation Trust of Australia merged in 2006 with the Australian Retirement Fund to form AustralianSuper.

SuperWrap (BT), formerly called Retirement Wrap, BT, is a retail, public offer superannuation fund managed by BT (formerly Bankers' Trust), now owned by Westpac with approximately $55.0 billion in funds under management and over 870,000 members. The product allows a member to 'wrap' their superannuation portfolio of shares, managed funds and insurance into one account and provides online access to consolidated reporting and tax statements for the whole portfolio. See: www.bt.com.au/personal/superannuation/solutions.html.

Tasmanian Retirement Benefits Fund (RBF) was established in 1904 and is the Tasmanian public sector scheme, a government and non-public offer fund available to public sector workers in the State with just over $4.0 billion in funds under management. See: www.rbf. superfacts.com.

Tasplan Superannuation Fund is an industry and public offer fund set up in 1987 in Tasmania, with approximately $3.3 billion in funds under management and 98,000 members. In 2016, the merger with the RBF Tasmanian Accumulation Scheme was announced. Should this proceed in 2017, the merged fund would have around 165,000 members, with approximately $6.5 billion in funds under management. See: www.tasplan.com.au

Telstra Superannuation Scheme was established in 1990 and has grown to become Australia's largest corporate superannuation fund. Originally set up for employees of Telstra and related telecommunications businesses, the fund is now a public offer fund with approximately $16 billion in funds under management, with approximately 100,000 members. See: www.telstrasuper.com.au.

TWU Superannuation Fund is an industry and public offer superannuation fund, established in 1984, and available to employees in the transport, logistics, related, and other industries with approximately $4.3 billion in funds under management, with approximately 123,000 members. See: www.twusuper.com.au.

NSW Treasury Corporation (TCorp), a statutory authority founded in 1983, is the financial markets partner of New South Wales public sector agencies. Originally set up to provide treasury functions, including borrowing, money market investments, and insurance functions, and issuance of bonds, in 2014 the NSW government, announced the bringing together of investment functions in TCorp, WorkCover (now called iCare), and State Authorities Superannuation Trustee Corporation (STC), and (TCorp), the State's three largest managers of financial assets. This was consummated in 2015, with $70 billion in funds under management. Responsibility for the investment objectives, risk management and asset allocation of the funds controlled by iCare, STC, and TCorp, however, remain with each of the separate entities and their respective Boards. See: https://www.tcorp.nsw.gov.au.

UniSuper is an industry and non-public offer superannuation fund available to higher education and research professionals with approximately $55.0 billion in funds under management, with approximately 400,000 members. UniSuper famously boasts that it declines to use asset consultants on asset allocation routinely. See: https://www.unisuper.com.au.

The Universal Super Scheme (MLC) is a retail and public offer fund offered to employees and employers across Australia. With approximately $46 billion in funds under management, the fund has over 1,100,000 members. Formed in 1886 as a life insurance business and eventually named the Mutual Life & Citizens Assurance Company Limited (MLC), in 1982 Lend Lease took a 50 per cent stake and full control in 1985. The following year, MLC's multi-manager, multi-style investment philosophy was introduced. This was strongly influenced by the asset consultant Frank Russell, which in turn inspired Lend

Lease CEO Dick Dusseldorp. In 2000 the business was sold entirely to the National Australia Bank, one of the big four Australian domestic banks. See: https://www.mlc.com.au/personal/superannuation/super-disclosure-and-governance/MLC-Super-Fund.

Victorian Funds Management Corporation (VFMC) is a public authority and body corporate established under the Victorian Funds Management Corporation Act 1994. VFMC's primary objective is to manage the long-term investment assets of Victorian State Government entities, including superannuation. It presently has $52 billion in funds under management. See: https://www.vfmc.vic.gov.au.

Victorian Superannuation Fund (Vic Super) is a public offer and public sector fund with approximately $16 billion in funds under management, with approximately 242,000 members. See: www.vicsuper.com.au.

Vision Super, previously called the Victorian Local Authorities Superannuation Fund, is a public offer and public sector fund with approximately 103,000 members across Australia, though concentrated in Victoria, with around $7.5 billion in funds under management. See: https://www.visionsuper.com.au.

WA Local Government Superannuation Plan, a public sector and public offer fund, has approximately 45,000 members and $2.5 billion in funds under management. See: www.wasuper.com.au.

Wealth Personal Superannuation & Pension Fund is a retail and public offer fund offered to employees and employers across Australia. With approximately $27 billion in funds under management, the fund has over 210,000 members. The trustee, formerly owned by National Mutual, is now owned by AMP (qv.) with AXA, in this instant providing fund management services. (Although AXA is a French multinational firm headquartered in Paris that engages in global insurance, investment management, and other financial services, these operations were acquired by AMP with certain continuing licensing agreements with AXA.). See: www.superguide.com.au/super-funds-guide/wealth-personal-superannuation-and-pension-fund-run-by-axa.

APPENDIX 7: SIGNIFICANT ASSET CONSULTANTS

Currently, the big four asset consultants advising the major and many other Australian superannuation and other investment funds are JANA, Frontier, Mercer and Willis Towers Watson. The next four in significance are also listed

Cambridge and Associates provides independent investment advice and research services to institutional investors and private clients worldwide, including Australia. See: www.cambridgeassociates.com.

Frontier Advisors: Established in 1994 as an asset consulting group within Industry Funds Services (IFS), in 1999 the IFS Board decided to spin off the consulting business into a new and separate company, Frontier Advisors. This was done to remove conflicts of interest that arise when a firm provides both investment advice and investment products. In July 2000 Frontier re-established as a standalone entity with no parent company, subsidiaries, or affiliated businesses. It is owned by four shareholders, AustralianSuper, CBUS, HESTA and FIRST Super and as at August 2016 had more than$230 billion in assets under advice. See: http://frontieradvisors.com.au.

JANA was established in 1987 as John A. Nolan and Associates, the founder principal and owner, to provide institutional investment advice to superannuation funds. The firm became a fully-owned subsidiary of National Australia Bank (NAB) Limited in December 2000 and in 2002 the firm developed its implemented consulting business. In February 2012, the JANA and MLC Implemented Consulting businesses combined. Then in April 2014, JANA and MLC Investment Management came together – all under the JANA name. See: http://www.jana.com.au.

Mercer advises large institutional clients in Australia. See: www.mercer.com.au.

Quentin Ayres was founded in 1994 and is owned by its executives. It specialises in domestic and international private equity and alternative asset investments. See: www.quentinayers.com.

Russell was formed when founder Frank Russell opened a brokerage firm in Tacoma, Washington, USA, and he was succeeded in 1958 by his son George, fresh from Harvard Business School, who developed in 1969 an evaluation tool for assessing performance of fund managers. By then known as Frank Russell and Associates, a decade later the firm expanded internationally and in 1986 an office opened in Sydney with Lend Lease as its major client, through MLC. In 1999 Northwestern Mutual acquired the firm, now known as Russell Investments. In 2014 the London Stock Exchange Group (LSEG) acquired the business. In 2016 TA Associates and Reverence Capital Partners complete acquisition of Russell Investments' asset management business from LSEG. Presently Russell globally advises around $38 billion in retirement savings under advice. See: https://russellinvestments.com/au.

Whitehelm Capital, formerly Access Capital Advisors, was formed in 1998 and specialises in infrastructure and private equity investments with around $16 billion in funds under advice. Prior to the global financial crisis, it was larger and famously convinced its super fund clients to invest as much as half of their portfolios in alternative assets including infrastructure, property, private equity and hedge funds. In the crisis, however, the "illiquidity premium" hit hard as clients wanted to sell an asset. See: www.fidante.com.au/im/WhitehelmCapital.htm.

Willis Towers Watson was formed in 2010 in a merger of equals, Towers Perrin and Watson Wyatt combined to form Towers Watson. In 2016 Willis Group and Towers Watson merged to become Willis Towers Watson. The business employs over 750 associates worldwide, has more than 1,000 pension funds and institutional investors as clients, and has assets under advisory of over US$2 trillion. Australia represents around $200 billion in retirement savings under advice. See: www.willistowerswatson.com.

Appendix 8: Major Superannuation Industry Associations

Association of Superannuation Funds of Australia (ASFA) is the peak policy, research and advocacy body for Australia's superannuation industry representing all superannuation fund sectors, service providers and fund members. A non-profit, non-political national organisation ASFA's mission is to protect, promote and advance the interests of Australia's superannuation funds, their trustees, and their members. See: http://www.superannuation.asn.au

Australian Council of Superannuation Investors is a research and advice body that advises institutional members, mostly industry funds, on environmental, social, and corporate governance (ESG) investment risk. See: www.acsi.org.au

Australian Institute of Superannuation Trustees (AIST) is a national not-for-profit organisation whose membership consists of the trustee directors and staff of industry, corporate and public-sector funds. As the principal advocate and peak representative body for the $700 billion not-for-profit superannuation sector, AIST plays a key role in policy development and is a leading provider of research. Each year, AIST hosts the Conference of Major Superannuation Funds (CMSF), in addition to numerous other industry conferences and events. See: www.aist.asn.au

Conference of Major Superannuation Funds (CMSF) – see AIST.

Fund Executives Association Ltd (FEAL) was established to further the professional development of superannuation fund executives. See: www.feal.asn.au

Financial Services Council of Australia (FSC) represents Australia's retail and wholesale funds management businesses, superannuation funds, life insurers, financial advisory networks, licensed trustee companies and public trustees. The Council has over 120 members who are responsible for investing more than $2.5 trillion on behalf of 11 million Australians. See: www.fsc.org.au

Industry Funds Management (IFM) –see IFMI.

IFM Investors (IFMI), from 1998 to 2013 known as Industry Funds Management, provides investment services for a number of large industry superannuation funds and manages funds across four asset classes – infrastructure, debt investments, listed equities and private capital. It is owned by 29 world-leading pension funds. See: www. fsc.org.au

Industry Funds Services (IFS) describes itself as the leading provider of financial product and advice services to industry super funds and union members. IFS is a wholly owned subsidiary of Industry Super Holdings Pty Ltd, which in turn is owned by a number of the major industry funds. See: https://ifs.net.au

Industry Super Australia (ISA) manages collective projects on behalf of Industry SuperFunds with the objective of maximising the retirement savings of five million industry super members. These projects include research, policy development, government relations and advocacy in addition to the well-known Industry SuperFunds Joint Marketing Campaign. See: www.industrysuperaustralia.com

Members' Equity (ME) bank, founded in 1994 as Super Member Home Loans, originally as a joint venture with National Mutual (later AXA), is now 100 per cent owned by 29 industry funds, and provides retail banking products and advice to the Australian market. See: www.mebank.com.au

SMSF Association is the peak professional body representing the SMSF sector throughout Australia. See: www.smsfassociation.com

Women in Super (WIS) was informally started in 1991 at that year's Conference of Major Superannuation Funds and then launched as an independent body in 1994 to network women in industry and other not-for-profit funds across the sector. The website describes their mission as "a superannuation system without gender bias". See: www. womeninsuper.com.au

Appendix 9: Superannuation Jargon Made Easy

There are unfamiliar terms and acronyms habitually referenced in discussions and debates on superannuation in Australia. On one superannuation website, that of the Western Australian Government Employees' Superannuation (GESB) fund, there is a section explaining much of the jargon. AustralianSuper's website also contains a glossary of terms. From these sources and others, such material has been garnered and masticated for here.

Accumulation Fund or Scheme, also called a defined contribution fund, is a type of super fund where an account balance builds up over time from an individual's employer contributions, their own personal contributions, as well as from investment earnings. How much an account grows depends on the number and amount of contributions received, the length of time the superannuation is invested, the fees and costs deducted, and the overall performance of the underlying assets that are invested The benefit a member receives is the total of their contributions plus or minus investment returns, less fees and tax.

Administration Fee is the fee charged by a fund to cover its administration costs.

Agency Cost or Agency Risk is the difference between the potential benefit the principal (such as a superannuation fund) would receive if the agent (such as an external investment manager appointed to manage funds) performed the task completely in the principal's best interest and the actual benefit the principal received. It is the same thing as principal risk.

Alignment refers to whether there is alignment between principal (such as a superannuation fund) and agent (such as an external investment manager appointed to manage funds) in the performance of a particular task. This can entail alignment in execution and incentives – including over and under performance.

Alternative Assets are unlisted investment vehicles that are 'alternatives' to the assets that are included more traditionally in large institutional investment portfolios. Advocates of alternatives believe they can play a valuable role in diversifying the investment portfolios to reduce overall portfolio risk and boost long-term returns to members. Alternative assets normally include private equity, infrastructure, absolute return funds (or hedge funds).

Allocated Pension is a type of retirement income arrangement under which an individual invests a lump sum and then draws down a regular pension to a value that takes account of expected cash flow needs and life expectancy. Income ceases when all capital has been used up.

Annuity is an arrangement where payments are made to a person at regular intervals in return for the investment of a lump sum. See also: retirement income account; deferred annuity.

Approved Deposit Funds (ADFs) are investment vehicles that can receive, hold, and invest certain types of rollovers until such funds are withdrawn or a condition of release is satisfied (depending on the preservation status of the assets). ADFs can be either single-member or multi-member.

Assets are the financial resources in which a fund invests on behalf of its members. Among other things, these may include shares, property, cash or bonds.

Asset Allocation is the investment mix of a superannuation fund in various assets, including Australian equities, international equities, cash, fixed interest, unlisted property, private equities, etc.

Asset Class is a category of financial securities that can be invested in. Examples include Cash, Fixed Interest, Property, Australian Shares and International Shares.

Asset Consultant is an advisor who helps superannuation fund investors with their long-term investment planning.

Assets Test, also known as Age Pension assets test or Centrelink assets test, is a means test that assesses the value of the assets owned by an individual or couple, to determine their eligibility for the Government Age Pension and other social security payments.

Assets Under Management: Investment managers and superannuation funds both look after "assets under management". The term refers to the assets in all classes that are managed.

Australian Business Number: Super funds and most businesses in Australia have an Australian Tax Office (ATO) registered Australian Business Number (ABN) which, in the case of superannuation, is used to identify the particular fund and to facilitate transfers between funds.

Average Contribution Rate (ACR) is the average percentage of an individual's salary contributed to a superannuation account.

Award or "industrial award" are industrial relations instruments made by industrial tribunals, which specify minimum pay and conditions of employment for different industries and occupations. Modern awards made by the Fair Work Commission (as it is now named), which cover employers and employees in industries and occupations throughout most of Australia, and specify default superannuation schemes for occupational superannuation contributions.

Award Superannuation refers to superannuation entitlements that are determined by a Federal or State industrial award. In some cases these entitlements may provide entitlements to employees, which are above the minimum Superannuation Guarantee requirement currently at 9.5 per cent of salary.

Bank Bills: Cash is always a short-term investment that may take various forms ranging from a simple cash deposit held at a bank, to tradable short-term securities such as bank bills that are traded between investors on the money market. Most large funds invest in bank bills and other short-term to medium-term investments. Cash investments such as bank bills carry a low level of investment risk and returns are generally very stable and relatively low.

Basis Point is the measurement of change in the value of an investment, equal to 1/100th of one per cent.

Beneficiary is the person a member has nominated to receive their superannuation benefits in the event of the member's death. The person must be either a related dependant or a financial dependant or the member's legal personal representative.

Bond at investment grade is a bond whose credit quality is considered to be among the most secure by any independent bond-rating agency. It is usually a (fixed interest) security issued by corporations, governments or their agencies, in return for cash from lenders or investors.

Cash Investments may take various forms, including a cash deposit held at a bank, term deposits or short-term securities such as bank bills that are traded between investors on the money market. Cash investments such as bank bills carry a low level of investment risk and generally achieve stable, although relatively low, returns.

Choice of Superannuation. Employees are able to choose their own superannuation fund under laws introduced by the Australian Government from 1 July 2005. This choice, however, does not apply in the case where a Federal enterprise agreement specifies only a particular scheme or schemes.

Commonwealth Government Super Co-contribution is a co-contribution and a Commonwealth Government initiative designed to help eligible individuals increase their retirement savings by boosting their super.

Completed Months of Service is the number of months of full-time equivalent service an individual has completed in their fund. Especially in defined benefit funds, this figure is used in the calculation of the Final Benefit.

Complying Fund is a regulated superannuation fund that complies with the operational standards specified in the Superannuation Industry Supervision (SIS) Act regulations. Unless a fund meets the SIS regulations, it is unable to accept Superannuation Guarantee contributions.

Compound Interest is when interest is earned on interest as well as on the initial investment. Compound interest differs from simple interest in that simple interest is calculated only as a percentage of the initial capital sum.

Concessional Contributions are any contributions made to a super account before tax is deducted, for example employer Superannuation Guarantee contributions or salary sacrifice contributions.

Consolidate: This is when an individual transfers their superannuation benefit from one super fund to another super fund. It is also known as a rollover or roll in.

Contribution Caps refer to contributions made to an individual's super account in a financial year. If a person contributes more than the caps, extra tax is liable. The cap amount, and how much extra tax might need to be paid, depends on age and whether the contributions are of different types. More recently, there is the rule concerning lifetime contribution caps.

Contribution Splitting allows a person to split their superannuation contributions with their spouse or partner. It means that a portion of an individual's super can be split into an account held by their spouse.

Corporate Superannuation Fund is a fund that is set up by a company to provide superannuation for its own employees.

Custodian is a company that safeguards and maintains assets on behalf of other people. Unlike a trustee, which "owns" the assets, a custodian is solely responsible for holding and safeguarding assets on behalf of others.

Default Super funds are those funds to which employers on behalf of employees make compulsory superannuation contributions. Should a member of a superannuation fund not actively choose a fund they prefer to be invested in, then they are allocated to a default product, usually with a conservative asset allocation mix. Since 2014, all superannuation funds in Australia need to offer a MySuper default – see that definition.

Defined Benefit Scheme: This style of super scheme means that an individual's final superannuation benefit is determined by applying a fixed or 'defined' formula, usually based on length of service, contributions, and final salary. This type of scheme is not market linked, as the benefit is defined and does not depend on investment market returns.

Defined Contribution Fund – see Accumulation Fund

Dependant includes an individual's spouse (or former spouse or de facto, including same-sex spouse), a child under 18 (including an adopted, step or ex-nuptial child), any person who is financially dependent on the individual, or any person with whom the individual has an interdependent relationship. Under the SIS Act, the term "dependant" also includes any person who the Trustee considers to have been wholly or partially financially dependent on the member at the time of a member's death and any person who the Trustee considers to have been in an "interdependency relationship" with the member at the time of the member's death.

Diversification is an investment approach that involves investing across a range of asset classes, rather than investing in only one type of asset. Diversification suggests that the positive performance of one asset class may help mitigate the negative performance of another. It is consistent with the saying, "do not put all your eggs in one basket".

Eligible Rollover Funds (ERFs) are super funds or approved deposit funds which are eligible to receive benefits automatically rolled over from other funds.

Execution Risk is the risk of performing a particular strategy.

ESG refers to environmental, social, and corporate governance issues.

Growth Asset Classes include higher risk asset categories, such as Shares and Property. Growth asset classes typically generate high returns with higher levels of volatility.

Hybrid Fund is defined here as a fund that straddles private and public sectors. First State Super, headquartered in Sydney, is an example. Originally a public sector fund, it became a public offer fund on 1 May 2006, opening up membership to anyone eligible to receive superannuation benefits. On July 2012 it merged with Health Super and considerably expanded its geographic reach across Australia.

Implemented Consulting, pioneered by Frank Russell & Co. (later called Russell Investments) and adopted by most asset consultants in Australia, is the implementation of a strategy usually by an asset consultant. In its broadest application, this comprises elements of policy formation, manager structure and selection, and performance monitoring. Effectively, it is a partnership between the trustees and/or managers of a fund and the consultant. Sometimes this might be for a whole portfolio or limited to investment decisions for only for an asset class (such are as alternatives). Implemented Consulting is flexible and tailored to individual client needs.

Inflation: increases in the cost of living, usually measured by the Consumer Price Index (CPI).

Insourcing refers to whether particular tasks, including investments, are performed internally ("insourced" or "in-house") or externally ("outsourced"). All superannuation funds consider what functions are best performed by what method. The "insourcing" debate in Australia in funds management has partly been driven by a desire to reduce external fees and lack of alignment between principal and agent.

Investment Choice/Investment Plan generally refers to a range of investment plans, each one with a different objective for target performance; from "growth" (high risk) through to "cash" (low risk). Investment plans each have a unique asset allocation, comprising different types of assets such as Shares, Property and Fixed Interest – so a superannuation fund member can choose a plan that suits their particular – or view of their – risk profile.

Investment Grade Bond is a bond with a credit quality considered to have a relatively low level of default risk by an independent bond-rating agency.

Investment Return and Risk: "return" can be defined as the gain or loss in the value of an investment and "risk" is the variability of those returns. When an investment is made, there is typically a trade-off between risk and return. Generally, the higher the potential return, the higher the potential risk. Similarly, investments offering lower returns tend to have a lower level of risk.

Investment Timeframe: refers to the period of time expected to hold an investment or portfolio. An investment timeframe is an important factor in determining particular risk profiles.

"Look through" transparency is where all fees, costs, and charges are fully disclosed on an investment.

Low Income Superannuation Contribution (LISC) arrangements provide that where an individual earns less than $37,000 a year and their employer (or they) make concessional (before-tax) super contributions, then they can expect a refund of the 15 per cent contributions tax deducted from their super account. The refund is paid direct into the superannuation account by the Australian Tax Office. From 1 July 2017, LISTO replaces LISC..

Low Income Super Tax Offset (LISTO), announced in the 2016/17 Commonwealth Budget, is a tax offset available to superannuation funds based on the tax paid on concessional contributions made on behalf of low income earners. The offset will mean that individuals with an adjusted taxable income up to $37,000 will receive a refund into their superannuation account of the tax paid on their concessional superannuation contributions, to a cap of $500. LISTO replaces the Low Income Superannuation Contribution (LISC).

Lump Sum is a benefit payable as a single cash payment or as several part payments rather than gradually drawing-down as a retirement income or annuity.

Management Expense Ratio (MER) are the expenses of an investment option in a superannuation fund (for example, management, investment, trusteeship) as a proportion of the investment option's net asset value.

Median is the number that appears exactly half way in a set of data. For example, five managers may have produced annual investment returns of 1 per cent, 2 per cent, 4 per cent, 10 per cent and 20 per cent. The median return is 4 per cent (the third of five figures). The average (or mean) is 7.4 per cent.

MySuper replaced default superannuation arrangements in Australia. Effective since 1 July 2013, super funds can offer "a simple, low cost default product called MySuper to improve the simplicity, transparency and comparability of default superannuation products." It comprises a uniform set of products intended for people who do not actively choose their fund. From January 2014 every new default superannuation account had to be in a MySuper product and all default funds must be transferred into a MySuper product by July 2017. Sales commissions cannot be paid on MySuper products. Some MySuper fees are limited to cost-recovery only; there must be a single investment product (which can be a lifecycle product), and standardised presentation of product information (including risk and fees) through a MySuper dashboard. Key features of MySuper were:

- new duties for trustees, including a specific duty to deliver value for money as measured by long-term net returns, and to actively consider whether the fund has sufficient scale;
- a single diversified investment strategy, suitable for the vast majority of members who are in the default option;
- reporting comparable data on long-term net returns published by APRA;
- restrictions on unnecessary or excessive fees, including:
  - banning commissions in relation to retail investment products and group insurance;
  - new standards for the payment of performance fees to fund managers;
  - a ban on entry fees charged to new members;
  - exit fees limited to cost recovery; and,
  - switching fees not payable to the trustee in their personal capacity;
- a fair and reasonable allocation of costs between MySuper and other products;
- standardised reporting requirements written in plain English; and,
- life, and total and permanent disability (TPD) insurance (where available, depending on occupational and demographic factors) offered on an opt-out basis.

Non-commutable Income Stream: a non-commutable income stream is one that pays a regular income from an individual's super, but does not allow lump-sum withdrawals.

Non-concessional Contributions: a contribution that is made from a person's after-tax income (as opposed to their employer's contributions, which are made before tax is deducted). It is also known as a personal contribution.

Ordinary time earnings refers to earnings in respect of ordinary hours of work, including over-award payments, shift-loading or commission, excluding earnings from a payment in lieu of unused sick leave, an unused annual leave payment, or unused long service leave payment, and certain lump sum payments made to the employee on the termination of his or her employment.

Outsourcing refers to whether particular tasks, including investments, are performed internally ("in-house") or externally ("outsourced").

Payroll Tax is the tax an employer withholds based on the wage or salary of the employee.

Pension: a pension is a type of income stream an individual might receive in retirement. This includes putting a person's super into a product such as an allocated pension, where they would receive a regular income drawn from their super.

Personal Contributions are contributions that an individual can make that are over and above the compulsory Superannuation Guarantee contributions that their employer must make on their behalf.

Pooled Superannuation Trusts (PSTs) are trusts in which regulated super funds, approved deposit funds and other PSTs invest.

Preservation is the legal requirement that certain superannuation benefits must be held in a superannuation or rollover fund until the member retires after reaching their preservation age. Only in very limited circumstances (for example, total and permanent disablement and severe financial hardship), can preserved amounts be released before the member reaches this age. All superannuation contributions made after 30 June 1999, including personal and investment earnings are considered preserved.

Preservation Age is the minimum age at which a person can access their super, provided they have permanently retired from the workforce. The preservation age is gradually increasing from 55 years. For those born before 1 July 1960, the preservation age is 55, increasing on a sliding scale to a maximum of 60 for those born after 30 June 1964.

Principal Risk is the difference between the potential benefit the principal (such as a superannuation fund) would receive if the agent (such as an external investment manager appointed to manage funds) performed the task completely in the principal's best interest and the actual benefit the principal received. It is the same thing as agency risk.

Private Equity is an investment in an unlisted company or enterprise.

Public Offer Fund is a super fund that anyone can join.

Restricted Non-preserved: restricted non-preserved benefits are those benefits which are not preserved, but cannot be cashed until a beneficiary meets a condition of release such as termination of employment.

Risk Profile: an individual's risk profile is a description of them, based on how much risk they are willing to take when they invest their money. Investors willing to take on a lot of risk, or "growth" investors, typically seek to maximise their longer term investment and are less worried about the possibility of a negative return. On the other hand, conservative investors typically seek more stable returns.

Rollover – see Consolidate.

Salary Continuance Insurance (SCI) provides a monthly income of a percentage of an individual's pre-disability income (subject to a maximum amount) for a certain period, where an individual becomes disabled due to sickness or injury.

Salary Sacrifice is a way to make before-tax (concessional) contributions to an individual's superannuation account. The money "sacrificed" is paid directly from salary into the individual's super account before they pay income tax. Within super, salary sacrifice is an arrangement between you and your employer where you choose to give up part of your before-tax salary and add it directly into your super account.

Self-Managed Super Funds (SMSF) is a private super fund that an individual can manage for themselves. SMSFs are regulated by the Australian Taxation Office and can have one to four members. All members must be trustees to ensure they are fully involved in the decision-making of the fund.

Small APRA Funds (SAF) are super funds regulated by APRA with less than five members. They have a trustee with an extended public offer licence.

Sovereign Risk originally meant the risk that a government could default on its debt (sovereign debt) or other obligations. This also refers to the risk generally associated with investing in a particular country, or providing funds to its government (also called country risk). The term is popularly applied to *any* risk to business profitability resulting from government policy changes. But this is not an accepted use of the term.

Standard Risk Measure (SRM): The Australian Superannuation Funds Association (ASFA) has produced a guide to enable members to compare the potential risk of various investment plans called the "Standard Risk Measure". The SRM is based on industry guidance developed to allow members to compare investment options that are expected to deliver a similar number of negative annual returns over any 20 year period. The SRM is not a complete assessment of all forms of investment risk. For instance, it does not detail what the size of a negative return could be or the potential for a positive return to be less than a member may require in order to meet their particular objectives. Further, it does not take into account the impact of administration fees and tax on the likelihood of a negative return.

Superannuation is the money saved in a fund during a person's working life, to be used in retirement.

Super Choice – see Choice of Superannuation

Superannuation Guarantee (SG), or the Superannuation Guarantee Charge or Levy, is the compulsory rate (defined by the Commonwealth government) of contributions an employer must make to each individual's superannuation account. As at late 2016, the rate is set at 9.5 per cent.

SuperStream is a package of administrative reforms adopted by the Australian government intended to reduce costs. It includes the introduction of consistent data standards in order to reduce manual handling; the use of tax file numbers as a unique identifier to help administrative processes, and mandatory consolidation of accounts within a fund. Since 2015 (for employers with more than 2o employees and a year later for all others) Superstream is the way businesses must pay employee superannuation guarantee contributions to super funds with payments and data sent electronically in a standard format between employers, funds, service providers, and the ATO. The data is linked to the payment by a unique payment reference number.

Superannuation Surcharge: This is an additional tax that applies where a member's adjusted taxable income (normally the member's taxable income plus surchargeable contributions) is over a specified threshold in a financial year. The government abolished the superannuation surcharge from 1 July 2005. It is important to note, however, that the abolition of the superannuation surcharge does not affect any superannuation surcharge tax liabilities owed before 1 July 2005.

Superannuation Guarantee Charge or levy is a penalty payable by an employer if the minimum Superannuation Guarantee contribution for any employee is not paid on time.

Tax File Number (TFN) is a unique number issued to individuals and organisations by the Australian Taxation Office to increase the efficiency in administering tax and other Commonwealth Government systems such as income support payments.

Transferred Service Benefit is such that where an individual was previously in another superannuation scheme, once they transfer to a new scheme, then this benefit is transferred, based on the past full-time employment accrued by the individual when they transferred.

Transition to Retirement is a strategy that allows an individual to access their superannuation benefit once they have reached their Commonwealth preservation age, in the form of a non-commutable income stream, while they continue to work full or part time.

Trust Deed is in the case of superannuation a legal document that sets out the rules governing the operation of a superannuation fund. Members are entitled to view a copy of their fund's trust deed, although they may be charged a fee to be sent a copy.

Trustee/s are the persons or corporate body that has legal responsibility for the running of a fund in accordance with the requirements laid out in the trust deed. The trustee has a duty to act in good faith and in the best interests of members, and is governed by the Australian Securities & Investments Commission (ASIC) and Australian Prudential Regulation Authority (APRA).

Unit Trust is a collective investment vehicle, established under a trust deed, that continually offers new units and stands ready to redeem existing ones from the owners.

Untaxed Scheme means that the government does not tax either concessional contributions that an individual or those their employer makes, or the investment earnings. Instead of paying tax upfront, tax is paid when a benefit is paid or rolled over to a taxed super fund or retirement income stream.

Unrestricted non-preserved are benefits for which a condition of release has previously been met, and may be accessed at any time (subject to a particular superannuation fund's rules).

Unique Superannuation Identifier (USI) is used to facilitate transfers in and out of accounts.

Vesting is the inclusion of all or part of the employer contributions in the benefit payment to a member who leaves his or her employment before being eligible for a retirement benefit. "Full vesting" means that the member is entitled to all of the employer contributions, while "partial vesting" means that only a portion of the employer's contributions are applied to the member's benefit. A "vesting scale" sets out the rate at which, over the period of employment, the employer's contributions vest in the member. In general, almost all superannuation funds now provide for full vesting for all their members.

Volatility is the degree of fluctuations in an investment, for example share prices, exchange rates, or interest rates. Volatility is one measure of risk.

Voluntary Contributions are additional contributions an individual can make that are over and above the compulsory Superannuation Guarantee that an employer must make on behalf of their employees. Contributions can be made after-tax (non-concessional contributions) or before-tax (concessional contributions), also known as salary sacrificing. They can also be regular or lump-sum payments.

APPENDIX **10**: ABBREVIATIONS

ABLF	Australian Builders' Labourers' Federation
ABN	Australian Business Number
ABS	Australian Bureau of Statistics
AC	Companion of the Order of Australia
ACCI	Australian Confederation of Commerce and Industry
ACM	Australian Chamber of Manufacturers
ACSPA	Australian Council of Salaried and Professional Associations
ACTU	Australian Council of Trade Unions
ADF	Approved Deposit Fund
AEU	Amalgamated Engineers Association
AFEI	Australian Federation of Employers and Industry
AFCC	Australian Federation of Construction Contractors
AFR	Australian Financial Review
AGEST	Australian Government Employees Superannuation Trust
AHA	Australian Hotels Association
AiG	Australian Industry Group
AIRC	Australian Industrial Relations Commission
AIST	Australian Institute of Superannuation Trustees
ALLA	Australian Labour Law Association
ALP	Australian Labor Party
AM	Member of the Order of Australia
AMIEU	Australasian Meat Industry Employees' Union
AMWU	Amalgamated Metal Workers' Union
AMWU	Amalgamated Manufacturing Workers' Union.
AMWSU	Amalgamated Metal Workers' and Shipwrights' Union

ANU	Australian National University
AO	Officer of the Order of Australia
APRA	Australian Prudential Regulatory Authority
APS	Australian Public Service
ARF	Australian Retirement Fund
ASE	Australasian Society of Engineers
ASFA	Association of Superannuation Funds of Australia
ASIC	Australian Securities Investment Commission
ASSLH	Australian Society for the Study of Labour History
ASU	Australian Services Union
ATF	Australian Teachers' Federation
ATO	Australian Tax Office
AUD	Australian Dollar
AUST	Allied Unions Superannuation Trust
AWOTE	Average Weekly Ordinary Time Earnings
AWU	Australian Workers Union
BCA	Business Council of Australia
BIRP	Building Industry Recovery Procedures
BLs	builders' labourers
BLF	Builders' Labourers' Federation
BUSS	Building Unions' Superannuation Scheme
BWIU	Building Workers' Industrial Union of Australia
CAGEO	Council of Australian Government Employee Organisations
CAI	Confederation of Australian Industry
CARE	Clerical and Retail Employees' Superannuation
CATU	Clothing and Allied Trades Union
C+BUS	Construction and Building Unions Superannuation

CBD	central business district (of a city)
CBUS	Construction and Building Unions Superannuation
CEPU	Communication Electrical and Plumbing Union
CFMEU	Construction Forestry Mining and Energy Union
CH	Companion of Honour
CIPR	comprehensive income product for retirement
CLR	Commonwealth Law Reports
CMSF	Conference of Major Superannuation Funds
Commission	the national wage tribunal, known over the years by various names
CPA	Communist Party of Australia
CPA (M-L)	Communist Party of Australia, Marxist-Leninist
CPI	Consumer Price Index
DB	defined benefit
DC	defined contribution
DLP	Democratic Labor Party
EPACn	Economic Planning Advisory Commission
ERF	Eligible Rollover Fund
ESG	environmental, social, and corporate governance
ETU	Electrical Trades Union
FACSIA	Family and Community Services and Indigenous Affairs
FCU	Federated Clerks Union
FEC	Federal Electorate Council
FEDFA	Federated Engine Drivers and Firemen's Association of Australia
FIA	Federated Ironworkers' Association
FLAIEU	Federated Liquor and Allied Industries Employees Union

FMWU	Federated Miscellaneous Workers' Union of Australia
FOFA	Future of Financial Advice
FSC	Financial Services Council
FSI	Financial System Inquiry
FSPU	Federated Storemen and Packers' Union
FSR	Financial Services Reform (Act)
GCL	Grand Companion of the Order of Logohu [Papua New Guinea]
GFC	Global Financial Crisis (since 2008)
HESTA	Health Employees Superannuation Trust of Australia
HSBC	Hong Kong and Shanghai Banking Corporation
IAG	Insurance Australia Group
IFM	Industry Funds Management
IFMI	IFM Investors
IFS	Industry Funds Services
ILO	International Labour Organisation
IMF	International Monetary Fund
IRC	Industrial Relations Commission
ISA	Industry Super Australia
JUST	Journalist Union Super Fund
KG	Knight of the Order of the Garter
LHMU	Liquor, Hospitality and Miscellaneous Union
LISC	Low Income Superannuation Contribution
LISTO	Low Income Super Tax Offset
LSE	London School of Economics and Political Science
LUCRF	Labour Union Co-operative Retirement Fund
MBA	Master Builders' Association
MBE	Member of the British Empire
MBFA	Master Builders' Federation of Australia

ME	Members' Equity
MIES	Meat Industry Employees Superannuation
MIM	Mount Isa Mines
MOA	Municipal Officers' Association
MTAA	Motor Traders Association of Australia
MTIA	Metal Trades Industry Association
MUA	Maritime Union of Australia
MUST	Manufacturing Unions' Superannuation Trust
NATSEM	National Centre for Social and Economic Modelling
NCC	National Civic Council
n.d.	not dated
NLA	National Library of Australia
NRMA	National Roads and Motorists Association
NSW	New South Wales
NUW	National Union of Workers
OAM	Medal of the Order of Australia
OECD	Organisation for Economic Cooperation and Development
OH&S	Occupational Health and Safety
OM	Order of Merit (UK Honour)
PAYG	Pay As You Go
PC	Member of the Privy Council
PGEU	Plumbers and Gasfitters Employees Union of Australia
PPE	Philosophy, Politics and Economics (the popular Arts degree at Oxford)
PPP	Private Public Partnership
PrC	Productivity Commission [an Australian government body]
PSA	Prices Surveillance Authority
PST	Pooled Superannuation Trusts

RBL	Reasonable Benefits Level
REST	Retail Employees Superannuation Trust
ROC	Return of Capital
RSE	Registrable Superannuation Entity
RTA	Retail Traders' Association
SAF	Small APRA Fund
SDA & SDAEA	Shop, Distributive and Allied Employees Association
SEC	State Electricity Commission
SG	Superannuation Guarantee
SGC/L SIS	Superannuation Guarantee Charge/Levy
SIS	Superannuation Industry Supervision (Act)
SMSF	Self-Managed Superannuation Fund
SPA	Socialist Party of Australia
SSR	Super System Review (Cooper Report)
STA	Superannuation Trust of Australia
SUA	Seamen's Union of Australia
TAFE	Technical and Further Education
TCF	Textile Clothing and Footwear
TDC	Trade Development Council
TDCS	Trade Development Council Secretariat
TPD	total and permanent disability
TWU	Transport Workers Union
UK	United Kingdom
UNE	University of New England
UNSW	University of NSW
WIS	Women in Super
WWF	Waterside Workers' Federation

BIOGRAPHIES OF KEY PERSONS MENTIONED IN THE BOOK

Anthony John "Tony" ABBOTT (1957-), political activist, journalist, lawyer, politician, and 28th Prime Minister of Australia, moved from close association with Bob Santamaria's National Civic Council to Liberal politics and he defeated prominent lawyer, leading company director, and Liberal moderate Kevin McCann for pre-selection for Warringah in the Federal parliament, a seat he has held since 1994. Educated in economics and law at the University of Sydney, he took the PPE Arts degree at Queen's College at the University of Oxford and then, as a trainee priest, he studied at St Patricks Seminary, Manly, not completing those studies. From 1998, he held ministerial office in the Howard government, as Minister for Employment Services, Minister for Employment and Workplace Relations, and Minister for Health and Ageing. He defeated Malcolm Turnbull as Opposition Leader in 2009 and relentlessly campaigned against Prime Ministers Rudd, Gillard, and Rudd again, becoming Prime Minister in 2013, after winning the election, his second as Opposition Leader (having almost won in 2010). His fortunes were partly tied to those of his Treasurer, Joe Hockey (q.v.), whom he appointed Shadow Treasurer in 2009. In office he seemed to lose direction and Malcolm (q.v.) Turnbull defeated him in a party room ballot as Prime Minister in September 2015.

Mark BISHOP (1954-), unionist, politician, and businessman, was a senator representing the ALP from Western Australia from 1996 to 2013. Earlier, he was an industrial officer, then secretary of the WA Branch of the shop assistants' union, the SDA. He was educated in law at the University of South Australia and in public policy at Harvard University, where he also completed the Trade Union Program. He played a role in securing CARE as the default super fund for the retail industry in WA, then reversed his position to favour REST.

Anna Christina BOOTH (1956-) has worked as a unionist, company director, and arbitration official. After graduating in 1977 in industrial relations with a Bachelor of Economics (Hons.) from the University of Sydney, she immediately began working as a Research Officer in the national office of the Clothing and Allied Trades Union. Eventually she became its National Secretary and, thereafter, National Secretary of the Textile, Clothing and Footwear Union of Australia (a merger on 1 July 1992 of various unions in the fabrics industry) and a Vice President of the ACTU. She resigned from her union positions in 1996 to take up a position in the private sector with Star Casino. As a union official, she played an important role in the foundation of the Australian Retirement Fund (ARF) as a general manufacturing industries superannuation trust. She was an inaugural member of the board of ARF (now merged into AustralianSuper). She has served on the boards of the Commonwealth Bank of Australia, the National Roads & Motorists Association (NRMA), the Centre for Policy Development, and the Commission for Children and Young People. She was a member of the Sydney Organising Committee for the Olympic Games (SOCOG), and chaired the Torch Relay Committee. Since February 2012, she has been a Deputy President of Fair Work Australia. Immediately prior to this appointment she was a director of the workplace-relations consulting firm CoSolve Pty Ltd, chair of listed law firm Slater & Gordon Ltd, and a non-executive director of retail and wholesale financial services companies Members' Equity Bank and Industry Funds Management (owned by the industry superannuation funds).

Christopher Eyles ("Chris") BOWEN (1973-), politician, graduated with a B.Ec. from the University of Sydney and began his political career as a research officer for the Hon. Janice Crosio, whom he eventually was to replace in 2004 as a Federal MP in western Sydney. Meanwhile he worked in various roles as a ministerial advisor to the NSW Labor Government. Several years after entering Parliament, Bowen was appointed in 2006 to the Labor front bench as Shadow Assistant Treasurer and Shadow Minister for Revenue and Competition Policy. In December 2007 Prime Minister Kevin Rudd appointed him Assistant Treasurer and Minister for Competition

Policy and Consumer Affairs. In June 2009 Bowen was promoted to cabinet as Minister for Financial Services, Superannuation and Corporate Law and Minister for Human Services. In April 2010 Bowen announced significant reforms to the financial-services sector, including banning of commissions for financial planners giving advice on retail investment products including superannuation, managed investments and margin loans; instituting a statutory fiduciary duty so that financial advisors must act in the best interests of their clients; and increasing the powers of the corporate regulator, ASIC. His reforms were partially a response to the high-profile collapse of Storm Financial, Westpoint, and Opes Prime – and the resultant losses for retail investors, but also reflected global concerns with financial governance following the GFC. The reforms were implemented on 1 July 2012. In September 2010, Bowen was appointed Minister for Immigration and Citizenship, and then in February 2013 Minister for Tertiary Education, Skills, Science and Research. But he resigned all Ministerial positions in March 2013 over concerns about the leadership of the Parliamentary Labor Party. He returned to Ministerial office as Treasurer when Kevin Rudd returned to the Prime Ministership in June 2013. After Labor's defeat in September 2013, he was briefly Acting Leader, then Shadow Treasurer after Bill Shorten was elected Labor Leader in October 2013. Whilst between Ministries, Bowen wrote *Hearts and Minds. A Blueprint for Modern Labor* (2013).

Garry BRACK (1950-), lawyer and employers' advocate, succeeded Alan Jones (q.v.) in the mid-1980s as head of the Employers' Federation of NSW, later renamed Employers' First and now the Australian Federation of Employers and Industries (AFEI). He vigorously opposed industry superannuation in the late 1980s, but eventually agreed in 1987 with the NSW Chamber of Manufactures and the Labor Council of NSW to co-found the ASSET Superannuation scheme as a 3 per cent default industry fund for NSW employers. With the merger of Asset into CARE in 2012, he briefly served on the board of trustees of CARE Super.

Wal BUCKLEY (-2004), unionist, was an active job delegate in the then Amalgamated Engineering Union [AEU]. He was instrumental in achieving the AEU's independence from the United Kingdom union of the same name, and went on to assist in the union amalgamations with the Boilermakers and Blacksmiths and the Sheet Metal Works, and later the Shipwrights. These were the formative years of the Amalgamated Metal Workers Union, now the Australian Manufacturing Workers Union. He was on the left of the union movement, but respected by employers like Bert Evans (q.v.).

Tasnor Ivan ("Tas") BULL (1932-2003), union official, was head of the Waterside Workers Federation (WWF), succeeding Charlie Fitzgibbon (q.v.) as national leader. Early in his working life, Bull became a waterside worker (stevedore) in Hobart and was soon a WWF job delegate. Later he worked in Melbourne and Sydney. In 1967 he was elected a Vigilance Officer for the WWF; in 1971 he was elected Federal Organiser, and later Assistant General Secretary. In 1984 he became national General Secretary, a post he held until 1992. He was prominent in the ACTU, becoming a Vice President in 1987, and Senior Vice President in 1991. His leadership occurred during a period of radical change on the waterfront due to technological advances and massive changes in how freight was handled, colloquially called containerisation. Such changes reduced the size of the workforce. Under the Hawke Government, Bull cooperated with the waterfront and industrial relations reforms while defending his members' interests. In 1993 the WWF amalgamated with the seamen's union (the SUA) to form the Maritime Union of Australia (MUA) and, in eventual consequence, Maritime Super, an industry fund. Bull joined the Communist Party of Australia (CPA) in 1951, but left in the late 1950s, disillusioned following the Soviet crushing of the Hungarian revolution. Close to Kelty (qv.) and Hawke (qv.), he supported the ALP Left, though from a critical spirit, in keeping with Fitzgibbon's similar political outlook. Following his retirement in 1993 Bull remained active in various left-wing and union causes, and published his autobiography *Life on the Waterfront* in 1998. One of his protégés was Greg Combet (1958-), the ACTU president from 2000-2007, and Minister in the Rudd and Gillard governments from 2007-2013.

Leonard James ("Jim") CALLAGHAN (1912-2005), Baron Callaghan of Cardiff, KG PC, politician, was Chancellor of the Exchequer, 1964 to 1967; Home Secretary, 1967 to 1970; Foreign Secretary, 1974 to 1976; and Prime Minister of Great Britain from 1976 to 1979. His nickname was "Sunny Jim". See Kenneth Morgan's biography.

Laurie CARMICHAEL (1925-), union leader, was one of the most impressive and inspiring union leaders from the left in the post-war era. A metal worker by trade, Carmichael rose to become Secretary of the Victorian Branch of the Amalgamated Engineering Union. A passionate member of the CPA, in the 1970s he was a strident militant, perceived particularly so by Senator James Robert "Diamond Jim" McClelland (1915-1999), when McClelland was Minister for Labour and Immigration at the end of the Whitlam Government. Political considerations kept Carmichael away from national leadership of his union (his colleagues feared he could lose an election for the ticket), though he was easily the dominant intellectual force in what became the AMWU. As National Research Officer, AMWU, he was a member of the Australia Reconstructed Mission visit to Europe in 1986. He became close to Bill Kelty (q.v.) and Paul Keating (q.v.), with whom he shared a love of Mahler's music. Kelty brought him into the ACTU as Assistant Secretary, where he argued strongly for the Accord and thereby the suite of policies and campaigns that underpinned the union superannuation campaigns. Years later, in his 2009 John Button Oration, Kelty claimed that "… the Accord could not have been achieved without Laurie Carmichael; the ALP could not so easily have won government in 1983, and it could not have governed so effectively without him." See Stutchbury's profile in the *AFR* in August 1984 and his interview in the Reeves and Dettmer book on his old union.

Patrick Martin ("Pat") CLANCY (1919-1987), trade unionist, union strategist, leader of the Building Workers Industrial Union and pro-Moscow communist, cautiously backed the Accord and saw the significance of industry super. He encouraged his successor, Tom McDonald, to support its development, including the formation of the Building Unions' Superannuation Scheme. Clancy was Assistant Secretary (1947) and Secretary (1953) of the NSW branch of the Building Workers' Industrial Union (now part of the CFMEU), then acting Federal Secretary (1971), and Federal Secretary (1973) until his retirement in 1985. See the biographical entry on Clancy by Suzanne Jamieson in the *Australian Dictionary of Biography*, 2007.

Peter Francis Salmon ("Peter") COOK (1947-2005), AM, unionist and politician, was the WA Trades and Labour Council Secretary from 1975 to 1983, and from 1981 to 1983 an ACTU Vice President; he was a Senator for Western Australia from 1983 to 2005. He served as a Minister under the Hawke and Keating governments, including as Minister for Resources, 1988 to 1991; Minister for Industrial Relations, 1990 to 1993; and Minister for Trade, 1993 to 1994. As Minister for Industrial Relations he had carriage of the SGC legislation.

Colin COOPER (-), Federal President, Australian Telecommunications Employees' Association, was a leading figure on the Left, from a pro-Marxist perspective, although from within the ALP. He was a member of the Australia Reconstructed Mission to Europe in 1986.

Jeremy COOPER (1960-), lawyer and financial services practitioner, was Deputy Chairman of the Australian Securities and Investments Commission from 2004 to 2009. He was appointed by Minister Nick Sherry (q.v.) to chair a wide-ranging review of Australia's superannuation system, now known as the Cooper Review. Since 2010, he has been Chairman, Retirement Income at Challenger Limited, a full-time executive role involving aspects of thought leadership, research, policy development and public advocacy of Challenger's philosophies in a range of areas.

Peter Howard COSTELLO (1957-) AC, barrister, politician, and businessman, was Treasurer from 1996 to 2007, throughout the entirety of the Prime Ministership of John Howard (q.v.). In superannuation, he was responsible for many changes, including eliminating Reasonable Benefits Limits, allowing greater choice of funds, and tinkerings to improve the strategic positioning of the self-managed superannuation fund side of the industry. Widely expected to succeed Howard, the latter held on too long as Prime Minister. After the government was defeated in the 2007 election he resigned from Parliament. He joined the Board in 2009 and became Chair in 2014 of the Guardians of the Australian Future Fund. His memoir was published by Melbourne University Press in 2008.

Terry COUNIHAN (-), Director, Consultation and Research Section, Trade Development Council Secretariat, Department of Trade, and Mission Manager, the Australia Reconstructed Mission to Europe in 1986. He was the son of Melbourne radical Noel Counihan (1913-1986).

Ian COURT (1948-), unionist, superannuation trustee, and funds management executive, was educated in economics at La Trobe University. He was a senior industrial officer with the ACTU (1982-1992) and then became Executive Chair of CBUS (1992-1998), then CEO of Development Australia Funds Management Ltd (1998-2004). He became the inaugural president of the Australian Institute of Superannuation Trustees (AIST) in 1993. Since then he has gained extensive experience as a non-executive director in a range of companies and industry sectors. He was a non-executive director and chair of ACTU Member Connect Pty Ltd, chair of the Industry Funds Management Investor Advisory Board and chair of the International Advisory Committee for the IFM Global Infrastructure Fund. Currently he is a non-executive director with AssetCo. Management Pty Ltd and its related Infrastructure PPP companies, SSSR Holdings Pty. Ltd., Praeco Pty. Ltd., and Western Liberty Group Holdings Pty. Ltd. He is Chair of the IFM Investors Shareholder Board and until 2016 non-executive director of Slater and Gordon Ltd., the law firm, and chair of ACTU Member Connect Pty Ltd.

Simon CREAN (1949-), unionist and politician, was a son of former Treasurer and Deputy Prime Minister Frank Crean (1916-2008). After graduating with commerce and law degrees from Monash University at the end of 1970, he started work with the Victorian Branch of the Storemen and Packers (FSPU). He eventually transferred to its national office, where he became Assistant General Secretary and General Secretary from 1976-1985. He joined the ACTU Executive in 1981 and became Senior Vice-President in 1983 and ACTU President in 1985, succeeding Cliff Dolan (q.v.). During the late 1980s he held memberships on the boards of Qantas and the Australian Industry Development Corporation. With Bill Kelty (q.v.) he played a major role in the development of superannuation policy from the early 1980s. Elected Federal Member for the Hotham in 1990, he held ministerial positions until 2013 on the front bench in both government and opposition. In the Hawke and Keating Governments, he served as Minister for Science and Technology, Minister assisting the Treasurer, Minister for Primary Industries and Energy, and Minister for Employment, Education and Training. In Opposition he held various roles, including Deputy Leader of the Opposition and Shadow Treasurer from 1998 until 2001, Leader of the Opposition between 2001 and 2003, and Shadow Treasurer for the period 2003-2004. He held senior portfolios in the Rudd and Gillard Governments until March 2013, when he resigned over leadership issues. He did not contest the September 2013 elections.

Richard Howard Stafford CROSSMAN (1907-1974) OBE, British Labour politician, intellectual, and former editor of *The New Statesman* journal 1970-1972, was a cabinet minister under Prime Minister Harold Wilson, and was the Secretary of State for Social Services, 1968-1970. A speech he gave in 1972 on superannuation and pension policy in the UK, "The Politics of Pensions", was read by Whitlam staffer Race Mathews (q.v.) and, together with the writings of Richard Titmuss (q.v.), constituted key sources of inspiration that led to the commissioning of the superannuation inquiry by Keith Hancock (q.v.) under the Whitlam Government. Andrew Burchell's essay "Crossman and Social Security", 2012, is instructive in discussing the issues that concerned Crossman.

Walter James "Wally" CURRAN (1932-2014) OAM, unionist, joined the meat workers' union, the AMIEU, in 1954 and was its Assistant Secretary for 16 years and then Secretary from 1973 to 1997. In the 1970s, the union set up and loaned money to establish the Meat Industry Employees Superannuation (MIES) fund. Curran, a member of the CPA, then the ALP Socialist Left in Victoria, was interviewed by Wendy Lowenstein (1927-2005) for the NLA Oral History Program for the "Communists and the Left in the arts and community oral history project" in 1995. For further biographical background and an assessment, see: Carney, Shaun (2014) "An Era of Activism has Gone with Wally Curran", *Herald Sun*, 27 March.

Brian John DALEY (1955-), actuary, union leader, and superannuation administrator, graduated with a Bachelor of Mathematics degree from the University of Newcastle, became active in the AMP Staff Officers' Association and in 1985 joined the Federated Miscellaneous Workers' Union as a Research Officer in the National Office. He became national Assistant Secretary, then Victorian Secretary of the Liquor Hospitality and Miscellaneous Union, a position he held for more than a decade, then National President of United Voice and National Officer (Superannuation). He is currently Capital Stewardship Officer for the ACTU. He has been actively involved in industry superannuation since the recognition of superannuation as an industrial issue in the 1980s and has played an important role in policy development and implementation. He was a representative of the ACTU to the Federal Government summit, which developed the Superannuation Guarantee contribution in the early 1990s. He joined AustralianSuper's Board on 1 July 2006 and was previously a Director of one of the predecessor funds, the Australian Retirement Fund (ARF) from 1991-2006. He is a director of Industry Super Property Trust (ISPT) and is on the Industry Superannuation Australia Advisory Council. His industry involvement has included service as a former director of Host Plus (1990-2015),

IFS (1996-2006), AIST and ASFA, the boards of HESTA and AGEST. In 2001, he was awarded the Centenary Medal for outstanding service to industrial relations and trade unions.

John Sydney ("Joe") DAWKINS (1947-) AO, politician and businessman, was Federal Treasurer under Paul Keating (q.v.) from 1991 to 1993.

Joseph ("Joe") DE BRUYN (1949-), union leader, was born in Roosendaal, Holland, in 1949. Abandoning an agricultural economics PhD in 1973, he felt the calling for involvement in the labour movement and began working for the Shop Distributive & Allied Employees' Association (SDA) as a research officer. Always close to Jim Maher (q.v.), he succeeded him in 1978 as Secretary/Treasurer. As a member of the Australia Reconstructed Mission to Europe in 1986, he participated in discussions on the evolution of the modern trade-union movement. Although he felt his members wanted direct wage increases rather than superannuation, he supported the position reached by Maher and Kelty (q.v.) in support of industry super. At first, Maher, de Bruyn, and John Maynes (q.v.) became inaugural members of the CARE Super board of trustees, hoping that this fund would apply to the retail and clerical industries, the latter covered by the Federated Clerks Union (FCU) of Australia. But the retailers, led by the NSW Retailers' Association, and probably quietly supported by the ACTU, favoured a discrete retail industry scheme. This ultimately led the SDA to support the REST scheme, and to abandon to the FCU and other unions the CARE fund, without the SDA's active involvement.

Clifford Ormond "Cliff" DOLAN (1920-2000) AO, union leader, was President of the ACTU from 1980 to 1985, during the period that the Prices and Incomes Accord was negotiated – first, from 1982 to 1983 between the ACTU and the Federal ALP, and second, subsequent iterations following the election of the Hawke Government in 1983. Starting his working life as an electrical apprentice, Dolan joined the Electrical Trades Union and became a full-time officer in the NSW branch in 1949; he was elected Federal Secretary in 1964. Although nominally on the right of the ALP, in 1969 Dolan supported Bob Hawke as ACTU President against the right's candidate, Harold Souter, as he believed Hawke was the best person to lead the modern trade union movement. Dour and cautious, he nonetheless conveyed great personal dignity and an unfailing desire to help people. He served on the ACTU Executive, becoming Vice-President and then, after Bob Hawke moved into Federal politics, becoming ACTU President. See Jenni Hewett's profile "Cliff Dolan: Sure Footed as he Plods Across the Industrial Centre Stage", *Sydney Morning Herald*, 26 December 1981, and [anonymous] "Vale Cliff Dolan: A Lifelong Commitment", *Workers Online*, No. 81, 8 December 2000.

Gerardus Jozef "Dick" DUSSELDORP (1918-2000) AO, was a Dutch-born engineer and migrant to Australia who was the founder of Civil and Civic, the financing arm of which later emerged as Lend Lease Corporation, one of Australia's largest companies and few of global reach in construction and investment management. In 1982 Lend Lease took a 50 per cent stake in Mutual Life & Citizens Assurance Company Limited (MLC) and full control in 1985. Dusseldorp saw steady growth in funds management as a balance to the volatility of the construction industry. Fascinated by funds management, intrigued by MLC's potential, and strongly influenced by the American-based asset consultant Frank Russell, in 1986 MLC's multi-manager, multi-style investment philosophy was introduced. Frank Russell, in turn inspired by its most famous Australian client (and only one at first) became – up to the early 2000s – one of Australia's most influential asset advisers. See: Lindie Clark's biography, *Finding a Common Interest: The Story of Dick Dusseldorp and LendLease*, 2002.

Albert Coulston ("Bert") EVANS (1931-) AO, D.Sc.Ec. (Hon), retired in October 1996 after 38 years' service with the Metal Trades Industry Association (MTIA), now the Australian Industry Group (AiG), the last 15 as Chief Executive. At one time an implacable opponent of the metal workers' union (AMWU), he saw them mellow during the Accord period. With Bill Kelty (q.v.) and Laurie Carmichael (q.v.), though initially with many reservations, he saw the merit of creating the Superannuation Trust of Australia (STA), which was formed as a joint venture between the employer associations and the unions. It thereby dislodged the manufacturing unions' scheme (MUST), which was exclusively owned by the unions. Evans was made a Member of the Order of Australia and further honoured in 1996 when he was made an Officer. In 1993 the Senate of the University of Sydney conferred upon him a Doctorate of Science in Economics, *honoris causa*. He served as Executive Chairman of STA for many years.

Martin FERGUSON (1953-) AM, union leader and politician, after obtaining a degree in economics at the University of Sydney, joined the Federated Miscellaneous Workers' Union under Ray Gietzelt (q.v.) as Research Officer; he later became Assistant General Secretary and General Secretary of the union, Vice-President of the ACTU from 1985 to 1990, and President of the ACTU from 1990 to 1996, succeeding Simon Crean (q.v.). He was a Member of the Australia Reconstructed Mission to Europe in 1986. He recruited Brian Daley (q.v.) to assist both his union and the ACTU in the forging of national superannuation policy. Elected Federal MP for Batman in 1996, he immediately was appointed to Labor's frontbench and, with Labor's election to office in 2007, served as Minister for Resources and as Minister for Tourism; he resigned all Ministerial positions in March 2013 over concerns about the leadership of the Parliamentary Labor Party and did not contest the September 2013 elections.

Dr Vincent William ("Vince") FITZGERALD (1944-) AO, public servant, public policy intellectual, and consultant is a former senior government official in Canberra in the Departments of the Treasury, Prime Minister and Cabinet, Finance (Deputy Secretary), Trade (Secretary), and Employment, Education and Training (Secretary). His 1993 report *National Saving: A Report to the Treasurer* was influential. With the Allen Consulting Group, he consulted to the Business Council of Australia and the government on superannuation and other issues. He was educated in economics at the University of

Queensland and at Harvard University where he obtained a PhD in economics.

Charles Henry ("Charlie") FITZGIBBON (1922-2001) AM, union leader, undertook the various roles of President and Vigilance Officer of the Newcastle Branch of the Waterside Workers' Federation (WWF) and served as national General Secretary, WWF, from 1961 to 1983 and Senior Vice-President of the ACTU from 1980 to 1983. He was made a Member of the Order of Australia in 1984. Bill Kelty (q.v.) credits him with setting up an important precedent for industrial superannuation through the stevedores' schemes created in the early 1970s in the aftermath of industrial disputes concerning containerisation. Tas Bull (q.v.) worked closely with Fitzgibbon in these matters. The C.H. Fitzgibbon Papers, 1929-1989, P102, are deposited with the Noel Butlin Archives Centre, ANU Archives. As part of the NLA/Labor Council of NSW Oral History Program, he was interviewed by Richard Raxworthy in 1986. See the National Library of Australia Oral History Collection, ORAL TRC 1948/19.

Bernard William ("Bernie") FRASER (1941-), economist, was born in Junee and educated at the UNE and the ANU. He joined the public service in 1961 and the Treasury Department in 1963. He was Secretary to the Australian Treasury from 1984 to 1989, then Governor of the Reserve Bank from 1989 to 1996. He worked closely with Paul Keating (q.v.) and was instrumental in the economic reforms and initiatives of the Hawke and Keating Governments. After he left the public sector, he played a major role with the industry funds, serving as an independent director or chair of a number, including CBUS and AustralianSuper, and also as a director of Members' Equity. From the late 1990s, he became the reassuring face of the industry funds in publicity materials and television and radio advertisements. See Lucinda Schmidt's profile in *The Melbourne Age*, 19 March 2008.

Norm GALLAGHER (1931-1999), unionist and Marxist-Leninist, led the militant Builders' Labourers' Federation (BLF) as Federal Secretary and as Victorian State Secretary. Raised in Melbourne, he joined the BLF in 1951. By 1970, he was elected as the BLF's Victorian State Secretary and sought to radically improve pay and conditions on building sites. His ideas were influenced through his membership and leadership of the pro-Maoist Communist Party of Australia (Marxist-Leninist) (CPA M-L), a breakaway from the CPA in the 1960s. Partly influenced by the NSW BLF but also acting independently, as Secretary of the union he acted to preserve distinct Melbourne boulevards such as Royal Parade from development and many historic buildings from destruction, including the Regent Theatre and the City Baths. Such positions, defensible in themselves, also widened public support for the union. A BLF black ban protected the historic Bakery Hill site in Ballarat, where huge mass meetings were held in 1854 during the Eureka rebellion, from development. The distinctive Eureka flag became the emblem of the BLF. Gallagher embraced controversy when he directed the Federal branch to sack the pro-CPA NSW leadership and take over that branch of the union in the mid-1970s. Gallagher was criticised for lifting some of the NSW branch's Green Bans. Gallagher fought the pro-SPA leadership of the Building Workers' Industrial Union (BWIU) both industrially and ideologically. Larger than life, he was brought down by hubris, corruption allegations, and legal action. He contested the development of the Building Unions' Superannuation Scheme fund, partly because he believed that the BWIU were too dominant in the fund and rejected the bosses' involvement. Following a Royal Commission into the BLF's business affairs, the union was deregistered. Gallagher was convicted of obtaining building materials from construction companies while he himself was building a holiday house in Gippsland. On appeal, a retrial was ordered but not before Gallagher had spent four months in gaol. By 1992-93 the officials, staff, and members of the BLF were exhausted, with Gallagher himself in ill health. Bereft of funds, the BLF was forcibly amalgamated into what is now called the Construction Forestry and Mining Employees' Union (CFMEU). Gallagher died in Melbourne in retirement. A sympathetic tribute was written by the former NSW BLF head Steve Black, "Norm Gallagher – A Tribute", 2000.

Patrick GERAGHTY (1928-2016) AM, seaman and union leader, was raised in Balmain, shipped out as a deckboy in 1947, and like many seamen in the post-war years was employed on British and Scandinavian ships, seeing much of the world in the process; his experiences led him to become an active unionist and communist. Trusted by the union's leadership, in 1961-1962 he acted as Federal returning officer in the union elections. In 1967 he left his job as bosun on the Calla Liverpool (sometimes referred to as Calta Moscow) and took office as Assistant Federal Secretary of the SUA, to work closely with the maritime legend, Federal Secretary E.V. Elliott (1902-1984). Geraghty represented the SUA in the 1969 Work Value Inquiry before Judge Gallagher, which helped create the historic aggregate wage for seafarers. He was also the driving force behind the creation of the Seafarers' Retirement Fund. Following Elliott's retirement in 1979, Geraghty took over as Federal Secretary, a position he held to retirement in 1991. See Rowan Cahill's profile in *The Hummer*, 1992.

Raymond ("Ray") GIETZELT (1922-2012) AO was General Secretary of the Federated Miscellaneous Workers Union (FMWU), popularly called the "missos", from 1955 to 1984. Originally sympathetic to the pro-communist Left, Gietzelt moved to a strong left position in the ALP, expunging communist influences, particularly after anti-communist campaigns in his union by his opponents in the early 1970s. He was close to Neville Wran (1926-2014), the NSW lawyer, QC, and Premier of NSW from 1976 to 1986; Lionel Murphy (1922-1986), the controversial Whitlam Government Attorney General and High Court Judge; and Bob Hawke (q.v.), whom he decisively backed as ACTU President in 1969 against the right-wing candidate, ACTU Secretary Harold Souter (1911-1994). Gietzelt ran a highly efficient, professional union, an exemplar for many others. He recruited Martin Ferguson (q.v.), whom he groomed as his successor. United Voice is the union formed from the merger of the LHMU and FMWU. See Gietzelt's memoirs, *The Memoirs of Ray Gietzelt: General Secretary of the Federated Miscellaneous Workers Union of Australia 1955-1984*, 2004, and Harriett Veitch's obituary in the *Sydney Morning Herald*, 20 December 2012.

Julia Eileen GILLARD (1961-), lawyer and politician, was the 27th Prime Minister of Australia. After completing degrees at Adelaide and Melbourne universities, and working as a lawyer, she was elected to the Federal parliament in 1998 as MP for Lalor, succeeding Barry Jones. Holding various Shadow Ministries from 2001, in 2006 she joined Kevin Rudd in successfully challenging the then ALP leadership of Kim Beazley and Jenny Macklin, to become Deputy Leader of the Opposition in 2006 and, from 2007, Deputy Prime Minister and Minister for Education and Minister for Employment and Industrial Relations. On 24 June 2010 she became Prime Minister of Australia after challenging Prime Minister Rudd for the top job. Widely popular among colleagues, self-deprecating and sharply attentive in private, she referenced her uncertainty in projecting her image by saying in the 2010 election campaign, which she narrowly won as the leader of a minority government, that "the real Julia Gillard" needed to be better known. Never quite overcoming her "Lady Macbeth" reputation for deposing Rudd, her reputation sank after reversing a promise not to introduce a carbon tax on her watch as Prime Minister. She was scurrilously attacked in social media. Administratively, she ran an effective government – things got done, legislation was passed, the nitty gritty was attended to – but she was criticised for lacking strategic direction and nous. Kevin Rudd revenged his vanquish by deposing her as Prime Minister in a ballot of Labor MPs on 26 June 2013. She retired from parliamentary politics at the election later that year.

Graeme Alexander "Sandy" GRANT (1944-), superannuation administrator and industry fund pioneer, as CEO of Jacques Martin, owned by Colonial Mutual, in the mid-1980s provided administration and consulting services to industry superannuation funds and thereby came to closely work with Bill Kelty (q.v.), Garry Weaven (q.v.) , Tom McDonald (q.v.) and others in providing assistance to the development of superannuation schemes as an avid supporter of the industry-fund model. He has been formally involved in the industry-fund sector since 1986. He worked for Industry Funds Services (IFS) as managing director, 1997-2004, and was chief executive of CBUS from 2004 to 2008. He retired from CBUS in early 2008 and thereafter became Chair of CARE Super for a term, where he is still a director, and served as a director of Members' Equity bank.

Keith Jackson HANCOCK (1935-) AO, academic economist and labour-relations expert, was the foundation Professor of Economics at Flinders University, and subsequently became Vice-Chancellor of the University. Barry Jones recalls Hancock and he conceiving the idea of the Chifley Memorial Lectures, sponsored by the Melbourne University Labour Club, from the early 1950s. See Jones' Light on the Hill Speech, *circa* 2000. Hancock was commissioned by the Whitlam Government to chair an inquiry into the merits of a review of a national system of superannuation; he reported in 1977, under the Fraser Government, which rejected his main recommendations supporting a national superannuation plan. Under the Hawke Government, he was commissioned to do a review of the industrial-relations system and reported in 1985. By the time legislation was introduced, at first in 1987, then again in 1988 (after elections the previous year), the Government had become more emboldened to look at ILO treaties as providing more certain and diverse "heads of power" to extend the jurisdiction of industrial law; significantly so in the field of superannuation. From 1987 Hancock served for 10 years as Deputy President and Senior Deputy President of the Australian Conciliation and Arbitration Commission and the Australian Industrial Relations Commission. On retirement, he became a Professorial Fellow in the National Institute of Labour Studies at Flinders University and an Honorary Visiting Fellow in the School of Economics at the University of Adelaide; he is now an Emeritus Professor there. His publications include (with S. Richardson) *Conciliation & Arbitration?: the Economic & Social Effects* (2003) and his essay "Wage Determination in the Twentieth Century Australian Economy" (2005). A *festschrift* edited by Joe Isaac and Russell Lansbury, was published in 2005: *Rewriting the Rules: Essays in Honour of Keith Hancock*. This Keith Hancock is not to be confused with Sir Keith Hancock (1898-1988), the Australian historian.

Greg HARRISON (1947-), unionist and tribunal member, was an official in the NSW Branch, then in the national office of the Amalgamated Metal Workers' Union, and the pioneer of the Manufacturing Unions' Superannuation Trust (MUST) scheme in the metal industry, which eventually folded into STA. From 1984 to 1989 he was Assistant National Secretary of the AMWU. He resigned from union roles to become a Commissioner of the AIRC, then Fair Work Australia, from 1989 to 2012.

Robert James Lee ("Bob") HAWKE (1929-) AC GCL, former Australian politician and trade unionist, was the 23rd Prime Minister of Australia and the parliamentary leader of the ALP from 1983 to 1991. Educated at the University of Western Australia, he was a Rhodes Scholar at Oxford University and started as a Research Officer at the ACTU in 1958. He was then elected as President in 1969, taking over from Albert Monk (1900-1975) who had been President for 20 years. Through Hawke, the ACTU modernised, expanded staff, and obtained extensive media publicity. The larrikin, thoughtful, sometimes argumentative and conciliatory Hawke became the public face of the union movement. The relationship between the ACTU and the ALP grew stronger, notwithstanding the travails of the Whitlam government, between 1972 and 1975, when there was more support of strike action than in the past. He was to learn some hard lessons from that period. Under Hawke, the ACTU established stronger links with white-collar unions and organisations, many of which merged or initiated merger talks with the ACTU. He served as ACTU President until 1980, when he entered the Federal Parliament. From 1983 to 1991, he was Prime Minister, until he lost a leadership vote to Paul Keating (q.v.).

Denis Winston HEALEY (1917-2015), Baron Healey of Riddlesden, CH, MBE, PC, politician, was Chancellor of the Exchequer from 1974 to 1979 and therefore in charge of economic policy under the Callaghan government. His memoirs, *The Time of My Life*, are amongst the best ever written by a former politician.

Dr. Kenneth Ross ("Ken") HENRY (1957-) AC, economist and public servant, worked from 1986 to June 1991 as a senior advisor to the then Treasurer, Paul Keating (q.v.). He went on, from 2001 to retirement in 2011, to be Secretary of the Treasury Department. He conducted the Henry review of tax policy for Federal Treasurer Wayne Swan from 2009 to 2010. In all his roles with Treasury, he played an important role in fashioning tax and superannuation policy. He is presently non-executive director and Chairman of the Board of the National Australia Bank.

Henry Bournes HIGGINS (1851-1929), lawyer, arbitration advocate, and politician, was elected a Protectionist candidate for a working class seat in Melbourne. In the John Christian Watson Labor government of 1904 he was made Attorney General. Deakin appointed him a justice of the High Court of Australia from 1906 to his death. In 1907, he was also appointed President of the newly created the Commonwealth Court of Conciliation and Arbitration, created to arbitrate disputes between unions and employers. See John Rickard's biography, 1994.

Joseph Benedict HOCKEY (1965-), lawyer, political adviser, Liberal politician, and diplomat, was MP for North Sydney in the Federal Parliament, 1996-2015; Shadow Treasurer, 2009 to 2013; and, under Prime Minister Tony Abbott, Treasurer of Australia, 2013 to 2015. In the Howard governments, he held ministerial office from 1998, including as Minister for Financial Services and Regulation, Small Business and Tourism, Human Services, and Employment and Workplace Relations. Earlier, he was a lawyer with Corrs Chambers Westgarth law firm and Director of Policy to the then Premier of New South Wales, John Fahey. He initiated the Financial System Inquiry chaired by David Murray.

John Winston HOWARD (1939-) OM AC, lawyer and politician, was the 25th Prime Minister of Australia. Elected MP for Bennelong from 1974 to 2007, he held various offices including as Federal Treasurer, 1977-1983; Deputy Leader of the Opposition, 1982-1985; Leader of the Opposition, 1985-1989 and again from 1995; Prime Minister,

1996-2007. In Opposition he shifted from protectionist, Menzies-like conservatism to more free market stances, particularly concerning industrial relations. An opponent of Labor's superannuation guarantee, he nonetheless supported the opening up of the Australian economy and many of the economic reforms in the early years of the Hawke government. He was one of the important modernisers both of his own party and of Australia. Intensely disliked by Keating (q.v.), and never tremendously popular, he was a shrewd judge of political trends and was genuinely interested in and a contributor to public policy debates. The title of his autobiography, *Lazarus Rising*, neatly summed up the vicissitudes of his career.

Terry JOHNSON (1942-2010), unionist, was National Secretary of the ETU, and a Member of the Australia Reconstructed Mission to Europe in 1986. He had been a full-time ETU official for 19 years from 1972-1991, starting as an organiser in the NSW Branch before being appointed in 1976 to the union's National Office as National Research and Industrial Officer. He became Assistant National Secretary in 1979 before rising to ETU National Secretary in 1986, a position he held until 1991. In 1962, prior to becoming an ETU official, he had completed his apprenticeship as an electrical fitter mechanic and from 1963 to 1972 he had worked at publisher John Fairfax & Sons, where he was shop steward. He supported industry super in a variety of industry funds. See [anonymous] (2010) "Vale Terry Johnson", *Livewire*, Quarterly Journal of the ETU, NSW Branch, Autumn, p. 16.

Alan Belford JONES (1941-) AO, had a varied career as a teacher, coach, employer advocate, speech writer, radio personality and, from the late 1970s to 1985, as Executive Director of the Employers Federation of NSW. It was during this time that he started his radio career. Both Simon Crean (q.v.) and Greg Sword (q.v.) remember memorable clashes with Jones on industrial relations, but found him surprisingly sympathetic to the principle of widespread superannuation coverage. At the Employers Federation he was succeeded by Garry Brack (q.v.). A detailed – though unfriendly – profile is Chris Masters' biography.

Dr Michael Stockton KEATING (1940-) AC, senior bureaucrat and economist, graduated in economics at Melbourne University and wrote a PhD at the ANU. As a senior bureaucrat, he was head of Employment and Industrial Relations, 1983-86; Finance, 1986-1991, and then on the recommendation of Paul Keating (q.v., no relation) head of Prime Minister and Cabinet, 1991-96. He was responsible for overseeing the Superannuation Guarantee legislation. Since retirement from the Commonwealth public service he has worked as an academic and independent researcher.

Paul John KEATING (1944-), politician and businessman, was elected Federal MP for Blaxland in 1969 and went on to become the 24th Prime Minister of Australia and the parliamentary leader of the ALP from 1991 to 1996. He served as Treasurer from 1983 to 1991, resigning in June 1991 and becoming Prime Minister in December 1991, defeating Bob Hawke (q.v.) in a ballot of members of the parliamentary Labor Party. His rapier wit, restless intelligence, and enterprising mind made him a compelling figure to pursue and explain the economic reforms of his time. Defeated at the 1996 elections, he actively pursued business interests, becoming Chair of the Australian operations of the investment bank Lazard.

William John ("Bill") KELTY (1948-) AC, trade unionist, was Secretary of the ACTU from 1983 to 2000. He studied economics at La Trobe University, along with Garry Weaven (q.v.) and David Morgan (q.v.), graduating with a Bachelor of Economics degree in 1969. He was particularly impressed with Professor Don Whitehead (q.v.), who inspired him to lift his grades and to think more about macro-economic issues, including superannuation, inflation and, especially, industrial relations. His professional union activity began as an industrial officer with the Federated Storemen and Packers' Union, 1970, a research officer with the Workers' Educational Association, Adelaide, 1974, and a research officer/advocate with the ACTU in 1974 where he worked closely with Harold Souter, the then Secretary, who retired in 1977. From 1977 to 1983, he was assistant secretary of the ACTU, and succeeded Peter Nolan (1934-2012) as ACTU secretary from 1983-2000, starting his new role on the eve of the Accord in January 1983. As Secretary, his impact was immediate, as he was one of the authors of the Accord between the unions and the Labor Government. He played an astonishing role in reaching out across the political spectrum, including to communist leaders like Laurie Carmichael (q.v.) and, to the right's Jim Maher (q.v.), who had been close to the National Civic Council and, until 1985 outside of the ALP for thirty years. Such alliances were built on personal rapport and respect, and were essential in his ability to carry the union movement with him on major reform questions, including industrial relations, union amalgamation, award modernisation, and the development of the modern Australian system of superannuation. He was a member of the Australia Reconstructed Mission to Europe in 1986, which was both an opportunity to explore what European unions were doing in a multitude of fields, including retirement savings, and to deepen friendships with a diverse mix of union leaders. He was close to both Hawke (q.v.) and Keating (q.v.). The partnership he forged with the latter invigorated and sustained the government, especially in taking the initiative in superannuation. Retiring from the ACTU in 2000, he served on superannuation boards and joined Linfox Group and various boards. Past appointments include: Director of the Reserve Bank, Chairman of the Superannuation Trust of Australia, director of the Australian Retirement Fund, and director of Industry Funds' Investments. He was made an AC in 2008 for services to the trade union movement, particularly through the establishment of the universal system of superannuation, through improvements to productivity and conditions in the workplace, and the development of youth training schemes.

John Charles KERIN (1937-) AM, economist, farmer, and politician, worked at the Australian Bureau of Agricultural and Resource Economics (ABARE) before being elected for the ALP as Federal MP for Macarthur in 1972. He lost the seat in the 1975 election, and returned to ABARE, before being re-elected as member for Werriwa in 1978 after Gough Whitlam's retirement. He served as Minister for Primary Industries (1983-1987), Minister for Primary Industries and Energy (1987-1991), Minister for Transport and Communications (1991), Minister for Trade and Overseas Development (1991-1993), and Treasurer (1991) in the Labor government of Bob Hawke. Since leaving politics in 1993, he has served with various bodies including the Australian Meat and Livestock Corporation, the CSIRO, the Poultry Cooperative Research Centre, the Australian Weed Research Centre, the CRC for Tropical Savannahs Management, UNICEF Australia and the National Ovine Johne's Disease Programme Advisory Committee. In 2001 he was appointed as a Member of the Order of Australia for services to the Australian Parliament. In the same year, he was awarded the Centenary Medal for services to Australian society in technological science and engineering. He has a long association with The Crawford Fund: after serving on the Crawford Fund Board and as chair of the Crawford Fund NSW and ACT Committees for some years, he was elected as Chair of the Crawford Fund Board in October 2010.

Cheryl KERNOT (1958-), née Paton, politician, academic and political activist, was a member of the Australian Senate, representing Queensland and the Australian Democrats, from 1990 to 1997, and led the Australian Democrats from 1993 to 1997. She supported the amendments to legislation that led to the Superannuation Guarantee legislation under Paul Keating in 1992. As the Democrats held the balance of power in the Senate, her support for such legislation was crucial. In 1997 she resigned from the Democrats, joined the ALP and won a seat in the House of Representatives, Dickson in Queensland, for a single term to 2001. Thereafter, after unsuccessfully standing as an independent in NSW for the Senate in 2010, Kernot has worked as a researcher and academic in the field of social policy, including at the UNSW.

William Albert ("Bill") LANDERYOU (1944-), unionist, politician and businessman, became an organiser of the Federated Storemen and Packers' Union (FSPU) in 1966, Victorian State Secretary in 1969 to 1975, Federal Secretary in 1974 to 1979, and Federal President in 1979 to 1982. He recruited Greg Sword (q.v.), Bill Kelty (q.v.) and Simon Crean (q.v.), amongst others, to the union, which played a major role in the development of industry super through the creation of the LUCRF scheme in the late 1970s. Elected to the Victorian Legislative Council in 1976, he served until resignation as an MP in 1992. After the formation of the Cain Labor Government in 1982, he became Victorian Minister for Economic Development and Tourism; later that year he became Minister for Industrial Affairs and Minister for Labour and Industry. Since retirement from politics, he has pursued private business interests.

John Terrence ("Terry") LUDEKE (1921-2013), lawyer and judge, was a controversial figure amongst unionists. Although he started active political life as an industrial officer for the Industrial Groups in the early 1950s, he moved away from such NCC sympathies. He worked as industrial advocate for the Australian Hoteliers' Association and went on to serve as a barrister for all sides, though mostly the employers. Appointed to the Commission as a judge, Ludeke was seen as prickly and opinionated. Others saw a man of independent mind who began to have doubts about the economic efficacy of compulsory conciliation and arbitration. In late 1983 he successfully persuaded his fellow justices to reject the proposed building-industry agreement, including its the Building Industry Recovery Procedures (BIRP) allowance. This spurred the unions to seek the allowance through superannuation, then deemed, through a quirk of interpretation of the law at the time, as a non-industrial matter and therefore for the industrial tribunals *ultra vires*. He dismissed the second 3 per cent superannuation claim in 1986 on "economic grounds", which provoked Keating (q.v.) and Kelty (q.v.) to call for legislation, by way of a superannuation guarantee, to provide minimum standards for superannuation. Thus, inadvertently, he played an important role in fathering the modern Australian superannuation system. In retirement, he wrote a short polemical book extolling the argument that in certain industries, such as parts of the mining industry, unions either were out of place or had to earn their place. See his *Line in the Sand: The Long Road to Staff Employment in Comalco*, 1996.

James ("Jim") MAHER (1927-2009) AO, joined the shop assistants' union SDA in 1946; by the time he retired as National President in 1995, the union was Australia's largest, with more than 230,000 members. He was Victorian State Secretary from 1973-1991 and National President from 1970-1995. He was also an ACTU Vice-President for more than 10 years, retiring as Senior Vice-President. After the election of the Hawke Government in 1983, he led the old Grouper, ex-NCC unions, the Ironworkers, Clerks, the Amalgamated Society of Carpenters and Joiners, and the SDA back into the Victorian Branch of the ALP in 1985. He received the Order of Australia (AO) in 1988 for his contribution to Australian and international trade unionism. Along with his deputy and protégé, Joe de Bruyn (q.v.), Maher was initially unsympathetic to the development of industry super – preferring "money in the pocket" for his low-paid workforce. He tried to forge an alliance with the Federated Clerks Union (FCU) in forming the Clerical and Retail Employees (CARE) scheme. Although CARE was established, opposition from retailers and probably, discreetly, the ACTU, led to the establishment of the REST scheme as the dominant super scheme for the retail industry. Maher became close to Bill Kelty (q.v.), and supported the ACTU Secretary's strategic initiatives in superannuation and industrial relations more generally. See the obituary by Michael Easson, "Maher Created a Powerful Force", published in the *Sydney Morning Herald*, 4 January 2010.

John William MacBEAN (1935-) AM, unionist and industrial tribunal member, was Secretary of the Labor Council of NSW, 1984-1988, and Senior Vice President, ACTU, 1985 to 1987. He was Deputy Head of the Australia Reconstructed Mission to Europe in 1986. He played an important role in forging a broad consensus for the Accord and, in NSW, consolidating the State public-sector superannuation schemes and improving eligibility and vesting benefits for blue-collar workers. See Marilyn Dodkin's chapter on MacBean, described him as "The Consensus Secretary", in her book *Brothers: Eight Leaders of the Labor Council of New South Wales*, 2001.

Tom McDONALD (1926-) AM, was born in Balmain, reared in Glebe, a carpenter by trade, a union member for 72 years to date, he was NSW State Secretary then a national official of the Building Workers' Industrial Union (BWIU) for 41 Years, including as National Secretary, 1985-1991, where he helped to form the Construction Forestry and Mining Union (CFMEU), an amalgamation of twenty unions. He was an ACTU Vice President. He was a member of the Australia Reconstructed Mission to Europe in 1986 and, earlier, a founding Trustee of the Building Unions' Superannuation Scheme, now CBUS, for 10 years, and instrumental in the formation of the building unions' superannuation. He was awarded Membership of the Order of Australia (AM) in 1993. In retirement from 1991, he and his wife Audrey published a memoir, *Intimate Union*, 1998, which covered a life of union and radical politics, including adherence to the pro-Moscow wing of the communist movement, something he saw as tragically flawed after communism's collapse in Eastern Europe. An update in a new book is their McDonald, Audrey & Tom *Dare to Dream. Stories of Struggle and Hope*, 2016. Well liked across the industrial and political spectrum, though regarded as militant he was considered a man of his word who stuck by agreements. As part of the NLA/Labor Council of NSW Oral History Program, he was interviewed by Richard Raxworthy in 1994. See National Library of Australia Oral History Collection, ORAL TRC 3128/8.

Mike McKAY (), unionist and superannuation administrator, worked in superannuation as an Industrial Officer at the ACTU. He was instrumental in the establishment of many of the Industry Funds and involved in the original Superannuation Guarantee Legislation. He subsequently held a series of senior roles within industry super (including as Chair of CBUS), joining consulting firm John Nolan and Associates (JANA) in 1992. Subsequent roles were in funds management, including HSBC Asset Management. He currently serves as the Chair of the Advisory Board at Mclowd Pty Ltd.

William Clements ("Bill") MANSFIELD (1942-2011), union leader and industrial tribunal member, spent a lifetime in industrial relations and was one of the most under-rated, if extremely professionally competent, union leaders of his time. Raised in Yarrawonga in northern Victoria, he left Wangaratta Technical College in year 10 at 15 years of age, subsequently qualified as a communications technician, and studied years 11 and 12 at night school. Active with the telecommunications employees' union, in 1963 he was appointed Assistant Secretary of the Victorian Branch of the Australian Telecommunications Employees Association. In 1966 he moved to the Federal office of the union, where he held various senior positions. He studied law part-time at the University of Melbourne, graduating in 1972 at the age of 30. In 1977 he was elected Federal secretary of the union, a position he held until in 1985 when he was elected ACTU Assistant Secretary, a position he held to 2002 when he was appointed a Commissioner of the Australian Industrial Relations Commission. He provided powerful backup to Bill Kelty (q.v.), Garry Weaven (q.v.), Iain Ross (q.v.) and other union leaders, and played important roles in union campaigns, including in the areas of training, education, OH&S, and superannuation. He was active representing the ACTU at the ILO and other fora.

Keith Douglas MARSHALL (1924-) AM, industrial-relations expert and tribunal member, was the Registrar, and later President, of the Victorian Industrial Relations Commission to 1982.

Charles Race Thorson ("Race") MATHEWS (1935-), politician, author, and cooperative economist, trained as a teacher and speech therapist before joining the staff of the Leader of the Opposition, the Hon. E.G. Whitlam, as Principal Private Secretary from 1967-1972. He played a major role in developing ALP policies prior to the ALP's victory in 1972 (and his own as Federal MP for Casey, which he held to 1975). In the early 1970s Mathews was attracted to the writings of Richard Crossman, the UK Labour politician, and to the advocacy of a national system of superannuation. This was part of the genesis of thinking that led to the commissioning of the Hancock

Inquiry on superannuation. After Federal politics, Mathews served in the Victorian Parliament as a MP from 1979 to 1992, including as a Minister from 1982 to 1988. Subsequently he wrote a PhD and published a number of books on the Fabian, cooperative, and Christian socialist traditions which are amongst the finest ever written in Australia. Note in particular his co-edit of *Whitlam Re-visited: Policy Development, Policies and Outcomes* (1992), and his own works, *Australia's First Fabians: Middle-Class Radicals, Labour Activists and the Early Labour Movement* (1993), and *Jobs of Our Own: Building a Stakeholder Society* (1999).

John Peter MAYNES (1923-2009) AM, union leader, after the ALP split in Victoria in 1955, became the most prominent member of the NCC block in the union movement and the leader of the Federated Clerks Union, as Federal President. According to Gerard Henderson's biography of Santamaria, he was the Industrial Officer of the NCC from 1957 to its split in 1982. He was a founding trustee director of CARE in 1986. See several tributes written in 2009: Gerard Mercer "John Maynes and the Movement" and John Lee "Grouper Who Defined an Era".

David Raymond MORGAN (1947-) AO, economist and business leader, worked at the International Monetary Fund in Washington in the 1970s and the Federal Treasury in the 1980s. He headed all major areas of the Treasury before being appointed the Senior Deputy Secretary during the Hawke-Keating Federal government, contributing to government policy for the financial sector, including the floating of the Australian dollar, financial deregulation more generally and the development of superannuation policy. He knew Bill Kelty (q.v.) and Garry Weaven (q.v.) at La Trobe, where they studied economics, with Morgan top of the class. He also received a Master of Science in Economics (with Distinction) and a Doctor of Philosophy (Economics) from the London School of Economics, and completed the Advanced Management Program at Harvard Business School. After a career in the public service in 1990 he became a banker, becoming CEO of Westpac Banking Corporation from 1999 to 2008. Subsequent company directorships included a stint as a non-executive director of BHP Billiton Ltd,. In 2008 he became a partner and Chairman of the Australian operations of the US-based specialist investment firm JC Flowers, subsequently becoming Executive Chairman for JCF Europe and Asia Pacific, and a member of the firm's Management Committee, based in London He is married to Roslyn Joan ("Ros") Kelly (1948-) AO, a former Minister in the Hawke and Keating governments.

Scott John MORRISON (1968-), geographer, political activist, and politician, grew up in Sydney's eastern suburbs, graduated in applied economic geography at the UNSW and worked in the tourism and property sectors, including with the Property Council of Australia and the Tourism and Transport Forum. From 2000 to 2004 he was NSW State Director of the Liberal Party and in 2007 was elected MP for Cook, covering Sydney's southern beachside suburbs. After serving as Minister for Immigration and Border Protection, then Minister for Social Security in the Abbott government, he was appointed Treasurer of Australia by Prime Minister Turnbull in September 2015. His 2016-17 Budget was controversial, especially among traditional Liberals, for trying to claw back generous superannuation tax concessions.

David Victor MURRAY (1949-) AO, businessman, was Chief Executive of the Commonwealth Bank from 1992 to 2005, including the period it privatised. He rose from teller and part-time student, activist in the then Commonwealth Bank Officers' Association, to the top, growing increasingly conservative along the way. Widely respected for his business acumen, he was Chairman of the Board of Guardians of the Australian Future Fund, 2006 to 2012. He was appointed by Treasurer Joe Hockey (q.v.) to conduct a review into the financial system, the Financial System Inquiry (FSI) which reported in 2014 and made sweeping proposals to change the superannuation industry, including consideration of auctions for default superannuation. In 2007 he was awarded an AO for service to the finance sector nationally and internationally through strategic leadership and policy development, to education, particularly fostering relations between educational institutions and business and industry, and to the community as a supporter of and fundraiser for cultural and church organisations.

Peter Ian NOLAN (1934-2012), unionist and tribunal member, started working life as an apprentice printer in Tasmania, rising to elected positions with the union. Later he departed for a role as Industrial Officer with the Victorian Trades Hall Council. He became the ACTU's assistant secretary in 1971, and then the first assistant secretary from 1975, then Secretary from 1977 to 1983, succeeding Harold Souter (1911-1994), who was ACTU Secretary from 1956 to 1977. He left initially as an industrial relations adviser to the Victorian government, then to an appointment as a Commissioner of the AIRC, from where he eventually retired. Nolan was succeeded by Bill Kelty (q.v.). See Malcolm Brown's obituary in the *Sydney Morning Herald*, 22 August 2012.

Christopher "Chris" NORTHOVER (1937-), union leader and superannuation pioneer, was for twenty-five years national Secretary of the Pulp and Paper Workers' Union, which in 1990 merged into what became the CFMEU. He was widely influential and his experience was drawn on in the establishment of LUCRF, CBUS, Print Super, and other industry schemes. He led the formation of the Pulp and Paper Workers' Scheme in 1974, one of the pioneering industry funds, now called First Super.

Michael O'SULLIVAN (1941-2013), union leader and super-annuation administrator, was a Director of CARE Super from 1996 to 2012 and president for a decade to 2011 of the Australian Council of Superannuation Investors (ACSI). After graduating in a degree in agricultural science, he felt the calling to apply Catholic thinking on social justice by joining the union movement. He became an official of the Federated Clerks Union in 1966 and active in anti-communist Labor affairs, contributing articles under pseudonyms for the *Bulletin* magazine. Mentored by John Maynes (q.v.), the latter was too slow to see that the union needed to modernise to survive. In 1988 in elections for Victorian State Secretary, O'Sullivan was defeated by Lindsay Tanner (q.v.), who came to value his judgement, acumen, and sincerity in representing workers. O'Sullivan became inaugural national President of the Australian Services Union (ASU) in 1993 and continued to play an active role in the union as long as his health allowed. See the obituaries by Keith Harvey and Michael Easson (both 2013). Nichola Clark in 2009 published a perceptive piece on his role with the ACSI. In the latter role, he was a credible and articulate spokesperson for better corporate governance and was frequently interviewed in the media, including television.

Cassandra PARKINSON (), teacher, was National Secretary of the TAFE Teachers' Association, Australian Teachers' Federation and Member of the Australia Reconstructed Mission to Europe in 1986, and served as Executive Director at Australian TCF Industry Training Board from 1989 to 1996. In this role she helped to develop the first national competency standards for the TCF and allied industry sectors, and Australia's first accredited qualifications for clothing-machine operators.

The Hon. Peter Sydney Maitland PHILIPS (1927-2009) AM, stockbroker and politician, representing the Liberal Party in the NSW Legislative Council from 1976 to 1988, wrote on superannuation and financial issues. He found it difficult to appreciate the inadequacies of the superannuation provisions in the late 1970s for ordinary workers and he perceived that the emerging union schemes at that time were moves by unions for more power.

Colin POLITES (1946-2003), lawyer, employers' advocate and tribunal member, the son of George Polites (qv.), played an active role in the industrial relations battles, including over superannuation, in the 1980s. Educated in law at the University of Melbourne, he was formerly a partner of Moule, Hamilton and Derham, and then Freehill, Hollingdale and Page (now Herbert Smith Freehills), for many years he represented employers in national wage cases. Appointed to the Australian Industrial Relations Commission as a Deputy President in

1989, he became Senior Deputy President in 1994. He succumbed to cancer after a long illness.

George POLITES (1918-) AC, from the late 1950s was the Industrial Advocate for the Victorian Employers' Federation, the leader of the Australian Council of Employers' Federations, and then the Director General of the Confederation of Australian Industry (CAI) from 1978 to 1983. A pragmatist and realist, he was honoured by conservative governments with membership in the Order of the British Empire (MBE) and Commandership in the Order of St Michael and St George (CMG). He was awarded, in the Hawke government's first Honours List, with the decoration of Companion of the Order of Australia (AC). He foresaw in the early 1980s, before the Accord agreements from 1983 onwards, that superannuation rights would become a major focus of union campaigns and urged employers to make reforms to existing schemes, lest reforms be imposed upon them. A number of conservative thinkers saw him as a member of the "Industrial Relations Club" of unions and employers favouring centralised wage fixing, as indeed he was – though shrewder and more interesting than the critics allowed. See Des Moore's complaints in "Public Interest or Vested Interest. The Role of the CAI in the Regulation of Australia's Labour Market" (1991).

Mavis June ROBERTSON (1930-2015) AM, was a feminist, former CPA activist (which she finally left in 1984), and superannuation administrator, who was widely respected across the labour movement's political spectrum, as well as by employers who credited her professional determination and industrious approach to industry superannuation. She became involved in the superannuation movement in 1984 when the building and construction unions, with the support of the ACTU, campaigned successfully for a retirement benefit to be paid by employers into one of two industry funds, BUSS (Building Unions' Superannuation Scheme) or AUST (Allied Unions' Superannuation Trust). She was appointed a trustee director of AUST by the pro-CPA FEDFA (Federated Engine Drivers and Firemen's Association), which later became part of the CFMEU (Construction, Forestry, Mining and Energy Union). She worked full-time first in Sydney in the newly formed Superannuation Unit, then later transferred to Melbourne, where she became National Coordinator for Industry Superannuation at the ACTU. As Fund Secretary of BUSS and AUST, she steered the merger in 1992 of these two funds to create CBUS, the first billion-dollar industry fund. As the CEO and later Chair of CBUS, she became a Vice President of ASFA (Association of Superannuation Funds of Australia). Other initiatives in which she was integral include a range of initiatives designed to enhance the work of industry funds and, more generally, the not-for-profit sector and the representative trustee system, such as the founding of each of the Conference of Major Superannuation Funds, the Australian Institute of Superannuation Trustees, Industry Funds Super, Australian Council of Superannuation Investors, and Women in Super. She was awarded membership in the Order of Australia in 1994, and was a life member of AIST, ASFA, Women in Super, and the CFMEU. Note the comprehensive interview with Mavis Robertson and interviewer Sara Dowse in 2003, National Library of Australia Oral History Collection, ORAL TRC 5030. See Tony Stephens' obituary in the *Sydney Morning Herald*, 27 February 2015.

Dr Iain James ROSS (1959-) AO, unionist, lawyer, and judge, studied law at the University of Sydney, joining the ETU as Research Officer prior to joining the Labor Council of NSW as Occupational Health and Safety Officer in the 1980s. He later moved to the ACTU as Legal Officer, becoming a key support to ACTU Secretary Bill Kelty (q.v.). Shy and reserved, he had a determined, formidable intellect, and an uncanny ability to simplify, explain, and persuade. Indeed, in interviews for this book, Kelty (q.v.), Keating (q.v.), McDonald (q.v.), Weaven (q.v.), and Kernot (q.v.) all praised his expertise in marshalling arguments and legal acumen in pursuing the ACTU's objectives in superannuation, particularly with the Superannuation Guarantee legislation. Ross was an elected ACTU Assistant Secretary from 1992 to 1994, and from 1994-2006 he was Vice President of the Australian

Industrial Relations Commission. He became an Adjunct Associate Professor of Law at the University of Sydney, 2004. After a period in private practice with the law firm Corrs Chambers Westgarth, he was appointed first to the County Court, then to the Victorian Supreme Court in 2009, and in 2010 became President of the Victorian Civil and Administrative Tribunal. He became Chair of the Council of Australian Tribunals and, from February 2012, President of Fair Work Australia, now named the Fair Work Commission. He is also a Judge of the Federal Court of Australia.

Kevin Michael RUDD (1957-), politician and professional bureaucrat, was the 26th Prime Minister for Australia from 2007 to 2010 and again from June to September 2013. (Although serving twice, he is recorded officially as 26th PM). He was ALP leader from 2006 to 2010 and during 2013. Majoring in Chinese language and history with first-class honours from the Australian National University, after a period in the Australian diplomatic service, he became Chief of Staff to Queensland ALP leader and Premier of Queensland Wayne Goss from 1981 to 1988. He won election to the House of Representatives in 1998 (having lost on his first attempt, in the Keating landslide defeat of 1996). One of Prime Minister Rudd's last major decisions before losing his position to his Deputy in June 2010 was to announce support for the Superannuation Guarantee gradually being phased in from 9 per cent to 12 per cent.

Dr Don RUSSELL (1949-), economist, diplomat, public servant and investment banker, was advisor to Paul Keating (q.v.) from 1985 to 1993, Australian Ambassador to Washington from 1993 to 1995 then Principal Advisor to Prime Minister Keating from 1995 to 1996. He went on to have several careers in investment banking and the public service. Between 1997 and 2000, he worked for Sanford C. Bernstein, a research and money management firm in New York. To 2010 he was Global Investment Strategist at BNY Mellon Asset Management Australia, a period which overlapped with being independent Chairperson of NSW State Super, from 2008. Then, from 2011 to

2013, he was the Secretary of the Commonwealth Department of Industry, Innovation, Climate Change, Science, Research and Tertiary Education. Since 1 July 2014 he has been Chief Executive of the South Australian Department of State Development. He wrote on some of his experiences in a paper: "The Role of Executive Government in Australia" (2003). He has a PhD from the London School of Economics, a MEc from the ANU, and a BEc (Hons) (First) from Flinders University and also holds the Chartered Financial Analyst designation (CFA) 2007.

Hon. Susan RYAN (1942-) AO, politician, feminist and administrator, was a Senator for the ACT representing the ALP from 1975 to 1988. In 1983, under Bob Hawke (q.v.), she became the first woman to hold a cabinet post in a Federal Labor Government. She served as Minister for Education and Youth Affairs, Minister Assisting the Prime Minister on the Status of Women and Special Minister of State. She served as CEO of the Association of Superannuation Funds of Australia from 1993 to 1997, President of the Australian Institute of Superannuation Trusteess from 2000 to 2007, a member of the Australian Council of Superannuation Investors from 2001 to 2007, a member of the ASX Corporate Governance Council from 2003 to 2007, and the Independent Chair of the IAG and NRMA Superannuation Plan to 2011. She became Australia's first Age Discrimination Commissioner on 30 July 2011.

Nicholas John ("Nick") SHERRY (1955-), union leader, politician, and businessman, was Senator for Tasmania from 1990 to 2012. He was influential with Cheryl Kernot (q.v.) in winning support for the SGL. Starting his working life while at university as a night cashier and auditor at the Wrest Point Hotel and Casino in Hobart, he joined the Federated Liquor and Allied Industries Employees' Union of Australia (FLAIEU), becoming its State Secretary between 1979 and 1990. In 1992, the FLAIEU amalgamated with the FMWU to form the Liquor Hospitality and Miscellaneous Union (LHMU), which became the United Voice union in 2011. As State Secretary he helped establish the HostPlus Superannuation Fund, an industry superannuation fund at that time only for hospitality industry workers, but now a full public-offer fund. He was a trustee of HostPlus from 1987-1990 and was also a trustee, manager, and company secretary of the Tasmanian ClubPlus Superannuation fund. Although he rose rapidly in the parliamentary Labor Party, depression and his inspiring recovery required him to take a break. In 2001 he was appointed Shadow Minister for Retirement Incomes and Savings, a position he held until 2004. In 2004 Sherry was appointed as the Shadow Minister for Finance and Superannuation, and in 2005 he was appointed as the Shadow Minister for Superannuation and Intergenerational Finance and Shadow Minister for Banking and Financial Services, positions he held until the 2007 election. Following the election of the Rudd Government, he was appointed Minister for Superannuation and Corporate Law, 2007-2009, then Assistant Treasurer, 2009-2010; then, under Prime Minister Julia Gillard, Minister for Small Business, 2010-2012. He retired from the Senate and public office in 2012. As Australia's first Minister for Superannuation, he set up the Review into the Governance, Efficiency and Structure and Operation of Australia's Superannuation System, also known as the Cooper Review, after its head, Jeremy Cooper. The Gillard Government released the Cooper Review on 5 July 2010. After relinquishing political office, he secured a number of roles, including Senior Advisor, Superannuation and Pensions to Ernst and Young and Citigroup, and a range of other board and advisory roles in the pensions area in Australia and globally.

Ian SILK (1958-), superannuation professional, CEO, and public policy thought leader, has led from its formative stages onwards, Australia's largest superannuation fund, AustralianSuper. After graduating with an economics degree, he tried his luck at forklift driving and cut his professional teeth working in industrial relations at what is now Melbourne Water, then home to about 5,000 blue-collar workers. After a period as an apolitical senior advisor in industrial relations on the staff of several Ministers in the Victorian government, he started in the superannuation industry, initially as a Senior Manager for Australian Administration Services, then as CEO of ARF which in 2006, following its merger with STA, became AustralianSuper Pty Ltd. He was a Director of the Association of Superannuation Funds of Australia from 2001 and was a Member of the Conference of Major Superannuation Funds Steering Committee. He is a member of the Financial Services Advisory Council to the Federal Treasurer, the Australian Government's Financial Literacy Board, ASIC's External Advisory Board and the Board of the Australian Council of Superannuation Investors (ACSI); and a Director on the Yooralla Board. He holds an ASFA Certificate of Superannuation Management. For a profile, see "Back to School with Ian Silk", InTheBlack, March 2013, http://www.itbdigital.com/people/2013/03/04/back-to-school-with-ian-silk-ceo-of-australiansuper/.

Ian SPICER (1938-) AM, was a former head of the Victorian Employers Federation and of the Australian Chamber of Commerce and Industry.

Wayne Maxwell SWAN (1954-), academic, ALP official, and politician, was Treasurer from 2007 to 2013 under the first Rudd administration and the Gillard administration. With the latter, he was Deputy Prime Minister from 2010 to June 2013, until Rudd again became Prime Minister. He returned to the backbench and was re-elected at the 2013 elections. He was the Federal MP for Lilley from 1993 to 1996, which he lost after one term. He was re-elected again in 1998 and every subsequent election. From 1978 to 1980, he was an advisor to Labor Leader Bill Hayden, then from 1983 to 1984 with Mick Young and Kim Beazley. He was also the State Secretary of the Queensland Labor Party from 1991 to 1993. As Federal Treasurer he commissioned the Henry (q.v.) review into taxation, which covered, *inter alia*, superannuation issues. In Opposition, he wrote a book on economic disparity in Australia: *Postcode: The Splintering of a Nation* (2005).

Gregory Brian ("Greg") SWORD (1948-) AM, union leader, superannuation pioneer, and administrator, came to the attention of

Bill Landeryou (q.v.) after speaking at an ALP Conference in Victoria, where in his capacity as National President of Young Labor from 1972 to 1974 he was defending some participants in a local controversy, coming to the attention of W.A. ("Bill") Landeryou, the then State Secretary of the Federated Storeman and Packers' Union (FSPU). He had studied engineering and had worked at the Victorian State Electricity Commission. But he quit that job in 1974 to work with Landeryou at the Victorian Branch of the FSPU. From the SEC, although he was just shy of 10 years' service, he received nothing in superannuation except for his own contributions. That began a burning desire for superannuation justice. He co-founded the Labour Union Co-operative Retirement Fund (LUCRF), originally set up for the Federated Storemen and Packers' Union (FSPU) officials. In the late 1970s, he extended coverage of the fund to workers in the skin and hide industries and retail distribution, and then more generally. He became the first full time CEO of the fund in 1978 until returning to the Union in 1982. He was elected in 1984 national General Secretary of the FSPU (from 1989, following amalgamations, called the National Union of Workers, or NUW). He was a member of the Australia Reconstructed Mission to Europe in 1986, which set the scene for the modernisation of the union movement, including an approach to wage fixation based on productivity increases and efficiencies in the workplace. He has served as the National and the Victorian Branch President of the ALP. After a brief stint as Chairman of the LUCRF Board and Chairman of Labour Union Insurances, from 2006 to retirement in 2014 he again served as the CEO of LUCRF Super. Other interests included serving as a trustee of the Caulfield Racecourse Reserve and the National Jockeys Trust. He has served as Chairman of St Vincent's Public Hospital, Melbourne.

Lindsay James TANNER (1956-) is a former lawyer, union leader, and politician, as well as an environmentalist, businessman, and investment banker. After graduating with Arts and Law degrees from the University of Melbourne, he worked for a Labor politician and the law firm Holding Redlich Lawyers. He was unexpectedly elected

Assistant State Secretary of the Federated Clerks' Union from 1987, then State Secretary from 1988 until 1993, when he left to successfully contest the Federal seat of Melbourne, which he held to 2010. After serving as Minister for Finance from 2007 to 2010, he decided to quit politics for personal reasons. He is active in the private sector, and an advisor to the investment bank Lazard. He wrote of his union experiences in *The Last Battle* (1996).

Malcolm Bligh TURNBULL (1954-), lawyer, journalist, entrepreneur, investment banker, and politician, graduated from Sydney University with a BA LLB, won a Rhodes Scholarship and completed a further law degree at Oxford. In the United Kingdom he worked as a barrister, returning to Australia and eventually to business, where he co-founded the internet business OzEmail in 1994. He also worked in investment banking, including as a partner of Goldman Sachs. A committed republican, he unsuccessfully led the pro-republic campaign in 1999. He entered Federal politics as the Member for Wentworth in 2004. In early 2006 he was appointed Parliamentary Secretary to the Prime Minister and a year later to Cabinet as the Minister for Environment and Water Resources; a position he held until the Federal Election on 24 November 2007. In Opposition he was at first Shadow Treasurer, then Leader from September 2008 to December 2009. He was Minister for Communications in the Abbott government and then Prime Minister, becoming the 29th Australian Prime Minister after defeating Tony Abbott in a party room ballot on 9 September 2009. He narrowly won re-election in July 2016.

Richard Morris TITMUSS (1907-1973) was a pioneering British social researcher and teacher in the academic discipline of social theory and administration. He was the founding chair of Social Administration at the London School of Economics from 1950 until his death in 1973. His thinking on superannuation and the development of a national superannuation scheme in the UK influenced UK politician Richard Crossman (q.v.), who in turn, through Race Mathews, (q.v.) influenced the ALP's thinking in the early 1970s.

Allan Raymond VOSTI (1915-2007) AM, industrial relations expert, served in the Australian Armed Forces during the Second World War. He progressed to the Department of Defence in the field of industrial relations. He was appointed as a Commissioner to the Australian Conciliation and Arbitration Commission and served the building and construction industry from 1972 to 1980. He became the inaugural Chairman of the Victorian Building Industry Disputes Board from 1981 to 1988. He was instrumental in the formulation of the Building Industry Recovery Procedures (BIRP) allowance in 1983. From 1989 he was involved in private arbitrations, working with the Australian Conciliation and Arbitration Commission. His papers are held in the Melbourne University Archives; see http://gallery.its.unimelb.edu.au/imu/imu.php?request=multimedia&irn=4995.

Stanley David Martin "Stan" WALLIS (1939-) AC, businessman, graduated from Melbourne university in accounting and went on to a stellar career in business, including to 1996 as CEO of AMCOR, the Australian-based multinational packaging company. He later served as Chair of Coles-Myer, and AMP, amongst other appointments. Treasurer Peter Costello (q.v.) appointed him Chair of the Financial System Inquiry which reported in 1997 which inter alia urged greater competition and choice between superannuation funds.

Barry John WATCHORN (1938-), employer-organisation leader, was known for his roles as a barrister, diplomat, senior public servant, and superannuation expert. He began his career in the public service, rising through the ranks to a position as senior officer with the Federal Department of Industrial Relations. He was posted to Nigeria between 1966 and 1968, and to Geneva as the Australian Government's representative to the International Labour Organisation and the OECD's Manpower and Social Affairs Committee between 1980 and 1983. He first became involved with superannuation when working for the Australian Chamber of Manufacturers (ACM), which later merged with the Metal Trades Industry Association (MTIA) to form the Australian Industry Group (AiG). Responsible for industrial relations activities at the ACM, he became involved in the employer campaign against award super in the early 1980s. Seeing the writing on the wall, Watchorn offered a settlement to the ACTU and the manufacturing unions: the establishment of a fund which could be operated on a cooperative basis. As a result, the Australian Retirement Fund (ARF) was born. Watchorn became a trustee of the ACM Training Centre Superannuation Funds in 1989 and of ARF in 1993. He was ARF Chairman at the time of its merger with the Superannuation Trust of Australia (STA) in 2006 to form AustralianSuper. He retired to become the Chair of CARE Super in 2008. See the anonymous article on Watchorn in *Industry*, 2008.

Sir Bruce WATSON (1928-2008) AC, miner and businessman, was trained as an electrical engineer at the University of Queensland, worked in the Tasmanian power industry before returning to Queensland to work for Mount Isa Mines (MIM) Holdings where he eventually rose to Managing Director (1980), Chief Executive Officer (1981) and Chairman (1983). He was knighted in 1985 in recognition of distinguished service to Queensland industry. In a 1979 article, "Union Involvement in the Provision of Superannuation", he saw that unions had a legitimate right to seek improvements in existing schemes and counselled his employer colleagues to be innovative in response. See: https://www.uq.edu.au/news/article/2008/11/uq-remembers-sir-bruce-watson-ac, accessed 20 September 2016.

Garry WEAVEN (1948-), union leader, economist, superannuation pioneer, investor, and administrator, grew up in Northcote, in Melbourne's inner-north. He was a member of the Socialist Club during his time at La Trobe University in the early 1970s, during which time he befriended Bill Kelty (q.v.). In the late 1970s he joined the Victorian Branch of the Municipal Officers Association (which became in 1991 part of the Australian Services Union) as a researcher, and later was elected Victorian State Secretary. He joined the ACTU in 1981, becoming Assistant Secretary in 1986. Within the ACTU he became a key architect and a major driving force behind the ACTU's success in reforming superannuation, advocating reform, and spreading industry superannuation funds throughout the workforce during the 1980s. He left the ACTU to join Westpac as a financial consultant in 1990, before setting up Industry Funds Services in 1994. IFS provided funds management, banking and legal support to the industry super funds that grew out of the union movement. IFS eventually became Industry Funds Management, then IFM Investors, owned by 30 super funds, including giants AustralianSuper, CBUS, HESTA and HostPlus, and now invests almost $50 billion on behalf of some 120 Australian and international investors (mainly superannuation funds), with a focus on "nation-building" infrastructure assets like airports, tollways and energy companies. He was Chairman of Pacific Hydro, a renewable energy company in Australia, Brazil and Chile, at one time owned by the IFM Australian Infrastructure Fund; and Director of ME Bank, which is owned by the same group of Australian superannuation funds. See "Money Movers No. 6, Garry Weaven", http://www. thepowerindex.com.au/money-movers/garry-weaven.

Donald Henry WHITEHEAD (1931-1980), economist and economic historian, BA (Oxon.), lectured in economic development at the University of Adelaide from 1958 to 1963. then became Senior Lecturer in 1964, then moved to the University of New England to teach Economic History in 1965 and then to La Trobe in 1967 as foundation Professor of Economics. He gave evidence in National Wage Cases on behalf of the employers, and was considered an expert on stagflation. One of his students at La Trobe was Bill Kelty (qv.), who credits Whitehead with inspiring him to become a good student. Despite their differing politics, Kelty greatly admired Whitehead's stimulating discussion on contemporary industrial issues and the development of tax wage trade-offs to curb the wage-prices inflation cycle. Jordon notes that in Whitehead joined La Trobe University as that University introduced a Bachelor of Economics degree. At La Trobe, Whitehead insisted on the Faculty teaching the history of economic thought. Named in his honour, the Donald Whitehead Building now houses the School of Law and Management at La

Trobe's Bundoora campus. For biographical references, see Anderson and O'Neil, 2009, p. 65; Jordon, 2004, p. 118; Schneider, 2007. See also Whitehead's book, *Stagflation and Wages Policy in Australia*, 1973, and Davidson's memoir in *The Economic Record*, 1980.

Ralph WILLIS (1938-) AO, economist, unionist, and politician, was ACTU Research Officer until 1972, when he was elected Federal MP for Gellibrand from 1972 to 1998. He was Shadow Minister for Industrial Relations, Economic Affairs and Treasury from 1976 to 1983. However, he was dropped from the last post to be replaced by Paul Keating (q.v.) in January 1983, as then Labor Leader Bill Hayden (1933-) tried to shore up his support against Bob Hawke (q.v.), who was to depose him as ALP Leader in February 1983. A Minister in the Hawke and Keating governments, Willis was briefly Treasurer in 1991 under Hawke, and again under Keating from 1993 to 1996. He served as Chair of CBUS to 2012.

Ted WILSHIRE (1943-) was a unionist, economist, and trade bureaucrat. After studying Political Economy at the University of Sydney and becoming close to the CPA, though apparently never as a member, he worked for the AWWU as National Research Officer. At heart a radical industry protectionist, he modified his views and sought to learn from European and other union experiences, including the development of national pension schemes. With the election of the Hawke Government in 1983, he joined the Department of Trade, becoming Executive Director of the Trade Development Council. In that position, he was a member of the Australia Reconstructed Mission to Europe in 1986. Wilshire played an important role in the Australian Left, on both sides of the dividing line within the ALP, in creating and sustaining a pro-Accord viewpoint. After an attack by unknown assailants in 1989, he was left with brain damage and dropped out of any significant roles in the labour movement. Some of his co-authored works include a pamphlet (with Bill Mountford) on *Australia on the Rack*, 1982, and, as joint editor with Greg Crough and Ted Wheelwright, *Australia and World Capitalism*, 1980.

REFERENCES

ACTU/TDC Mission to Western Europe (1987) *Australia Reconstructed, A Report by the Mission Members to the ACTU and the TDC*, Australian Government Publishing Service, Canberra.

ACTU records, www.actu.org.au/Images/Dynamic/oldsite/public/papers/1991may/1991may.rtf, accessed 28 May 2013.

ACTU (2005) History of Super. Melbourne: Australian Council of Trade Unions, http://www.actu.asn.au/super/about/super_history.html, accessed 5 April 2013.

Alcock, Pete, Glennerster, Howard, Oakley, Ann & Sinfield, A. (2001) *Welfare and Well Being: Richard Titmuss's Contribution to Social Policy*, The Policy Press, Bristol.

Allen, Geoff (2012) "Business Council of Australia. Its Origins and Early Years", in Sheehan, Mark & Sekuless, Peter (2012), editors, *The Influence Seekers: Political Lobbying in Australia*, Australian Scholarly Press, pp. 76-95.

Anderson, Kym, & O'Neil, Bernard (2009) *The Building of Economics at Adelaide, 1901-2001*, University of Adelaide, Adelaide.

[anonymous] Editorial (1979) "Who Will the Storemen Send Packing?", *Superfunds*, No. 67, June, p. 2.

[anonymous] Editorial (1980) "The 1980s", *Superfunds*, No. 70, March 1980, p. 3.

[anonymous] (1984) "Superannuation Coverage", *Superfunds*, No. 89, December, pp. 27, 29, 31.

[anonymous] Editorial (1985) "Consultation or Chaos?", *Superfunds*, No. 90, March, p. 3.

[anonymous] (1986) "Union-Sponsored Industry Funds", *Superfunds*, No. 95, June, pp. 13, 25, 28.

[anonymous] Editorial (1986) "Fishing Up the Moon", *Superfunds*, No. 96, September, p. 2.

[anonymous] (1990-91) "Year in Review", *Superfunds*, No. 132, December 1990-January 1991, p. 15.

[anonymous] (1991) "McKay's Reflection on Industry Funds", *Superfunds*, No. 141, September, pp. 17-20.

[anonymous] (1992) "CMSF '92: Home Ownership Simplification and Art Works", *Superfunds*, No. 147, April , pp. 5, 8.

[anonymous] (1992-1993) "1992: The Superannuation Year that Was", *Superfunds*, No. 155, December 1992- January 1993, pp. 22-3.

[anonymous] (1992-1993) "1993: Super Shootout", *Superfunds*, No. 155, December 1992- January 1993, pp. 32-3.

[anonymous] (1994) "REST Assured – It's Bigger and Busier", *Superfunds*, No. 173, August, pp. 14-16.

[anonymous] (2000) "Vale Cliff Dolan: A Lifelong Commitment", *Workers online*, No. 81, 8 December, http://workers.labor.net.au/81/news1_cliff. html, accessed 26 May, 2013.

[anonymous] (2008) "Barry Watchorn Retires from AustralianSuper", *Industry* [Australian Industry Group], Edition 45, Winter, p. 8.

[anonymous] (2010) "Vale Terry Johnson", *Livewire*, Quarterly Journal of the ETU, NSW Branch, Autumn, p. 16.

APRA (2007) "A Recent History of Superannuation in Australia", *APRA Insight*, Issue 2, 2007 http://www.apra.gov.au/Insight/upload/History-of-superannuation.pdf, accessed 8 April 2013.

APRA (2016) *Annual Superannuation Bulletin*, APRA, Sydney, June 2015, reissued 23 August 2016, http://www.apra.gov.au/Super/Publications/ Documents/2016ASBPDF201506.pdf, accessed 9 September 2016.

Argy, Fred (2003) *Where to From Here? Australian Egalitarianism Under Threat*, Allen & Unwin, Crows Nest, NSW, Australia.

Artis, Michael John, & Cobham, David P. (1991), editors, *Labour's Economic Policies 1974-1979*, Manchester University Press, Manchester.

ASFA (2016) "Alternative Default Models", Submission to the Productivity Commission, October, https://www.superannuation.asn.au/.../ASFA_ submission_PC_Superannuation_Alternatives, accessed 3 November 2016.

Australian Prudential Regulation Authority (2007) *A Recent History of superannuation in Australia*, APRA Insight, Issue 2. http://www.apra. gov.au/Insight/upload/History-of-superannuation.pdf, accessed 23 March 2013.

Australian Treasury (1984) "Issues and Broad Options Concerning National Superannuation", An Internal Discussion Paper Prepared by the Inter-Departmental Committee on Retirement Incomes, October, typescript, pp. 5-8. [Copy of extracts provided by Mr Keating].

Australian Treasury (2001) "Towards Higher Retirement Incomes for Australians – A History of the Australian Retirement Income System Since Federation", *Economic Roundup*, 1 January.

Australian Treasury (2009) "Australia's Future Tax System, The Retirement Income System: Report on strategic issues, May 2009", http://taxreview.treasury.gov.au/content/downloads/retirement_income_report_stategic_issues/retirement_income_report_20090515.pdf.

Barr, William M., & Conley, John M. (1992) *Fortune & Folly. The Wealth & Power of Institutional Investing*, Business One Irvin, Homewood, IL, USA.

Bateman, Hazel, & Piggott, John (1998) "Mandatory Retirement Saving in Australia", *Annals of Public and Cooperative Economics*, Vol. 69, No. 4, December, pp. 547-69, http://info.worldbank.org/etools/docs/library/76548/march2000/proceedings/pdfpaper/preliminary/bateman.pdf, accessed 5 June 2013.

Bateman, Hazel, & Piggott, John. (1999) "Mandating Retirement Provision: the Australian Experience", *The Geneva Papers on Risk and Insurance*, Vol. 24, pp. 95-114.

Bateman, Hazel., Kingston, Geoff., & Piggott, John. (2001) *Forced Saving: Mandatory Private Retirement Provision*, Cambridge University Press, London.

Bateman, Hazel (2001) "Disclosure of Superannuation Fees and Charges", Discussion Paper for AIST, UNSW Centre for Pensions and Superannuation, August, 43 pp.,

http://pension.kiev.ua/files/cpsdp200304.pdf, accessed 5 June 2013.

Bateman, Hazel (2002) "Retirement Income Strategy in Australia", *Economic Analysis and Policy*, Vol. 32, pp. 49-70.

Bateman, Hazel, & Kingston, Geoff. (2010) "The Henry Review and Super and Saving", *The Australian Economic Review*, Vol. 43, pp. 437-48.

Bauer, Rob and Frehen, Rik (2008). The Performance of US Pension Funds: New Insights into the Agency Costs Debate", http://ssrn.com/abstract=965388, accessed 5 April 2013.

Black, Steve (2000) "Norm Gallagher – A Tribute", *The Hummer*, Journal of the Sydney Branch of the ASSLH, Vol. 3, No. 5, www.asslh.org.au/hummer/vol-3-no-5/norm-gallagher, accessed 25 May 2013.

Bogle, John (1999) *Common Sense on Mutual Funds*, John Wiley & Sons, Inc., New York.

Bogle, John. (2005) *The Battle for the Soul of Capitalism*, Yale University Press, New Haven & London.

Bongarzoni, Carlo (1989) "Superannuation Regulation and the Fund Member", *Superfunds*, No. 113, March, p. 1.

Bongarzoni, Carlo (1990) "Debate Yes; Confusion No!", *Superfunds*, No. 124, March, p. 3.

Borowski, Allan (2005) "The Revolution that Faltered: Two Decades of Reform of Australia's Retirement Income System'", *International Social Security Review*, Vol. 58, No. 4, pp. 45-65, *The Revolution that faltered: two decades of reform of Australia's retirement income system*, accessed 23 January 2013.

Borowski, Allan (2008) "Back at the Crossroads: The Slippery Fish of Australian Retirement Income Policy", *Australian Journal of Social Issues*, Vol. 43, No. 2, Winter, pp. 311-34.

Bramston, Troy (2016) *Paul Keating. The Big-Picture Leader*, Scribe Publications, Brunswick [Australia].

Brown, Malcolm (2012) "Union Man [Peter Nolan] Earned Broad Respect", *Sydney Morning Herald*, August 22.

Bowen, Chris (2013) *Hearts and Minds. A Blueprint for Modern Labor*, Melbourne University Press, Carlton.

Bull, Tas (1998) *Life on the Waterfront. An Autobiography*, Harper Collins, Sydney.

Burchell, Andrew (2012) "Crossman and Social Security", Warwick University, August, http://www2.warwick.ac.uk/services/library/mrc/explorefurther/digital/crossman/urss/socialsecurity, accessed 26 May 2013.

Burgmann, Meredith (1984) "Australian Trade Unionism in 1983", *The Journal of Industrial Relations*, Vol. 26, No. 1, August, pp. 91-8.

Burke, Edmund (1790; 2003) *Reflections on the Revolution in France*, Turner, Frank M., editor, Yale University Press, New Haven and London.

Cahill, Rowan (1992) "A Note on the Career of Patrick Geraghty", *The Hummer*, ASSLH, Sydney Branch, No. 33, March-April, http://asslh.org.au/hummer/no-33/geraghty/, accessed 30 May, 2013.

Callaghan, P. S. (1983) "Idealism and Arbitration in H.B. Higgins' New Province for Law and Order", *Journal of Australian Studies*, Vol. 7, No. 13, pp. 55-66.

Carmichael, Laurie (2013) "The Struggle Continues: Laurie Carmichael

Talks with Andrew Dettmer", in Reeves Andrew, & Dettmer, Andrew (2013), editors, *Organise, Educate, Control: The AMWU in Australia, 1852–2012*, Monash University Publishing, Clayton, pp. 173-90.

Carney, Shaun (2014) "An Era of Activism has Gone with Wally Curran", *Herald Sun*, 27 March.

Clare, Ross. (2012) "The Equity of Government Assistance for Retirement in Australia", Association of Superannuation Funds, Sydney, www.superannuation.asn.au, accessed 1 June 2013.

Clark, Gordon L. (2012) "From Corporatism to Public Utilities: Workplace Pensions in the 21st Century", *Geographical Research*, Vol. 50, No. 1, February, pp. 31-46.

Clark, Lindie (2002) *Finding a Common Interest: The Story of Dick Dusseldorp and Lend Lease*, Cambridge University Press, Cambridge.

Clark, Nichola (2009) "Keeping Shareholder Activism Alive", *Company Director Magazine*, publication of the Australian Institute of Company Directors, September, http://www.companydirectors.com.au/director-resource-centre/publications/company-director-magazine/2000-to-2009-back-editions/2009/september/profile-keeping-shareholder-activism-alive, accessed 26 September 2016.

Clausewitz, Carl von (1832, 1984) *On War,* Howard, Michael, & Paret, Peter, editors, Princeton University Press, New Jersey.

Cochrane, George (1991) "Industry Funds Guide for 1991", *Superfunds*, No. 141, September, pp. 14-16.

Cochrane, George (1992) "Inside Industry Funds", *Superfunds*, No. 152, September, pp. 14-16, 18.

Cohen, M.D., March, J.G., & Olsen, J.P. (1972) "Garbage Can Model of Organizational Choice", *Administrative Science Quarterly,* Vol. 17, No. 1, March, pp. 1-25.

Coleman, A D F, Esho N & Wong, M (2006) "The Impact of Agency Costs on the Investment Performance of Australian Pension Funds", *Journal of Pension Economics and Finance*, Vol. 5, No. 3, pp. 299-324.

Colvin, John, & McCarry, Greg (1986) "Superannuation and Industrial Law", *Australian Law Journal*, Vol. 60, pp. 501-12.

Commonwealth Government, Treasury (2001) Economic Roundup, *Towards Higher Retirement Incomes for Australians – A History of the Australian Retirement Income System Since Federation,* Towards higher retirement incomes for Australians – A History of the Australian retirement income system since Federation, accessed 23 March 2013.

Commonwealth of Australia (2002) *Intergenerational Report, 2002-2003*, Budget Paper No. 5, Canberra, Info Access Network.

ComSuper (2008) *A History of Commonwealth Superannuation*, Australian Government Belconnen, http://www.comsuper.gov.au/pages/about/history.htm, accessed 6 April 2013.

Connolly, David (1989-1990) "The Coalition and Retirement Income", *Superfunds*, No. 122, December 1989-January 1990, pp. 21, 23.

Cook, Peter (1991) "The Accord: An Economic and Social Success Story", address given to the LSE in June 1991, reprinted in Crosby, Michael & Easson, Michael (1992), editors, *What Should Unions Do?*, Pluto Press in conjunction with the Lloyd Ross Forum, Leichhardt, pp. 152-70.

Cooper, Jeremy (2010a) "Super System Review, Final Report Part One: Overview and Recommendations", www.supersystemreview.gov.au, accessed 1 June 2013.

Cooper, Jeremy (2010b) "Super System Review, Final Report Part Two: Recommendation Packages", www.supersystemreview.gov.au, accessed 1 June 2013.

Corden, M.W. (1968) *Australian Economic Policy Discussion: A Survey*, Melbourne University Press, Parkville.

Costa, Michael, & Duffy, Mark (1991) *Labor, Prosperity and the Nineties. Beyond the Bonsai Economy*. The Federation Press, Leichhardt, NSW.

Costa, Michael, & Duffy, Mark (1993) "Labor and Economic Rationalism", in James, Chris, Jones, Chris, & Norton, Andrew (1993), editors, *A Defence of Economic Rationalism*, Allen & Unwin, St Leonards, NSW, pp. 121-31.

Costello, Peter, with Coleman, Peter (2008) *The Costello Memoirs*, Melbourne University Press, Carlton.

Covick, Owen (2002) "What *Can* Governments Do to Lift National Savings?", in Covick, Owen (2002), editor, *Policies to Boost Australian Saving: How? And Why?*, Wakefield Press, Kent Town, SA, Australia, pp. 24-39.

Covick, Owen (2002), editor, *Policies to Boost Australian Saving: How? And Why?*, Wakefield Press, Kent Town, SA, Australia.

Cox, Eva (2011) 'Women Lumped with Thick End of Retirement Edge', October, http://www.crikey.com.au/author/evacox, accessed 2 June, 2013.

Cox, James F. & Schleier, John (2010) *Theory of Constraints Handbook*, McGraw-Hill, New York.

Crosby, Michael, & Easson, Michael (1992), editors, *What Should Unions Do?*, Pluto Press in conjunction with the Lloyd Ross Forum, Leichhardt, NSW, Australia.

Crossman, R H S (1972) "The Politics of Pensions", *The Eleanor Rathbone Memorial Lecture,* Liverpool.

Crough, Greg, Wheelwright, Ted & Wilshire, Ted (1980), editors, *Australia and World Capitalism*, Penguin Books, Ringwood, Vic, Australia.

Dabscheck, Braham (1989) *Australian Industrial Relations in the 1980s*, Oxford University Press Australia, Melbourne & Oxford.

Dabscheck, Braham (1990) "Enterprise Bargaining: A New Province for Law and Order?", *The Australian Quarterly*, Vol. 62, No. 3, Spring, pp. 240-55.

D'Alpuget, Blanche (1977) *Mediator. A biography of Sir Richard Kirby*, Melbourne University Press, Carlton, Victoria.

D'Alpuget, Blanche (1982) *Robert J. Hawke. A Biography*, Schwartz in conjunction with Lansdowne Press, Sydney.

Daley, Brian (1991a) "Industry Funds: Where They Are Heading", *Superfunds*, No. 141, September, pp. 22-4.

Daley, Brian (1991b) "Divided Over SGL", *Superfunds*, No. 143, November 1991, pp. 6-7.

Daley, Brian (1992a) "How the Award System Works Under the SGC", *Superfunds*, No. 152, September, pp. 20-2.

Daley, Brian (1992b) "Industry Funds' Investment Strategy is on Target", *Superfunds*, No. 152, September, pp. 36-7.

Davidson, F.G. (1980) "Donald Whitehead", *The Economic Record*, Vol. 56, Issue 154, September, pp. 281-4.

Davis, Kevin, & Harper, Ian (1992), editors, *Superannuation and the Australian Financial System*, Allen & Unwin, St Leonards, NSW.

Dawkins, John (1992) "Security in Retirement – Planning for Tomorrow Today", Statement by The Honourable John Dawkins, M.P., Treasurer of the Commonwealth of Australia, 30 June.

Deloitte (2015) "The Dynamics of the Australian Superannuation System. The Next Twenty Years, 2015-2035", https://www2.deloitte.com/au/en/pages/financial-services/articles/dynamics-australian-superannuation-system-2015.html, accessed 2 June 2016.

Devlin, Michael W. (1986) "Industrial Relations and the Superannuation Industry, Blushing Bride and Reluctant Bridegroom", *Superfunds*, No. 96, September, pp. 11, 13.

Dixon, Daryl (1990) "Superannuation and Government over the Next Three Years: What Can We Expect?", *Superfunds*, No. 126, May, pp. 25-6, 28.

Dixon, John (1983) "Australia's Income-Security System: Its Origins, Nature and Prospects", *International Social Security Review*, Vol. 36, pp. 19-24.

Dodkin, Marilyn (2001) "John MacBean: The Consensus Secretary", in Dodkin, Marilyn (2001) *Brothers: Eight leaders of the Labor Council of New South Wales*, University of New South Wales Press, Sydney, pp. 175-88.

Dorey, Peter (2001) *Wage Politics in Britain: The Rise and Fall of Incomes Policies Since 1945*, Sussex Academic Press, Brighton, UK.

Dowling, Joseph (1992) "Super Makes Kernot a Rising Star", *Superfunds*, No. 152, September, pp. 34-5.

Drew, Michael, & Stanford, Jon (2002) "The Economics of Choice of Superannuation Fund", *Accounting, Accountability and Performance*, Vol. 8, No. 1, pp. 1-20.

Drew, Michael, & Stanford, Jon (2003a) "Principal and Agent Problems in Superannuation Funds", *Australian Economic Review*, Vol. 36, Issue 1, March, pp. 98-107.

Drew, Michael, & Stanford, Jon (2003b) "A Review of Australia's Compulsory Superannuation Scheme After a Decade", Discussion Paper No. 322, University of Queensland, March, 26 pp., http://www.uq.edu.au/ economics/abstract/322.pdf, accessed 24 September 2016.

Drew, Michael, & Stanford, Jon (2003c) "Returns from Investing in Australian Equity, Superannuation Funds, 1991 to 1999", *Service Industries Journal*, Vol. 23, No. 4, pp. 12-24.

Drucker, Peter (1976) "Pension Fund Socialism", *The Public Interest*, No. 42, Winter, pp. 3-46.

Drucker, Peter (1976) *The Unseen Revolution: How Pension Fund Socialism Came to America*, Harper & Row, New York.

Dunnin, Alex (2008) *A History of Super in Australia*, Rainmaker Information, http://www.selectingsuper.com.au/_2006_SSHB_History_of_Super_in_ Australia.html, accessed 6 April 2013.

Easson, Michael (1995) "ILO to the Rescue?", *Economic and Labour Relations Review*, Vol. 6, No. 1, June, pp. 149-57.

Easson, Michael (2010) "Maher Created a Powerful Force", *Sydney Morning Herald*, 4 January, www.smh.com.au/national/obituaries/maher-created-a-powerful-force-20100103-ln9t.html, accessed 25 May 2013.

Easson, Michael (2013) "[Michael O'Sullivan] Union Leader Guided by Principles", *Sydney Morning Herald*, 15 January.

Easson, Michael (2013) "Industrial Relations Policy", in Bramston, Troy (2013), editor, *The Whitlam Legacy*, The Federation Press, Leichhardt, pp. 223-34.

Edwards, A. & Magarey, S. (1995), editors, *Women in a Restructuring Australia: Work and Welfare*, Allen & Unwin, Sydney.

Edwards, John (1996) *Keating. The Inside Story*, Viking, Ringwood, VIC, Australia.

Elder, John Richard (1994) "The Australian Building Construction Employees & Builders Labourers Federation and the NSW Building Industry", Thesis for Master of Industrial Relations, University of Sydney, http://hdl.handle.net/2123/2155, accessed 26 May 2013.

Epstein, Lee, & Segal, Jeffrey A. (2000) "Measuring Issue Salience", *American Journal of Political Science*, Vol. 44, No. 1, pp. 66-83, http://epstein.usc.edu/research/salience.pdf, accessed 5 April 2013.

FACSIA (1983) "A Compendium of Legislative Changes in Social Security 1908–1982", Occasional Paper No 12, 1983, reprinted in 2006, http://www.facsia.gov.au/research/op12/sec1.htm, accessed 7 April 2013.

FACSIA (2006), "A Compendium of Legislative Changes in Social Security 1983-2000", Occasional Paper 13 June, http://www.facsia.gov.au/internet/facsinternet.nsf/research/ops-ops13.htm, accessed 7 April 2013.

Fallick, Les (1990) "The Accord: An Assessment", *The Economic and Labour Relations Review*, Vol. 1, No. 1, June, pp. 93-106.

Falls, Caroline (1993) compiler of various views, "The Year Ahead for Superannuation", *Superfunds*, No. 155, December 1992- January 1993, pp. 24, 27, 29-30.

Fitzgerald, Vince, & Harper, Ian (1992) "Banks, Super Funds and the Future of Financial Intermediation", in Davis, Kevin, & Harper, Ian (1992), editors, *Superannuation and the Australian Financial System*, Allen & Unwin, St Leonards, NSW, pp. 40-58.

Foenander, Orwell de R. (1959) *Industrial Conciliation and Arbitration in Australia*, Law Book Company, Sydney.

Ford, Bill, & Plowman, David (1989), editors, *Australian Unions. An Industrial Relations Perspective*, Second Edition, Macmillan Company of Australia, Crows Nest, NSW.

Frazer, Andrew (1997) "Major Tribunal Decisions in 1996", *Journal of Industrial Relations*, Vol.39, No.1, March, pp. 77-95.

Freebairn, John (1998) "Compulsory Superannuation and Labour Market Responses", *Australian Economic Papers*, Vol. 37, pp. 58-70.

Gallagher, P. & Preston, A. (1993) *Retirement Income Modelling and Policy Development in Australia* Treasury Retirement Income Modelling Task Force, Canberra, http://rim.treasury.gov.au/content/pdf/CP933.pdf, accessed 23 March 2013.

Gardner, Margaret (1986) "Australian Trade Unionism in 1985", *Journal of Industrial Relations*, Vol. 28, No. 1, March, pp. 133-41.

Ghilarducci, Teresa (1992) *Labor's Capital. The Economics and Politics of Private Pensions*, The MIT Press, Cambridge, MA, USA.

Gietzelt, Ray (2004) *The Memoirs of Ray Gietzelt: General Secretary of the Federated Miscellaneous Workers Union of Australia 1955-1984*, The Federation Press, Sydney.

Gill, Howard (1979) "Industrial Relations and Superannuation", *Superfunds*, No. 69, December, pp. 6, 8, 10.

Golat, Theodore (2016) "Banks' Wealth Management Activities in Australia", *Bulletin of the Reserve Bank of Australia*, September Quarter, pp. 53-9, www.rba.gov.au/publications/bulletin/2016/sep/7.html.

Goldratt, Eliyahu M., & Cox, Jeff (1986) *The Goal: A Process of Ongoing Improvement*, North River Press, Great Barrington, MA, USA.

Goldratt, Eliyahu M. (1994) *Theory of Constraints* North River Press, Great Barrington, MA, USA.

Grant, Sandy (1989) "Industry Superannuation – Current Position, Future Developments", *Superfunds*, No. 117, July 1, pp. 38-9, 48.

Grattan Institute (2014), *Super Sting* report, https://grattan.edu.au/report/super-sting-how-to-stop-australians-paying-too-much-for-superannuation, accessed 20 September 2016.

Gray, Warren (1989) "2001: A Superannuation Odyssey", *Superfunds*, No. 112, February, p. 1.

Green, Roy (1996) "The 'Death' of Comparative Wage Justice in Australia", Research Paper Issue 27, Employment Studies Centre, University of Newcastle, Australia, 27pp.

Griffin, G & Giuca, V (1986) "One Peak Council: The Merger of ACSPA and CAGEO with the ACTU", *Journal of Industrial Relations*, Vol. 28, No. 4, pp. 483-503.

Hajer, Maarten A. & Wagenaar, Hendrik (2003), editors, *Deliberative Policy Analysis: Understanding Governance in the Network Society*, Cambridge University Press, Cambridge.

Hall, Peter A. (2008) "Systematic Process Analysis: When and How to Use It", *European Political Science*, Vol. 7, No. 3, pp. 304-17, http://www.palgrave-journals.com/eps/journal/v7/n3/abs/2210130a.html, accessed 6 April 2013.

Hamilton, Frances (1991) "Why Compliance is Vital for a Level Playing Super Field", *Superfunds*, No. 141, September, pp. 25-7.

Hancock, Keith (1998) "The Needs of the Low Paid", *Journal of Industrial Relations*, Vol. 40, No. 1, March.

Hancock, K J (2005) "Wage Determination in the Twentieth Century Australian Economy", in Isaac, Joe and Lansbury, Russell D. (2005), editors, *Labour Market Deregulation*, Federation Press, Annandale, NSW, Australia, pp. 182-90.

Harbord, Graham (1987) "Major Tribunal Decisions in 1986", *Journal of Industrial Relations*, Vol. 29, No. 1, March, pp. 66-74.

Harrison, Greg (1986) "Superannuation – A Union's Viewpoint, *Superfunds*, No. 95, June 1986, pp. 12, 14.

Harvey, Keith (2013) "Strove to Better Workers' Lives", *Sydney Morning Herald*, 28 January.

Hawke, Hon. R.J.L. (1983) "Statement to the National Economic Summit", House of Representatives *Hansard* (Parliament of Australia), 3 May.

Hawke, Bob (1994) *The Hawke Memoirs*, William Heinemann Australia, Port Melbourne.

Healey, Denis (1989) *The Time of My Life*, Michael Joseph, London.

Hely, Susan (1991a) "Can Iain Ross Fill Garry Weaven's Shoes?", *Superfunds*, No. 137, May, pp. 9-10, 12.

Hely, Susan (1991b) "What Troubles Trustees", *Superfunds*, No. 138, June 1991, pp. 20-4.

Hely, Susan (1991c) "Where Industry Funds are Leading Superannuation", *Superfunds*, No. 141, September, pp. 28-30.

Hely, Susan (1991d) "ACTU Congress on Superannuation", *Superfunds*, No. 142, October, p. 3.

Hely, Susan (1992a) "The Continuing Role for Award Superannuation", *Superfunds*, No. 145, February, p. 5.

Hely, Susan (1992b) "The Superannuation Gospel According to Sandy Grant", *Superfunds*, No. 145, February, pp. 14-16.

Hely, Susan (1992c) "The First for an Economic Statement... No Mention of Super...", *Superfunds*, No. 146, March, pp. 6-7.

Hely, Susan (1992d) "Briare McElhome: HOSTPLUS' New Fund Secretary", *Superfunds*, No. 152, September, pp. 27-8.

Henderson, Gerard (1983) "The Industrial Relations Club", *Quadrant*, Vol. 27, No. 9, September, pp. 21-9.

Henderson, Gerard (2015) *Santamaria. A Most Unusual Man*, The Miegunyah Press, Melbourne University Publishing Limited, South Carlton, Victoria.

Henry, Ken, Chair, et. al. (2010) Australia's Future Tax System Review, http://taxreview.treasury.gov.au/content/Content.aspx?doc=html/home.htm, accessed 3 February 2015.

Hewett, Jennifer (1981) "Cliff Dolan: Sure Footed as He Plods Across the Industrial Centre Stage", *Sydney Morning Herald*, 26 December, www.news.google.com/newspapers?nid=1301&dat=19811226&id=JalWAAAAI BAJ&sjid=PecDAAAAIBAJ&pg=6616,8082297, accessed 26 May, 2013.

Hewitt, Jennifer (2016) "The Government Comes from Behind on Superannuation", *Australian Financial Review*, 15 September.

Higgins, H.B. (1922) *A New Province for Law and Order*, Constable, London (originally published in the *Harvard Law Review* in 1915).

Hirschman, Albert O. (1970) *Exit, Voice, Loyalty: Responses to Decline in Firms, Organizations, and States*, Harvard University Press, Cambridge, MA, USA.

Holley, William H., Jennings, Kenneth M., & Wolters, Roger S. (2011) *The Labor Relations Process*, 10th edition, Cengage Learning, Mason, OH, USA.

Honeyman, Victoria (2006) *Richard Crossman: A Reforming Radical of the Labour Party*, I.B. Tauris, London.

Horne, Donald (1964) *The Lucky Country*, Angus & Robertson, Sydney.

Howard, John (2010) *Lazarus Rising. A Personal and Political Autobiography*, Harper Collins Australia.

Howe, Brian (1989-1990) "Labor's Retirement and Incomes Policy Achievements and Prospects", *Superfunds*, No. 122, December 1989-January 1990, pp. 19-20.

Huntley, Pat (1978) *Inside Australia's Largest Trade Union*, Ian Huntley Pty. Ltd., Braddon [ACT]

Ingles, D. (2009) "The Great Superannuation Tax Concession Rort", Research

Paper No. 61, The Australia Institute, www.tai.org.au, accessed 3 June 2013.

Ingles, D., & Fear, J. (2009) "The Case for a Universal Default Superannuation Fund", Policy Brief No 3, The Australia Institute, www.tai.org.au, accessed 3 June 2013.

Irving, Terry (1994) "Labourism: A Political Genealogy", *Labour History*, No. 66, May, pp. 1-13.

Isaac, Joe, & Lansbury, Russell (2005), editors, *Labour Market Deregulation. Rewriting the Rules. Essays in Honour of Professor Keith Hancock*, The Federation Press, Annandale, NSW, Australia.

Jamieson, Suzanne (2007) "Clancy, Patrick Martin (Pat) (1919–1987)", *Australian Dictionary of Biography*, National Centre of Biography, Australian National University, http://adb.anu.edu.au/biography/clancy-patrick-martin-pat-12320/text22131, accessed 25 May 2013. This article was first published in hardcopy in *Australian Dictionary of Biography*, Volume 17, (MUP), 2007.

Jefferson, Therese (2012) "Private Retirement Savings in Australia: Current Policy Initiatives and Gender Equity Implications", *Australian Bulletin of Labour*, Vol. 38, Issue 3, September, pp. 234-50.

Jones, Barry (2000) "Light on the Hill Speech", mimeo, Calare FEC, Bathurst, *circa* 2000.

Jordon, Matthew (2004) *A Spirit of True Learning: The Jubilee History of the University of New England*, UNSW Press, Kensington.

Kaine, Sarah (2015) "Women, Work and Industrial Relations in Australia in 2015", *Journal of Industrial Relations*, Vol. 58, No. 3, pp. 324–39.

Keating, Michael (2015) "The Financial System Inquiry. Part 2: Superannuation and Retirement Incomes", in *Pearls and Irritations*, blog compiled by John Menadue, 20 January, http://johnmenadue.com/blog/?p=3004, accessed 20 August 2016.

[Keating, Paul] (1987) "Mr Keating Responds to ASFA", *Superfunds*, No. 100, September, pp. 9-10.

Keating, The Hon. P.J., Treasurer (1988) *Reform of the Taxation of Superannuation* Australian Government Publishing, Canberra, 25 May.

Keating, Paul (1991) "A Retirement Incomes Policy", Address to the Australian Graduate School of Management, 25 July, typescript, 17pp.

Keating, Paul (2004) "Superannuation Policy: Commentary on an Interview with Paul Keating, Former Prime Minister", *Journal of Australian Political Economy*, Vol. 53, pp. 9-16.

Keating, Paul. (2007a) "Pension Adequacy and Private Provisioning", *Global Pension and Investment Forum*, conducted at the meeting of the Global Pension and Investment Forum, Monte Carlo, Monaco.

Keating, Paul (2007b) "The Story of Modern Superannuation", speech delivered to the Australian Pensions and Investment Summit, 31 October, http://www.keating.org.au/shop/item/the-story-of-modern-superannuation-31-october-2007, accessed 1 September 2016.

Keating, Paul (2012) "Speaking Notes to the ASFA 50th Anniversary Conference", Association of Superannuation Funds of Australia, 28 November, typescript, 13pp.

Kelly, Paul (1992) *The End of Certainty*, Allen & Unwin, Sydney.

Kelly, Paul (2011) *The March of Patriots, The Struggle for Modern Australia*, Melbourne University Press, Carlton (first published in 2009, updated in 2011).

Kelly, Rosemary (1997) "Superannuation and the Marketisation of Retirement Incomes", *Labour & Industry: A Journal of the Social and Economic Relations of Work*, Vol. 8, Issue 1, pp. 57-79.

Kelty, Bill (1984) "An Incomes and Prices Policy for Australia", in Aldred, Jenny (1984), editor, *Industrial Confrontation*, Australian Institute of Political Science and Unwin & Allen, North Sydney, pp. 42-8.

Kelty, Bill (2009) "Romance in Politics – the Public Good", the inaugural John Button Oration, http://johnbuttonprize.org.au/about/news/post/-romance-in-politics-the-public-good-bill-kelty-s-inaugural-john-button-oration, accessed 26 May 2013.

Kemp, D.A. (1983) "The National Economic Summit: Authority, Persuasion and Exchange", *The Economic Record*, Vol. 59, Issue 3, September, pp. 209-19.

Kemp, R. (1999) "The Government's Approach to Superannuation", Speech by The Hon. Rod Kemp, Assistant Treasurer, to the Australian Society of Certified Practicing Accountants, Brisbane, 28 May, http://treasurer.gov.au/assistanttreasurer/speeches/ATSPI2.asp, accessed 28 August 2013.

Kerin, John (1991), Treasurer, "Second Reading Speech: Appropriation Bill (No. 1) 1991-92", House of Representatives, Debates, 20 August, p. 13, http://parlinfo.aph.gov.au/parlInfo/search/display/display.w3p;query=Idper cent3Aper cent22chamberper cent2Fhansardrper cent2F1991-08-20per cent2F0024per cent22, accessed 28 May 2013.

Kernot, Cheryl (1993) Senator Cheryl Kernot, Australian Democrat Treasury

Spokesperson, contribution to "Super Policies", *Superfunds*, No. 157, March, p. 6.

King, J E (2007), editor, *A Biographical Dictionary of Australian and New Zealand Economists*, Edward Elgar Publishers, Cheltenham, UK.

Kingston, G, Piggott, J, & Bateman, H. (1992) "Customised Investment Strategies for Accumulations in Superannuation", in Davis, Kevin, & Harper, Ian (1992), editors, *Superannuation and the Australian Financial System*, Allen & Unwin, St Leonards, NSW.

Kitney, Geoff (1991) "Government May Legislate to Implement Super", *The Australian Financial Review*, 26 April, pp. 1, 8.

Knight, E.S. et al. (1982) *Superannuation Planning in Australia*, Third Edition, CCH Australia Limited, North Ryde.

Knox, David (1985) "The Present and Future of Occupational Superannuation in Australia", *Superfunds*, No. 91, June, pp. 23, 25, 27, 29, 31, 33-4.

Lally, Tony (1989-1990) "Evaluation of Industry Superannuation in Australia", *Superfunds*, No. 122, December 1989-January 1990, pp. 41-2.

Landau, C.E. (1987) "The Influence of ILO Standards on Australian Labour Law and Practice", *International Labour Review*, Vol. 126, No. 6, November-December, pp. 669-90.

Landeryou, W.A. (1978) "The Union Attitude to Superannuation", *Superfunds*, No. 65, December, pp. 30-1.

Langton, Glenn (1986) "Superannuation as an Industrial Relations Issue", *Superfunds*, No. 95, June, pp. 5-7.

Lee, John (2009) "Grouper Who Defined an Era"[obituary to John Maynes], *The Melbourne Age*, August 22. http://www.theage.com.au/national/grouper-who-defined-an-era-20090821-etvi.html, accessed 25 May 2013.

Lindblom, Charles E. (1959) "The Science of Muddling Through", *Public Administration Review,* Vol. 19, No. 2, pp. 79-88.

Lindblom, Charles E. (2001) *Politics and Markets,* Yale University Press (2001).

Lockery, Ken (1992) "SGL – What is ASFA Saying?", *Superfunds*, No. 146, March, pp. 8-9.

Lovan, Robert W., Murray, Michael, & Schaffer, Ron (2004), editors, *Participatory Governance: Planning, Conflict Mediation and Public Decision-Making in Civil Society*, Ashgate Publications Ltd., Aldershot, UK.

Lucas, Harry W. (1977) *Pensions and Industrial Relations*, Pergamon, London.

Ludeke, John Terrence (1996) *Line in the Sand: The Long Road to Staff Employment in Comalco*, Wilkinson Books, Melbourne.

McCallum, John (1991) "The Three Historic Phases of Australian Superannuation", *Superfunds*, No. 142, October, pp. 35-9.

McCallum, Ron, & Wood, Karen J. (1995) "Crafting the Law: The High Court and Superannuation as an Industrial Matter", *Australian Journal of Labour Law*, Vol. 8, No. 2, August, pp. 121-36.

McCallum, Ron (1994) "The Internationalisation of Australian Industrial Law: The Industrial Relations Reform Act, 1993", *Sydney Law Review*, Vol. 16, pp. 122-35.

McDonald, Audrey & Tom (1998) *Intimate Union: Sharing a Revolutionary Life. An Autobiography*, Pluto Press, Sydney.

McDonald, Tom (2011) "A New Super Vision. The Changing World of Superannuation", typescript, 5 April, 10pp.

McDonald, Audrey & Tom (2016) *Dare to Dream. Stories of Struggle and Hope*, self-published, Sydney.

McDougall, Bruce (1989a) "Member Trustees Make Big Impact in Fund Management", *Superfunds*, No. 116, June, pp. 22-3.

McDougall, Bruce (1989b) "Union Leader is a Real Super Man [profile of Garry Weaven]", *Superfunds*, No. 118, August, pp. 20-1.

McDougall, Bruce (1989c) "Brian Howe – From Pulpit to Super Reformer", *Superfunds*, No. 120, October, pp. 27, 30.

Macken, Jim (1986) "Why Retirement Income Will Be An Enduring Issue", *Superfunds*, No. 95, June, pp. 8, 10-11.

March, J G & Olsen, J P (1989) *Rediscovering Institutions: The Organisational Basis of Politics*, The Free Press, New York.

Masters, Chris (2007) *Jonestown: The Power and Myth of Alan Jones*, Allen & Unwin, North Sydney.

Mathews, Race, Emy, Hugh & Hughes, Owen (1992), editors, *Whitlam Revisited: Policy Development, Policies and Outcomes*, Pluto Press, Sydney.

Mathews, Race (1993) *Australia's First Fabians: Middle-Class Radicals, Labour Activists and the Early Labour Movement*, Cambridge University Press, Cambridge.

Mathews, Race (1999) *Jobs of Our Own: Building a Stakeholder Society*, Pluto Press, Sydney, and Comerford & Miller, London.

Mees, Bernard, & Brigden, Cathy (2017) *Workers' Capital. Industry Funds and the Fight for Universal Superannuation in Australia*, Allen & Unwin, North Sydney

Megalogenis, George (2012) *The Australian Moment. How We Were Made for These Times*, Viking, Camberwell, Victoria.

Mercer (2015) *Melbourne Mercer Global Pension Index*, Australian Centre for Financial Studies, October, www.globalpensionindex.com/wp-content/uploads/Melbourne-Mercer-Global-Pension-Index-2015-Report-Web.pdf., accessed

Mercer, Gerard (2009) "John Maynes and the Movement", *Quadrant*, Vol. 53, No. 9, September, pp. 92-4.

Mills, Stephen (1993) *The Hawke Years. The Story from the Inside*, Viking, Richmond Victoria.

Minifie, Jim (2014) *Super Sting: How to Stop Australians Paying Too Much for Superannuation*, The Grattan Institute, Melbourne, April, 57 pp., http://grattan.edu.au/wp-content/uploads/2014/04/811-super-sting.pdf, accessed 24 September 2015.

Minifie, Jim (2014) "How to Halve our Super Fees", *The Australian*, 28 April.

Minto, Jim (2016) "ASFA Oration", 9 November 2016, www.superannuation.asn.au/media/speeches, accessed 14 December 2016.

Mitchell, William F. (1998) "Macroeconomic Policy in Australia 1983-1996", Centre of Full Employment and Equity, The University of Newcastle, http://e1.newcastle.edu.au/coffee/pubs/wp/1998/98-03.pdf, accessed 6 September 2015.

Moore, Des (1991) complaints in "Public Interest or Vested Interest. The Role of the CAI in the Regulation of Australia's Labour Market", H.R. Nicholls Society, Vol. 8, http://archive.hrnicholls.com.au/archives/vol8/vol8-12.php, accessed August 2016.

Moore, Matthew (1987) "Judge Asks", *The Sydney Morning Herald*, 30 July, http://news.google.com/newspapers?nid=1301&dat=19870730&id=ritW AAAAIBAJ&sjid=c-QDAAAAIBAJ&pg=6175,10343519, accessed 26 May 2013.

Morgan, Kenneth O. (1997) *Callaghan: A Life*, Oxford University Press, Oxford.

Mountford, Bill & Wilshire, Ted (1982) *Australia on the Rack* [pamphlet], Amalgamated Metal Workers and Shipwrights' Union (Australia), National Council, Surry Hills, NSW.

Mulvey, Charles (1984) "Wage Policy and Wage Determination in 1983", *Journal of Industrial Relations*, Vol. 26, No. 1, August, pp. 112-9.

Mulvey, Charles (1985) "Wage Policy and Wage Determination in 1984", *Journal of Industrial Relations*, Vol. 27, No. 1, March, pp. 68-75.

Munton, Joel Len (1985) "'Intruder' Upsets ASFA Talk on Builders' Scheme", *Australian Financial Review*, 20 February.

Murray, David, Chair, *et. al.* (2014) Report of the Financial System Inquiry, http://fsi.gov.au/publications/final-report, accessed 7 July 2015.

Nairn, Bede (1973) *Civilising Capitalism, The Beginnings of the Australian Labor Party*, Australian National University Press, Canberra.

Ney, Steven (2009) *Resolving Messy Policy Problems*: *Handling Conflict in Environmental, Transport, Health and Ageing Policy*, Earthscan Ltd, Sterling, VA, USA.

Nolan, David (1985) "Superannuation from the Employers' Viewpoint", *Superfunds*, No 92, September, pp. 33-35.

Noonan, Gerard (1985) "The Significance of the Super Deal", *The Australian Financial Review*, 13 September, pp. 1, 8.

North, Douglass C. (1996) *Institutions, Institutional Change and Economic Performance*, Cambridge University Press, Cambridge.

Oakes, Laurie (1991) "The Super Champ", 6 August column in *The Bulletin*, reproduced in Oakes, Laurie (2011) *Power Plays: The Real Stories of Australian Politics* [a collection of published articles], updated edition, Hachette, Sydney.

Oakes, Laurie (2011) *Power Plays: The Real Stories of Australian Politics* [a collection of published articles], updated edition, Hachette, Sydney.

O'Brien, Kerry (2015) *Keating*, Allen & Unwin, Crows Nest, NSW.

Ostrom, Elinor (1990) *Governing the Commons*: *The Evolution of Institutions for Collective Action*, Cambridge University Press, Cambridge.

Owen, Mary (1984) "Superannuation Was Not Meant For Women", *The Australian Quarterly*, Vol. 56, No. 4, Summer, pp. 363-73.

Paatsch, Dean & Smith, Graham (1992) "The Regulation of Australian Superannuation: An Industrial Relations Law Perspective", *Corporate and Business Law Journal*, Vol. 5, pp. 131-64.

Palmer, Ray (1983) "Hawke's 1983 Initiatives – A Trial Balance", *Superfunds*, No. 85, December, pp. 9-10, 12-14, 16-18.

Pemberton, Joanne, & Davis, Glyn (1986) "The Rhetoric of Consensus",

Politics, The Australian Journal of Political Science, Vol. 21, No. 1, pp. 55-62.

Petridis, A (1987) "Wage Policy and Wage Determination 1986", *Journal of Industrial Relations*, Vol. 29, No. 1, March, pp. 75-83.

Philips, P.S.M. (1979) "Union Superannuation Funds", *Superfunds*, No. 69, December, pp. 24, 26-9.

Pittard, Marilyn & McCallum, Ron (1994) "Superannuation Funds, Interlocking Corporations and Industrial Disputes", *Australian Business Law Review*, Vol. 21, No. 1, February, pp. 71-4.

Plowman, David & Weavan, Garry (1989) "Unions and Superannuation", in Ford, Bill, and Plowman, David (1989), editors, *Australian Unions. An Industrial Relations Perspective*, Second Edition, Macmillan Company of Australia, Crows Nest, NSW, Australia, pp. 251-68.

Polites, George (1980) "Superannuation as an Industrial Relations Issue", *Superfunds*, No. 71, June, pp. 4, 6.

Polites, Colin G. (1984) "Major Tribunal Decisions 1983", *Journal of Industrial Relations*, Vol. 26, No. 1, pp. 105-11.

Quinlivan, Beth (1990) "Award Super: Key Issues to Debate", *Superfunds*, No. 128, August, pp. 22-3.

Quinlivan, Beth (1990-91) "Mavis Robertson... An Alternative Path to Super", *Superfunds*, No. 132, December 1990-January 1991, pp. 12-3.

Quinlivan, Beth (1991) "Administering Industry Funds", *Superfunds*, No. 141, September, pp. 11-2.

Quinlivan, Beth (1992) "Merging Industry Super Funds", *Superfunds*, No. 152, September, pp. 29-31, 33.

Radaelli, Claudio M. (1995) "The Role of Knowledge in the Policy Process", *Journal of European Public Policy,* Vol. 2, No. 2, June, pp. 159-83.

Reeves Andrew, & Dettmer, Andrew (2013), editors, *Organise, Educate, Control: The AMWU in Australia, 1852–2012*, Monash University Publishing, Clayton.

Rice, M., & McEwin, I. (2002), 'Superannuation Costs and Competition', Investment and Financial Services Association Limited Ltd, Sydney, accessed at www.ifs.com.au. accessed 7 August 2013.

Rice Warner (2012) "Superannuation Market Projections Report 2012", Sydney.

Rice Warner (2014) "Superannuation Market Projections Report 2012", Sydney, http://ricewarner.com/superannuation-market-projections-2014-

report-show-two-dominant-themes-growth-and-cost-fees, accessed 26 May 2015.

Richards, David, and Smith, Martin J. (2004) "Interpreting the World of Political Elites", *Public Administration*, Vol. 82, No. 4, pp. 777-800, http://onlinelibrary.wiley.com/doi/10.1111/j.0033-3298.2004.00419.x/abstract, accessed 7 April 2013.

Richardson, S. & Hancock, K. J. (2003) *Conciliation & Arbitration?: the Economic & Social Effects*, National Institute of Labour Studies, Adelaide.

Rickard, John (1984) *H.B. Higgins. The Rebel as Judge*, George Allen and Unwin, Sydney.

Roach, O.F. (1980) "An Overview- The Next Ten Years," *Superfunds*, No. 71, June 1980, pp. 8, 10, 12-13.

Robinson, I. (1992) "Superannuation – A Policy Perspective", in Davis, K & Harper, I (1992), editors, *Superannuation and the Australian Financial System*, Allen & Unwin, St. Leonards, NSW, Australia.

Robinson, Paul (1986) "Employers Warn on Metal Unions' Super Scheme", *The Age* (Melbourne), 24 March, p. 3.

Rothman, G. & Tellis, D. (2008) "Projecting the Distribution of Superannuation Flows and Assets", Retirement and Intergenerational Modelling and Analysis Unit, Department of Treasury, Canberra, http://rim.treasury.gov. au, accessed 4 June 2013.

Rothman, G. (2009) "Assessing the Equity of Australia's Retirement Income System", Retirement and Intergenerational Modelling and Analysis Unit, Department of Treasury, Canberra, http://rim.treasury.gov.au, accessed 4 June 2013.

Rothman, Honourable Justice Stephen (2011) "Reflections from Queens Square", paper delivered at the ALLA conference, 5 December, http://www.supremecourt.lawlink.nsw.gov.au/agdbasev7wr/supremecourt/documents/pdf/rothman_051211.pdf, accessed 26 May 2013.

Russell, Don (2003) "The Role of Executive Government in Australia", Papers on Parliament, No. 41, December (a paper first presented as a lecture in the Department of the Senate Occasional Lecture Series at Parliament House on 25 October 2002), http://www.aph.gov.au/About_Parliament/Senate/Research_and_Education/pops/pop40/russell, accessed 9 September 2013.

Rutledge, Martha (1986) "Neild, John Cash (1846-1911)", *Australian Dictionary of Biography*, Volume 10, Melbourne University Press, Carlton, pp. 672-3.

Schmidt, Lucinda (2008) "Profile: Bernie Fraser", *The Melbourne Age*, 19 March, www.theage.com.au/news/money/profile-bernie-fraser/2008/03/17/1205602290290.html, accessed 30 May 2013.

Schneider, Michael (2007) "Frank Geoffrey Davidson; Donald Henry Whitehead", in King, J E, editor, *A Biographical Dictionary of Australian and New Zealand Economists*, Edward Elgar Publishers, Cheltenham, UK.

Scott, Andrew (2013) "Australia Reconstructed", in Reeves Andrew, & Dettmer, Andrew (2013), editors, *Organise, Educate, Control: The AMWU in Australia, 1852–2012*, Monash University Publishing, Clayton, VIC, Australia, pp. 137-51.

SDA (2012) "Submission to the Productivity Commission concerning Default Superannuation Funds in Modern Awards", www.pc.gov.au/__data/assets/pdf_file/0013/116302/sub024-default-super.pdf, accessed 28 May 2013.

Sharp, R. (1992) "The Rise and Rise of Superannuation under Labor", *Journal of Australian Political Economy*, Vol. 30, pp. 24-41.

Sharp, R. (1995) "Women and Superannuation: Super Bargain or Raw Deal?", in Edwards, A & Magarey (1995), editors, *Women in a Restructuring Australia: Work and Welfare*, Allen & Unwin, Sydney.

Sheridan, Thomas (1975) *Mindful Militants. The Amalgamated Engineering Union in Australia, 1920-1972*, Cambridge University Press, Cambridge. The union until 1972 was part of the UK Amalgamated Engineering Union.

Sheridan, Tom (1998) "Regulating the Waterfront Industry 1950-1968", *Journal of Industrial Relations*, Vol. 40, No. 3, pp. 441-60.

Silk, Ian (2015) 'ASFA Oration', 25 November, file:///C:/Users/measson/Downloads/asfa2015_Ian_Silk_Industry_oration.pdf, 4 pp.

Simon, Herbert A. (1957) *Models of Man,* Wiley, New York.

Smith, Matthew (2016) "What's Eating Asset Consultants", 2 June, http://finsia.com/news/news-article/2016/06/02/what-s-eating-asset-consultants, accessed 20 September 2016.

Solomon, D.J. (1979) "Wages Superannuation – Government, Union or Employer?", *Superfunds*, No. 68, September, pp. 8, 10-11.

St Anne, Christine (2012) *A Super History: How Australia's $1 Trillion+ Superannuation Industry Was Made*, Major Street Publishing, Highett, Vic, Australia.

Stackpool, J E (1988) "Industrial Relations Legislation in 1987", *Journal of Industrial Relations*, Vol. 30, No. 1, March, pp. 163-74.

Stephens, Tony (2015) "Mavis Robertson: Fighter for the Rights of Many, Has Died", *Sydney Morning Herald*, 27 February.

Stilwell, Frank (1986) *The Accord – and Beyond: The Political Economy of the Labor Government*, Pluto Press, Sydney.

Stutchbury, Michael (1984) "Laurie Carmichael: Union and Political Operator Extraordinaire", *The Australian Financial Review*, 31 August, pp.33, 36.

Swan, Wayne (2005) *Postcode: The Splintering of a Nation*, Pluto Press, North Melbourne.

Sword, Greg (1992) "Superannuation as a Recruitment Tool", in Crosby, Michael, & Easson, Michael (1992), editors, *What Should Unions Do?*, Pluto Press in conjunction with the Lloyd Ross Forum, Leichhardt, pp. 225-31.

Tanner, Lindsay (1996) *The Last Battle*, Kokkinos Press, Carlton.

Taylor, Mike (2010) "Industry Super Funds Stumble on the Secret of Success", *Money Management*, 18 October, http://www.moneymanagement.com.au/opinion/superannuation/archive/industry-super-funds-stumble-on-to-the-secret-of-s, accessed September 2013.

Tingle, Laura (1992) "Senator Sherry Sounds Out Super in 180 Submissions and 15 Days of Hearings", *Superfunds*, No. 147, April, pp. 19-20.

Tsebelis, George (2002) *Veto Players: How Political Institutions Work*, Princeton University Press, Princeton.

Twomey, Cyril (1985) "Building Unions Superannuation", *Superfunds*, No. 90, March, pp. 14-15, 17, 19.

Twomey, Cyril (1990) "Investment Strategies of Industry Funds", *Superfunds*, No. 130, October 1990, pp. 34, 37.

Tyndale, Philippa (1988) "Industry Superannuation off the Boil, but Still Simmering", *Superfunds*, No. 110, November, pp. 40, 42-3.

Various (1984) "National Superannuation Policy Statement", *Superfunds*, No. 89, December, pp. 14-15.

Various (1990) "Award Super – Round 2: Where the Players Stand [summary of positions]", Info Source Supplement, *Superfunds*, No. 123, February 1990, p. 1.

Various (1990) "Award Super – Round 2", *Superfunds*, No. 124, March, pp. 30-3, 36-7.

Various (1991) "Industry Funds Investing to Meet Members' Expectations", *Superfunds*, No. 141, September, pp. 37-9.

Various (1992) "Superannuation Guarantee Charge – Senate Select Committee Hearings", *Superfunds*, No. 149, June 1992, pp. 8-9.

Various (1992) "Super Saviour or Saboteur? What the Superannuation Movement is Saying About Treasurer Dawkins' Latest Changes", *Superfunds*, No. 151, August, pp. 7-10.

Various (1992-1993) "News and Trends", *Superfunds*, No. 155, December 1992- January 1993, p. 6.

Veitch, Harriett (2012) "Kingmaker Fought for Democratisation of Unions", *Sydney Morning Herald*, 20 December.

Watson, B.D. (1979) "Union Involvement in the Provision of Superannuation", *Superfunds*, No. 69, December, pp. 12-4.

Watson, Don (2002) *Recollections of a Bleeding Heart. A Portrait of Paul Keating PM*, Knopf, Sydney.

Way, Nicholas (1994a) "Under Fire, But Smooth as Silk", *Superfunds*, No. 176, November, p. 69.

Way, Nicholas (1994b) "Retail Sector Soars in Award Super Stakes", Superfunds, No. 174, August, p. 7.

Weaven, Garry (1985) "Superannuation: The Great Leap Forward. An Outline of the ACTU's Strategy for the Establishment of Universal Superannuation Coverage", *Superfunds*, No. 92, September, pp. 4-5, 7, 8-9, 11, 12, originally mimeo, ACTU, Melbourne.

Weaven, Garry (1989) "Superannuation and Retirement Incomes Policy. The Crucial Role of Unions", *Superfunds*, No. 116, June, pp. 24-5.

Weaven, Garry (2016) 'Workers' Capital: The Story of Industry Funds and Australia's Superannuation Revolution', Foenander Lecture at the University of Melbourne, 15 November 2016, 20 pp.

Weeks, Phillipa (1993) "Major Tribunal Decisions in 1992", *Journal of Industrial Relations,* Vol. 35, No. 1, pp. 97-109.

Western Australian Sub Division of ASFA, Benefits Study Group (1981) "Portability and Vesting – Getting Off the Fence", *Superfunds*, No. 77, December 1981, pp. 9-12.

Whitehead, Donald Henry (1973) *Stagflation and Wages Policy in Australia*, Longman, Camberwell, Victoria, Australia.

Whitehead, Donald Henry (1977) "Comment", *Economic Papers*, Vol. 56, pp. 35-8.

Whittle, Bruce (1987) "Twenty Five Years Retrospect", *Superfunds*, No. 100, September, pp. 16-17.

Whitwell, Greg (1986) *The Treasury Line*, Allen & Unwin, Sydney.

Whitehead, Noel (2002) "Constructing the Public-Private Divide. Historical Perspectives and the Politics of Pension Reform", Working Paper No. WP102, Oxford Institute of Ageing Working Papers, August, www.ageing.ox.ac.uk/files/workingpaper_102.pdf, accessed 26 May 2013.

Willis, Graham (1991) "Divided Over SGL", *Superfunds*, No. 143, November 1991, pp. 6-7.

INDEX